THE EVERYTHING

Giant Book of Crosswords

Dear Reader,

Words are fun! That's why I created Funster.com, a Web site devoted to word play and puzzles. I discovered just how addictive word games can be from all of the dedicated players who frequently visit Funster .com. Solving word puzzles like crosswords is creative play that leads to many of those satisfying "aha!" moments that keep people coming back for more.

But crossword puzzles are not just for fun. Researchers have determined that we can give our brains a boost by exercising them regularly. Solving crossword puzzles is a great way to get a mental workout. Studies show that this can improve our memory and cognitive abilities as we age. Crossword puzzles might be addictive, but they can also be part of a healthy lifestyle. Excellent!

I've stuffed this book full of a huge number of crossword puzzles that will keep you entertained for a long, long time. So grab a pencil (or pen, if you dare), put your brain in gear, and jump into this giant world of crossword puzzling fun.

Charles Timmerman

Welcome to the EVERYTHING® Series!

These handy, accessible books give you all you need to tackle a difficult project, gain a new hobby, comprehend a fascinating topic, prepare for an exam, or even brush up on something you learned back in school but have since forgotten.

You can choose to read an *Everything*® book from cover to cover or just pick out the information you want from our four useful boxes: e-questions, e-facts, e-alerts, and e-ssentials. We give you everything you need to know on the subject, but throw in a lot of fun stuff along the way, too.

We now have more than 400 *Everything*® books in print, spanning such wide-ranging categories as weddings, pregnancy, cooking, music instruction, foreign language, crafts, pets, New Age, and so much more. When you're done reading them all, you can finally say you know *Everything*®!

PUBLISHER Karen Cooper

DIRECTOR OF ACQUISITIONS AND INNOVATION Paula Munier

MANAGING EDITOR, EVERYTHING SERIES Lisa Laing

COPY CHIEF Casey Ebert

ACQUISITIONS EDITOR Lisa Laing

EDITORIAL ASSISTANT Hillary Thompson

Visit the entire Everything® series at *www.everything.com*

THE EVERYTHING®

GIANT

BOOK
OF
CROSSWORDS

From easy to challenging—
more than 300 puzzles to
entertain you around the clock

Charles Timmerman
Founder of Funster.com

Adams Media
New York   London   Toronto   Sydney   New Delhi

Dedicated to Suzanne and Calla.

Adams Media
An Imprint of Simon & Schuster, Inc.
57 Littlefield Street
Avon, Massachusetts 02322
Copyright © 2008 by Simon & Schuster, Inc.

An Everything® Series Book.
Everything® and everything.com® are registered trademarks of Simon & Schuster, Inc.

First Adams Media trade paperback edition MONTH YEAR [ED: Fill in on-sale month/year (all caps)]

ADAMS MEDIA and colophon are trademarks of Simon and Schuster.

For information about special discounts for bulk purchases, please contact Simon & Schuster Special Sales at 1-866-506-1949 or business@simonandschuster.com.

The Simon & Schuster Speakers Bureau can bring authors to your live event. For more information or to book an event contact the Simon & Schuster Speakers Bureau at 1-866-248-3049 or visit our website at www.simonspeakers.com.

Manufactured in the United States of America

12 2021

Library of Congress Cataloging-in-Publication Data has been applied for.

ISBN 978-1-59869-716-2

Contents

Contents

Acknowledgments

I would like to thank each and every one of the more than half a million people who have visited my Web site, Funster.com, to play word games and puzzles. You are the inspiration for this book.

Many thanks goes to my agent, Jacky Sach, for her expert help and guidance over the years.

It is a pleasure to acknowledge the fine folks at Adams Media who made this book possible. In particular, my editor, Lisa Laing, is always a joy to work with.

Introduction

▶ WHAT DO Rosa Parks, Richard Nixon, Jesse Owens and crossword puzzles have in common? They were all born in the year 1913. In that year a journalist named Arthur Wynne published a "word-cross" puzzle in the Sunday edition of the *New York World*. Though it was diamond shaped, it had all of the features of crossword puzzles that we know and love today. The name evolved into *crossword* as the paper continued to publish the popular word puzzles.

It wasn't until 1924 that the first book of crossword puzzles was published. That was when the crossword craze really began. It joined other fads of the Roaring Twenties like goldfish eating, flagpole sitting, yo-yos, and pogo sticks. Of course, not all of these fads survived (perhaps fortunately).

Besides crossword puzzles, some really beautiful things came out of the 1920s. In music, jazz surged in popularity and George Gershwin's *Rhapsody in Blue* was performed for the first time. In literature, F. Scott Fitzgerald published some of his most enduring novels, including *The Great Gatsby*. In design, it was the beginning of Art Deco. That's how the world was when crossword puzzles came of age.

Crossword puzzles became popular closer to a time when entertainment required *active* participation. In those days, people actually played sports rather than watched them, told each other stories rather than turned on the television, and even sang songs rather than listened to an MP3. Like entertainment of yesteryear, crossword puzzles require your active participation. And this is a refreshing change for those of us who still enjoy a mental workout.

Today, nearly every major newspaper runs a crossword puzzle. Entire sections of bookstores are devoted to crossword puzzle books. (Thanks for choosing this one!) Indeed, crosswords are the most common word puzzle in the world.

Why do crossword puzzles continue to be so popular? Only you can answer that question since there are as many reasons to work a crossword puzzle as there are solvers. But perhaps it has something to do with the convenient marriage of fun and learning that crossword puzzles offer. Enjoy!

PUZZLES

Section 1: Mildly Tricky Puzzles

Mildly Tricky 1

ACROSS

1. Immature salamanders
5. Damon and Lauer
10. F.B.I. workers: Abbr.
14. Enlist again
15. Should, with "to"
16. FedEx, say
17. Coordinate
18. Lodge resident
19. Heap
20. Cling
22. Golden
24. Hem again
27. Sun follower?
28. "Over the Rainbow" composer Harold
31. Fallen space station
33. Windows predecessor
37. Korean carmaker
38. Cut, perhaps
41. "Uncle Tom's Cabin" girl
42. Any doctrine
43. Pale
44. Nourished
46. "Now I ___ me down . . ."
47. Oolong, e.g.
48. Mother ___
50. Knox and Dix: abbr.
51. Firth of Clyde island
54. Scuff up, e.g.
55. San ___, Calif.
57. Physique, informally
59. West Indies, e.g.
61. Goes postal
65. Book before Job
69. Autumn birthstone
70. Two-door car
73. Designer Gernreich
74. Stuffing ingredient
75. Snouted animal
76. College grad
77. Pres. Jefferson
78. Mine entrances
79. Delicate

DOWN

1. Author Bombeck
2. Nourish
3. Heinie
4. Domain
5. He took two tablets
6. Arctic bird
7. Letters before F?
8. "Take ___ Train"
9. Play a guitar
10. Quaking trees
11. Karmann ___
12. Knight fight
13. Graf ___
21. Ask for more Time?
23. CD-___
25. "Without Me" rapper
26. Cleverness
28. Japanese dog
29. Choir's platform
30. University in Beaumont, Tex.
32. Directs (to)
34. Dutch pottery
35. Egg-shaped
36. Authority
39. "Can't Help Lovin' ___ Man"
40. ___ Moines, Iowa
45. Knights' ladies
49. BBC's Italian counterpart
52. White poplars
53. Denials
56. Starry
58. Formal pronouncements
60. Lecherous looks
61. Asea
62. Brilliantly colored fish
63. Palm starch
64. "The Wind in the Willows" character
66. Hippy entertainment?
67. P.T.A. concern: Abbr.
68. Frost-covered
71. Reuters competitor
72. Orchestra's place

Solution on page 320

Mildly Tricky 2

ACROSS

1. Pie nut
6. Sailing ropes
10. Defrost
14. Earth tone
15. "Aladdin" parrot
16. Ethereal: Prefix
17. Biased writing?: Abbr.
18. McDonald's arches, e.g.
19. Went out, as a fire
20. "Swan Lake" princess
22. All together
24. Code-breaking gp.
25. "Zip-___-Doo-Dah"
26. Crag
27. Mandolin's ancestor
30. ___ cit. (footnote abbr.)
32. "Too-ra-loo-ra-loo-___"
34. Sugar suffix
35. "Oklahoma!" aunt
37. Approaches
41. Kidney enzyme
43. From ___ Z
44. Big name in chips
45. ___ Park, CO
46. Gallows loop
48. Nasdaq debut: Abbr.
49. Drink slowly
51. Certain degree
52. Balance
53. Busy mo. for the IRS
56. Put on board, as cargo
58. Chemical suffix
60. "Listen up!"
62. ___-tung
65. Domesticate
66. Prefix with phobia
68. Do watercolors
70. Maple genus
71. Major-___
72. Is ___ (probably will)
73. "All ___ are off!"
74. Formerly, once
75. Plant again

DOWN

1. Baked Hawaiian dish
2. Opposite of endo-
3. Neighbor of Niger
4. Francis of "What's My Line?"
5. Aeries
6. Flooring square
7. Ming of the NBA
8. Goaded, with "on"
9. Norman native
10. "Hooray for me!"
11. Bank job
12. "You ___ Beautiful"
13. Dentist's request
21. Towering
23. Villain
25. Common solvent
27. Folk tales
28. Applications
29. Big top
31. Pearl Buck heroine
33. "Yesterday's Spy" author Deighton
35. Store, as fodder
36. Cheer (for)
38. End in ___
39. Exercise room count
40. Aperture
42. Plural ending
47. Big Apple ballpark
50. Memorial Day event
52. Record again
53. Take ___ at (try)
54. Serenity
55. Convened again
57. Designer's concern
59. Without face value
61. His and ___
62. Debatable
63. Poses
64. Prefix with derm
67. Apt. divisions
69. Drag

Solution on page 320

Mildly Tricky 3

ACROSS

1. Ballpark figures
5. Rapscallion
10. Macho man
14. Cad
15. Vacillate
16. Excessively
17. Vasco da ___
18. . . . . miss is as good as ___
19. Slangy dissents
20. Bewitched
22. River of song
24. Car with a bar
25. Wobbles
26. Ford flops
29. "I cannot ___ lie"
30. Symbol of freshness
31. Beach souvenir
32. Actor Gulager
35. "Desire Under the ___"
36. Pillow covers
37. Cager's target
38. River at Ghent
39. Alex Haley saga
40. Bamboo eater
41. Challenges
42. Baby
43. More precipitous
46. Rolling in dough
47. Midshipmen's rivals
48. Cowboy
52. Battery fluid
53. Newswoman Zahn
55. Car until 1957
56. Houston university
57. Propelled a boat
58. In ___: stuck
59. Feminine suffix
60. Oklahoma city
61. "Airplane!" actor Robert

DOWN

1. Coax
2. Bellyache
3. Cougar
4. Like some stockings
5. Groups of bees
6. Small role
7. Ardent
8. Brooks of "The Producers"
9. Takes advance orders for
10. Beethoven's "Moonlight ___"
11. Macbeth, for one
12. Theater worker
13. Prescribed amounts
21. Greasy
23. In good health
25. Abounds
26. Henry James biographer Leon
27. Tyne of "Judging Amy"
28. Jazzman Zoot
29. "___ enough!"
31. Blacksmith, at times
32. Hoodwinks
33. Miner's find
34. ___ the crack of dawn
36. Touchy subject
37. Rosh ___
39. Awestruck
40. Small indentation
41. Political pundit Myers
42. Noisy insect
43. Heart-stopping incident
44. Implied
45. Decree
46. Game needs
48. Singer Ives
49. Indian prince
50. Anthem opening
51. Resistance units
54. Nonpro sports gp.

Solution on page 320

Mildly Tricky 4

ACROSS

1. Rope fibers
6. Atomizer output
10. Foot: Prefix
14. WWII torpedo craft
15. Decorative case
16. Impulse transmitter
17. Faux pas
18. Invitation letters
19. Rock group
20. "The Gold Bug" author
21. ___-dokey
23. Town in County Kerry
25. Again, in music
26. Ghost's cry
27. Cowboy's moniker
28. Sauntered
32. Drains
33. "Amadeus" director Forman
34. Sounds of doubt
35. "Steal This Book" author Hoffman
40. Nile queen, for short
41. "___ Married an Axe Murderer" (Mike Myers comedy)
42. Minuscule
43. Losing streak
45. Part of Ascap: Abbr.
46. Elbow
47. Frosts, as a cake
49. Remove the pits from
50. Badge wearer
53. Bad review
54. "She Done ___ Wrong"
55. Crops up
57. The "C" in U.P.C.
58. Bank acct. entry
61. Roman historian
62. A bit cracked?
64. Rip-offs
66. Black, in poetry
67. Hairless
68. Aegean region
69. Fishing luck
70. Auto shaft
71. Begin

DOWN

1. Dickens's Uriah
2. Longest river entirely in Spain
3. "Don't stop!"
4. Kung ___ shrimp
5. Flashing lights
6. French mothers
7. "The ___ Bitsy Spider"
8. Explorer, e.g.
9. First-rate
10. Sunscreen ingredient
11. Praise
12. Beneficiary
13. Book end?
22. Josh
24. Santa ___, Calif.
26. Fundamental
28. Gremlins and Pacers
29. Pepper grinder
30. ___ cheese
31. Come into view
32. Drives off
34. City near Oberhausen
36. A/C units
37. ___ one's time
38. "Come Back, Little Sheba" playwright
39. Checked out
44. Sherlock Holmes prop
46. Unbeatable foe
48. Winter melon
49. Accomplished
50. Biblical spy
51. African antelope
52. Turning point
54. Crowd
56. "Auld Lang ___"
57. Ring up
58. Actor Andrews
59. Arab chieftain
60. H.S. junior's test
63. Florida port, for short
65. Army bed

Solution on page 320

Mildly Tricky 5

ACROSS

1. Development developments
6. "Shoo!"
10. "Dr. Who" network
13. __-garde
14. Anderson of "WKRP in Cincinnati"
15. Henry VIII's sixth
16. __-car
17. Butcher's cut
18. Early Chinese dynasty
19. Man of mystery
20. Light refractor
22. Meat cuts
23. Board game
24. All you can eat
26. Highest point
29. College, to an Aussie
30. Axes
31. Squelched
35. Ancient Egyptian symbols
39. Old cable inits.
40. Except
41. "Gotcha!"
42. Pack
44. Cast member
46. Body that includes SHAPE
47. Toupee, slangily
49. Was restless
51. Hot and dry
55. Ado
56. Belittle
57. Better-chosen
59. Keystone character
62. Bitter end?
63. Asian range
64. In the least
66. Actress Winslet
67. Big bash
68. Water wheel
69. "Little Women" woman
70. __ buco
71. "__ for the Misbegotten"

DOWN

1. Wrong
2. Partner of "done with"
3. Tailless cat
4. Suffix with absorb
5. Paper clip alternative
6. "Kate & __"
7. Courts
8. Japanese cartoon art
9. Yang's counterpart
10. Pesto ingredient
11. Pickling liquid
12. Unrefined
15. Fear
21. Regrets
22. Architect Maya
23. Metric system letters
25. Grayish brown
26. __ of the Apostles
27. Breathe hard
28. __ account
32. Disney division
33. Egyptian boy king
34. Oklahoma native
36. Ayatollah's predecessor
37. Cracker spread
38. Like show horses
43. Razorfish, e.g.
44. __ Khan
45. Baptism, e.g.
46. A.T.M. maker
48. Suffix with fail
50. Albania's capital
51. Decaf brand
52. At right angles to the keel
53. Rash
54. Nostrils
55. Fifth-century pope
58. Butter servings
59. Corn syrup brand
60. Hodgepodge
61. Blueprint
63. ET carrier
65. Male turkey

Solution on page 320

Mildly Tricky 6

ACROSS

1. Argentine plain
6. Golf shot
10. U.S.MC rank
13. Flax fabric
14. Prevalent
15. Advertising award
16. Literary device
17. "Take ___ from me"
18. Wash
19. "Baseball Tonight" channel
20. One, to Juan
21. On the schedule
23. Tack on
26. ___ Fox
27. Andean animals
30. Altar area
32. Actor Lew
33. "David Copperfield" woman
35. Not us
39. Confederate soldier, for short
40. Most quickly
43. Tic-tac-toe loser
44. Aide: Abbr.
46. A Flintstone
47. Courtyards
49. French roast
51. What a poor winner does
52. Neb. neighbor
54. French city on the Strait of Dover
57. Springlike
59. Fourposter, e.g.
60. Banned pollutants
64. Apple computer
65. Clearasil target
67. Wash gently against
68. Tarzan's transport
69. Stage assistant
70. Sheik's land, in song
71. Inquire
72. Mysterious: Var.
73. "Siddhartha" writer

DOWN

1. Ballet bend
2. Affectations
3. Queue before Q
4. Mark Twain, e.g.
5. ". . . have you ___ wool?"
6. Construction site sight
7. Make a pass at
8. "See ___ care!"
9. Enlivens, with "up"
10. Batter's position
11. Fin
12. Dorm denizen
15. Bordeaux wine
20. Delivery co. with brown trucks
22. Dieters' units: Abbr.
24. Free ticket
25. Challenged
27. Byron poem
28. Caustic solutions
29. Wall St. figures
31. ___ de deux
33. Kind of column
34. "A Chorus Line" tune
36. Bar mitzvah dance
37. Sartre's "No ___"
38. Extinct birds
41. Frequently, in poetry
42. Anklebones
45. Hypnotic state
48. Extra
50. Volga feeder
51. Roam (about)
52. 18-wheelers
53. Guzzled
55. Baseball's Doubleday
56. Skeptical
57. Cheer starter
58. Doily material
61. IRS staffers
62. Streisand, in fanzines
63. Eye infection
66. Actor's prompt
67. "Well, ___-di-dah!"

Solution on page 320

Mildly Tricky 7

ACROSS

1. Classic computer game
5. French port
10. FDR's dog
14. Golfer Isao ___
15. "Old MacDonald" refrain
16. Opposed to, in dialect
17. Golf hazard
18. Fowl place
19. Be a monarch
20. Agree out of court
22. Heretofore
24. Writer Joyce Carol ___
27. 24 horas
28. Desert havens
31. ___ Lingus
33. Actor John of "The Addams Family"
37. Deed
38. Main course
41. ___ Bell
42. Big ___, Calif.
43. "The Catcher in the ___"
44. Cowboys' org.
46. "Welcome" site
47. Persia, now
49. List of corrections
51. Anger
52. Pop singer Leo
54. Candied veggie
55. Took out
57. It's south of Eur.
59. Site of ancient Greek games
61. Courtroom fig.
64. Bony
68. Backgammon equipment
69. Funnel-shaped
73. Michener tale, e.g.
74. ___ instant
75. "Guitar Town" singer Steve
76. Bra size
77. Shea team
78. Play for time
79. Sen. Cochran of Mississippi

DOWN

1. Floor coverings
2. In days of ___
3. Card game
4. Walk quietly
5. Special Forces cap
6. "Flying Down to ___"
7. Fair-hiring abbr.
8. Lisa, to Bart
9. Lugged
10. China, Japan, etc.
11. "Son of ___!"
12. Disney's "___ & Stitch"
13. Again
21. Kind of surgery
23. Estuary
25. Automat, e.g.
26. Rev.'s address
28. Gobi refuge
29. Integra maker
30. Leave the straight and narrow
32. Put a new handle on
34. Dravidian language
35. Words of empathy
36. Eminent
39. Bill ___, the Science Guy
40. Eastern newt
45. Puts on cargo
48. Puts in order
50. Campaigned
53. TV's "Mayberry ___"
56. Patronizes, as a restaurant
58. Track events
60. Runway figure
61. Take ___ view of
62. Trig function
63. "Begone!"
65. Apiece
66. Juan's water
67. Sgt. Friday's force
70. Cereal grain
71. FDR measure
72. Annex

Solution on page 321

Mildly Tricky 8

ACROSS
1. Blockhead
5. Mall units
10. Deception
14. Violinist Leopold
15. Seven-time AL batting champ Rod
16. "Jane ___"
17. Analogy words
18. Cosmetician Lauder
19. Pet lovers' org.
20. Tar
22. Most cheeky
24. Beg
27. Mon. follower
28. City on the Rhine
31. Grand Coulee, e.g.
33. Pierces
37. "Holiday ___"
38. In layers
41. Auto racer Fabi
42. Handheld computer, briefly
43. CIA predecessor
44. "___ a chance!"
46. Happy hour hangout
47. "___ tu" (Verdi aria)
48. "Relax, and that's an order!"
50. Gold: Prefix
51. Singer Reese
54. Brain scan, for short
55. Threadbare
57. "___ in the Family"
59. Discontinue
61. "Eureka!"
65. Present and future
69. Fit
70. Thomas of "That Girl"
73. Continental coin

74. Bellicose deity
75. Suffix with sect
76. Aborigine of Japan
77. Barber's cry
78. English Channel feeder
79. "Cut it out!"

DOWN
1. Platform
2. Any of three English rivers
3. "I ___ Song Go Out of My Heart"
4. ___ l'oeil
5. Happening place
6. Consumes
7. Food scrap
8. Chick's sound
9. Saccharine
10. Six-line poem

11. Ballyhoo
12. Circle parts
13. Butcher's stock
21. ___ the good
23. U.S.S.R., now
25. "___ Fideles"
26. ___ es Salaam
28. Two-footed animal
29. Conductor Previn
30. Escargot
32. Household
34. Up, in baseball
35. Lollapalooza
36. Rueful
39. OT book
40. Hairstyles
45. Brusque
49. Common Mkt.
52. Most recent

53. Capone and Capp
56. Trojan hero
58. Green beans
60. Do penance
61. Larger ___ life
62. Aesop's also-ran
63. "Jeopardy!" host Trebek
64. Hawaiian tuber
66. Diamonds, e.g.
67. Brain-teasing Rubik
68. Progresso product
71. Backboard attachment
72. Escape

Solution on page 321

Mildly Tricky 9

ACROSS

1. Some Art Deco works
6. Straight ___ arrow
10. Ready money
14. Bullwinkle, e.g.
15. "The ___ Ranger"
16. Chip in
17. Clobber, biblically
18. "The Dukes of Hazzard" spinoff
19. It means nothing to the French
20. Plaza Hotel imp
22. 1984 Jeff Bridges film
24. Quart divs.
25. Espied
26. Doc bloc
27. Amazes
30. Small bird
32. "Falcon Crest" actress Alicia
34. Up-to-date
35. Comparable to a beet
37. Fright
41. Astrological ram
43. Cenozoic, e.g.
44. Lash ___ of old westerns
45. French beans?
46. Dispatches
48. Bumped into
49. "Send help!"
51. Mama bear, in Madrid
52. Give a darn
53. Nutritional abbr.
56. Inlets
58. Bean counter, for short
60. Exposed to oxygen
62. More loved
65. Enraged
66. ___-American relations
68. Attach a patch
70. Legal scholar Guinier
71. Warner Bros. creation
72. Choppers, so to speak
73. "At once!"
74. Garage sale warning
75. Synthetic fiber

DOWN

1. Bad ___ (German spa)
2. The Eternal City
3. Hard work
4. Bars, in law
5. "Now you ___ . . ."
6. Sheltered, at sea
7. George W., to George
8. Win by ___
9. Lipton competitor
10. Author John Dickson ___
11. Soul
12. Cook, as clams
13. Redhead's dye
21. Jet-setters' jets, once
23. Chronicles
25. Audiophiles' purchases
27. Amo, amas, ___ . . .
28. Sported
29. Trim, as text
31. Angers
33. ___ carte
35. Categorize
36. Dapper ones
38. First word of Virgil's "Aeneid"
39. Remorseful one
40. Allot, with "out"
42. Some Caltech grads
47. Carp cousin
50. Nap
52. Lifework
53. Train tracks
54. Rid of vermin
55. "Gladiator" setting
57. Linda Ronstadt hit song
59. Ziti, e.g.
61. Mine entrance
62. Puts on
63. Gershwin biographer David
64. Mechanical learning
67. "___ won't!"
69. Stanley Cup org.

Solution on page 321

Mildly Tricky 10

ACROSS

1. XXX x X
4. It's rounded up in a roundup
8. Bleats
12. Feathery scarves
14. Pass along
15. Crooked
16. Coastal flier
17. Adjust, as wheels
18. Mlle., in Madrid
19. Wicker material
21. Miffed, with "off"
23. Charged atom
24. Openings
26. Pollster's discovery
28. Investigate
31. The Spartans' sch.
32. Conjointly
33. Aug. follower
36. Flaky mineral
40. Pester
41. Relevance
44. Comic Conway
45. Clove hitch, e.g.
47. Latvian, e.g.
48. "The ___ Mutiny"
50. They: Fr.
52. Stirs up
54. Performed
57. Calf muscle
59. ___-tzu
60. Anatomical pouches
62. Stick on
66. Lo-cal
68. Tijuana toast
70. "The Time Machine" people
71. Not a copy: Abbr.
72. Think out loud
73. Queen of Jordan
74. "The Witches" director Nicolas
75. Ward (off)
76. Prime meridian std.

DOWN

1. "Good buddy"
2. Mrs. Dithers, in "Blondie"
3. Defeatist's word
4. Loki's daughter
5. Best
6. Storms
7. Physics unit
8. Air gun ammo
9. Eagle's nest
10. Susan of "Goldengirl"
11. Bear
13. Arrives, as darkness
14. Attacked, in a way
20. Sleep disorder
22. Sot's problem
25. ___ Rica
27. ___ and Coke
28. Cellarlike
29. "This ___ outrage!"
30. Full of energy
31. Range units: Abbr.
34. Blowup: Abbr.
35. Corolla part
37. "How sweet ___!"
38. Movie
39. Home of Iowa State
42. Charlie Rose's network
43. Reconnoiterer
46. Ascot
49. "Pride and Prejudice" author
51. Mormons, initially
53. "The Cloister and the Hearth" author
54. "It's ___ nothing"
55. 1943 conference site
56. Comic Fields
57. Land's end?
58. Singer K. T. ___
61. Beginning
63. Sleep like ___
64. Whispers sweet nothings
65. Trumpeter Al
67. Bird-to-be
69. German conjunction

Solution on page 321

Mildly Tricky 11

ACROSS

1. Lawn mower brand
5. Opposing group
10. EMT's skill
13. Gulf sultanate
14. Tree with triangular nuts
15. Author ___ Neale Hurston
16. Clash of clans
17. Be in harmony
18. Reassuring words
19. Except if
21. Run wild
23. Academy frosh
25. Romanov rulers
26. Pick
28. Moo ___ pork
29. "___ Were the Days"
30. CPR experts
32. City on the Rhone
36. Protection
37. Christmas buy
38. Goddess of the hunt
39. Once, once
40. Skater Thomas
41. Violinist Zimbalist
42. ___ Bartlet, president on "The West Wing"
43. Primps
45. Interviewer
48. Obeys
49. Twilight
51. Shrewd
55. Delhi wrap
56. Broad valleys
58. Cameo stone
59. Winnow
60. Low-budget prefix
61. No longer green
62. Capp and Capone
63. Attack
64. The "Y" of Y.S.L.

DOWN

1. Bean curd
2. Augur
3. Julia of "The Addams Family"
4. Banked
5. Degrades
6. Not pos.
7. Concise
8. "Original Gangster" rapper
9. Dagger holders
10. Promising one
11. Eggs on
12. Garden tool
15. "___-Dee-Doo-Dah"
20. Blackthorn fruits
22. The Spartans' sch.
24. Complained
26. "Moonstruck" actress
27. Swine
28. Skunk feature
29. Menlo Park inits.
31. Playing marble
32. Biography
33. Kitten's plaything
34. Change for a five
35. '60s war zone, briefly
38. Exploits
40. Mocks
42. "West Side Story" gang member
44. Sanity
45. Be of use
46. Feudal workers
47. Make a sweater
48. Serf
49. She, in Italy
50. Carp cousin
52. Colgate, e.g.: Abbr.
53. Use a keyboard
54. Former spouses
57. Brian of rock

Solution on page 321

Mildly Tricky 12

ACROSS

1. "Go back," in word processing
5. "Miracle on 34th Street" store
10. Gator kin
14. One of the Fab Four
15. Birdlike
16. Etna output
17. "__ Blue"
18. Backward-looking
19. Tel __, Israel
20. Kind of tank
22. Set of advantages
24. Rembrandt van __
25. Shutterbug's setting
27. Support, with "up"
29. Anticipated
30. Shoulder muscles, for short
34. DI doubled
35. Puts forth, as effort
38. Belafonte song opener
39. Storekeeper's stock: Abbr.
40. Bridle part
41. Acorn, eventually
43. Its cap. is Sydney
44. Retain
46. Win over
48. Fight enders, briefly
49. College application part
51. Film director's cry
52. Legume
54. Prefix with linear
56. Upper limit
57. Italian cheese
60. Signs of spring
63. The Miners of the Western Athletic Conf.
64. Inmate who's never getting out

67. Dirt
69. Buster Brown's dog
70. Desktop pictures
71. "Swan Lake" garb
72. Rob Roy, for one
73. Radium discoverer
74. Like a bug in a rug

DOWN

1. The WB rival
2. Thumbs-down votes
3. Fool
4. Veteran
5. California county
6. Opposite of sans
7. Op. __
8. Shostakovich's "Babi __" Symphony
9. Muzzle

10. Held on to
11. Sitarist Shankar
12. "Metamorphoses" poet
13. Bat's home
21. Laid-back
23. Pea container
25. It's a wrap
26. Begin a journey
27. Evergreens
28. Tears apart
29. Sense
31. Sri __
32. 1980s–'90s ring champ
33. Scatters, as seed
34. Emcee's need
36. Greek letters
37. Anatomical pouch
42. Shish __
45. Defensive wall

47. It makes MADD mad
50. Craving
53. Is
55. Baby's woe
56. Code name
57. Dead-end jobs
58. Aural
59. "Let __!"
60. Actor Santoni
61. Sentence subject, usually
62. In __ (undisturbed)
65. Post-op stop
66. In favor of
68. Big galoot

Solution on page 321

Mildly Tricky 13

ACROSS

1. And so forth
4. Tournament passes
8. The time being
13. Dull sound
15. Fluff
16. Rap sheet listing
17. Daughter of Zeus
18. High hairstyle
19. Put a new price on
20. Perry White, e.g.
22. Confess, with "up"
24. Hair goops
25. Sped
26. Iroquois tribe
28. Dorm unit
30. Deaden
34. Not at work
37. "___ Daughter" (1970 film)
40. Reef material
41. Geom. figure
42. SeaWorld star
44. Batman and Robin, e.g.
45. Make a shambles of
48. Heavenward
50. The Trojans of the NCAA
51. Parodied
53. Diplomacy
55. Charlotte ___, Virgin Islands
58. Skill
62. Thai currency
65. Actress Dawber
66. Ripper
67. Outdo
69. Created
71. "Dream Along With Me" singer
72. Director Kurosawa
73. Malayan sailboat
74. Ballyhoo
75. Flung
76. Under the weather
77. "___ Doubtfire"

DOWN

1. Heavens
2. Bara of the silents
3. Three-dimensional
4. Fuzzy image
5. Kennel sound
6. Finish with
7. Vermont ski resort
8. "All Things Considered" airer
9. Wild marjoram
10. Evening, in ads
11. Brat's stocking stuffer
12. Bits of work
14. Discourage
21. Aroma
23. Penpoint
26. Brando's birthplace
27. Calendar mo.
29. Yiddish plaints
31. Language of Pakistan
32. Art Spiegelman's rodent
33. Convention group
34. Fall mos.
35. Send packing
36. Kukla, ___ and Ollie
38. Arrest
39. Walloped, old-style
43. Charlottesville sch.
46. Level of achievement
47. Run smoothly
49. Behold: L.
52. Drivel
54. Piece of land
56. Reading lights
57. ___ ware (Japanese porcelain)
59. "___ With a View"
60. Leg bone
61. Brings (out)
62. Dinghy or dory
63. Egyptian cross
64. Next in line?
66. Furniture wood
68. Fido's foot
70. Bespectacled dwarf

Solution on page 322

Mildly Tricky 14

ACROSS
1. Burn
5. It may be furrowed
9. Milk: Prefix
14. Classic theater name
15. Part of BYOB
16. Cop ___
17. Novelist Wister
18. Smog
19. Be a bad winner
20. Humorist Shriner
21. "East of Eden" son
22. Grand Ole ___
23. Architects' output
26. Three-card monte, e.g.
29. Elsie's chew
30. Lands' End competitor
34. "Casablanca" cafe
37. Hungarian wine
40. Long-distance letters
41. Pallid
42. Relinquished
43. Ref. book
44. Batting stat
45. "Oh boy!"
46. Popular mints
47. Involve
49. Punch-in-the-stomach reaction
50. Hoo-ha
52. Holy
56. Influence
59. Due
61. U-turn from SSE
62. Arctic, for one
64. Summon
65. Prefix with photo
66. Andean animal
67. Merkel and O'Connor
68. Authentic
69. Singing Carpenter
70. Shut (up)
71. Habeas corpus, e.g.

DOWN
1. Throng
2. Mandel of "St. Elsewhere"
3. Skaters' jumps
4. Rembrandt van ___
5. Manually
6. Engine sounds
7. Anise-flavored liqueur
8. Small songbirds
9. Fall behind
10. Self-confidence
11. Hoof sound
12. Eye drop
13. Like Cheerios
24. Nasty
25. Gloomy guy
27. Attired
28. Prince ___ Khan
31. Arabian prince
32. Bank no.
33. Things to pick
34. Exceptional
35. Library I.D.
36. Voucher
37. Auto racer Fabi
38. Peculiar
39. Door opener
42. Pepsi, e.g.
43. Dict. entries
45. Hodges of the Dodgers
46. Miler Sebastian
48. On fire
49. First-born
51. Easy out
52. Commenced
53. Curl one's lip
54. Zhou ___
55. Lived
56. 11th U.S. president
57. Kareem's alma mater
58. Regan's dad
60. Diminish
63. Actress Grey
65. Credit-tracking corp.

Solution on page 322

Mildly Tricky 15

ACROSS
1. Rich earth
5. P.M. periods
9. Oriental nursemaids
14. ___ mater
15. Al or Tipper
16. Grammy winner Jones
17. Bismarck's state: Abbr.
18. Fifth-century pope who was sainted
19. Grab
20. Biological groups
22. Together
24. They get the lead out
26. Attack a sub?
27. "Let's Make ___"
29. Fight back
34. Doesn't just close
37. ___ bean
39. Cafeteria carrier
40. 1953 Leslie Caron film
41. Choir voices
42. Curling place
43. One-named supermodel
44. Film unit
45. "Beau ___"
46. Annoy
48. Markets
50. ___ Tafari (Haile Selassie)
52. Goes up and down
56. "Hold on!"
61. Couch
62. Moorehead of "Bewitched"
63. Cries of surprise
65. Clapton who sang "Layla"
66. Angry
67. Amusement park lure
68. Spanish painter
69. Carafe size
70. British gun
71. Kennedy and Turner

DOWN
1. "Tootsie" Oscar winner
2. More mature
3. Appliance maker
4. Cleans up financially
5. Shining brightly
6. Antagonist
7. "Star Trek: T.N.G." counselor
8. Paris bisector
9. Having handles
10. Big name in faucets
11. Dry, as a desert
12. Mist
13. Son of Noah
21. 1975–'76 World Series champs
23. Gogol's "___ Bulba"
25. French explorer La ___
28. Lo-cal brews
30. Treadmill ordeal
31. Bit of eye makeup
32. Director Gus Van ___
33. Moppet
34. Boo-boo
35. Gimlet garnish
36. "Dear me!"
38. Double agents
41. Tapestry
45. Elation
47. Pencil topper
49. Reduce
51. ___ Tower
53. Kilmer's last words
54. Bizarre
55. Religious factions
56. Sirens do it
57. Prefix with culture
58. ___ the kill
59. Head, to Henri
60. IOU
64. "Fables in Slang" author

Solution on page 322

Mildly Tricky 16

ACROSS

1. "___ Anything" ("Oliver!" song)
5. Boast
9. Kind of rap
12. Appearance
13. Sovereign
15. "Mona ___"
16. Venus de Milo's lack
17. Bridge bid, briefly
18. "Me, myself ___"
19. Pigpens
21. Actress Scala
22. Blue-green
23. Maryland athlete, for short
26. Noted plus-size model
28. Start to fall
31. Eye drops
33. ___ a beet
37. "___ on a Grecian Urn"
38. Busy place
39. Pesos
40. Flat bread?
42. Prefix with surgery
44. Bunch
45. Spuds
47. Go down
49. Blue Angels formation
50. /
51. Medicinal plant
52. Antiquity, once
53. "Hamlet" soliloquy starter
55. Cub Scout groups
57. Ski resort near Snowbird
60. Business letter abbr.
62. Harbor sights
66. Binge
67. What "there is nothin' like"
70. Bermuda, e.g.
71. Olympic sled
72. Printing flourish
73. Where there's smoke
74. Altar affirmation
75. Mouth part
76. Pack (down)

DOWN

1. "___ corny . . ."
2. Gossip
3. Moore of "G.I. Jane"
4. Beginning
5. "My man!"
6. Baseball score
7. "Shake ___!"
8. Bottled spirits
9. Twining stem
10. Meat package letters
11. Armor
14. Gad about
15. Triangular sails
20. Actor Green of "Buffy the Vampire Slayer"
24. Bridle attachments
25. Finish a drive?
27. Hosp. scan
28. Law school class
29. Archetype
30. Five: Prefix
32. Employ again
34. Search (into)
35. Spinning
36. Spread seed
39. "Death, Be Not Proud" poet
41. Having a valid will
43. Orange peel
46. Letter after pi
48. Okla. neighbor
51. E-mailer
54. Actress Arthur and others
56. Work period
57. Gudrun's husband
58. Garish
59. Like some restaurant orders
61. Dear, to Donizetti
63. Site in el mar
64. Jack Horner's find
65. Ooze
68. "O Sole ___"
69. Gee preceder

Solution on page 322

Mildly Tricky 17

ACROSS

1. Scottish inlets
6. "Man ___ Mancha"
10. Passenger inquiries abbr.
14. Wharton's "___ Frome"
15. Impoverished
16. Victor's cry
17. Humpback, e.g.
18. Slip ___ (blunder)
19. 1492 caravel
20. Place to sign
22. Fly in the ointment
23. Blows it
24. Observant ones
26. Gordon of "Oklahoma!"
29. From head ___
31. Spanish eye
32. Forbidden
34. Spoke (up)
38. Rope fiber
40. Corn
42. Prefix with second
43. Porterhouse, e.g.
45. Mix
47. Caustic chemical
48. Some beans
50. Even (with)
52. Fashion designer Giorgio
55. Chowder morsel
56. "Beowulf" beverage
57. Tied
63. "___ sow, so shall . . ."
64. Carson's successor
65. Mournful poem
66. "The Cosby Show" actor Richmond
67. Bull's-eye hitter
68. Prolonged attack
69. Other, in Oaxaca
70. Roy Rogers's real surname
71. Diviner's deck

DOWN

1. Bawdy
2. Roman emperor after Galba
3. Converse
4. Summer top
5. Pooh-pooh
6. Milky gems
7. Centers of attention
8. "Crazy" bird
9. Silver, in heraldry
10. Genius
11. Bale binder
12. Jordanian money
13. Hose woes
21. Fantasize
25. Alley ___
26. ___ scale
27. "Leaving on ___ Plane"
28. Arrive
29. Slaves away
30. Exude
33. "Ali ___ and the 40 Thieves"
35. Feeler
36. "A Day Without Rain" singer
37. Live wire, so to speak
39. Rose Bowl site
41. Organic compounds
44. "___-Tiki"
46. It may prove paternity
49. Gives way
51. Aviator Earhart
52. Brazilian novelist Jorge
53. Change, as a clock
54. City leader
55. $100 bill
58. Calf meat
59. "Just you wait, ___ 'iggins . . ."
60. Swerve
61. Frozen waffle brand
62. Putin's refusal

Solution on page 322

Mildly Tricky 18

ACROSS

1. 24-hr. conveniences
5. El ___
8. "Tosca" tune
12. Masterstroke
13. "Yes ___?"
14. Bucephalus, e.g.
15. Turnpike charge
16. QB Flutie
17. Lulus
18. Uncomfortable
20. Central point
21. "Fiddler on the Roof" matchmaker
22. Police dept. employee
23. Jerks
26. Most optimistic
30. Bewitch
31. Scribe
34. Knight club
35. Come to light
37. Coquettish
38. Great white ___
39. Linguist Chomsky
40. Cozily warm
42. Mail order abbr.
43. World records?
45. Numbered works
47. Mil. authority
48. Spoken for
50. Similar to
52. Uses a shortcut
56. Toyota rival
57. "___ my way"
58. Any day now
59. Hitching post
60. Kittens' cries
61. Atmosphere
62. Lump
63. Fingers, for short
64. Some M.I.T. grads

DOWN

1. Broadway opener
2. Screwdriver, for one
3. Think (over)
4. Spreads out
5. Zagreb resident
6. Occupied, as a lavatory
7. Venetian bigwig
8. Never
9. Buy by Benny
10. "Able was ___ I saw . . ."
11. Internet pop-ups, e.g.
13. Danish city
14. Loudness units
19. Fiesta Bowl site
22. Put on
23. Journalist Alexander
24. 1992 also-ran
25. Like some symmetry
26. Beams
27. Wild West family
28. Listerine alternative
29. Looks after
32. Sgts., e.g.
33. Extinct flightless bird
36. Squarely
38. Ballyhoos
40. Koppel of "Nightline"
41. Subway coins
44. Daub
46. Wild
48. Domesticated
49. Acknowledges
50. Laze
51. "What's gotten ___ you?"
52. ___ Valley, CA
53. A party to
54. ___ synthesizer
55. Aims
56. Witch

Solution on page 322

Mildly Tricky 19

ACROSS
1. Get ___ on the back
5. Porn
9. Low islands
13. Apollo astronaut Slayton
14. Buddies
15. Record company
16. Actress Laura
17. Big furniture retailer
18. "There ___ free lunches"
19. Mesabi yield
21. Drives back
23. Nine-digit I.D.
24. Links numbers
26. Boulder hrs.
27. ___ Paese
28. Common article
30. Sound of relief
34. Peres's predecessor
37. Wild hogs
39. The first "T" of TNT
40. Old-womanish
41. Column's counterpart
42. Navel type
44. Big name in bouquets
45. Iranian currency
47. Pillages
48. Chore
50. Floral necklace
51. Hebrew letter
52. Farm female
54. Actor McGregor
56. Alternatives to Macs
59. Golf shoe features
62. Beg
64. On the way out
65. Nincompoop
67. ___-bitty
68. High points
69. Incantation opener
70. At liberty
71. Link
72. Low voice
73. Some evergreens

DOWN
1. ___ Ababa
2. Equals
3. Ohio city
4. Dollywood's state: Abbr.
5. Kind of notebook
6. Manufacturer
7. Suffix with glob
8. Ivan the Terrible, for one
9. Insertion marks
10. Biblical murder victim
11. Cravings
12. ___-mo
15. Swimmer's regimen
20. First game of a doubleheader
22. Part of EMT: Abbr.
25. Rat
27. Puppeteer Baird
29. Hems' partners
31. "Pay ___ mind"
32. Sand
33. Makes haste
34. Huck Finn's conveyance
35. Architectural pier
36. Auction actions
37. Highland hillside
38. Mum
43. ___ de plume
46. "Okay if ___ myself out?"
49. Wailed
51. Tropical rays
53. Tail motions
55. River dams
56. ___ dish (lab item)
57. Handle the food for a party
58. Eye sores
59. Chanel of fashion
60. Describe
61. Attempt
63. Jazz phrase
64. Shoot the breeze
66. Ring org.

Solution on page 323

Mildly Tricky 20

ACROSS

1. Pigeon's home
5. Quire member
10. Flexible, electrically
14. Seed covering
15. "The ___ Sanction"
16. "Star Wars" princess
17. Docs for dachshunds
18. Europe's "boot"
19. Raggedy ___ (dolls)
20. Farm call
22. Abandons
24. Categorize
27. ACLU concerns
28. Atlanta-based public
    health agcy.
31. ___-foot oil
33. Certain herring
37. Attorney F. ___ Bailey
38. Audition tape
39. Repair shop substitute
41. "It was ___ mistake!"
43. The "L" of XXL
45. Corduroy feature
46. Some Ivy Leaguers
48. Fly high
50. Cousin ___ of "The
    Addams Family"
51. "Star Wars" sage
52. Trunks
53. Dispirited
54. Sold-out sign
56. Teachers' favorites
58. Clarion blast
62. Gillette razors
66. Actress Downey
67. "Love Story" author
70. "Portnoy's Complaint"
    author
71. Toothpaste holder

72. Popular exercise system
73. Baseball brothers' name
74. Goddess of discord
75. Befuddled
76. Word of warning

DOWN

1. Cleveland cagers, briefly
2. Black-and-white cookie
3. Grammy winner Puente
4. Someone ___ (not mine)
5. Cinque follower
6. Big success
7. "Goodness gracious!"
8. Conger catchers
9. Assignation
10. Banned apple spray
11. Penny
12. Loud noises
13. ___ in Charlie
21. Over there, poetically
23. Exxon, formerly
25. Film units
26. Novelist Janowitz
28. Ali, once
29. Holdup
30. String quartet member
32. Midsection
34. "Hee ___"
35. Diarist Nin
36. Atlanta-based airline
39. Auto dealer's offer
40. No longer working: Abbr.
42. Facilitate
44. Hiker's snack
47. "___ of Eden"
49. "Lovely" Beatles girl
52. Clawed

55. Bob Marley fan
57. Fine fiddle
58. ___ de force
59. Prefix with dextrous
60. Dundee denials
61. "Now he belongs to the
    ___"
63. Caramel candy brand
64. Heaps
65. Close
66. I-95, e.g.: Abbr.
68. Vigoda of "Fish"
69. Mauna ___

Solution on page 323

Mildly Tricky 21

ACROSS

1. Prefix with chemical
6. Hostage situation acronym
10. A, in communications
14. ___ and aahed
15. Seat of Allen County, Kan.
16. Stallion, once
17. "And ___ grow on"
18. Marshes
19. "I've Got ___ in Kalamazoo"
20. Traffic tangle
22. Dancer Duncan
24. "Help ___ the way!"
26. "___ Rosenkavalier"
27. Finalize, with "up"
28. ___ Andy ("Show Boat" role)
31. "___ la la!"
33. Actor Herbert
35. Attorneys' org.
36. Jack who ate no fat
38. City in Georgia
42. Soothing ointment
44. HBO rival
45. Be crazy about
46. Pub perch
47. Chair designer Charles
49. Kitten's cry
50. DiCaprio, to fans
52. Religious sch.
53. Eccentric wheels
54. Car co. bought by Chrysler
57. TV's "___ Sharkey"
59. Farm feature
61. Nature's alarm clock
63. Cow catcher
66. Losing proposition?
67. Optimistic
70. Indiana's state flower
72. Mahler's "Das Lied von der ___"
73. ___ Domini
74. Swung around
75. Political cartoonist Thomas
76. Aria, e.g.
77. Fitzgerald and others

DOWN

1. Nanki-___ of "The Mikado"
2. Long, long times
3. "In that case . . ."
4. Keep
5. Scents
6. Bro or sis
7. Court
8. Cold
9. Mortarboard attachment
10. Mil. school
11. NBC's peacock and CBS's eye
12. Distress signal
13. Attorney-___
21. Chicago locale, with "the"
23. Inviting smells
25. Like Eric the Red
28. Elliot of the Mamas and the Papas
29. Blind as ___
30. ___ Alto, Calif.
32. Laughs
34. "Spy vs. Spy" magazine
36. Pick
37. Weighty books
39. Deep sleep
40. City near Provo
41. Kind of conference
43. Tennessee athlete, for short
48. Disney's "___ and the Detectives"
51. Met productions
53. Sportscaster Howard
54. Eve of "Our Miss Brooks"
55. Shearer of "The Red Shoes"
56. Sorority members
58. Maine college town
60. Run out, as a subscription
62. "Let it stand"
64. Aretha's genre
65. ___-Day vitamins
68. NBC weekend revue
69. "___-hoo!"
71. Football gains: Abbr.

Solution on page 323

Mildly Tricky 22

ACROSS

1. Halloween mo.
4. "Dracula" author Stoker
8. Fuselage fastener
13. Light: Prefix
15. College in New Rochelle, NY
16. John who wrote "Butterfield 8"
17. Dashed
18. Amphitheater level
19. Grief
20. Fragrant compounds
22. Palindromic diarist
24. Day laborer
25. Caterpillar rival
26. Writer Shelby
28. Frosh, next year
30. Partner of cease
34. ___-Man (arcade game)
37. Flies high
40. Dayan of Israel
41. Prefix with meter
42. Fissile rock
44. Mother Teresa, e.g.
45. Altercation
48. Arrow part
50. Multivolume ref.
51. Enamored of
53. General ___ chicken
55. Nobodies
58. "Frasier" character
62. ___ contendere
65. "___ Haw"
66. Corkscrew pasta
67. A Muse
69. Goya's "The Duchess of ___"
71. Like two peas in ___
72. ___-Kettering Institute
73. 500 sheets
74. Anger, with "up"
75. Edison rival
76. Club ___ (resorts)
77. "Dear old" guy

DOWN

1. ___ out (declined)
2. Picked
3. Rich cake
4. Bridle parts
5. "Vive le ___!"
6. Concerning
7. Mme. Curie
8. 16½ feet
9. "God willing!"
10. Caesar's farewell
11. Ending with switch
12. Mountain pool
14. Prognosticators
21. Classic cars
23. "Waking ___ Devine" (1998 film)
26. Former Iranian leaders
27. Moon lander, for short
29. Opposite of neg.
31. "Money ___ object!"
32. Andrew of "Melrose Place"
33. Baby-sit
34. "The other white meat"
35. In unison, musically
36. Ice cream holder
38. "Go team!"
39. Bed supports
43. Flunking letters
46. All told
47. "This instant!"
49. ___ avail
52. Book before Esth.
54. Ravi Shankar's instrument
56. Update the arsenal
57. Martinique volcano
59. Cholesterol, e.g.
60. "___ Gay"
61. Sympathized (with)
62. Cozy home
63. Escutcheon border
64. Indochina country
66. Butts
68. "Put ___ Happy Face"
70. Defective

Solution on page 323

Mildly Tricky 23

ACROSS
1. Conceal
5. "Where there's ___ . . ."
10. Restaurant freebie
14. Getting ___ years
15. Not presto
16. Actress Raines
17. "Cool Runnings" vehicle
18. Ankle bones
19. "___ my lips!"
20. "Ditto"
22. 1992 Elton John hit
24. Ethereal
25. Uses for support
26. Toils (away)
29. Brace
30. Word of mouth
31. Be silent, in music
32. In shape
35. France's Cote d'___
36. Cry of terror
37. "Beloved" author
    Morrison
38. Sleep stage, briefly
39. "The Last Supper,"
    for one
40. Batman's sidekick
41. Quotes
42. In order that
43. Deadlock
46. Restrooms, informally
47. Least cooked
48. In excess of
52. Turkish officials
53. Debunk?
55. Gutter locale
56. Naldi, of silents
57. Do-nothing
58. Prefix with -stat
59. Bakery employee

60. Bel ___ cheese
61. Lith. and Ukr., formerly

DOWN
1. "Bonanza" brother
2. "To Live and Die ___"
3. Per ___ (daily)
4. Undertaking
5. Changes
6. All in
7. About, contractually
8. OCS grads
9. Dillydallied
10. Sublet
11. Bread spreads
12. Grassy plain
13. Burdened
21. Cad
23. ___ monde

25. Maj.'s superior
26. Exchange blows
27. Loll
28. Calla lily, e.g.
29. Heroic tales
31. Crowd quorum
32. Watch chains
33. "What's ___ for me?"
34. Baseball's Martinez
36. Surpass
37. Browning devices
39. Fail to see
40. Gad about
41. Rubicon crosser
42. "La Nausée" novelist
43. Farsi speaker
44. Wizardry
45. Babble
46. Comes in second

48. Lounging slipper
49. Cries of triumph
50. Affirm
51. Revivalists
54. Room in a harem

Solution on page 323

Mildly Tricky 24

ACROSS

1. Patronize, as a restaurant
6. "The Purple People Eater" singer Wooley
10. Educator's org.
13. Generals' insignia
14. Puff of a joint
15. Broadway award
16. Fifty minutes past the hour
17. Working without ___
18. Grafted, in heraldry
19. Arnaz of "I Love Lucy"
20. High season, on the Riviera
21. Restaurant patrons
23. Accent
26. Bohemian
27. Rugged ridges
30. Juno, to the Greeks
32. Fertile soil
33. Small deer
35. Florida's Miami-___ County
39. "Do Ya" rock grp.
40. Helmsman
43. Broadway's "Five Guys Named ___"
44. Parts of a min.
46. Alpine stream
47. Moving about
49. Made a hole in one
51. Magician's cry
52. Jutlander
54. Lustrous fabric
57. Brawls
59. Actor Chaney
60. Juan's "another"
64. Years in Spain
65. ". . . unto us ___ is given": Isaiah
67. Loud, as a crowd
68. "___ we forget . . ."
69. "And Then There Were ___"
70. "Beetle Bailey" character
71. The "Superstation"
72. Takes to court
73. Highway curves

DOWN

1. Founded: Abbr.
2. Suit to ___
3. Beach shades
4. Manet and Monet
5. General of Chinese menu fame
6. Condition
7. Sharpens
8. Barely make, with "out"
9. ___ noire
10. Trio trebled
11. Door
12. Affirmative votes
15. Foursome
20. Triage sites, briefly
22. Bern's river
24. "___ of the D'Urbervilles"
25. Sex researcher Hite
27. Amber brews
28. Patton, to Scott
29. Fair-hiring org.
31. Compass dir.
33. Studies
34. "___ the land of the free . . ."
36. Quantities: Abbr.
37. "I dare you!"
38. Architect Saarinen
41. Inventor's monogram
42. Pink, as a steak
45. Most reasonable
48. Ladies of Spain
50. Mediocre mark
51. Ballpoint, e.g.
52. Star in Cygnus
53. At ___ for words
55. By oneself
56. Softens, with "down"
57. ___ liquor
58. Lacking
61. Rocky peaks
62. Foam at the mouth
63. Loads from lodes
66. Nearly worthless coin
67. Enzyme ending

Solution on page 323

Mildly Tricky 25

ACROSS

1. Job for a dermatologist
5. Cut, as a log
9. Par ___
14. Internet auction site
15. Dr. Seuss's "Horton Hears ___"
16. ___ la Plata
17. Yvette's evening
18. Throat trouble
19. Dry (off)
20. Wine cask
21. Effeminate
22. Dirty
24. Couturier's concerns
26. Mauna ___
27. Worldwide (abbr.)
29. LP successors
30. Year in Nero's reign
33. Bridges
36. Tic-tac-toe win
38. Hiker's path
40. Soave, e.g.
41. Mil. stores
42. O.T. book
43. Houston ballplayer
45. CBS logo
46. "Land ___!"
47. La ___, Bolivia
48. Prof.'s degree
50. Applaud
52. Little, in Lille
53. Suck up
57. Turkish inn
60. "The Simpsons" storekeeper
61. Subside, with "down"
62. Animal life
63. Briefs, briefly
65. "Star Wars" knight
66. Ant
67. Small, medium or large
68. Fictional circumnavigator
69. Billiards shot
70. ___ Piper
71. "Trick" joint

DOWN

1. Adam and Mae
2. Approximately
3. Wet, weatherwise
4. Son of Odin
5. Least risky
6. Out of kilter
7. Reporter's query
8. Holiday quaffs
9. Most bohemian
10. Quartet member
11. "___ Russia $1200" (Bob Hope book)
12. Pigged out (on)
13. "___ blu dipinto di blu"
21. Swamps
23. Approved
25. Cruise ship
28. Ran
29. Trig function
30. Dearth
31. Bad habit, so to speak
32. Afflictions
33. Exchange
34. Leaning tower site
35. 1998 animated bug film
37. Prefix with acetylene
39. Harvests
44. Run
46. "Elephant Boy" boy
49. Color
51. Ended, as a subscription
52. Glazier's items
54. Classic theater
55. Chain of hills
56. Neutral shade
57. "___ Camera"
58. Fall bloomers
59. Recipe amt.
60. Axlike tool
62. Opposite of masc.
64. The Henry who founded the Tudor line
65. NYC airport

Solution on page 324

Mildly Tricky 26

ACROSS
1. Lbs. and ozs.
4. ___ of Arc
8. Early 12th-century date
12. Groundbreakers?
14. Emperor after Nero
15. Linen vestments
16. Periodic table no.
17. Riyadh residents
18. Archaeological site
19. Saunters
21. Least taxing
23. Speedy
26. Hosp. staffer
27. Itsy-bitsy
30. Bigwig
32. Bridge positions
36. Assns.
37. Park place?
39. Fan setting
40. Ingot
41. A Bobbsey twin
42. Cushion
43. Thurman of "The Avengers"
44. Compass pt.
45. Lacking a key, in music
47. Eager
48. Coup ___
50. "Oy ___!"
51. Calf-length skirts
52. "Kapow!"
54. Chocolate tree
56. Asthmatic's device
60. Put on the line
64. Borscht vegetable
65. Acknowledge, in a way
68. Numbers game
69. Author ___ Stanley Gardner
70. Posture problem
71. Dick and Jane's dog
72. Olympian's quest
73. Sore
74. Pair

DOWN
1. Kapow!
2. Dog in Oz
3. Stitches
4. Cookie holder
5. Suffix with pay
6. French cleric
7. Kind of cavity
8. Yacht lot
9. Sleuth's find
10. Wading bird
11. "___ It Romantic?"
13. Rears
14. [How shocking!]
20. Palindromic cheer
22. Velocity
24. Chekhov's first play
25. N, E, W, or S
27. "And so ___"
28. Bleep out
29. "Snowy" bird
31. Yellow fruit
33. Swung around
34. Marisa of "My Cousin Vinny"
35. Tchaikovsky ballet roles
37. Gangster's gun
38. "My ___ Sal"
41. Birth-related
46. IBM rival
47. Newsstands
49. Lessened
51. ___ tai
53. Bright bunch
55. Field yield
56. "___ to differ!"
57. Agrippina the Younger's son
58. "War is ___"
59. Campus military org.
61. Didn't return
62. Sufficient, in verse
63. Inflict upon
66. Homer Simpson outburst
67. Plaything

Solution on page 324

Mildly Tricky 27

ACROSS

1. Arafat's gp.
4. "Last one ___ a rotten egg!"
8. "Immediately!"
12. Angelic headgear
14. It's a wrap
15. Ancient alphabetic character
16. During
17. Bonehead
18. Where water became wine
19. Principles
21. Radiator sound
23. Alt. spelling
24. Navy builder
26. Suave competitor
28. Bridge support
31. West of "My Little Chickadee"
32. "M*A*S*H" clerk
33. Tach readings
36. Makes "it"
40. Afternoon hour on a sundial
41. Land
44. Corp. VIP
45. "Not guilty," e.g.
47. Cutup
48. Exposed
50. Brit. legislators
52. Eternal
54. Tend to the turkey
57. Enlightenment, in Zen
59. Matterhorn, e.g.
60. Old English letters
62. Times up
66. Cutting remark
68. Consume
70. Romance lang.
71. Latin lesson word
72. Hag
73. Explorer Hernando de ___
74. Kind of bean
75. Add to the staff
76. Gaping mouth

DOWN

1. Excellent, in modern slang
2. Poor, as excuses go
3. "Chocolat" actress
4. "___ be my pleasure!"
5. Bing, bang, or boom
6. Words of resignation
7. Complete collections
8. ___ de Triomphe
9. Debonair
10. One year's record
11. Oyster's prize
13. Black Sea port
14. Rope fiber
20. Aquarium fish
22. Health resort
25. "It ain't over till it's over" speaker
27. Collecting Soc. Sec.
28. Excursion
29. Bus or air alternative
30. Adams of "The Ernie Kovacs Show"
31. Chinese food additive
34. The "p" in m.p.g.
35. Angry with
37. "God's Little ___"
38. Orders to plow horses
39. Lays down the lawn
42. IV units
43. Film critic Roger
46. Qty.
49. Outs
51. Second of April?
53. Flip out
54. Rum cakes
55. "Remember the ___!"
56. Deodorant type
57. Lewis with Lamb Chop
58. Fur trader John Jacob
61. "Rambling Wreck From Georgia ___"
63. Basic bit
64. "Bye-bye"
65. Deliberate
67. Jamboree grp.
69. French article

Solution on page 324

Mildly Tricky 28

ACROSS

1. Cut
6. Cosby's "I Spy" co-star
10. Siamese sound
14. Dispatch boat
15. Suffix with utter
16. Bread spread
17. Red vegetables
18. Neap, e.g.
19. Foot part
20. Sizes up
22. Woolly
24. Ananias, e.g.
25. Locked (up)
26. Synagogue
29. Belgian river
31. Painting surface
35. Juries
37. Astronaut Armstrong
39. "You're it!" game
40. Four Monopoly properties: Abbr.
41. Painkiller
43. Be in arrears
44. Follower: suffix
45. Defeat
46. Honeybunch
48. Sea swallows
50. "___ the mornin'!"
52. Dict. entries
53. Klutz's cry
55. Diana of the Supremes
57. 1884 Helen Hunt Jackson novel
60. "Cornflake Girl" singer
64. Prayer start
65. Name of 12 popes
67. Catch
68. High school subj.
69. The "A" in ABM
70. Scatter
71. Make yawn
72. Bringing up the rear
73. Safecrackers

DOWN

1. Netherlands Antilles island
2. December 24 and 31
3. Contends
4. 1967 Oscar winner Parsons
5. Martini's partner
6. Supplies the food for
7. Les Etats-___
8. Digital readout, for short
9. "The Old Wives' Tale" playwright
10. Grosse ___, Mich.
11. Arm bone
12. Four-sided fig.
13. Mies van der ___
21. Refuses
23. "The Ice Storm" director
25. Hunted animals
26. Nautical pole
27. Writer Bret
28. Racer Al
30. Put an ___ (halt)
32. Alibi
33. Greeted at the door
34. Curved moldings
36. "Rent" composer Jonathan
38. Not alfresco
42. Double-play pair
47. Armand of "The Marrying Man"
49. Piece of pasta
51. "To your health!"
54. Like some bulls
56. Spacek of "Carrie"
57. L.B.J. in-law
58. Exchange premium
59. Othello, for one
60. Sounds of reproof
61. Actress Helgenberger
62. Calif. neighbor
63. Bastes
66. "___ pig's eye!"

Solution on page 324

Mildly Tricky 29

ACROSS

1. Many, many years
4. Blood: Prefix
8. Lens
13. Exchange premium
15. Picked from a lineup
16. Yellowstone animal
17. Geom. figure
18. Greek sandwich
19. "Hill Street Blues" actor Joe
20. Pennsylvania university
22. Nigerian native
24. Gush
25. Prevent legally
26. R-rated
28. Punch
30. Admirers, collectively
34. Bern's river
37. In stitches
40. Immune system component
41. Musical syllable
42. Retell
44. Kenan's Nickelodeon pal
45. November birthstone
47. Beginner
48. Zaire's Mobutu ___ Seko
49. "Later"
51. Blue-green
53. Some potatoes
56. Othello's people
60. Badgers
63. Republicans, for short
64. "Yay!"
65. Felt poorly
67. Extremely
69. Catcher Tony
70. Hardly Mr. Right
71. Arthurian lady
72. Prom-night safety gp.
73. Imparts
74. Wash
75. Arid

DOWN

1. "Guitar Town" singer Steve
2. Curved moldings
3. Not, in Nuremberg
4. Lofty
5. Popular ice cream maker
6. Promotion basis
7. Building material
8. "Pygmalion" monogram
9. Not really sing
10. "Now!"
11. Unit of loudness
12. Falling flakes
14. Idle
21. Main mail ctr.
23. Big galoot
26. ___ shooting
27. Chess ending
29. Chicago hrs.
31. Astronaut Slayton
32. Bullfight cheers
33. Fr. miss
34. Memo abbr.
35. Suffix with buck
36. Deeply absorbed
38. Twisted
39. They make busts
42. Popular shirt label
43. Plaything
46. Liqueur flavoring
48. Busybodies
50. Jokester
52. I love: Lat.
54. Shack
55. ___ can of worms
57. Mountain nymph
58. Time off, briefly
59. Disreputable
60. Table salt, to a chemist
61. Suffix with concession
62. Narrow valley
64. Jekyll's alter ego
66. Stat for infielders
68. Mo. or Miss.

Solution on page 324

Mildly Tricky 30

ACROSS

1. Workout sites
5. Stick-in-the-mud
9. Allegation
14. In apple-pie order
15. The same: Lat.
16. Prefix meaning "sacred"
17. "Back in the ___"
18. Biblical verb
19. Hearing-related
20. Chemical cousin
22. Pershing's WWI command
24. Believer's suffix
25. Corkwood
27. Superman foe ___ Luthor
29. French dear
31. Washington's ___ Stadium
33. Rumple
37. Kind of sauce
38. Actress Shearer
40. Swiss capital
41. "___ which will live in infamy": FDR
43. "___ Married an Axe Murderer" (Mike Myers comedy)
44. 1973 Rolling Stones #1 hit
45. "Ciao!"
46. Linoleum layer
48. Byrnes of "77 Sunset Strip"
49. Direction from which el sol rises
50. Mangy mutt
51. A+ or C-
53. 601, in old Rome
55. Avid
57. Cost-of-living stat
60. Cached

62. Delaware tribe
65. Hullabaloo
67. Diehard
69. "All ___ are off!"
71. Arctic abode
72. "Whip It" rock group
73. "The jig ___!"
74. Paint layers
75. Plow pullers
76. Hairdo

DOWN

1. Wildebeest
2. "___ Can" (Sammy Davis Jr. autobiography)
3. Come together
4. Disco light
5. Beethoven opera
6. Smells
7. Receive
8. Jewish youth org.
9. Rub raw
10. "Charlie's Angels" costar Lucy
11. Ethereal: Prefix
12. Some nest eggs, for short
13. Snakes do it
21. Fictional weaver
23. Antlered animal
26. Wardrobe
28. Marvel Comics group
29. Musical endings
30. Marriott competitor
32. Flunk
34. Goaded
35. Derogatory
36. Germ
37. Bargain event

39. Queue after Q
40. Fruitless
42. Got ready to drive
47. Incited
50. Early second-century year
52. Language of the Koran
54. Mass confusion
56. Animated
57. Trendy
58. ___ stick
59. Seat of Allen County, Kan.
61. Pedestal part
63. Cuban cash
64. Pins and needles holder
66. In demand
68. Annoy
70. Tanning lotion letters

Solution on page 324

Mildly Tricky 31

ACROSS

1. Bitty bite
4. Town
8. Corn bread
12. Hip bones
14. Cavalry sword
15. Historic Hungarian city
16. Photos
17. Singer Cleo
18. Actor Connery
19. Hunting dog
21. Big name in diamonds
23. Tricks
26. Kit ___ bar
27. Flavor
30. Fleur-de-___
32. Pelvic bones
36. Cow-headed goddess
37. Pinpoint
39. Brick carrier
40. Abbr. on a shingle
41. Atlas page
42. One of the Cyclades
43. Baton Rouge sch.
44. Big Apple sch.
45. "To do" list
47. Thwart
48. Neighborhoods
50. Kipling's "Gunga ___"
51. Armada
52. French nobleman
54. Old Testament book
56. Kodaks, e.g.
60. Ford classics
64. Above
65. Pan-fry
68. In ___ of
69. "___ a man with seven wives"
70. Good ___

71. "Peter Pan" pirate
72. Butterfly snarers
73. Two-wheeled carriage
74. Popular ice cream maker

DOWN

1. Bites
2. "Would ___ to you?"
3. Ancient Briton
4. Cote call
5. Where: Lat.
6. Pull apart
7. Fraternity man
8. 100 centimos
9. Decorative molding
10. Around
11. Sea eagles
13. Minute Maid Park team
14. Some cameras, for short
20. Prefix with Asian
22. Diamond bags
24. Ran for one's wife?
25. Order to attack, with "on"
27. Province in Tuscany
28. From Nineveh: Abbr.
29. Resentment
31. Refused
33. Uncle Tom's wife
34. Riveter of song
35. Not for minors
37. Delay
38. Shelley's "___ Skylark"
41. Conductor Kurt
46. Medical research agcy.
47. Thrashes about
49. Whizzes
51. Presidents' Day mo.
53. Spanish houses
55. Bouillabaisse, e.g.
56. Brother of Abel
57. "Don't look ___!"
58. ___ & Chandon (champagne)
59. Accessory for Miss America
61. "The ___ of the Ancient Mariner"
62. Achievement
63. Chop ___
66. Acapulco article
67. Mystery writer Josephine

Solution on page 325

Mildly Tricky 32

ACROSS

1. Songwriter Coleman et al.
4. Boutique
8. Silent film star
13. Champagne Tony of golf
15. Singer Irene
16. Newsman Roger
17. "___ was in the beginning . . ."
18. Bickering
19. Laid up
20. Gymnast Mary Lou
22. Resistance unit
24. Sunrise direction, in Sonora
25. Fire remnants
26. Bless
28. Any day now
30. Deadly
34. Bed board
37. The two
40. "Cool!"
41. "That hurts!"
42. Help settle
44. San Francisco's ___ Hill
45. Bowler's pickup
47. Add-on rooms
48. Greek letters
49. John Irving hero
51. Org. for Annika Sorenstam
53. "The magic word"
56. March honoree, for short
60. Catches in the act
63. Special attention, for short
64. Japanese floor covering
65. Home planet
67. Shamu, e.g.
69. "I have ___ good authority"
70. Toast choice
71. Advertising sign
72. Quito's country: Abbr.
73. Ivan and Nicholas
74. An earth sci.
75. "48___"

DOWN

1. Santa ___, Calif.
2. Acceptances
3. Most common U.S. surname
4. Car radio button
5. Derby, for one
6. Betelgeuse's constellation
7. Prefix with logical
8. ___ polloi
9. Actress Bening
10. Civil War soldiers
11. Artist Mondrian
12. Kind of shoppe
14. Swear (to)
21. Bear, in Madrid
23. Thickness measure
26. + end
27. Hawaiian goose
29. U.K. award
31. ___ Christian Andersen
32. Yours, in Tours
33. Arcing shots
34. Method: Abbr.
35. Cuts off
36. Like gossiping tongues
38. Up to, briefly
39. Oscar winner Berry
42. Blackbird
43. Cooking meas.
46. Eminem, e.g.
48. Flat peppermint candy
50. Caress
52. Fed. property overseer
54. As a companion
55. Rocky debris
57. Quilt part
58. Love, in Lourdes
59. Singer Turner and others
60. Former Speaker Gingrich
61. Contented sighs
62. La ___ tar pits
64. Sharp flavor
66. Elevs.
68. Dove's sound

Solution on page 325

Mildly Tricky 33

ACROSS

1. "___ I can help it!"
6. Critters in litters
10. Photocopier problems
14. Barely ahead
15. Approve
16. Bassoon relative
17. Sired, biblically
18. Answer to "Shall we?"
19. "Billy Budd" captain
20. City on the Rio Grande
22. Toughened
24. Buckeyes' sch.
25. Like Easter eggs
26. Actor Ron
27. Diamond irregularity
30. Chiang ___-shek
32. Korean War fighter
34. Bagel topper
35. Marry again
37. Marine ___
41. Endure
43. "Foucault's Pendulum" author
44. Sees the sights
45. Honeydew, e.g.
46. Pub pastime
48. Mire
49. Cut the grass
51. Jamaican music
52. Nimble
53. Cover
56. Broke down
58. "Phooey!"
60. Timeless
62. Clog
65. Boughpot
66. H.H. Munro's pen name
68. Observant one
70. Kind of sch.
71. Beholder
72. "Lord, ___?": Matthew
73. Classic theater name
74. Falls behind
75. Star

DOWN

1. Essence
2. European auto
3. Forum garb
4. Lined up
5. Elaborate parties
6. Game on horseback
7. Strings of islands?
8. Singer Cline
9. Modus operandi
10. "By ___!"
11. White poplar
12. Edible mushroom
13. Down at the heels
21. Home of the Blue Devils
23. Fiats
25. Molded, as metal
27. Deception
28. Ear part
29. Leaf angle
31. Struck with wonder
33. Moo ___ gai pan
35. Celebrity
36. Nerd
38. Country bumpkin
39. Coll. figure
40. Army NCO
42. ___ Perignon
47. President before Wilson
50. Pop maker
52. Unseat
53. Crowbar, e.g.
54. Author Calvino
55. Neuter
57. Desert drainage basin
59. Architectural order
61. ___ Martin (cognac brand)
62. Gentlemen
63. Gas, e.g.: Abbr.
64. Folk singer Seeger
67. Beer barrel
69. Kid

Solution on page 325

Mildly Tricky 34

ACROSS
1. Campus bigwig
5. Coal waste
9. Baseball commissioner Bud
14. ___ Canal
15. Game-stopping call
16. "Maria ___"
17. "A Doll's House" heroine
18. Bit attachment
19. Gondola's route
20. African fly
22. Close call
24. Puts under
26. Jeanne d'Arc, e.g.: Abbr.
27. Tre + quattro
29. French star
34. For face value
37. Hindu hero
39. Betting group
40. Conclude, with "up"
41. Broadcaster
42. "Return of the Jedi" creature
43. Actress Singer of "Footloose"
44. Outlaws
45. Maternally related
46. Batting coach's concern
48. Mixes
50. Electrical unit
52. Swears
56. Theatrical
61. Intensify
62. Draw a bead on
63. Nintendo rival
65. Ward of "Sisters"
66. Cathedral topper
67. "Hold on ___!"
68. "Members ___"
69. Injures
70. Ancient portico
71. Refusals

DOWN
1. Fender bends
2. Jagged, as a leaf's edge
3. Broadcast
4. Immaculate
5. Avenue
6. Commit perjury
7. Idi ___
8. Hereditary factors
9. Hush-hush
10. Jack of "Rio Lobo"
11. Director Riefenstahl
12. "Much" preceder
13. Guys' partners
21. Suffix with gang
23. Go on ___ (rampage)
25. Narrow groove
28. Brings home
30. Legal hunting period
31. Corn Belt state
32. Rioter's take
33. Actress Sommer
34. Cobblers' tools
35. Brisk pace
36. Prefix with legal
38. Hostess Perle
41. Red as ___
45. Art Deco artist
47. Jalopies
49. Cornell's home
51. Kudrow and Bonet
53. Dictation taker
54. Gown fabric
55. Neuters
56. Short race
57. Kelly of morning TV
58. Mideast chief: Var.
59. Old-time schoolteacher
60. "___ la vie"
64. Prefix with thermal

Solution on page 325

Mildly Tricky 35

ACROSS
1. Beer, slangily
5. Parachute part
9. Put ___ to (end)
14. Cat's scratcher
15. "___ from Muskogee"
16. Pope of 1605
17. E pluribus ___
18. Joke response, informally
19. Playwright Jean
20. Forbid
21. Suffix with electro-
22. Designer letters
23. Sister of Apollo
26. Bring down the house
29. Grief
30. Lethargy
34. Young hooter
37. Push roughly
40. Diplomat: Abbr.
41. Try, as a case
42. Pages (through)
43. Done, in Dijon
44. Follower of sigma
45. Miata automaker
46. Calf-length skirts
47. Confer holy orders on
49. Nickname
50. ___ Fifth Avenue
52. Antares, e.g.
56. Holds close
59. Bout enders, in brief
61. Singer Sumac
62. Bubbling
64. Harvest
65. Fingerboard ridge
66. Dismiss
67. ___ facto
68. Gray wolf
69. Call to a bellhop
70. Big East team
71. ___ Bator, Mongolia

DOWN
1. Diving acronym
2. Of an arm bone
3. Intimidate
4. Personal ad abbr.
5. Herding dog
6. Gives the go-ahead
7. Break in friendly relations
8. Postpone
9. H.S. math
10. Farm machine
11. Honky-___
12. Field team
13. Feel sorry for
24. Basin accessory
25. Bon ___ (witticism)
27. Off-road travelers, briefly
28. Actress Caldwell
31. Bill stamp
32. All: prefix
33. Diamond stats
34. "___ be in England": Browning
35. Wash's partner
36. Extol
37. "___ who?"
38. Ate
39. One ___ kind
42. Long and lean
43. Little lies
45. "Mamma ___!"
46. Wrestling venue
48. Specify
49. Tyrant
51. Do a full monty
52. Friars' fete
53. Austrian province whose capital is Innsbruck
54. Tiny creature
55. Betray, in a way
56. Fair share, maybe
57. Above, in Berlin
58. Attend
60. Military cap
63. Auction offering
65. Grippe

Solution on page 325

Mildly Tricky 36

ACROSS
1. Actress Berger
6. "Handsome ___ handsome does"
10. "Don't have ___, man!"
14. Less cordial
15. Broad valley
16. Rail bird
17. Blakley of "A Nightmare on Elm Street"
18. Grand in scale
19. Speaker of Cooperstown
20. Rub the wrong way
22. Hard to miss
24. Ample shoe width
25. "___ cost to you!"
26. "___ before beauty"
27. On ___ with (equal to)
30. Louse-to-be
32. Cap with a pompom
34. ___ Aviv
35. Red-tag events
37. Striped cat
41. Put off, as a motion
43. Circuit
44. Goddesses of the seasons
45. Money in the bank, say
46. Beethoven dedicatee
48. A Gershwin
49. Freight weight
51. Artist Yoko
52. Poetic nights
53. Faucet
56. The Amish, e.g.
58. Roast hosts, briefly
60. Accept
62. Bounded
65. Beginning of the end?
66. "___ Little Kindness"
68. Ticked off
70. Feminine suffix
71. "Magnet and Steel" singer Walter
72. Prayer wheel priests
73. Pro ___
74. Small dent
75. In the air

DOWN
1. Dubbed one
2. MBA course
3. Cloud number
4. Wobble
5. Rocky ridge
6. ___ fixe
7. Chump
8. Elite group
9. Trigonometric ratio
10. ___ spumante
11. Jazz pianist Chick
12. Rocket gasket
13. Squander
21. Horne who sang "Stormy Weather"
23. Detest
25. Gorged oneself
27. "___ girl!"
28. Shooter's ammo
29. Linen vestments
31. "Winnie ___ Pu"
33. ___ Zedong
35. Bristly
36. Rotate
38. Camembert's kin
39. Building near a silo
40. Affirmative votes
42. Allow
47. "___ Like It Hot"
50. Took home after taxes
52. Observation
53. Spud
54. Guam's capital
55. Computer command
57. Welsh dog
59. "Cheers" waitress
61. Home of Zeno
62. Singer k. d. ___
63. "Tickle me" doll
64. Unheeding
67. TV chef Martin
69. Summer hrs.

Solution on page 325

Mildly Tricky 37

ACROSS

1. Low-___ diet
5. Pepsi rival
9. Loos who wrote "Gentlemen Prefer Blondes"
14. "A Death in the Family" author James
15. Rent-___
16. Raison ___
17. Rover's reward
18. Delhi dress
19. Exterior
20. Suffix with drunk
21. Der ___: Adenauer
22. "The Wizard of Oz" dog
23. Milan opera house
26. Swing around
29. Surgery sites, for short
30. Unmitigated
34. Appetizing
37. ___ Gras
40. Bovine bellow
41. Black cuckoos
42. Borders
43. Amount to make do with
44. "Far out"
45. Sail holders
46. Tender areas
47. Cubic meters
49. Cries at fireworks
50. Chemical endings
52. Primal therapy sounds
56. Turkish leader
59. Rat-___
61. Long.'s opposite
62. Sculptor Henry
64. Say ___ (deny)
65. Colleen's country
66. Like windows
67. Ness, e.g.
68. "The Sweater Girl" Turner
69. Coasters
70. Feudal serf
71. TV's talking horse

DOWN

1. Conspiracy
2. Ancient Greek marketplace
3. Tears apart
4. Buzzer
5. Cellist Pablo
6. Central Florida city
7. Go-___
8. Great Lakes tribesmen
9. "Much ___ About Nothing"
10. It's gender
11. "What's ___ you?"
12. Waste allowance
13. Dynamic leader?
24. Camp beds
25. Station closing?
27. Boys
28. Mentalist Geller
31. From the States: Abbr.
32. Carrot on a snowman, perhaps
33. Chuck
34. Blackens
35. Biol. subject
36. A or B, on a record
37. ER workers
38. F.B.I. employee: Abbr.
39. ___ ipsa loquitur
42. "___ on Down the Road"
43. Come in last
45. Chess pieces
46. Nasdaq unit: Abbr.
48. Brought up
49. Overture follower
51. A votre ___
52. Beelzebub
53. "Are you calling me ___?"
54. Chateau-Thierry's river
55. Lieu
56. Concert equipment
57. Hockey score
58. Fine-tune
60. Big gobblers
63. Begley and Bradley
65. "A Nightmare on ___ ___ Street"

Solution on page 326

Mildly Tricky 38

ACROSS

1. Flat-bottomed boat
5. ___ terrier
9. Accident
12. Spherical
14. Markers
15. Peacock constellation
16. Particular
17. Burrito wrappers
19. Bunyan's tool
20. Young salmon
22. Matching furniture set
23. Beaux
25. Classified
26. Vacation destination
28. Kind of counter
29. Blessed ___
30. Harangue
32. Crossed (out)
33. Neighbor of Nigeria
34. The Colonel's place, initially
37. Noshes
39. Kind of eclipse
41. Go-carts
43. Rita of "West Side Story"
44. Infernal
45. Hood release?
47. "Get ___ of yourself!"
48. Bucks and bulls, e.g.
49. Agnus ___
52. Luau serving
54. Correct, as text
56. Make ready, briefly
57. Not of the cloth
58. Bridget Fonda, to Jane
59. "___ out!" (ump's call)
60. American, abroad
61. Two-stripers (abbr.)

DOWN

1. Coin collector?
2. Heart of the matter
3. Fanatical
4. "Scream" director Craven
5. Squelch
6. Mentholated cigarettes
7. Mongolian tent
8. Approx.
9. Rock salt
10. Personification
11. Sat
13. Richard of "L.A. Law"
15. Dive
18. "Let me repeat . . ."
21. Cambridge sch.
24. Came out on top
25. Withdraw gradually
26. "Oedipus ___"
27. Apple picker
28. Cubism pioneer Juan
30. Private eyes
31. Bic filler
33. "Roseanne" star
34. Mired
35. Booster
36. ___-Magnon
37. Lug
38. "I ___ vacation!"
39. Ease up
40. Dot-com's address
41. Bring back on staff
42. Penitent
43. G.I. chow in Desert Storm
44. Diaper, in Britain
45. Michael of "Monty Python"
46. Smart ___
48. Movie-rating org.
50. Abbr. on a business letter
51. March 15, e.g.
53. Carry on, as a trade
55. Tape rec. jack

Solution on page 326

Mildly Tricky 39

ACROSS

1. Accumulate
6. A deer, a female deer
9. According to
14. Like some floors
15. "Sweet as apple cider" girl
16. Exhibited
17. Yarns
18. Western org.
19. "___ Johnny!"
20. Salt Lake City collegians
21. "As I Lay Dying" character
22. Lyric poems
23. Chipped in
25. Patriotic org.
27. Clarinet cousins
30. Greek god of the winds
35. CD predecessors
38. First name in whodunits
40. Animal skin
41. Like granola
43. Riddle-me-___
44. Hindu queen
45. "Chestnuts roasting ___ open fire"
46. Athens rival
48. FDR or JFK
49. Lady of Spain
51. Hotelier Helmsley
53. Greek "H"
55. Diamond protectors
58. Memorial Day solo
61. Enzyme suffixes
64. Be-boppers
66. Advance furtively
67. ___ Tin Tin
68. 200-milligram unit
69. ___ a time
70. Mork's planet
71. "It's the end of ___"
72. Endures
73. Born, in Bordeaux
74. Employee benefits

DOWN

1. Aleutian island
2. Mazda model
3. ___ wrench
4. Takes care of
5. '60s campus grp.
6. Singer Celine
7. Harem rooms
8. Alleviates
9. On dry land
10. Molt
11. Look (over)
12. Female sheep
13. ER workers
21. Work like ___
24. Abba of Israel
26. Battery size
28. Lawman Wyatt
29. Appropriate
31. ___-Locka, Fla.
32. Advance
33. 1997 Peter Fonda role
34. Arrest
35. "Gentlemen Prefer Blondes" author Anita
36. Window section
37. ___ Lee of Marvel Comics
39. "From ___ to Eternity"
42. Ambient music composer Brian
44. ___ fever (was sick)
46. Posed
47. Rug rats
50. Adjusts, as a clock
52. Esoteric
54. Composer Copland
56. Kitchen gadget
57. Grim
58. Actress Louise
59. Citrus coolers
60. Developer's map
62. Beget
63. Three-time speed skating gold medalist Karin
65. RR stops
66. Impresario Hurok
68. Limit

Solution on page 326

Mildly Tricky 40

ACROSS

1. Smudge
5. Window parts
10. Inquires
14. Investment firm T. ___ Price
15. Sarge's superior
16. Booty
17. Barley beards
18. Sit in on
19. Help for the stumped
20. "___ Rides Again" (1939 western)
22. Speechifies
24. Artist's prop
27. Matchsticks game
28. Primp
31. Be bedridden
33. "For ___ sake!"
37. "___ Abner"
38. Checked for prints
41. Shoulder muscle, informally
42. Duke's conf.
43. "Lord, is ___?"
44. "Shoo!"
46. Burns' negative
47. Neet rival
49. Carbonate
51. Suffix with Capri
52. Broke off
54. Daily grind
55. Discussion group
57. Balloon filler
59. Moray catcher
61. Reagan Supreme Court appointee
64. Electric eye, e.g.
68. Mata ___
69. ___ nova
73. Cockney greeting
74. Flightless flock
75. Alaska Peninsula native
76. Auctioneer's closing word
77. Superman's alter ego
78. Cassettes
79. Health resorts

DOWN

1. Actor Pitt
2. "The West Wing" actor
3. Has
4. Blue book filler
5. Kills, as a dragon
6. Chit
7. Israeli airport
8. 52, in old Rome
9. Attack
10. Red-faced
11. Houlihan portrayer
12. "Citizen ___"
13. Certain NCO's
21. "Amazing" magician
23. Tear
25. Less complicated
26. On, as a lamp
28. 747, e.g.
29. Puerto ___
30. Castilian hero
32. Emissary
34. Fitted piece
35. Delight
36. Bethlehem product
39. Actress Hagen
40. Dah's partner
45. Home on the range
48. No dreamer
50. McClanahan of "The Golden Girls"
53. Early sixth-century date
56. James of "Gunsmoke"
58. Capital near Casablanca
60. Atty.-to-be exams
61. Chiang Kai-___
62. Arrived
63. Make ___ for it
65. Feed, as pigs
66. ___ podrida
67. Fishing gear
70. Schnozz ending
71. Equinox mo.
72. Seek damages

Solution on page 326

Mildly Tricky 41

ACROSS

1. Walkers, for short
5. V-shaped fortification
10. "The Nazarene" author
14. Lined up
15. Prefix with meter
16. "Begone!"
17. Zero, on a court
18. Unyielding
19. Kind of marketing
20. Get mad
22. Rubbed out
24. Blacken
25. Kenyan tribe
27. "Check this out!"
29. Bit of Braille
30. Understand
34. ___ Fail (Irish coronation stone)
35. Discharges
38. This, in Toledo
39. Fink
40. Insult, in slang
41. "___ show time!"
43. 1960–61 world chess champ
44. Linear, for short
46. Word before Nevada or Leone
48. ___ Miss
49. Pried (into)
51. ___ v. Wade
52. Leonine locks
54. Commercial makers
56. Howard of "Happy Days"
57. Like a good egg
60. Washington airport
63. Old-time actress Velez
64. Disables
67. Nest eggs, briefly
69. Singer Anita
70. Hearty steak
71. Guitar accessory
72. Journalist Ernie
73. Organic compound
74. Exceeded the limit

DOWN

1. Amigo
2. Archer of myth
3. Hawk's opposite
4. Candy
5. Harder to find
6. "National Velvet" author Bagnold
7. MBA, for one
8. Friend, in France
9. Bumps
10. "Silk Stockings" star
11. Tom Jones's "___ a Lady"
12. ___ slaw
13. Worked on a bed
21. Assessed
23. Joplin work
25. Cal. pages
26. Clothing
27. Baby grand, e.g.
28. Fills
29. Hanker for
31. ___ Martin
32. No longer fresh
33. Ashen
34. Scientologist ___ Hubbard
36. PX patrons
37. Narrow waterway: Abbr.
42. Margaret Mead study site
45. Marksman
47. Long, long time
50. H.S.T.'s successor
53. Monkeyshines
55. Island south of Sicily
56. Visit anew
57. Unappetizing food
58. New York's Giuliani
59. "Be ___!" ("Help me out!")
60. E-mail, e.g.
61. "I don't give ___!"
62. Supergarb
65. Rocket interceptor, briefly
66. "Who, me?"
68. Grass patch

Solution on page 326

Mildly Tricky 42

ACROSS

1. Autumn pear
5. Range: Abbr.
9. Egg __ yung
12. Ersatz fat brand
14. Half a train?
15. Life stories
16. Stallone title role
17. "The Night Watch" painter
19. "__ Maria"
20. Marsh of mystery
22. Roman official
23. Ancient Greek coin
25. Miss a step
26. Of last month
28. Contradicts
29. Chessman
30. "Alas!"
32. EMT's skill
33. Poison
34. A Chaplin
37. Defeatist's word
39. Schlepper
41. Irish accent
43. Warning
44. Study intently
45. Nova __
47. Orgs.
48. "Forget it!"
49. Calendar square
52. Saturated with
54. Online publication
56. Telephone button
57. Curve
58. Stinks
59. Cobbler's tool
60. Carry on
61. Cheese choice

DOWN

1. Adriatic wind
2. Norway's patron saint
3. Academic term
4. Hack
5. Jazz singer Carmen
6. Not our
7. Hurler Hideo
8. Cry hard
9. Limited
10. Lots and lots
11. Blender maker
13. Generic
15. Golfer's headache
18. Domain
21. Classic muscle car
24. __-tac-toe
25. Terrarium plant
26. Merchandise I.D.
27. Back talk
28. Lure
30. Exhausted, with "in"
31. Prefix with skeleton
33. Hardware item
34. Stabilized
35. Indeed
36. Richard Gere title role
37. __ beef
38. Visibly horrified
39. Rag
40. Egg: Prefix
41. Give as a gift
42. Market again
43. Bamboozle
44. Former Turkish title
45. Playground equipment
46. __ Nast
48. "I had no __!"
50. "Diana" singer
51. "Okay, Aunt Bee," Opie-style
53. "Charlotte's Web" author's monogram
55. Last of 26

Solution on page 326

Mildly Tricky 43

ACROSS

1. Greyhound vehicle
4. Jar tops
8. "I wanna!"
13. Lennon's in-laws
15. "Don't bet __!"
16. "Silas Marner" novelist
17. Between jobs
18. Stress, for one
19. Big name in insurance
20. Part of S.W.A.K.
22. Little bit
24. Corp. heads
25. Flubbed
26. Liveliness
28. "Peter Pan" dog
30. "__ by Starlight"
34. Bitterness
37. Table scraps
40. 1988 Olympics site
41. Myrna of "The Thin Man"
42. The tiniest bit
44. 201, to Caesar
45. Tuckered out
47. "The Persistence of Memory" artist
48. Mischievous Norse god
49. Taken care of
51. To be, in ancient Rome
53. Sacred scrolls
56. Made bovine noises
60. Diminish
63. "Cakes and __"
64. Canal site
65. Ages and ages
67. "I cannot tell __"
69. "Put __ writing"
70. Sonata section
71. Go for the gold
72. Pastrami purveyor
73. Dread
74. Afrikaner
75. __ Speedwagon

DOWN

1. Idaho's capital
2. Below
3. Like some renewable energy
4. Burden
5. Gerund maker
6. Food regimens
7. Rein, e.g.
8. Grassland
9. Office holder
10. Itty-bitty bug
11. Pre-stereo
12. Greek vowels
14. Greek moon goddess
21. Author LeShan
23. A.M.A. members
26. Kind of seal
27. "__ small world!"
29. The "N" in NCO
31. Bonkers
32. Gambler's need
33. Et __ (and others)
34. Le Sage's "Gil __"
35. Captive of Hercules
36. Singer Lovett
38. __ Maria liqueur
39. Shoe bottoms
42. "I'm __ you!"
43. "__ the season to be jolly"
46. Has in mind
48. Soviet leader Brezhnev
50. "Are you a man __ _ mouse?"
52. Wee, in Dundee
54. Gentle as __
55. Sun: prefix
57. Horse opera
58. Author Zola
59. Aquarium fish
60. Theda of the silents
61. Long, long time
62. Chinese mafia
64. Equal
66. Barfly
68. Multipurpose suffix

Solution on page 327

Mildly Tricky 44

ACROSS

1. "An apple ___ . . ."
5. "Darn!"
9. Sgt., e.g.
12. In ___ land (spacy)
13. Safe havens
15. Congers
16. "Famous" baker
17. Spares, e.g.
18. Patricia of "Hud"
19. Real
21. Comics shriek
22. 007 foe
23. Start of Massachusetts' motto
25. London art gallery
27. Kansas motto word
30. Mornings, for short
32. Jazz singer Vaughan
36. "Sprechen ___ Deutsch?"
37. Antifur org.
39. Sister of Venus
40. "Judith" composer
42. Yemen's capital
44. Asterisk
45. Must
47. Taxpayer I.D.s
49. Soul, to Sartre
50. "___ Is Born"
51. Harden
52. Farm measures
54. Hacienda room
56. Opera set in Egypt
58. NBA segment
61. Engine need
63. Has a feeling
67. Le Pew of cartoons
68. Gunk
70. Official proceedings
71. Drop from the eye
72. Antisub device
73. Computer info
74. Heavens
75. After-bath wear
76. Lebanese, e.g.

DOWN

1. Jai ___
2. "___ Yankees"
3. ___ vera
4. Arafat of the P.L.O.
5. Has status
6. "___ Lay Dying"
7. Whitehall whitewall
8. Comes down hard?
9. ___-do-well
10. Extended family
11. Capital on a fjord
14. "___ silly question . . ."
15. Makes beloved
20. Ginger cookie
24. "I could ___ horse!"
26. "Ash Wednesday" monogram
27. Yoga posture
28. Fathers
29. Article of faith
31. Parsonage
33. Pave over
34. "What's in ___?"
35. Hounds' quarries
38. "___ Beso" (Paul Anka song)
39. ___ Clemente
41. Lou Grant portrayer
43. "The Thin Man" canine
46. ___ la la
48. Marquis de ___
51. Salt
53. The Great White North
55. Defeat
57. Grenoble's river
58. Places for rent: Abbr.
59. Go after
60. Fix, in a way
62. Prefix with type
64. Harry Potter's lightning bolt, e.g.
65. Kett, of the comics
66. Swedish auto
69. Fairy queen

Solution on page 327

Mildly Tricky 45

ACROSS

1. Is cockeyed
6. "Livin' la Vida ___"
10. Drying chamber
14. NBA Hall of Famer Thomas
15. Suffix with origin
16. Sexologist Shere
17. Country singer Tucker
18. Steals from
19. "The Simpsons" tavern
20. "Survivor" shelter
21. British raincoats
23. Breakfast dish
25. Beethoven's cry
26. Cellular letters
27. Auditing org.
28. "___ Cheerleaders" (1977 film)
32. Tops
33. Seed coverings
34. Capitol Hill VIP: Abbr.
35. Star in Perseus
40. "Go, ___!"
41. Aardvark morsel
42. Arias, usually
43. Fresh-mouthed
45. "Fancy that!"
46. ___ of time
47. Experts
49. Give a makeup to
50. Append
53. ___ Alamos, N.M.
54. The "S" in R.S.V.P.
55. Sisters' daughters
57. Walk in water
58. Consumer protection org.
61. With the bow, in music
62. Perfectly
64. One-named Spanish singer
66. 5K, e.g.
67. Hillside shelter
68. Pamplona runners
69. Thom ___ shoes
70. ___ Fein
71. Crockpot concoctions

DOWN

1. Baltic country: Abbr.
2. Biblical twin
3. "___ it the truth!"
4. Aye canceler
5. Tribal healers
6. Durable wood
7. Western Indians
8. Corn holder
9. Cases for insurance detectives
10. Words of woe
11. Garlicky mayonnaise
12. Animal in a roundup
13. Exams
22. Rm. coolers
24. ___ Hari (spy)
26. French income
28. Tests for srs.
29. Length x width, for a rectangle
30. Spanish aunts
31. "___ for the poor"
32. Elaine ___ ("Seinfeld" role)
34. Wise guys
36. Aspiring atty.'s exam
37. Auctioneer's last word
38. Automobile pioneer
39. "Schindler's ___"
44. Bush's alma mater
46. Chooses
48. NBC sportscaster Bob
49. Free from, with "of"
50. Cost ___ and a leg
51. 1933 physics Nobelist Paul
52. Bing Crosby's record label
54. Sheet material
56. "Fargo" director Joel
57. Alert
58. Empty
59. It may be furrowed
60. Head honcho
63. ___-Wan Kenobi
65. Boiling

Solution on page 327

Mildly Tricky 46

ACROSS
1. Astonish
5. Sorts
9. Wagering locale, for short
12. Stubborn beasts
14. ___ me tangere (touch-me-not)
15. Adriatic seaport
16. Really dug
17. Lawyers' charges
18. Approved
19. Deem necessary
21. Dampen
22. Go backpacking
23. Men
24. Entre ___ (confidentially)
26. Exit
28. Mass seating
29. "I'm freezing!"
30. Jazzman Baker
33. Astronaut's insignia
35. Right-hand page
40. "Where the heart is"
41. Kama ___
43. Expert
44. Prefix with red
46. Litigant
47. Overabundance
48. ___ Diavolo (seafood sauce)
50. Kissers
52. Pure
56. Salon worker
57. Mr. Ziegfeld
60. Possess
61. Rx watchdog
63. Wound
65. Computer operating system
66. Klinger player on "M*A*S*H"
68. Cursed
69. ___-poly
70. Pinza of "South Pacific"
71. Temptress
72. Vardalos of "My Big Fat Greek Wedding"
73. Bad impression?
74. Intellect

DOWN
1. Boffo show
2. Student getting one-on-one help
3. "___ Gold" (1997 film)
4. Nine, in Nantes
5. Like Beethoven's "Pastoral" Symphony
6. Big name in movie theaters
7. Artist Paul
8. Bridesmaid, often
9. Jack of "The Great Dictator"
10. Arduous journeys
11. Waits
13. Backbone
15. Physicist Niels
20. Hamlets
25. Patriotic chant
27. Dog's warning
28. Wing: Prefix
29. Just
30. "The Sweetheart of Sigma ___"
31. Darlin'
32. "Unbelievable" rock band
34. Alphabet trio
36. Roe
37. ___-de-sac
38. Capote, to friends
39. Away
42. Disney mermaid
45. Astern
49. Called the game
51. Fourth estate
52. Butter maker
53. Capital of Vietnam
54. Spanish city
55. Alluring
56. "Mack the Knife" singer
57. Italian flowers
58. Sophia of "Two Women"
59. Upright, as a box
62. Stun
64. Triathlon leg
67. Balderdash

Solution on page 327

Mildly Tricky 47

ACROSS

1. Sorvino of "Mighty Aphrodite"
5. Capitol feature
9. Distinctive doctrines
13. Alamogordo's county
15. "Yeah, sure"
16. Chesterfield, e.g.
17. Beeped
18. OT book
19. "___ and the King of Siam"
20. Dampens
22. Before now
24. Look after
26. ___-Cat (off-road vehicle)
27. Municipal bldg.
28. Atlantic catch
29. Blabbed
32. LAX posting
34. Uru. neighbor
35. Slippery as ___
37. Less loony
41. Bingo call
43. Greek island
45. ___ Scotia
46. Begin's co-Nobelist
48. Fountain drinks
50. "Oh, brother!"
51. Lust, for one
53. Delta deposit
54. "Brokeback Mountain" director Lee
55. Part of NATO
58. Aussie hopper, for short
60. Nullifies
62. Nomads
64. Blessing
65. Soprano Berger
66. Fashion
68. Stared stupidly
72. "Good going!"
73. K.C. Royal, e.g.
74. Omit in pronunciation
75. No-win situations
76. Like Jack Sprat's diet
77. Bolshevik Trotsky

DOWN

1. Finish, with "up"
2. "Give ___ rest!"
3. Rule, for short
4. "___ there yet?"
5. Conks out
6. Delivery room doctors, for short
7. Allots, with "out"
8. C_2H_6
9. Suffix with poet
10. ___ boom
11. "Olympia" painter
12. Bart or Brenda
14. One-named folk singer
21. Roger Rabbit et al.
23. Decomposes
24. Somewhat, colloquially
25. Nosed (out)
28. Hacks
30. Meadows
31. Floor models
33. Dapper guy?
36. City near Sacramento
38. Bedouin
39. Rogers's partner
40. "You ___?"
42. "If I Ruled the World" rapper
44. Artillery burst
47. Radial, e.g.
49. Straight man
52. Everyday
55. "___ we all?"
56. Shinto temple gateway
57. Cavalry soldier
59. "___ Mio"
61. As a whole
63. Fannie ___ (securities)
64. Universal Postal Union headquarters
67. Narcs' org.
69. Cobbler
70. Tokyo, formerly
71. ___ of iniquity

Solution on page 327

Mildly Tricky 48

ACROSS

1. Red sky at morning, e.g.
5. Dossier
9. Dandy
12. The "B" of N.B.
13. Take ___ breath
15. Menlo Park middle name
16. Don of talk radio
17. Bit of regal regalia
18. King of tragedy
19. Pushover
21. Photo
22. Cotton bundle
23. "What are the ___?"
25. Salinger dedicatee
27. Wilkes-___, Pa.
30. Egypt and Syria, once: Abbr.
32. Song syllables
36. Brit. record label
37. Gangster's gal
39. Walk a beat
40. Cheerful tune
42. Mrs. Gorbachev
44. "Three men in ___"
45. Looked lecherously
47. Fish that complains a lot?
49. "It's no ___!"
50. So far
51. ___ Xing
52. Street show
54. NYC cultural center
56. Score after deuce, in tennis
58. "Comin' ___ the Rye"
61. Energy unit
63. Hole-enlarging tool
67. "The Clan of the Cave Bear" author
68. Deceive
70. Pedestal part
71. Move, to a realtor
72. Copenhageners
73. Book before Daniel: Abbr.
74. Ltr. additions
75. Radio operators
76. Kind of room

DOWN

1. Japanese sashes
2. Bulletin board notice
3. Sufficient, informally
4. Trojan War sage
5. Destined
6. Dictator Amin
7. Jump
8. More chilling
9. Dog biter
10. Egg-shaped
11. Reduce, as expenses
14. D.C. fund-raisers
15. Montana neighbor
20. Same, in footnotes
24. Toni Morrison novel
26. NYC subway overseer
27. Beautiful, in Bologna
28. Gallic girlfriends
29. Life of ___
31. Wonderland girl
33. Pianist Rubinstein
34. No-goodnik
35. "Tiny Alice" playwright
38. California's Fort ___
39. Average
41. Vibrating effect
43. Actress Thompson
46. D.D.E.'s command
48. ___-dieu
51. Outcast
53. Wreath for the head
55. Blend
57. Refuse
58. Ball field covering
59. Shades
60. Fam. members
62. Actress Rowlands
64. Labyrinth
65. Barbara of "I Dream of Jeannie"
66. Korean soldiers
69. President pro ___

Solution on page 327

Mildly Tricky 49

ACROSS

1. Peak
6. 76ers' org.
9. Gushes
14. Cowboy contest
15. "Tasty!"
16. Omega's opposite
17. Poet Dickinson
18. Dallas sch.
19. Cartoon skunk Pepe
20. Harry Potter has one
21. Own (up to)
22. Retailer's gds.
23. Model Campbell
25. Couple
27. Fox comedy series
30. Country music?
35. Boob tubes
38. Consider again
40. Broad
41. Greek city-state
43. Annoy
44. "That's it!"
45. Grand Dragon's group
46. Salad leaf
48. Morning moisture
49. Double curve, as in yarn
51. Acquired relative
53. L.B.J.'s veep
55. Betel palm
58. Like Solomon
61. Steinbeck's "To __
    _ Unknown"
64. Cut ___ (dance)
66. "Sonnets to Orpheus" poet
67. Have dinner
68. Circumvent
69. Adam of "Chicago Hope"
70. Big bang maker
71. City near Dayton
72. Casual attire
73. Approvals
74. Glacial ridge

DOWN

1. All hands on deck
2. Kind of candle
3. Minneapolis suburb
4. Once in a blue moon
5. Plaything
6. Big Board inits.
7. Mooches
8. Imperative
9. Yellowish-pink
10. Begged
11. Omar of "The Mod
    Squad," 1999
12. "This is fun!"
13. Observed
21. Bona ___
24. Red planet
26. "This means ___!"
28. Skinny
29. "La Traviata" composer
31. Prefix with night or light
32. Posterior
33. Advantage
34. Cat call
35. Toll rds.
36. Electric unit
37. Cabbage salad
39. Like, with "to"
42. Pasta suffix
44. Chicago footballer
46. Biblical verb ending
47. Prince who inspired
    "Dracula"
50. Lusters
52. Drives dangerously
54. Must
56. Model T starter
57. War hero Murphy
58. Telegram
59. Actress Chase
60. Scrape, as the knee
62. Icky stuff
63. Chooses, with "for"
65. Reverse, e.g.
66. British rule in colonial
    India
68. English Channel feeder

Solution on page 328

Mildly Tricky 50

ACROSS

1. Ticker tapes?
5. Karate school
9. CEO's degree
12. "Psycho" actress Miles
13. Finland, to the Finns
15. Will of "The Waltons"
16. "If ___ be so bold . . ."
17. Cheapskate
18. Count ___, villain in Lemony Snicket books
19. Arthur Miller's salesman
21. Amateur radioer
22. The "E" of B.P.O.E.
23. Engine cover
26. Stadium sounds
28. Thurman of "Pulp Fiction"
31. Alpha's opposite
33. Decrease
37. Prickly husk
38. Veto
39. Aleve alternative
40. "The Three Sisters" sister
42. Corrupt
44. Stowe novel
45. In disagreement
47. Author Roald
49. "How was ___ know?"
50. Behemoth
51. Vowel quintet
52. "Le Coq ___"
53. O. Henry's "The Gift of the ___"
55. Stars and Stripes, e.g.
57. PC "brains"
60. Marseilles Mrs.
62. Open, as a bottle
66. "I see," facetiously
67. "Steady ___ goes"
70. Words of woe
71. Composer ___ Carlo Menotti
72. Become narrower
73. Mouth-puckering
74. North Pole toymaker
75. Pyramid, essentially
76. Offended

DOWN

1. Bad to the bone
2. ___ sabe
3. Fat unit
4. Doctor's order
5. Mil. award
6. Yvette's "yes"
7. Tease
8. 1998 British Open champ
9. Pell-___
10. Schnozzola
11. Barks
14. "___ la Douce" (1963 film)
15. Spoils
20. Alcove
24. Excludes
25. Boxer Oscar ___ Hoya
27. Solo of "Star Wars"
28. Depth charge target
29. Prefix with task
30. Lingo
32. Move effortlessly
34. Bitter
35. Connect with
36. "Star Wars" planet
39. Playwright Fugard
41. "Born Free" author Joy
43. Innocent
46. Crime scene evidence
48. Hilo feast
51. Draws a bead on
54. B-school entrance exam
56. Grind, as teeth
57. Hamster's home
58. Pop singer Collins
59. Letters on a B-52
61. Former Bruin Phil, to fans
63. ___ En-lai
64. Asian river
65. Flippant
68. Border
69. Tarzan creator's monogram

Solution on page 328

Mildly Tricky 51

ACROSS

1. Command to Fido
4. Dudes
8. Studies
13. Barber's job
15. Without purpose
16. Hang back
17. Notes after do
18. Adjective follower
19. Wood finish
20. Kind of band
22. "Ben-Hur" studio
24. Little devils
25. Juan of Argentina
26. Continue
28. Autograph
30. Greenhouse area
34. Mimicking bird
37. Shipping dept. stamp
40. Initial venture
41. Debt acknowledgment
42. Baby blues
44. Call ___ day
45. Croesus' kingdom
47. Debussy's "Clair de ___"
48. Fed
49. Chekov player on "Star Trek"
51. Compulsive desire
53. Quenches
56. Actress Winger
60. Desire
63. Kind of feeling
64. "Honest!"
65. Dialect
67. Mend
69. Full house, e.g.
70. Israeli native
71. Sow sound
72. Black-and-white treat
73. Devereux's earldom
74. Do in
75. ___ Bingle (Crosby moniker)

DOWN

1. Razor sharpener
2. Cara of "Fame"
3. Track official
4. Helsinki native
5. Prefix with meter
6. Showy feather
7. "The Playboy of the Western World" author
8. ACLU concerns
9. Erode
10. Composer Khachaturian
11. What icicles do
12. Dict. entries
14. Brunch cocktail
21. Black cuckoo
23. Speed meas.
26. Prepare to propose
27. Punch lines?
29. Test for coll. seniors
31. Fedora feature
32. "I could ___ horse!"
33. Actress Cannon
34. Half of half-and-half
35. Toy that goes "around the world"
36. Classic art subject
38. Heart of a PC
39. Patron saint of France
42. Beach toy
43. Emeritus: abbr.
46. Coming up
48. "Tommy" rockers
50. Stifle
52. LPs' successors
54. "Great job!"
55. Amazon sales, e.g.
57. Santa Claus feature
58. Hindu queen
59. Passion
60. Sagacious
61. Nabokov heroine and others
62. Penpoints
64. Pitch-black
66. Upper limit
68. Genetic initials

Solution on page 328

Mildly Tricky 52

ACROSS

1. Ness, e.g.
5. ___ Arabia
10. Frigate's front
14. 1998 Sarah McLachlan hit
15. Entices
16. Dandy
17. Ingenuity
18. Anxiety
19. Confront
20. Schindler portrayer
22. Puget Sound city
24. Builder's backing
26. "Citizen Kane" studio
27. Heartache
30. Vienna's land: Abbr.
32. "Peer ___"
36. Cambodia's Lon ___
37. Ugly duckling, eventually
39. Book before Jeremiah
41. Assert
43. Comment to the audience
45. ___ sapiens
46. Mortise insertions
48. Period in office
50. Ottoman governor
51. Drink with sushi
52. Tempe sch.
53. Heads-up
55. Big wine holder
57. Lansbury Broadway role
59. Gives in
63. Home wrecker
67. Fr. miss
68. "Same here!"
70. "Thank Heaven for Little Girls" musical
71. Jewish month
72. Varnish resin
73. Feds
74. Lass
75. Tasty
76. Actress Lamarr

DOWN

1. Croquet area
2. "Garfield" canine
3. Commend
4. Annoyance
5. Bias
6. Hot time: Abbr.
7. "A God in Ruins" author
8. Dissuades
9. "Wicked Game" singer Chris
10. Fizzling-out sound
11. Iranian money
12. "___ bitten, twice shy"
13. Itsy-bitsy
21. Blockheads
23. Clothes
25. Lukas of "Witness"
27. Annoying insect
28. Wanders
29. Actress Massey
31. Condos, e.g.
33. Derisive cry
34. Weeper of myth
35. Whip wielder
38. Existed
39. Ending with cash or bombard
40. Hall-of-Famer Wilhelm
42. Moo goo gai pan pan
44. "Te ___" (hymn)
47. Campbell of "Scream"
49. Cry from a crib
52. Number one Hun
54. Pants measure
56. Aconcagua's range
58. Bypass
59. "___ Wanna Do" (Sheryl Crow hit)
60. Disparaging remark
61. Unload, as stock
62. "___ lively!"
64. Thin coin
65. Elderly
66. Streaked
67. Computer storage unit, informally
69. 1979 nuclear accident site: Abbr.

Solution on page 328

Mildly Tricky 53

ACROSS

1. The ___ Prayer
6. "___ and away!"
10. "Harper Valley ___"
13. "I don't give ___!"
14. ___-Rooter
15. Oscar Madison, e.g.
16. Amazed
17. Copycat
18. Create
19. "Dracula" director Browning
20. Less tanned
22. "Water Lilies" painter Claude
23. Edges
24. Buckeyes
26. Bathhouse
29. Denver summer hrs.
30. "___ I care!"
31. Bacteriologist Salk
35. Room connector
39. Bygone airline
40. "Obviously!"
41. LAX watchdog
42. Radio host John
44. Fess up to
46. "___ Ha'i"
47. Priestly garb
49. Fairy king
51. Baffled
55. High-fiber food
56. Chronic nag
57. "Awake and Sing!" playwright
59. Automobile sticker fig.
62. Places
63. Sacred bird of the pharaohs
64. Beach
66. Not genuine: Abbr.
67. Golfer Ballesteros
68. Consumed
69. "60 Minutes" network
70. Kind of fall
71. Treasure ___

DOWN

1. Cafe au ___
2. "___ you don't!"
3. Highway
4. ___ Jones
5. Enter
6. Russian range
7. Bishop of Rome
8. In ___ (not yet born)
9. ___ favor (please, in Spanish)
10. Primary strategy
11. Arcade coin
12. Assists
15. Peanut butter choice
21. Key related to F# minor: Abbr.
22. ___-Atlantic
23. Brit. fliers
25. "___ Pinafore"
26. Suffragist Carrie
27. "___ forgive our debtors"
28. Diagonal
32. Hardly ordinary
33. Book before Deut.
34. Hawaiian tuna
36. Way, way off
37. Composer Schifrin
38. Reclined
43. Most hearty
44. Stomach muscles, briefly
45. Civil wrong
46. Actor Affleck
48. Fan setting
50. Hound dog
51. Jellied garnish
52. Green ___
53. Ars gratia ___
54. Clearheaded
55. Assail
58. La Scala star
59. Marquand's Mr.
60. Before: Abbr.
61. Characteristic carrier
63. AOL, e.g.: Abbr.
65. Guffaw syllable

Solution on page 328

Mildly Tricky 54

ACROSS
1. Looped handle
5. Metrical feet
10. Kemo ___ (the Lone Ranger)
14. Innocent's claim
15. Serve
16. Where she blows
17. NY Met, e.g.
18. Declaim
19. Delhi princess
20. If nothing else
22. Tidy up
24. "___ say more?"
25. Rise
28. Popular record label
30. 16th century Italian poet
34. Common allergen
37. "The Sound of Music" backdrop
39. Set down
40. Auto racer Luyendyk
41. Binge
43. Haul
44. CBS forensic drama
45. Chimney residue
46. Outpourings
48. Sheer linen
50. Cheers
52. Break time
54. Throws
58. Kind of blue
61. Trap
63. G.I. addresses
64. "A Bell for ___"
67. Annual theater award
68. Ache (for)
69. Go ___ for: defend
70. Competed
71. Ballpoints

72. "Stars and Stripes Forever" composer
73. "No ifs, ___ or buts!"

DOWN
1. Kofi of the UN
2. Nick of "48 HRS."
3. Commemorative marker
4. Terrier type
5. They're exchanged at weddings
6. Main arteries
7. Curator's deg.
8. Burbank's sci.
9. "Goodnight" girl of song
10. Layers
11. At the drop of ___
12. Curse
13. "___ go bragh!"

21. Billion follower
23. Tolkien creatures
26. Catch off guard
27. Racer Yarborough
29. ___ many words
31. Falling-out
32. Confident
33. Baseball's Mel and others
34. Agreement
35. Approximately
36. 53, in old Rome
38. Termite, e.g.
42. Frost or Burns
43. Ladies' man
45. Close, as an envelope
47. Chest muscles, briefly
49. Rental agreements
51. Circus sites
53. Box score numbers

55. Polio vaccine developer
56. Took a stab at
57. Tournament favorites
58. "Li'l Abner" cartoonist
59. Mayberry boy
60. City on the Rhine
62. ___ care in the world
65. Scooby-___ (cartoon dog)
66. "Aladdin" monkey

Solution on page 328

Mildly Tricky 55

ACROSS

1. Russian country house
6. Haus wife
10. Shakes up
14. Wheel turners
15. Column crossers
16. "___ Ben Adhem" (Leigh Hunt poem)
17. Cat chorus
18. One of the Aleutians
19. Columnist Maureen
20. Meddle
21. Blue hue
23. Takes to task
25. Birth control method, for short
26. Second-century date
27. Journalist Nellie
28. Witch's laugh
32. Born's partner
33. Neural transmitters
34. Boo follower
35. Eye-related
40. "___ Only Just Begun"
41. Barley beard
42. Gospel writer
43. Gobs
45. Napoleon's marshal
46. Hermit
47. ___-friendly
49. Meal
50. Speed: Abbr.
53. Juilliard subj.
54. Barbarian
55. Catherine of ___
57. Triangular sails
58. Axlike tool
61. Puerto ___
62. Primatologist Fossey
64. Antique shop item
66. Decorated, as a cake
67. Mont Blanc, par exemple
68. Ancient Indo-European
69. Roams
70. Barely makes, with "out"
71. Heartbeat

DOWN

1. Humid
2. Downsizer
3. Satiate
4. Chop
5. Goes after
6. Whistle-blower's exposure
7. Roster
8. Parrot's cry
9. Functional
10. Will's wife
11. Manhattan Project project
12. Spur wheel
13. Like dishwater
22. "___ pasa?"
24. Adriatic resort
26. Old pal
28. Crow calls
29. Figure skater's jump
30. Inlet
31. Was in on
32. Leafy shelter
34. Fruit of the Loom competitor
36. Alka-Seltzer sound
37. Yellowfin, e.g.
38. Alibi ___ (excuse makers)
39. Dick Francis book "Dead ___"
44. Japanese wrestling
46. Camera protection
48. Fountain treat
49. Massage
50. Airline to Rio
51. "Fear of Flying" author Jong
52. Spiked
54. Gregory of "Tap"
56. Mount Olympus dwellers
57. Jest
58. Of a certain hydrocarbon group
59. "Buenos ___"
60. Area
63. Genre
65. S.A. country

Solution on page 329

Mildly Tricky 56

ACROSS

1. Seize suddenly
5. P.D. alerts
9. Red gem
13. Actor Calhoun
14. Grimace
15. Skater Sonja
16. "___ Angel" (Mae West film)
17. Annapolis initials
18. Pliocene, e.g.
19. Marine food fish
21. Quagmire
23. From A ___
24. Zorro's marks
26. Law, in Lyon
27. Columnist Marilyn ___ Savant
28. Anchorage-to-Fairbanks dir.
30. Ladder step
34. Earth color
37. Muralist Rivera
39. Comic book punch sound
40. Itinerary
41. Sch. in Troy, NY
42. Adorable one
44. Pear-shaped fruit
45. Big mug
47. Rose feature
48. Bolt
50. Triumph
51. Madison or Monroe: Abbr.
52. 11th-century date
54. FBI employee
56. "Count me out"
59. Singer Easton
62. Retiree's title
64. Imitating
65. Bog
67. A.B.A. member: Abbr.
68. Mrs. F. Scott Fitzgerald
69. Vaudeville's Seven Little ___
70. Spillane's "___ Jury"
71. Big-eyed birds
72. Mid 12th-century date
73. Henna and others

DOWN

1. Mill fodder
2. Juliet's beloved
3. Ball's partner
4. Invite letters
5. Diverts
6. Rapper's entourage
7. Hardly a daring do
8. Clothing line
9. Fix
10. Spanish articles
11. Popular pens
12. Slangy assent
15. Lifesaver, say
20. Portuguese islands
22. Cassini of fashion
25. Taking potshots
27. Dog doc
29. Dresden denial
31. "What've you been ___?"
32. Film ___
33. Broadway star Verdon
34. "Carmina Burana" composer Carl
35. Radiator part
36. Bigger than big
37. Cologne crowd?
38. Gas pump number
43. Sounds of doubt
46. Double
49. Corrects
51. Son of Mary Stuart
53. Star in Lyra
55. Actress Streep
56. ___-gritty
57. ___ drop of a hat
58. 19th president
59. Erupt
60. San Francisco's Nob ___
61. Letters on a radio switch
63. Foray
64. Nitrogen-based dye
66. Quadrennial games org.

Solution on page 329

Mildly Tricky 57

ACROSS

1. Prefix with China
5. "___ who?"
9. Short flight
12. Nary a soul
14. Arbor Day honoree
15. "American Gigolo" star
16. Jazz dance
17. ___ moss
18. Raise, as kids
19. Actor Borgnine
21. Opposite of a ques.
22. Fashion magazine
23. Ball holder
24. Dental exam
26. Coin flips
28. Chemical endings
29. Get an ___ (ace)
30. Single-edged knife
33. And others, briefly
35. Sedate
40. "East of Eden" brother
41. Attire
43. Competent
44. She had "the face that launched a thousand ships"
46. Open ___ of worms
47. Roly-___
48. Frigid
50. Manage
52. Mexican dish
56. Trillion: Prefix
57. Quick swim
60. Like Nash's lama
61. G.I.'s address
63. "Bewitched" witch
65. Forensic concerns
66. Princes, e.g.
68. Copier additive
69. Pet on "The Flintstones"
70. "Cogito ___ sum"
71. Brown ermine
72. "Absolutely!"
73. "Don't go!"
74. Criteria: abbr.

DOWN

1. Atlas enlargement
2. ___ Dame
3. "Lorna ___"
4. "This one's ___!"
5. "The racer's edge"
6. "He's ___ nowhere man" (Beatles lyric)
7. Bear young, as sheep
8. Begins, as work
9. Scoundrels
10. Papal vestment
11. Israel's Shimon
13. Big name in printers
15. Some college tests, for short
20. In a corner
25. Off course
27. Switch positions
28. Actress Skye
29. ___-Lorraine
30. "___, humbug!"
31. Bauxite, e.g.
32. Chat room chuckle
34. N.R.C. predecessor
36. CD alternative
37. Blood typing system
38. Afflicted
39. Susan of "L.A. Law"
42. Dorm annoyance
45. Nada
49. Stops
51. Trousers
52. Some like it hot
53. "___ Get Your Gun"
54. Wherewithal
55. "The Sun ___ Rises"
56. South Pacific kingdom
57. Forbidding words
58. "___ you loud and clear"
59. Labor's partner
62. Left on board?
64. Specks
67. Kind of sauce

Solution on page 329

Mildly Tricky 58

ACROSS
1. Police
5. "Born Free" lioness
9. Very, in music
14. Hydrocarbon suffixes
15. Moon valley
16. Brings up
17. Russo of "Tin Cup"
18. Indigo
19. Oncle's wife
20. Brownish
21. ___ good example
22. ___-majeste
23. Warned
26. Hydrant attachment
29. Canon camera
30. Collar
34. Beasts of burden
37. Bus. aides
40. ___ Paulo, Brazil
41. Caribbean and others
42. Chips in
43. Guy
44. Moray, e.g.
45. Came up
46. Ms. enclosures
47. Declare
49. Chicago hrs.
50. Dregs
52. Unwed fathers
56. Morales of "La Bamba"
59. Quaker pronoun
61. Make doilies
62. Leopard markings
64. 50-and-over org.
65. Speck
66. Trig functions
67. Awful-tasting
68. Snarl
69. "This is only ___"
70. "___ Tu" (1974 hit)
71. Arid

DOWN
1. Magna ___
2. Actress Tatum
3. Pasta often served with vodka sauce
4. Atlanta-to-Miami dir.
5. Rubs out
6. Like notebook paper
7. Buttonhole
8. Koran deity
9. Carney of "The Honeymooners"
10. Undercoat
11. All there
12. "Liberal" studies
13. "Aha!"
24. Roger of "Cheers"
25. How-___ (instructional books)
27. Feed bag contents
28. 12th graders: Abbr.
31. Those: Sp.
32. After-Christmas event
33. "Little piggies"
34. On a deck, perhaps
35. Views
36. "Do the Right Thing" pizzeria
37. Year, in Spain
38. John, Paul and George: Abbr.
39. "Didn't I tell you?"
42. Johnson of "Laugh-In"
43. Chess ending
45. "___ we having fun yet?"
46. Fed. stipend
48. Upper crusts
49. Thin pancakes
51. Ward (off)
52. Hostess Mesta
53. Gem
54. Golden Horde member
55. Cubic meter
56. She, in Italy
57. Barbecue rod
58. Excellent
60. "Aquarius" musical
63. Retired flier
65. Booker T. & the ___

Solution on page 329

Mildly Tricky 59

ACROSS

1. "Today" rival, briefly
4. Discovery
8. Spoil
13. Nope's counterpart
14. Two-time Grand Slam winner
15. Boredom
16. Producer: Abbr.
17. Wombs
18. Inclined
19. Popular vodka, informally
21. Ball girl
23. ___ bath (therapeutic treatment)
24. Shortly
27. Downy
29. Spa
31. On time
35. Corp. money managers
38. Muscle spasms
40. "Faust," e.g.
41. Cornfield sound
42. King Arthur's father
44. Playing marble
45. Fish basket
48. Influence
49. May honorees
50. Pay
52. Fine fiddle
54. Crossed (out)
56. Winter vehicle
59. Blabs
62. Domino dot
64. Coming-out
66. Apple laptop
68. Golfer Mediate
71. Bikini part
72. Father: prefix
73. First, second, reverse, etc.
74. Decline
75. Actor Buddy
76. Oscar's cousin
77. "Yeah, ___!"

DOWN

1. Workout sites
2. Civilian clothes
3. Chef protector
4. Blubber
5. "___ Got a Secret"
6. Dweeb
7. Hangs on a clothesline
8. Come together
9. Like some shopping
10. ___ Brith
11. Em, to Dorothy
12. Airhead
14. Soprano Tetrazzini
20. Places for experiments
22. Conk
25. "___, Brute!"
26. I.O.U.'s
28. To and ___
30. Pronunciation symbol
32. "Take ___ your leader"
33. Baby buggy
34. Fancy marbles
35. Inits. on a Soyuz rocket
36. Casino card game
37. "The Virginian" author Wister
39. Clothes lines
43. O'Neal of "Love Story"
46. It doesn't look good
47. Unilever soap brand
49. Cheese nibblers
51. Get-up-and-go
53. Fusses
55. Sad song
57. Monk's home
58. Prefix with prop or jet
59. "Egad!"
60. Basic rhyme scheme
61. Flower holders
63. Limerick, e.g.
65. Forbidden: Var.
67. Family
69. Engine part
70. Blubber

Solution on page 329

Mildly Tricky 60

ACROSS

1. "I'd hate to break up ___"
5. "Diary of ___ Housewife"
9. Classic drama of Japan
12. Carson predecessor
13. Loses color
15. "Gone With the Wind" plantation
16. To be, in Bordeaux
17. British biscuit
18. Distinctive flair
19. Political body
21. Brooch
22. Snitched
23. Midterm, say
25. Soissons seasons
27. Leg up
30. Airport info: Abbr.
32. Orchestra section
36. Directional suffix
37. Dover specialty
39. Eye bank donation
40. Barber's motion
42. Not relaxed
44. Wings: Lat.
45. Invigorating drinks
47. Muscle condition
49. Prince Valiant's son
50. Inscribed pillar
51. "Saving Private Ryan" craft: Abbr.
52. Attempts
54. 1944 battle site
56. Sneaker, e.g.
58. "___ for All Seasons"
61. "You've got mail" co.
63. Nail polish
67. Abhor
68. Lasso
70. "Damn Yankees" seductress
71. Robert of "The Sopranos"
72. Madrid mister
73. Disfigure
74. 10th anniversary gift
75. Gardener's spring purchase
76. Fr. holy women

DOWN

1. "Planet of the ___"
2. Fill up
3. Make, as a living
4. Goodies
5. Church areas
6. Brit's raincoat
7. Crooked
8. Naysayer
9. "The Lion King" lion
10. Algerian seaport
11. Put up, as a picture
14. Dispatched
15. Mosaic piece
20. Asian holidays
24. "Canterbury" story
26. Leandro's love
27. Defeats
28. "Ready ___ . . ."
29. Cat-___-tails
31. Leases
33. China's Zhou ___
34. "The Wreck of the Mary ___"
35. Composer Saint-___
38. Extra play periods, for short
39. 100 yrs.
41. Light lager
43. Drunkards
46. Jazz man
48. British school
51. Sarge's superiors
53. Kingdoms
55. Unseen "Mary Tyler Moore Show" character
57. Got wind of
58. "We want ___!"
59. French Sudan, now
60. Solar deity
62. Bucolic byway
64. Castle defense
65. "Night" author Wiesel
66. Flees
69. Bunion's place

Solution on page 329

Mildly Tricky 61

ACROSS
1. Coke competitor
6. Son of, in Arabic names
9. Tempest
14. Above it all
15. Part of T.G.I.F.: Abbr.
16. Swiss mathematician
17. Father-and-daughter Hollywood duo
18. Jazz instrument
19. To the rear
20. Cinematographer Nykvist
21. Amount of medicine
22. Places
23. Swelling
25. ___-fi
27. Zippy flavors
30. Neighbor of Zambia
35. Strike caller
38. Type of mutual fund
40. ___ fixe
41. Fall guys
43. Across the street from: Abbr.
44. Psychic Edgar
45. Pawn
46. "In the Land of Israel" author
48. Crosses (out)
49. Busybodies
51. Palace dweller
53. Philip of "Kung Fu"
55. Build
58. Moonshine containers
61. Calif. neighbor
64. Mushroomed
66. French landscape painter
67. "Wanna ___?"
68. First lady after Hillary
69. Edmonton hockey player
70. Mantra syllables
71. Cheri of "Saturday Night Live"
72. Like Oscar Madison
73. Life story, in brief
74. Reached

DOWN
1. Football gear
2. Student at the Sorbonne
3. Studied, with "over"
4. Shakespearean verse
5. Conditions
6. Assuming that's true
7. Bikini parts
8. Vetoes
9. Protect, as freshness
10. Marching band member
11. Oil of ___
12. Whistle blowers
13. Chain-wearing "A-Team" actor
21. "Hawaii Five-O" nickname
24. Staffs
26. Bounder
28. Latch (onto)
29. Lethargy
31. Transcript fig.
32. African antelope
33. Head case?
34. Cans
35. Sounds of disgust
36. 1969 landing site
37. Fashion designer Rabanne
39. Lhasa ___
42. Bout stopper, for short
44. Old Russian autocrat
46. ___ Wednesday
47. Court cry
50. Danish, e.g.
52. Smooth, in music
54. Bigwig
56. Salad oil holder
57. ___ cotta
58. ___ de vivre
59. www addresses
60. Decamps
62. Notes after do
63. "Wishing won't make ___"
65. "Hold it!"
66. Dot follower
68. Captain's journal

Solution on page 330

Mildly Tricky 62

ACROSS

1. "Now hear __!"
5. Ordered
9. Bounders
13. Monastery head
15. Berserk
16. Eye layer
17. Afrikaners
18. Fraternal gp.
19. Highway exit
20. Unnamed ones
22. Advances
24. Pine exudation
26. __ generis
27. Attempt
28. Aries animal
29. Costa __
32. Go one better
34. Mandela's org.
35. Mock
37. Paul of "American Graffiti"
41. Carol
43. Closet wood
45. Actress Teri
46. Pants parts
48. Metes (out)
50. Nigerian native
51. Rock's __ Jovi
53. Proof of pmt.
54. Auction action
55. __-de-lance
58. "2001" computer
60. Corset tightener
62. Apple pie order?
64. Vega's constellation
65. "Woe __!"
66. Prefix with logical
68. Santa's assistants
72. Gratuities
73. Was a passenger
74. Playground feature
75. "__ Rebel" (1962 #1 hit)
76. Give the cold shoulder
77. Comedian Mort

DOWN

1. Bar bill
2. "Sex and the City" shower
3. "Can __ dreaming?"
4. Out of __
5. Coddle
6. Gig need
7. Condemns
8. Barely make
9. Medical breakthrough
10. Sailor's "stop!"
11. Take exception
12. Foolish
14. Casual top
21. Early computer
23. Six-stringed instrument
24. Babbled
25. Host
28. Captain, e.g.
30. Prompted
31. Slashed words?
33. Cribbage piece
36. After-bath powder
38. Down East
39. Ann __, Mich.
40. Trampled, with on
42. Isr. neighbor
44. Answer
47. London district
49. Gawks
52. Depths
55. Confidence
56. Beast of Borden
57. Wheelchair-accessible routes
59. Enticed
61. Phones
63. Arizona city
64. Leopold's partner in crime
67. University Web address suffix
69. __ Dolorosa
70. Old English letter
71. French seasoning

Solution on page 330

Mildly Tricky 63

ACROSS

1. Salad veggie
5. Indications
10. Wren or hen
14. "Once ___ a time . . ."
15. Expect
16. Comply
17. Tie up
18. Compel
19. Jay's rival
20. Hire
22. Kitchen gadgets
24. Cook's canful
26. Mole
27. Token taker
30. Believer's suffix
32. "September ___" (Neil Diamond hit)
36. Actress Novak
37. A deadly sin
39. Web browser command
41. Footnote abbr.
43. Steep slope
45. Surfer's sobriquet
46. Highway divider
48. Arizona city
50. Tomcat
51. Office fill-in
52. "Acid"
53. "___ directed"
55. Con's opposite
57. Taro root
59. Pathetically inept person
63. Shuttle plane
67. Bill of fare
68. Like a horse or lion
70. Aquarium
71. ___ nitrate
72. African antelope
73. City east of Santa Barbara

74. Lab container
75. Having chutzpah
76. Quick

DOWN

1. Rubik creation
2. ___ arms (angry)
3. King ___
4. Ultimate purpose
5. Morley of "60 Minutes"
6. ___ Jima
7. "The World According to ___"
8. Most pleasant
9. Prepare, as tea
10. Be an omen of
11. Building beam
12. Guns, as an engine
13. Blonde's secret, maybe
21. Highlander
23. Old ___, Conn.
25. Frisbee, e.g.
27. Kind of milk
28. Lama's land
29. Ammonia derivative
31. Death row reprieves
33. Aged
34. Cheek cosmetic
35. Comaneci, of Olympic fame
38. Admiral's org.
39. Engine speed, for short
40. Young socialites
42. Barely lit
44. Boorish
47. Computer programs, for short
49. BMW competitor

52. Place
54. In a way
56. Nagano noodles
58. Pops
59. 18-wheeler
60. "Dragonwyck" author Seton
61. Lackluster
62. Bump on a log
64. ___ California
65. Merkel and O'Connor
66. Burlesque bit
67. Dallas cager, for short
69. Ltr. holder

Solution on page 330

Mildly Tricky 64

ACROSS

1. Crimson Tide, briefly
5. Bounce back
9. "How adorable!"
12. NYSE debuts
13. Cabbage
15. Have ___ in one's bonnet
16. Singer Eartha
17. Lustful looker
18. Italian money
19. Alleviated
21. Over there, old-style
22. Onion relative
23. Reddish-brown
26. Elite seats
28. Greek letters
31. Chicago airport
33. ___ cum laude
37. "Born in the ___"
38. Fizzy drink
39. Mill site
40. Fontanne's theater partner
42. "___ World Turns"
44. Agitated state
45. Hidden
47. Sought damages
49. UN working-conditions agcy.
50. Blackboard
51. "___ Doone" (1869 novel)
52. Equal: prefix
53. Table d'___
55. ___ Linda, Calif.
57. High point
60. Clairvoyance, e.g.
62. Assumed name
66. Crowd noise
67. Letter before beth
70. David, for one
71. Cartoonist Addams, for short
72. Durable fabric
73. "Typee" sequel
74. Syllables from Santa
75. Chinese dollar
76. "This won't hurt ___"

DOWN

1. Two-wheeler
2. Capital of Western Samoa
3. Witty sayings
4. Daisylike bloom
5. Comedian Philips
6. Gear part
7. Sacred
8. Enthusiastic corrida cry
9. He loved Rose
10. "The Way We ___"
11. Half a fortnight
14. Cartoonist Peter
15. Very attentive
20. Twosomes
24. Young pig
25. Little ones
27. Clock-setting std.
28. Cancels
29. Customary
30. Father Christmas
32. "Midnight Cowboy" character
34. Bottled spirits
35. Symbols of hardness
36. Playground retort
39. "___ evil . . ."
41. Ties up
43. Pitch
46. Newcomer, briefly
48. Lady of Spain
51. Stahl of "60 Minutes"
54. Afternoon affairs
56. Foil maker
57. Bow
58. Pacific salmon
59. Author of "Killer Spy"
61. Andean land
63. Metric unit
64. Mine, in Marseille
65. Common dog's name
68. Links org.
69. Biddy

Solution on page 330

Mildly Tricky 65

ACROSS

1. Algebra or trig
5. Svelte
9. Klingon on the Enterprise
13. Birthplace of seven U.S. presidents
14. South American rodent
15. Flaxlike fiber
16. Actress Schneider
17. Pitch-black
18. Pain-relief brand
19. Daughter of King Minos
21. Harsh
23. Boy
24. The scarlet letter
26. Some TV sets
27. Grasp
28. Wall St. deal
30. "What ___ blow!"
34. Shoestrings
37. World-weary
39. Suffix with brom-
40. Shackles
41. Sun, e.g.
42. Saul's successor
44. Back when
45. New Haven student
47. Paradises
48. Feminist Lucretia
50. ___-relief
51. Branch
52. Police alert, for short
54. Benjamin Disraeli, e.g.
56. London forecast
59. To be returned
62. Shooting marble
64. Siouan speakers
65. Normandy river
67. Tree trunk
68. River of Lyon
69. Santa's team, e.g.
70. Warner ___
71. Fellow
72. Agile
73. Protected

DOWN

1. Fable finale
2. Now, in Nogales
3. Not bold
4. Georgetown athlete
5. Keyboard instrument
6. Like a highway
7. "Eeeuuwl"
8. Baseball's Say Hey Kid
9. Solidarity leader
10. Hebrew measure
11. Split
12. Agent's amount
15. All-night bash
20. Stylish
22. Freudian subjects
25. Court order
27. ___ X
29. Paul Bunyan's ox
31. In person
32. Chief Norse god
33. Marries
34. Actor Neeson
35. Jason's ship
36. Codger
37. Gaucho's weapon
38. Channel swimmer Gertrude
43. Nav. officer
46. "Dancing Queen" group
49. Aptitude
51. Heart line
53. Affectation
55. "Lou Grant" star
56. Plant life
57. ___ Olay
58. "Silly" birds
59. Will-___-wisp
60. Shootout time, maybe
61. Drops off
63. Recedes, as the tide
64. Web address ender
66. Agent

Solution on page 330

Mildly Tricky 66

ACROSS
1. Alums
6. Golfer's concern
10. ___-mutuel
14. Poet W. H. ___
15. A little, musically
16. Any thing
17. Parisian thanks
18. Pass over
19. Honey holder
20. Twosomes
22. Wood in Hollywood
24. "Uh-huh"
26. Miracle-___
27. Inc., abroad
28. Deuces
31. Capek play
33. Credit-tracking corp.
35. 18-wheeler
36. Edible pods
38. Lots
42. Poe's middle name
44. However, briefly
45. "Dallas" matriarch Miss ___
46. Encounters
47. Madras dresses
49. Heart chart, for short
50. Energy
52. Actor Ayres
53. Personal: prefix
54. "Silent" prez
57. Sleuth, informally
59. Auto parts giant
61. Oakland's county
63. Fraternity letter
66. El ___, Tex.
67. Don Juan's mother
70. Moran and Brockovich
72. Reformer Jacob
73. ___-Cola
74. Ignited again
75. Signs, as a contract
76. ___ to one's ears
77. Squalid

DOWN
1. Pinup's leg
2. Felt bad about
3. Not ___ eye in the house
4. Rots
5. Derogatory
6. Family M.D.'s
7. Seoul soldier
8. Cake topper
9. Warhol's genre
10. 12-point type
11. Wake Island, e.g.
12. Send, as payment
13. Fix firmly
21. Cutty ___: Scotch brand
23. Spanish constructions
25. Smarts
28. Airport conveyance
29. Cunning trick
30. Eye amorously
32. 1986 Indy 500 winner Bobby
34. ___-Mart
36. Kind of inspection
37. Philosopher Kierkegaard
39. Took off
40. Kind of torch on "Survivor"
41. Kind of lily
43. Off-road transport, for short
48. "___ a Teen-age Werewolf"
51. Florence ruling family
53. "Amen!"
54. Bay of Naples isle
55. Actor Delon
56. Corrective eye surgery
58. Church law
60. Wharves
62. Forest growth
64. "___ 18"
65. Lively, in mus.
68. Euro forerunner
69. Cook in the microwave
71. Farm enclosure

Solution on page 330

Mildly Tricky 67

ACROSS

1. Do in, as a dragon
5. Alternative to Charles de Gaulle
9. Obstreperous
14. Helen's mother, in Greek myth
15. "___ life!"
16. Character of a people
17. Actor Estrada
18. Skin: Suffix
19. "___ we dance?"
20. ___ Kippur
21. Albanian money
22. Tampa neighbor, informally
24. Walk over
26. Opposite of vert.
27. Speak like Daffy
29. Beach attraction
30. Chang's twin
33. Stares
36. Prince ___ Khan
38. ___ Lama
40. Perlman of "Cheers"
41. Interjections from Rocky
42. Daddy-o
43. Angiogram image
45. Weirdo
46. Art able to
47. Memo letters
48. "Later!"
50. Job detail, briefly
52. Never, to Nietzsche
53. Chooses
57. Brewer Coors
60. After expenses
61. Ad ___
62. Pen
63. God of thunder
65. Coffin
66. Decide at the flip of ___
67. Ditty
68. Cross inscription
69. Chili con ___
70. Egg on
71. Average

DOWN

1. Weavers' reeds
2. Dormouse
3. Stop on ___
4. Talk, talk, talk
5. Nash and others
6. Really smell
7. Env. contents
8. Southern roots
9. Give an answer
10. Alternative
11. "Huh?"
12. 1996 also-ran
13. Designer monogram
21. Novelist Gould
23. Fri. preceder
25. Skirt fold
28. John of "Miracle on 34th Street"
29. Methods: Abbr.
30. North Carolina college
31. Siestas
32. Central point
33. Tennis's Steffi
34. "Hey, mate!"
35. Persian sprite
37. "Skip to My ___"
39. Lickety-split
44. Eisenhower's boyhood home
46. Breton, for one
49. "You betcha!"
51. Looked intently
52. Away
54. Material for uniforms
55. "___ is human"
56. Curtain fabric
57. Alms box
58. Christian, of fashion
59. Internet initials
60. Faux pas
62. WWII female
64. "Ben-___"
65. Coal container

Solution on page 331

Mildly Tricky 68

ACROSS

1. Tabula ___
5. Deep Blue's game
10. Seaweed, e.g.
14. City rds.
15. Friendliness
16. "___ yellow ribbon . . ."
17. Flying mammals
18. "Singin' in the Rain" director Stanley
19. Aardvark's fare
20. Graceland, e.g.
22. Withdraws
24. "Must've been something ___"
26. Some AL batters
27. False gods
30. ___ Cruces, N.M.
32. When tripled, a 1970 war film
36. Certain Wall Streeter, briefly
37. Flying jib, e.g.
39. Neighbor of Francia
41. "___ fair in love . . ."
43. Speck in the ocean
45. Baby blues
46. Ogle
48. River to the Seine
50. German direction
51. Mmes., in Madrid
52. RR stop
53. ___ Domingo
55. Cole nicknamed "King"
57. Beanery sign
59. Medal giver
63. Latke ingredient
67. Dalai ___
68. Toward the back
70. Ages
71. "I smell ___!"
72. Former Big Apple mayor Abe
73. Aussie hoppers
74. Decrease gradually
75. Flies alone
76. Cubs slugger Sammy

DOWN

1. Broccoli ___ (leafy vegetable)
2. Gardner and others
3. Paving stone
4. Attack
5. West Pointer
6. Med. group
7. Half of zwei
8. Chargers
9. Lip-___
10. Hardly any
11. Come-on
12. Catches on to
13. Walkman batteries
21. Former Soviet news agency
23. Ballpark figs.
25. "___ Coming" (1969 hit)
27. False god
28. City on the Rhone
29. Less inept
31. Apportion
33. Ajar, in poems
34. Synthetic fabric
35. "___ of robins in her hair"
38. Islet
39. Aliens, for short
40. About
42. Mme., across the Pyrenees
44. "___ kleine Nachtmusik"
47. "This comes ___ surprise"
49. "___ perpetua" (Idaho's motto)
52. Home music system
54. Fall bloomers
56. Saudis, e.g.
58. ___-ski
59. ___-kiri
60. Arabian Peninsula land
61. "Tiny" Archibald
62. Actual
64. Ending for buck
65. New Mexico art center
66. Bones
67. Perry Mason's field
69. ___, amas, amat

Solution on page 331

Mildly Tricky 69

ACROSS

1. Bridge coup
5. Cal. entry
9. Whole bunch
12. Nigeria's largest city
14. Jacob's first wife
15. ___ mater
16. Aromatic flavoring
17. Food
18. Feels poorly
19. Loire River city
21. Six-pointers, for short
22. Ice sheet
23. Band booking
24. Farm sounds
26. Have in mind
28. Lo ___ (noodle dish)
29. Civil War gp.
30. ___ colada
33. Lascivious look
35. Twisted
40. Smokes
41. House of the Seven
    Gables site
43. Hawaiian island
44. Govt. debt
46. "Bye"
47. Big gulp
48. L.A. clock setting
50. Ivory source
52. VW model
56. Borscht ingredient
57. African antelope
60. Gulf of ___, off the coast
    of Yemen
61. "Eureka!"
63. Buffalo team
65. Apple leftover
66. Rookie: var.
68. Spartacus, e.g.

69. Dresden's river
70. Mtn. stat
71. Misanthrope
72. Bay area airport letters
73. Fair to middling
74. Sots' spots

DOWN

1. What "yo mama" is
2. Hawaiian island
3. Winery process
4. The majority
5. 1936 candidate Landon
6. Fossil fuel blocks
7. Cowpoke's pal
8. Graduate record?
9. Duplicity
10. Acrylic fiber
11. Headquartered

13. Summons from the boss
15. Nutty
20. Dirties
25. Like a short play
27. Slangy turndown
28. Sail holder
29. Invent
30. Agt.'s take
31. "Am ___ your way?"
32. Vietnam's ___ Dinh Diem
34. ___ Lilly & Co.
36. City in SW Russia
37. Motor City gp.
38. Rapa ___ (Easter Island)
39. Cutting remark
42. Pouts
45. Antipollution org.
49. Union members
51. Put away

52. Steps off
53. Violinist Busch
54. ___-Croatian
55. Koko's dagger
56. Exposes
57. Persona non ___
58. "When pigs fly!"
59. Addicts
62. Hawaiian city
64. Spill the beans
67. Ab ___ (from the
    beginning)

Solution on page 331

Mildly Tricky 70

ACROSS

1. Sprightly dances
5. Larry King employer
8. Breezy
12. Bypass
13. "Pet" that's a plant
14. Oblivion
15. Opera's ___ Te Kanawa
16. "Blast it!"
17. Running wild
18. Intermissions
20. Enormous birds of myth
21. Bridge declaration
22. Bombast
23. Public flaps
26. Mail fee
30. Director Jean-___ Godard
31. Lean against
34. "There oughta be ___!"
35. Itsy-bitsy bits
37. Mountain pass
38. Kind of wave
39. TV handyman Bob
40. Lead source
42. ___ Harbour, Fla.
43. Breastbone
45. "Mourning Becomes Electra" playwright
47. May celebrant
48. Budapest-born conductor
50. "Let's go!"
52. Corroborates
56. New moon, e.g.
57. Minnesota ___
58. "Pipe down!"
59. Jazz instruments
60. Cries of surprise
61. Nevada county
62. Condo, e.g.
63. "Kidnapped" author's inits.
64. Hurry up

DOWN

1. One-liner, e.g.
2. "___ the Mood for Love"
3. Surrounded
4. Recipe direction
5. Heart-to-hearts
6. Dressed to the ___
7. Badgers
8. Former Ford minivan
9. Suffix with arthr-
10. Greek R's
11. "Are we there ___?"
13. Jewel box
14. "___ Theme" ("Doctor Zhivago" tune)
19. Copycats
22. Geometric suffix
23. Poles, e.g.
24. Do the job
25. French school
26. Barbershop emblem
27. Accused's need
28. President Nasser
29. "The Seven Year Itch" actor Tom
32. Ponzi scheme, e.g.
33. "My mama done ___ me"
36. Squirrel-like monkey
38. Jargons
40. Doublemint, e.g.
41. At a minimum
44. Canonical hour
46. Choice word
48. Lesley of "60 Minutes"
49. Preminger and Graham
50. Detective Charlie
51. Long garment
52. Get an ___ effort
53. "Star Trek" navigator
54. Clucking sounds
55. "Oops!"
56. Nittany Lions sch.

Solution on page 331

Mildly Tricky 71

ACROSS

1. Composer Berg
6. Farming prefix
10. Garlands
14. Trailblazer Daniel
15. "Pumping ___"
16. Courtroom affirmation
17. Eat away
18. "___ of Our Lives"
19. "Off the Court" author
20. Banned insecticide
21. Barely passing grades
23. Octad plus one
25. "___ Miserables"
26. Telecom giant
27. Country rtes.
28. Mary Hartman portrayer Louise
32. ___ Nostra
33. "___ Irish Rose"
34. Saturn, for one
35. Heat unit
40. Swabs
41. Gibbon, e.g.
42. Be in pain
43. Conundrum
45. X, at times
46. "A Lesson From ___"
47. Followers: suffix
49. Carpet fibers
50. "Bobby Hockey"
53. Articulate
54. 7, on a phone
55. Caught but good
57. After curfew
58. T-shirt size: Abbr.
61. Fork feature
62. "Like ___ not"
64. Flightless South American birds
66. Reply to "Are not!"
67. Ditto
68. Gin's partner
69. Pizzas
70. Unruly crowds
71. Caterpillar hairs

DOWN

1. In for the night
2. "___ of the Flies"
3. Dismiss unceremoniously
4. &
5. Pokes fun at
6. Staffers
7. Mardi ___
8. Singer Orbison
9. Beginnings
10. Shark's offering
11. Loom bar
12. "___ to Be You"
13. Outbuildings
22. Always, in verse
24. Dapper
26. Bridge expert
28. Light source
29. "Peek-___!"
30. Doesn't guzzle
31. Zaire's Mobutu ___ Seko
32. Ann and May
34. Malicious
36. "Stop!"
37. E.P.A. concern: Abbr.
38. First South Korean president
39. Chaos
44. Ascend
46. Maintains
48. Extreme cruelty
49. NYC subway
50. From the keg
51. "Spider-Man" director Sam
52. Dentist's directive
54. Cuts back
56. Thirteen popes
57. Bausch & ___
58. Fast time
59. Greek earth goddess: Var.
60. Suffix with opal
63. "___ Te Ching"
65. Garden tool

Solution on page 331

Mildly Tricky 72

ACROSS

1. Subway Series team
5. Fort Worth sch.
8. Bonkers
13. Chills and fever
14. ___ longa, vita brevis
15. Cram for an exam
16. Soup crackers
18. Cheers
19. 401, in old Rome
20. Mdse.
21. Inclined
22. Quills
24. Sporty Mazda
25. Milne's "Mr. ___ Passes By"
26. Nourish
27. HBO alternative
30. F sharp equivalent
33. "To thine own ___ be true"
34. Prosperity
35. Actress Graff
36. Final: Abbr.
37. 2:1, e.g.
38. "La Dolce ___"
39. Wire measures
40. Put ___ to (finish)
41. S.A.T. company
42. Bit
43. Do-it-yourselfer's purchase
44. Not presto
46. Overtakes
49. Hair salon item
50. Cycle starter
51. Auction action
53. One end of the spectrum
54. Tall, skinny guy
56. Atlas blowups
57. Actor Carney
58. "Spare tire"
59. Perfect places
60. Darned spot
61. Play mates?

DOWN

1. Gender abbr.
2. "Good grief!"
3. Garden bulb
4. Put in rollers
5. Bicycle built for two
6. Green garnish
7. Battleship letters
8. Type of mutual fund
9. Not suitable
10. Private chat
11. Sought damages
12. Photo ___ (media events)
15. Conviction
17. Light
21. Refines, as ore
23. Bucky Beaver's toothpaste
26. Guy
28. Central street
29. Blockhead
30. Fork over
31. Move like a moth
32. Releases
33. Romeo, to Juliet
34. Desires
37. Kind of bread
39. Sacred songs
42. Estuaries
43. Kind of chop
45. Actress Burstyn
46. Wing: Prefix
47. Deadly virus
48. "___ Marner"
49. Peel
52. Bankruptcy cause
53. Compete
54. Dracula, at times
55. U.S.MC rank

Solution on page 331

Mildly Tricky 73

ACROSS

1. Arizona Indian
5. Israeli guns
9. Stick (out)
12. Island strings
13. Bo of "10"
15. Mozart's "___ fan tutte"
16. Overcast
17. Neither sharp nor flat
18. Hurried
19. More vigorous
21. Cardinal's insignia
22. Rooney of "60 Minutes"
23. R.p.m. indicator
26. Fab Four film
28. Former Portuguese colony
    in India
31. Embarrassment
33. Perth ___, N.J.
37. "___ bin ein Berliner"
38. Sound from Santa
39. Like hen's teeth
40. Kiss
42. Hoarse
44. Table salt, to a
    chemist
45. Lighthearted
47. Belgrade native
49. Cumberland ___
50. Biblical mount
51. High nest: Var.
52. Baseball execs
53. Whimper
55. Artist Chagall
57. 451, in old Rome
60. Muslim pilgrimage
62. Doughnut-shaped
66. Claim on property
67. "Darn ___!"
70. Catchall abbr.
71. Workplace watchdog,
    briefly
72. TV, radio, etc.
73. "Terrible" czar
74. ___ Beta Kappa
75. 52 cards
76. Like dry mud

DOWN

1. Actor Jackman
2. Gumbo
3. Ring
4. "The best ___ to come"
5. Japanese vegetable
6. Buddhist discipline
7. Annoys
8. Boil
9. Enlist in
10. Employed
11. Neat
14. MacLachlan of "Twin
    Peaks"
15. Johnny Appleseed's real
    surname
20. Allergy reaction
24. Task
25. "That is so funny"
27. Fond du ___, Wis.
28. The Bee Gees brothers
29. Eyes
30. Mark Twain/Bret Harte
    play
32. Like some tree trunks
34. North Carolina fort
35. Philosopher William of ___
36. Pound sounds
39. Damascus's land
41. Staying power
43. Salon job
46. Go quickly
48. Ernie's "Sesame Street"
    pal
51. In seventh heaven
54. Impulse
56. Stand-up guy?
57. Hoof sound
58. Gossip, slangily
59. Where Samson slew the
    Philistines
61. Carved gem
63. 1972 Kentucky Derby
    winner ___ Ridge
64. "Out of Africa" author
    Dinesen
65. Manhattan sch.
68. Driver's need: Abbr.
69. "Mighty ___ a Rose"

Solution on page 332

Mildly Tricky 74

ACROSS

1. Increased
6. Res ___ loquitur
10. Bears' hands
14. Record player
15. Outscore
16. Designer von Furstenberg
17. Beautify
18. Opposite of bueno
19. Charades, e.g.
20. "Go ahead, ask"
22. Poor movie rating
24. ___ Mawr, Pa.
26. Holiday quaff
27. Conclusion
28. "___ delighted!"
31. Steal from
33. Watch chain
35. Wall Street order
36. Overhangs
38. "___ kidding!"
42. Have dinner at home
44. Bird: prefix
45. Contemptible ones
46. Secluded valleys
47. Assail
49. Census datum
50. A.F.L.'s partner
52. Chair part
53. Ref. book
54. Bankroll
57. Econ. yardstick
59. Notre ___
61. Tinsel, e.g.
63. Dressing choice
66. ___ monster
67. ___ fide
70. Bold one
72. Slippery
73. "___ Excited" (Pointer Sisters hit)
74. Grads
75. Artifice
76. Clock sound
77. Center

DOWN

1. "___ Lazy River"
2. Many profs.
3. "Tush!"
4. Attire
5. Philanthropist
6. "Big Blue"
7. ___ green
8. Drawing room
9. Many, many
10. Cribbage pieces
11. Playing marble
12. John Lennon hit
13. Bergen's bumpkin
21. Banks on a runway
23. Altruist's opposite
25. Exploding stars
28. "___ to differ!"
29. Twofold
30. Memory unit
32. Cut at an angle
34. Audi rival
36. Ship's flag
37. Located
39. Not yet final, at law
40. Ten sawbucks
41. Student's book
43. Business abbr.
48. Culture medium
51. In the least
53. National park in Alaska
54. Bet
55. Farewell
56. Guys' partners
58. Interest piquer
60. Lady
62. Zany Martha
64. Gunk
65. Skirt lines
68. Defense advisory org.
69. "All systems go"
71. Letter run

Solution on page 332

Mildly Tricky 75

ACROSS

1. Draft org.
4. History, with "the"
8. Syrian president
13. "That feels good!"
14. ___-Detoo ("Star Wars" droid)
15. Alabama march city
16. Absorbed, as a loss
17. Free to attack
18. Prepared to sing the national anthem
19. Witherspoon of "Legally Blonde"
21. His, to Henri
23. Sun. talks
24. Soak
27. Mideast capital
29. Monica of tennis
31. Declared
35. Pokes
38. Acorn sources
40. Court actions
41. "___ Gang"
42. Banal
44. Dernier ___
45. Barter
48. Adolescent
49. Droops
50. Lampoon
52. Mall component
54. ___ Stanley Gardner
56. Most cunning
59. "The wolf ___ the door"
62. "Cheers" role
64. Halloween option
66. Comforter stuffing
68. Badger
71. Botanist Gray
72. Blank look
73. Sea eagles
74. Asian holiday
75. "The Gondoliers" girl
76. Sofer of soaps
77. ". . . ___ shall die"

DOWN

1. German river
2. Completely full
3. See-through
4. Ante-
5. One whose name is followed by "esq."
6. In order
7. Carries
8. Balaam's mount
9. Leave port
10. ___ gin
11. Eros, to Romans
12. June honorees
14. Coeur d'___
20. Meeting: Abbr.
22. Airline to Stockholm
25. Coagulate
26. Valentine symbol
28. 40 winks
30. Irving Berlin's "Blue ___"
32. Ten: Prefix
33. Puppeteer Tony
34. Medical suffix
35. Scribbles
36. Atmosphere
37. Fresh kid
39. Editors' marks
43. Carbon compound
46. They practice girth control
47. "To ___ is human . . ."
49. Merlin, e.g.
51. Chicago trains
53. Marriage and others
55. Peter, pumpkinwise
57. Defunct defense gp.
58. Electric dart shooter
59. Superlative suffix
60. Construction ___
61. Nabokov heroine and others
63. A ___ pittance
65. "Play Time" actor/director
67. "Citizen X" actor
69. Cape ___, Mass.
70. Caribbean, e.g.

Solution on page 332

Mildly Tricky 76

ACROSS
1. Garret
5. Circus prop
10. Neat as ___
14. Intestinal sections
15. To have, in Le Havre
16. Scrawny
17. Change the decor of
18. Mother of Perseus
19. College QB, often
20. Birthplace of St. Francis
22. Villain, at times
24. Author Silverstein
26. Cleo's killer
27. "Me, too!"
30. Harvest goddess
32. Online periodical, for short
36. One of eight Eng. kings
37. Alaskan city
39. Charred
41. Suggestions on food labels: Abbr.
43. Gaucho gear
45. Ballet leap
46. Iron-based
48. Capital of Latvia
50. A Caesar
51. John ___ (the Lone Ranger)
52. Sailor's affirmative
53. Dull finish
55. Mil. training academy
57. Stops up
59. "C'est magnifique!"
63. "Pretty nice!"
67. Chaplin prop
68. Ushered
70. You can dig it
71. "Pardon me"
72. Pigeon's perch
73. Brood
74. Cosmonaut Gagarin
75. Lhasa ___ (Tibetan dogs)
76. Each

DOWN
1. Italian bread
2. Arena shouts
3. Some narcs
4. Eastern philosophy
5. ___ Hawkins Day
6. New Deal program, for short
7. Charged atoms
8. Jungle vines
9. Kilmer classic
10. E.g., e.g.
11. Fleshy fruit
12. "Are you ___ out?"
13. MoMA site
21. Leg part
23. Blunted blade
25. Togo's capital
27. Esne
28. More eccentric
29. Cognizant
31. Arctic explorer Robert
33. Capt.'s superior
34. "Give it ___!"
35. "Understand?"
38. Killer whale
39. Droop
40. "___ Dinah": Frankie Avalon hit
42. ___ Lanka
44. Bound
47. Baal, e.g.
49. Bullets, e.g.
52. Out for the night
54. Inhaler target
56. Kind of lily
58. Queen ___ lace
59. Diamond Head locale
60. Dilly
61. Prefix with sphere
62. Appends
64. Betty of cartoons
65. Brand for Bowser
66. Bottomless
67. Small island
69. "Can ___ now?"

Solution on page 332

Mildly Tricky 77

ACROSS

1. Stride
5. "Put ___ on it!"
9. Prom-night safety gp.
13. Airline to Israel
14. Fall tool
15. Craze
16. Drenches
17. Inhabitants: Suffix
18. Some wedding guests
19. China, Japan, etc.
21. Social classes
23. Boat mover
24. Hive dwellers
26. "___ Loves You"
27. Jail, slangily
28. ___ chi ch'uan
30. Carol
34. Ice cream holders
37. Curses
39. "___ any drop to drink":
    Coleridge
40. "___ of Two Cities"
41. "Exodus" hero
42. LaBelle or LuPone
44. With it
45. Palm fruits
47. Out of bed
48. Tiny fraction of a min.
50. Arthur of "The Golden
    Girls"
51. Actor Alastair
52. Amazement
54. Drink like a fish
56. ___-jongg
59. Not moving
62. Tell
64. Dad's rival
65. Garden intruder
67. Copied
68. Pindar, for one
69. Cap-___
70. Glided
71. Panhandles
72. Peccadilloes
73. Catcher Tony

DOWN

1. Basil-based sauce
2. Hawaii hi
3. Escapade
4. ". . . or ___!"
5. Up and about
6. Starbucks buy
7. Mamie's man
8. Fam. tree member
9. Stir-fries
10. "Green Gables" girl
11. Code signals
12. "___ Kapital"
15. Beat to a pulp
20. Humiliated
22. "Q ___ queen"
25. Ogle
27. "Fantasia" frame
29. "Lucky Jim" author
31. Football stats: Abbr.
32. Memo
33. Sheepish look
34. "High Hopes" lyricist
35. "Miss ___ Regrets"
36. Back of the neck
37. Dinner and a movie,
    perhaps
38. More nimble
43. Order between "ready"
    and "fire"
46. Beame and Burrows
49. Gentle stroke
51. Dark suit
53. Left on a map
55. ___ a million
56. Syrup flavor
57. Dined at home
58. Gossipy Hopper
59. Page, e.g.
60. Calc cousin
61. "___ the night before . . ."
63. Coarse file
64. Quoits target
66. Prefix with center

Solution on page 332

Mildly Tricky 78

ACROSS
1. Partner of Lewis or Lois
6. Fancy-schmancy
10. "___ Network" (1980s comedy series)
14. Great Lakes tribesmen
15. Novelist Jaffe
16. "___ Silver, away!"
17. Forbidding words
18. Cries of surprise
19. Lambs: Lat.
20. Boards
22. Got uptight
24. "Dang!"
25. Cartel city
26. Brownish purple
29. Sweater eater
31. Significant others
35. Tara family
37. Old 45 player
39. D.D.E.'s predecessor
40. Long sandwich
41. Indy entry
43. D.D.E.'s command in WWII
44. Three, in Torino
45. Mosque figure
46. Yak, yak, yak
48. Keep an ___ the ground
50. Goldfinger portrayer Frobe
52. "No problem!"
53. Catch sight of
55. Chemistry Nobelist Otto
57. Roofing pro
60. In need of company
64. 2:00 or 3:00
65. In the blink ___ eye
67. Bogged down
68. Bruins' sch.
69. Madam
70. Calm
71. Nonverbal okays
72. "Giant" author Ferber
73. Exigencies

DOWN
1. Formally surrender
2. Scientology's ___ Hubbard
3. "___ Misbehavin'"
4. Stock up on again
5. Relatively cool sun
6. Right away
7. ___ and aahs
8. ___-Cat (winter vehicle)
9. "___ la vista!"
10. Singer Twain
11. Smokes
12. Daly of "Judging Amy"
13. Emptiness
21. 2001 Sean Penn film
23. Where Mark Twain is buried
25. Fashionable
26. Mail, in Marseille
27. "Star Trek" lieutenant
28. Pole tossed by Scots
30. Central idea
32. Eta follower
33. ___ Park, Colo.
34. Tale
36. Melodic
38. Card game also called sevens
42. Sly
47. Kind of strength
49. Colorful fish
51. Girl in a Beach Boys song
54. Space explorer
56. Macho dude
57. Avoid
58. Kooky
59. "___ Lang Syne"
60. Croquet area
61. Escutcheon border
62. Anthropologist Margaret
63. Breyers rival
66. Craze

Solution on page 332

Mildly Tricky 79

ACROSS

1. Blue-ribbon position
6. Old French coins
10. Unguent
14. Sharp
15. "Mama" speaker
16. Ancient Greek theaters
17. Potato, for one
18. Lady of La Mancha
19. ___ Tzu
20. Impose, as a tax
22. Da ___, Vietnam
24. Wood sorrel
25. San ___, Italy
27. Impassive
29. Follower
33. Thesis introduction?
34. Cry out for
35. Pipe problem
37. "Me too"
41. Actor Benicio ___ Toro
42. Floor pieces
44. Short time?
45. Faulty
48. "___ 'er up!"
49. Disencumbers
50. ___ constrictor
52. Opinion opener
54. Odd
58. Folk singer Phil
59. Charlemagne's domain: abbr.
60. Inaugural ball, e.g.
62. Devours
66. Sommelier's prefix
68. Donny and Marie, e.g.
70. Stir up
71. ". . . ___ after"
72. First king of Israel
73. "Sesame Street" regular

74. "Mon ___!"
75. Verb type: Abbr.
76. Fit for a king

DOWN

1. ___ morgana (mirage)
2. Hosp. areas
3. Burnishes
4. Took the wheel
5. More to the point
6. Byrnes of "77 Sunset Strip"
7. Masked critter
8. Arm bones
9. Viewpoints
10. Derek and Diddley
11. Kind of committee
12. Nikon rival
13. Taj ___
21. Refine, as metal

23. "Naked Maja" painter
26. "___ by land . . ."
28. ___ and outs
29. Time ___ half
30. Consider
31. Prefix with port
32. Shire of "Rocky"
36. Horse of the Year, 1960–64
38. Female friend, in France
39. Calf-length skirt
40. Part of M.I.T.: Abbr.
43. Pizzeria order
46. Mom and pop store org.
47. Spiritual, e.g.
49. Do a museum job
51. Graf's husband
53. Generous one
54. Did a smithy's job

55. Rome's ___ Fountain
56. "Walk Away ___" (1966 hit)
57. Cuban boat boy Gonzalez
61. Adjoin
63. Belted out, as a tune
64. Voice of America org.
65. Rind
67. Sch. named for a televangelist
69. Kind of camera: Abbr.

Solution on page 333

Mildly Tricky 80

ACROSS

1. Star in Virgo
6. Pesticide brand
10. Mil. jet locale
13. Devastation
14. Hockey legend Gordie
15. Light beige
16. Lyric poem
17. Tex. neighbor
18. Restaurateur Toots
19. Ending with hard or soft
20. ___ de France
21. Inventor's goal
23. Break
26. Foxx of "Sanford and Son"
27. Give consent
30. Toll road
32. Fawner
33. Largest of the Marianas
35. When repeated, a food fish
39. Submissions to eds.
40. Austere
43. Jewel
44. "Beetle Bailey" dog
46. Be in harmony
47. Kitchen gadget
49. Cap'n's mate
51. Window dressing
52. Corned beef concoction
54. African desert
57. Least colorful
59. Apply gently
60. Ottawa-based law enforcement gp.
64. Artist's medium
65. Pigeon-___
67. Paramecium propellers
68. Roswell sightings
69. Bakery fixture
70. Agreement
71. Green
72. Hair division
73. Entices

DOWN

1. Sullivan had a really big one
2. Dad
3. Songwriter Novello
4. Emergency situation
5. Bandage brand
6. Wild Asian dog
7. Fountain orders
8. Barn bird
9. ___ tide
10. Felt sore
11. Palm leaf
12. Songwriter Bacharach
15. Favor
20. "Rocks"
22. "Raiders of the Lost ___"
24. "Grand" ice cream brand
25. Outpouring
27. Prefix with sphere
28. Go for
29. Play list
31. "___ Believer" (Monkees hit)
33. Makes progress
34. Metro area
36. Home of the Taj Mahal
37. Listen to
38. '50s Hungarian leader Nagy
41. Bedwear, briefly
42. Tenn. neighbor
45. Dwell (on)
48. Simple wind instrument
50. Cries of surprise
51. ___ Four (Beatles)
52. Israeli port
53. Give the O.K.
55. "Doe, ___ . . ."
56. Lacked, briefly
57. Come down hard
58. Car roof with removable panels
61. Roman 152
62. Baseball glove
63. Shells out
66. Eggs, to Caesar
67. Chicago pro

Solution on page 333

Mildly Tricky 81

ACROSS

1. "The Clan of the Cave Bear" author
5. Israeli dances
10. Skelton's Kadiddlehopper
14. Site in el mar
15. Blow one's top
16. "Divine Secrets of the ___ Sisterhood"
17. Pell-___
18. Furious
19. Lass
20. Friendly
22. Door frame part
24. Electrical pioneer
25. Bring back
28. Diamond pattern
30. Gas additive
34. Suspects
37. Impose, as a duty
39. Fair-hiring abbr.
40. Curve
41. Nonsense
43. Worldwide (abbr.)
44. F.B.I. employee: Abbr.
45. Karate blow
46. Throat part
48. Vagabond
50. "Mornings at Seven" playwright Paul
52. Conversationalist
54. "Dead Souls" novelist Nikolai
58. "Count me in!"
61. On the line
63. Simon or Diamond
64. Bring out
67. "Put ___ writing"
68. Child's plea
69. Bold one
70. Political columnist Charen
71. Kirghiz range
72. ___ und Drang
73. Joule fragments

DOWN

1. Draw a bead on
2. 1972 Bill Withers hit
3. New York Harbor's ___ Island
4. Space cadet's place
5. Cure
6. Cantankerous
7. Toupee, slangily
8. Follower of Mar.
9. Engraving tools
10. Young swan
11. Cafe au ___
12. Governess Jane
13. Shopaholic's heaven
21. Homer's boy
23. Actress Judith
26. Oval
27. #2
29. Barbarian
31. Egg producers
32. Abominable Snowman
33. Lounge
34. Construction beam
35. Lily of Utah
36. Airing
38. Quash
42. Castle, in chess
43. Lickety-split
45. Jam-pack
47. Assns.
49. And others
51. Stimulating drink
53. West Yorkshire city
55. Croc's cousin
56. Approving
57. Horne and Olin
58. Atahualpa, e.g.
59. Breakfast, lunch or dinner
60. Actress Lollobrigida
62. School session
65. "Can't Help Lovin' ___ Man"
66. S.A. country

Solution on page 333

Mildly Tricky 82

ACROSS

1. Introduction to physics?
5. "Erie Canal" mule
8. Chicago mayor Richard
13. "Dies ___" (hymn)
14. Acapulco gold
15. Strauss opera
16. Erodes
18. Fly
19. Fed. benefits agency
20. My ___, Vietnam
21. 1986 sci-fi sequel
22. Ancient Palestinian
24. British guns
25. Abbr. on a bank statement
26. Accomplishes
27. "Isn't ___ bit like you and me?" (Beatles lyric)
30. Mosey
33. Come down
34. NaCl
35. Vichyssoise ingredients
36. "Gimme ___!" (start of an Iowa State cheer)
37. Cleveland suburb
38. Do-it-yourselfers' needs
39. Eugene O'Neill's daughter
40. Like some old buckets
41. Coach Parseghian
42. Car
43. D.C. insider
44. Arcade flubs
46. Go-getters
49. Cherry-colored
50. Old Portuguese coin
51. Cool, once
53. Detective Lupin
54. Guaranteed
56. Prepare
57. Neighbor of Aus.
58. Have ___ (be connected)
59. Breathers
60. Three, in Napoli
61. Big cross

DOWN

1. Architect ___ van der Rohe
2. Clear, as a disk
3. Bye-byes
4. JFK's UN ambassador
5. Voiced
6. Bandleader Shaw
7. British john
8. Ray of the Kinks
9. From Mars, say
10. Usurer
11. CPR experts
12. "___-haw!"
15. Like potato chips
17. Actress Graff and others
21. Tone deafness
23. Jockey's wear
26. "Hawaii Five-O" nickname
28. "Waiting for the Robert ___"
29. ___ all-time high
30. ___-Seltzer
31. Eshkol's successor
32. Program trials
33. Taoism founder
34. Black Panther Bobby
37. Dance energetically
39. Beginning
42. Dress styles
43. South Dakota's capital
45. "___ my case"
46. More factual
47. Safari sight
48. Prefix with comic
49. Canadian Indian
52. Await judgment
53. Cabinet dept.
54. Cpl.'s superior
55. Remote

Solution on page 333

Mildly Tricky 83

ACROSS

1. Inhabitants: Suffix
5. "The Thin Man" dog
9. Expert
14. Taboo
15. Lowlife
16. Pulitzer-winning biography of a Civil War general
17. Belgian composer Jacques
18. Leaf
19. Opera about an opera singer
20. Sanford of "The Jeffersons"
22. Campers, for short
24. Ballpark fig.
25. Gives a hoot
27. Popeye's Olive ___
29. "Good buddies"
31. Duty
33. "Okay, Aunt Bee," Opie-style
37. Before: prefix
38. More modern
40. Instant
41. Wonderland cake message
43. Samovar, e.g.
44. Daughter of Lear
45. Toys with tails
46. It doesn't hold water
48. "___ Pinafore"
49. Historic Hungarian city
50. High-speed Internet inits.
51. Sends forth
53. TV adjunct
55. Big name in stationery
57. "Good" cholesterol, briefly
60. Center
62. Chew out
65. Kind of board
67. At a distance
69. Computer units
71. Big buttes
72. Spanish house
73. ___ to one's ears
74. Missouri river
75. "Blazing Saddles" Oscar nominee Madeline
76. End-of-week cry

DOWN

1. Bach's "Mass ___ Minor"
2. Actress Spelling
3. Chemical endings
4. Comfort
5. Slander
6. Bathroom item
7. Yank
8. New World abbr.
9. Like craft shows
10. ___ volente (God willing)
11. "If all ___ fails . . ."
12. Chest muscles, briefly
13. Suckling spot
21. Noble partner
23. ___ populi
26. Germ-free
28. Greek harp
29. Diet guru Jenny
30. Midler of "The Rose"
32. "Rule, Britannia" composer
34. Black billiard ball
35. Rip-offs
36. Kind of room
37. Yappy dog, briefly
39. Milquetoast
40. Seismograph pickup
42. Griffin of game shows
47. Experienced
50. Actress Joanne
52. "Not right now"
54. Go after
56. Disconcert
57. ___ sapiens
58. Membership fees
59. Actress Bonet
61. Support
63. Triangle tone
64. Needle case
66. Binge
68. LAX watchdog
70. Tanning lotion letters

Solution on page 333

Mildly Tricky 84

ACROSS

1. Bakery attraction
6. Large amount
10. Nintendo's Super ___
13. Bolshevik leader
14. Lasso
15. Double agent
16. Hole-___
17. Spanish snack
18. Others, to Ovid
19. Duffer's cry
20. Profs' helpers
21. Dogie catcher
23. Perches
26. Commits perjury
27. Oblique
30. Mtn. stats
32. Two-time U.S. Open winner Fraser
33. "Nobody doesn't like ___ Lee"
35. Biting
39. "___ Poetica"
40. "The Bartered Bride" composer
43. "Norma ___"
44. Back talk
46. Galway Bay's ___ Islands
47. Without ___ in the world
49. "L'___ c'est moi": Louis XIV
51. Maria of the Met
52. Filly's mother
54. Melodious
57. "Thy Neighbor's Wife" author
59. Lt.'s inferior, in the Navy
60. Je ne ___ quoi
64. The "A" in Chester A. Arthur
65. Gillette brand
67. Reach
68. Miles per hour, e.g.
69. Equine color
70. Cousin of a mink
71. ". . . ___ he drove out of sight"
72. Unit of loudness
73. 1,000 kilograms

DOWN

1. Arabic letter
2. Ashcroft's predecessor
3. ___ about (approximately)
4. 20 Questions category
5. "Wheel" buy
6. Mex. misses
7. Seashore
8. Computer program, for short
9. "Agreed!"
10. "It's the truth!"
11. Inventor Howe
12. Chair
15. Poughkeepsie college
20. Preschooler
22. Cover girl Carol
24. Change for a fin
25. Kitchen wrap
27. Miscellanies
28. Antitoxins
29. Girl
31. PC connection
33. "We make the world's best mattress" sloganeer
34. ___ glance
36. Asian sea
37. ___ avis
38. Golf ball props
41. Calf's call
42. Some batteries
45. Calm
48. Near
50. French possessive
51. Comedian Bill, familiarly
52. Of the cheek
53. Winged
55. Aired again
56. Absurd
57. Biblical weed
58. Canal zones?
61. Env. notation
62. Transcontinental hwy.
63. Achy
66. Also
67. Acquired

Solution on page 333

Mildly Tricky 85

ACROSS

1. Lots
5. Actress Eleniak
10. Data
14. Barn topper
15. Flowing tresses
16. Egyptian canal
17. Dentist's request
18. Little ones
19. School grps.
20. Israeli desert
22. Wall Street worker
24. Abound
27. Big bird
28. Versatile truck, informally
31. More cunning
33. Shreds
37. Ariz. neighbor
38. Shredded
39. Rang out
41. Deuce topper
43. Cut's partner
45. Criminals break them
46. Florid
48. Not theirs
50. Computer giant
51. Panama, e.g.: abbr.
52. Aegean vacation locale
53. Takes too much, briefly
54. C.I.O.'s partner
56. "George of the Jungle" elephant
58. Wrestling pair
62. A Gabor sister
66. ___ weevil
67. Levels
70. Subatomic particle
71. Icelandic epic
72. Pitcher Hideki ___
73. ___-Cuban music
74. Prod
75. Jeans material
76. Charon's river

DOWN

1. "___ calling"
2. Rubberneck
3. Ten C-notes
4. "John Brown's Body" poet
5. CPR expert
6. Beam
7. Durante's "___ Dinka Doo"
8. More acute
9. State in NE India
10. Cosby show
11. Loony
12. Achievement
13. Parts of lbs.
21. Sleeveless garment
23. Tackle box item
25. Run off to the chapel
26. Pianist Hess
28. "Do ___ others as . . ."
29. Gibbs of country music
30. Makes level
32. Belgian painter James
34. Suffix with president
35. Texas town
36. Stitched
39. Capital of Western Australia
40. Mil. awards
42. China's Sun ___-sen
44. Mardi Gras, e.g.: Abbr.
47. "___ does it!"
49. Appear
52. Actress Bloom
55. Stinky
57. Dads
58. Bustle
59. Alan of "M*A*S*H"
60. Happy
61. Average
63. Knack
64. Flat-bottomed boat
65. Strong as ___
66. Entreat
68. Baseball stat
69. Total

Solution on page 334

Mildly Tricky 86

ACROSS

1. K–12, in education
5. Cube creator
10. Tobacco mouthful
14. Emulated Pinocchio
15. Torment
16. Change places
17. New Year's Day game
18. Snapshot
19. "Whatcha ___?"
20. Photographer Adams
22. Comebacks
24. Window feature
27. Mythical bird
28. Immunization letters
31. Certain tides
33. Ski lift
37. Indonesia's ___ Islands
38. Arp's art
39. Dough
41. Pro ___
43. Where the deer and the antelope play
45. "Venerable" English writer
46. ___ Island Ferry
48. Lodges
50. Cloak-and-dagger org.
51. Bone: Prefix
52. La ___ opera house
53. Absorb, with "up"
54. Big inits. in trucks
56. Used a loom
58. Difficult spot
62. New York Harbor's ___ Island
66. Short skirt
67. 1983 Nicholas Gage book
70. A goodly number
71. As a result
72. Some Bosnians
73. Affix one's John Hancock
74. "Gee whillikers!"
75. Psychoanalyst Fromm
76. ___ II (razor brand)

DOWN

1. Seat of Coffee County, AL
2. Animal with a mane
3. Chops
4. Runs in neutral
5. Eminem's genre
6. "Gross!"
7. Crude dude
8. Buries
9. Former capital of Japan
10. U.S.N rank
11. Catcall
12. "We try harder" company
13. Cyst
21. The Swedish Nightingale
23. Eight: prefix
25. Commit to memory
26. Terhune's "___ Dog"
28. Small amounts, as of cream
29. Prefix with -plasm
30. Bluefin and yellowfin
32. Wall Street worry
34. Weave's partner
35. Baldwin and Guinness
36. AM/FM device
39. ___ Park, Calif.
40. Pile
42. Baseball's Mel
44. Chew (on)
47. Brain tests, briefly
49. Bank
52. Tackle box gizmo
55. Reagan attorney general Edwin
57. Horror film locale: Abbr.
58. "Farmer in the Dell" syllables
59. Blame
60. Mrs. Addams, to Gomez
61. Hatcher of "Desperate Housewives"
63. Den
64. Swenson of "Benson"
65. In ___ (together)
66. Bus. get-together
68. Peacock network
69. Common language suffix

Solution on page 334

Mildly Tricky 87

ACROSS

1. Director Welles
6. Aid and ___
10. Smear
14. Hajji's destination
15. Greek "I"
16. "Casablanca" heroine
17. Borders on
18. Litter's littlest
19. Sign of healing
20. Knocking sound
22. Indian music
23. Chianti, e.g.
24. Near ringer
26. Lurch
29. Corpulent
31. Commando's weapon
32. Scalawag
34. Garlic unit
38. New York Shakespeare Festival founder Joseph
40. Eastwood's "Rawhide" role
42. Victor's cry
43. Golf great Sam
45. Flute player
47. "Les Girls" actress Taina
48. Surgeon's assistant
50. Sadat's predecessor
52. Fleet of warships
55. Shopping outlet
56. Boor
57. Honey
63. ___ dixit
64. Vena ___
65. Tiny bit
66. Faint, with "over"
67. Chopped down
68. Negatively charged particle
69. "Das Rheingold" goddess
70. "Fatal Attraction" director Adrian
71. Mary Poppins, e.g.

DOWN

1. Epps of TV's "House"
2. Country's McEntire
3. Rabbit's tail
4. Musical interval
5. More spiteful
6. ___-ground missile
7. Boxing match
8. 2001 erupter
9. Spill the beans
10. British P.M. before Gladstone
11. Highway to Fairbanks
12. Accepted practice
13. Storied royal elephant
21. Bother
25. Computer key
26. Golf targets
27. Summons to prayer
28. Like a yellow banana
29. Navel variety
30. Toot
33. Openings
35. Has debts
36. Meadow mouse
37. M.I.T. graduate
39. Slender cigar
41. French legislature
44. Lemon
46. Rutgers' river
49. Scamp
51. Breastbones
52. Similar
53. Rodeo performer
54. Pondered
55. Civil War general
58. Like candles
59. Fifty-fifty
60. Ibuprofen target
61. Clickable image
62. Counting-out word

Solution on page 334

Mildly Tricky 88

ACROSS

1. Pop the question
4. Author ___ Neale Hurston
8. Art able to
13. Vocalized
15. Like two peas in ___
16. Amtrak's "bullet train"
17. Clairvoyant
18. Conceal, as a card
19. "Yippee!"
20. Wings it
22. Ms. Ullmann
24. Pad
25. Dissuade
26. Threaten
28. Data entry acronym
30. Light-footed
34. Arctic bird
37. Academy Award
40. Icy
41. Unit of conductance
42. Crook
44. Student's stat.
45. Nat and Natalie
48. At an angle
50. "Psst!"
51. Zhivago portrayer
53. Horse's motion
55. Lumberjack
58. African grassland
62. Ticker tapes?
65. Joined together
66. Hair dryer brand
67. Overplay
69. Nothin'
71. Start to type?
72. Wombs
73. Gives a hand
74. Fresh kid
75. "Singin' in the Rain" director Stanley
76. "Star ___"
77. "Pipe down!"

DOWN

1. Syrian president Bashar al-___
2. "Blue ___ Shoes"
3. Genuflected
4. Nukes
5. ___-Locka, Fla.
6. Esther of "Good Times"
7. Mgmt.
8. Crow's call
9. Campus life
10. Classic soft drink
11. Trudge
12. New Mexico art colony
14. "Peer Gynt" composer
21. Get-up-and-go
23. Vehicle with sliding doors
26. Coffee shop order
27. Smoke, for short
29. Prime meridian std.
31. Drivel
32. Not on tape
33. Jittery
34. Gremlins and Pacers
35. "Here comes trouble!"
36. Caffeine source
38. River island
39. Period of power
43. Neighbor of Ga.
46. Start of a correction
47. Half a dozen
49. VCR alternative
52. Not many
54. Potato sack wt., maybe
56. ___ work (road sign)
57. Firefighter Red
59. Dens
60. Washington who sang the blues
61. Loyalty
62. Barak of Israel
63. Green Hornet's aide
64. FBI guys
66. Wine holder
68. Wrestling win
70. Ike's initials

Solution on page 334

Mildly Tricky 89

ACROSS

1. Auto financing co.
5. Blood: Prefix
9. ___ de mer
12. Accumulated
14. "Beowulf," e.g.
15. Actor Lugosi
16. ___ nous
17. Change for a twenty
18. Region of Saudi Arabia
19. Liqueur flavorers
21. ___ de cologne
22. Beach composition
23. Middle X of X-X-X
24. Does lacework
26. ___ Pieces
28. ___ carotene
29. Poetic adverb
30. Unadulterated
33. "The doctor ___"
35. Opera highlights
40. Legs, slangily
41. French political divisions
43. Associate
44. Feel
46. Discharge
47. Couple
48. Magazine no.
50. Beanies
52. Spread out
56. Cinco follower
57. Basic version: Abbr.
60. Eatery
61. Appropriate
63. Bacon serving
65. Furnace output
66. Fatty treat for birds
68. Baggy
69. Come together
70. Unlocks, poetically
71. ___ ray
72. Canadian prov.
73. When doubled, an old sitcom goodbye
74. Bosc, for one

DOWN

1. "Super!"
2. Food from heaven
3. Bit of tomfoolery
4. Junkyard dogs
5. Angry, with "up"
6. Fencing swords
7. "___ Lisa"
8. Make certain
9. Big buttes
10. Dress style
11. Greases
13. Golfer Calvin
15. Corner of a diamond
20. Composer Erik
25. Samples
27. Bambi's aunt
28. First lady before Mamie
29. Inveigle
30. Some MPAA ratings
31. Abu Dhabi's fed.
32. L.B.J.'s successor
34. The Beatles' "___ the Walrus"
36. Emulates Eminem
37. Dockers' gp.
38. "Float like a butterfly, sting like a bee" boxer
39. Damascus' land: Abbr.
42. Escalator part
45. Frozen Wasser
49. Time of the year
51. Sacred song
52. Doofus
53. Hymn of praise
54. Make ___ buck
55. Soaks, as flax
56. Dutch painter Jan
57. Excelled
58. Seed coat
59. Gloomy, in poetry
62. Insect stage
64. "General Hospital," e.g.
67. Nashville sch.

Solution on page 334

Mildly Tricky 90

ACROSS
1. Cut
4. Snow remover
8. Don't just stand there
13. Allies' foe
15. Gossipy Barrett
16. Hiding place
17. Pub offering
18. "In memoriam" item
19. ___ of roses
20. Paragons
22. Pennies: Abbr.
24. German mister
25. Marsh plant
26. Do a cobbler's job
28. Inner: Prefix
30. Mars, for one
34. Calif. airport
37. Fern-to-be
40. Bingo relative
41. PC hookup
42. ___ preview
44. "Hold on a ___!"
45. Boxer Roberto
48. Noted bankruptcy of 2001
50. Old what's-___-name
51. More hackneyed
53. Centers of activity
55. Lives
58. Maker of the game Asteroids
62. Homeowner's pmt.
65. Cedar Rapids college
66. Easygoing
67. Big ape
69. Musical ending
71. Ricelike pasta
72. Terra ___

73. "Sometimes you feel like ___ . . ."
74. Chicken ___
75. Bandleader Kay
76. Kid's building toy
77. Alphabet trio

DOWN
1. ___ lazuli
2. Rust, e.g.
3. Longed (for)
4. Old hands
5. High toss
6. In reserve
7. Light bulb units
8. Big TV maker
9. Diner sign
10. Entr'___
11. Blacken

12. Okla., before 1907
14. Fright site?
21. Microscope part
23. Boar's mate
26. TV exec Arledge
27. Chem class
29. Stat for infielders
31. Deep cut
32. "That's ___ haven't heard"
33. Medicos
34. Digital displays, for short
35. In ___ (stuck)
36. More, in adspeak
38. Stimpy's cartoon pal
39. Viscounts' superiors
43. Kitchy-___
46. Italian for "to the tooth"
47. Different
49. College sports org.

52. ___ center
54. "There, there"
56. Hometown-related
57. Sierra ___
59. Golden
60. Tore down
61. Latin I translation
62. Ridicule
63. Helen of ___
64. Gangsters' guns
66. Ancient Roman censor
68. Needlefish
70. Grooved on

Solution on page 334

Mildly Tricky 91

ACROSS
1. Mil. addresses
5. "That was close!"
9. ___ Island
14. Chicago exchange, for short
15. Govern
16. Jazz pianist Blake
17. Wash's partner
18. 1816 Jane Austen novel
19. Richard's first veep
20. On the loose
22. Singer Ocasek
24. Dry, as wine
25. Toady
26. Complacent
28. Circle or square
31. Bradley University site
35. Kilmer of "At First Sight"
38. Fishhook attachment
40. Stirs up
41. Stick in one's ___
43. Courtroom event
45. Pedal pushers
46. Carnival attractions
48. "Balderdash!"
50. China's Chou En-___
51. One of the Seven Dwarfs
53. Goof-up
55. Busiest
57. ___ Pointe, Mich.
61. Witch
64. When repeated, a Latin dance
65. Street vendor
66. Artist Max
68. +
70. Cut
71. Stroke of luck
72. Racetrack stops
73. Mine, in Marseilles
74. "___, With Love"
75. Entr'___
76. ___ of the above

DOWN
1. Home products seller
2. Golfer Calvin
3. Some tests
4. Skedaddles
5. Expecting
6. Actor Cronyn
7. "Slippery" tree
8. Has on
9. Firefighter, at times
10. Drill sergeant's syllable
11. Kimono sashes
12. In ___ straits
13. Fair-hiring org.
21. Stadium sounds
23. Little devil
27. Flub
29. Cop's collar
30. Beethoven dedicatee
32. Cambodian money
33. Intestinal sections
34. ___ spumante (wine)
35. Some RCA products
36. Seed covering
37. Stow, as cargo
39. Bert of "The Wizard of Oz"
42. Blubber
44. Generous gifts
47. Haunting image
49. Promise
52. Derisive cry
54. Dennis of the NBA
56. Phi Beta ___
58. Replay feature, for short
59. Attach a patch
60. Baseball Hall-of-Famer Banks
61. Bulk
62. Folkie Guthrie
63. Wildebeests
65. Any miniature golf shot
67. Compete in a slalom
69. Driver's need: Abbr.

Solution on page 335

Mildly Tricky 92

ACROSS

1. Broadway dud
5. Scott of "Charles in Charge"
9. Whiskey drinks
14. Crowd sound
15. Dubliner's country
16. Fool's month
17. Three-time speed skating gold medalist Karin
18. "Diary of ___ Housewife"
19. Capital of Nord, France
20. "You betcha!"
22. Stopped
23. Gen. Robert ___
24. Male deer
25. Buck topper
28. Man of steel?
32. Jumps (out)
33. "Grand Hotel" star
34. Like ironic humor
35. Good for what ___ you
36. Durable dos
37. "Beowulf" beverage
38. Mischievous
39. B-ball
40. Muslim sect
41. South Australia's capital
43. Timmy's dog
44. To be, in old Rome
45. Judges' seat
46. "No way!"
49. Erodes
53. Make ___ for (justify)
54. "Hey . . . over here!"
55. Poi ingredient
56. Power glitch
57. Start of Massachusetts' motto
58. Old French coins
59. Observe furtively
60. "Witness" director Peter
61. Trent of the Senate

DOWN

1. Glenn of the Eagles
2. Isolated
3. Acorn sources
4. Takes advance orders for
5. Check payee, maybe
6. Anouk of "La Dolce Vita"
7. "Dies ___"
8. Multivolume ref.
9. Italian seaport
10. Narcotic
11. www addresses
12. Anger
13. Rosebud, e.g.
21. Martinique et Guadeloupe
22. Atkins diet no-nos
24. Injures
25. Addis ___, Ethiopia
26. Aquatic nymph
27. Spanish diacritic
28. ___ diem (seize the day)
29. Actress Verdon and others
30. Teheran native
31. Singer Gorme
33. Crystal-lined stone
36. Aplomb
37. Sweet wine
39. Faded star
40. Without
42. "C'mon!"
43. Second of two
45. Operatic villains, often
46. Mama ___ of the Mamas and the Papas
47. Bra size
48. ___ a one
49. Feudal serf
50. City on the Brazos
51. In ___ (stuck)
52. Baseball's "Walking Man" Eddie
54. Church bench

Solution on page 335

Mildly Tricky 93

ACROSS

1. Blood components
5. [Uh-oh!]
9. Letters on a brandy bottle
12. Nixon chief of staff
13. Eclectic mixes
15. 2000, e.g.
16. To ___ (exactly)
17. Matching furniture set
18. Cut ___ (dance)
19. In abundance
21. Suffix with president
22. "Holy ___!"
23. Gladly
25. Urban renewal target
27. Botch
30. ___ Kosh B'Gosh
32. Chart anew
36. UN working-conditions agcy.
37. Kojak, to friends
39. Two-fisted
40. Biography
42. Japanese beer brand
44. Baseball's Musial
45. At hand
47. Bridge, in Bretagne
49. Clearasil target
50. 1950s Ford flop
51. Author Rand
52. Spanish queen
54. Middles: Abbr.
56. Enter
58. Emcee
61. "What have we here?!"
63. S.A.T.'s
67. Berlin-born Sommer
68. Dolphins' home
70. Fortune 500 abbr.
71. Dismissed, with "off"
72. Orange ___ tea
73. Fork part
74. Movie format
75. Cereal grasses
76. ___ gin fizz

DOWN

1. Chase flies
2. "I could ___ horse!"
3. Cambodian currency
4. Ancient
5. "Take a look!"
6. Eskimo knife
7. 53, in old Rome
8. Fertilizer ingredient
9. ___ Beach, Fla.
10. First king of Israel
11. Bacchanal
14. Broker's advice
15. Complains
20. Laughfest
24. Adversaries
26. Self-proclaimed psychic Geller
27. Pooh's creator
28. Fibber's admission
29. Resting places
31. Melodramatic
33. Gaynor of "South Pacific"
34. French actor Delon
35. Prefix with -gon
38. Cow chow
39. Beaujolais, e.g.
41. Built
43. ___ Kong
46. Diner order
48. Peter, Paul and Mary, e.g.
51. More pale
53. Puts on the books
55. Cavort
57. Theater awards
58. Grasped
59. Norwegian king
60. Cargo platform
62. Tasting of wood, as some wines
64. Agitate
65. Bond adversary
66. Graf ___
69. A Stooge

Solution on page 335

Mildly Tricky 94

ACROSS
1. Mozart's "Il mio tesoro," e.g.
5. "Family Ties" mom
10. Reasons
14. Lays down the lawn
15. Harvests
16. Lug
17. 1974 Sutherland/Gould spoof
18. "___ kidding!"
19. Paris airport
20. Parachute material
22. Loses it
24. Letters on Sputnik
27. Bog
28. Mortarboard
31. Lunchbox treats
33. Baum princess
37. "___ Lazy River"
38. Went under
39. German subs
41. Created a web site?
43. Choreographer Twyla
45. Sieben follower
46. Royal residence
48. Ritzy
50. Singer Orbison
51. Sluggish
52. Skin problem
53. Verb ending
54. Coll., e.g.
56. "Pay ___ mind"
58. As a substitute
62. Make sense
66. Program
67. Streamlined
70. Comedian Carvey
71. Seat of Allen County, Kan.
72. Bridal path
73. City on the Rhone
74. Junk e-mail
75. Mrs. Gorbachev
76. Baseball's "Walking Man" Eddie

DOWN
1. Org.
2. Cordlike
3. Pastoral poem
4. Org.
5. "___ tu" (Verdi aria)
6. Moon vehicle, for short
7. Yin's opposite
8. Lampoons
9. First name in cosmetics
10. Command to a horse
11. Angel's instrument
12. Christmas season
13. Artful
21. Sgts. and cpls.
23. Haughty one
25. Box
26. Phnom ___
28. Astrological transition point
29. Shock
30. Sao ___
32. Cousin of a giraffe
34. Animal group suffix
35. Computer shortcut
36. A Musketeer
39. Surprise win
40. Eye inflammation
42. Pester
44. Rice-a-___
47. Dermatologist's concern
49. Mandlikova of tennis
52. Comic's Muse
55. Composer Franck
57. Strange to say
58. Breakfast restaurant chain
59. Vincent Lopez's theme song
60. Did the butterfly, e.g.
61. He loved Lucy
63. Belafonte song opener
64. Spanish articles
65. Huff and puff
66. ___ boom bah
68. Golfer Ernie
69. Mauna ___

Solution on page 335

Mildly Tricky 95

ACROSS

1. Wyo. neighbor
5. Disney collectibles
9. Seine city
14. Nike competitor
15. Asian nurse
16. Exxon alternative
17. Peddle
18. Dawdling
19. Senior member
20. "Hamlet" setting
22. Reliable
23. Kind of slicker
24. Unit of loudness
25. French satellite launcher
28. Keep up
32. ___ Yello (soft drink)
33. "Common Sense" pamphleteer
34. 6, on a telephone
35. D.C. bigwigs
36. ___ Haute, Ind.
37. Kind of mile: Abbr.
38. Women's ___
39. Chores
40. Congo's old name
41. Weather
43. Des ___
44. Diving birds
45. An amoeba has one
46. Warns
49. Epitome
53. "Beats me!"
54. Face, slangily
55. Shrek, for one
56. Singing chipmunk
57. Suffix with differ
58. Winter wear
59. Ponders
60. "___, old chap"
61. Food label abbr.

DOWN

1. Central church area
2. Daredevil Knievel
3. Coal holders
4. Extremists
5. "Breakfast at Tiffany's" author
6. Atlanta campus
7. Water-skiing locale
8. Bashful
9. Italian innkeeper
10. Add up (to)
11. Rogers and Clark
12. "Body Count" rapper
13. PlayStation maker
21. El ___
22. Biblically yours
24. Couples
25. Enough
26. Lubricate again
27. "Well, ___!"
28. Pre-euro German money
29. With full force
30. Accustom
31. Jottings
33. Annoyers
36. Armored vehicles
37. Finalize
39. Old Germans
40. "J'accuse" author
42. 1964 Hitchcock thriller
43. Liverpool's river
45. Co-conspirator of Brutus
46. Sandler of "Big Daddy"
47. Doozie
48. Ltr. holders
49. Some crossword clues
50. Gershwin's "___ Plenty o' Nuttin'"
51. Wax
52. Cheesy sandwich
54. Architect I. M. ___

Solution on page 335

Mildly Tricky 96

ACROSS

1. Milo of "The Verdict"
6. Rights org.
10. Some TVs
14. Phylum subdivision
15. Conductance units
16. Kotter of "Welcome Back, Kotter"
17. Port-au-Prince is its capital
18. V
19. Loyal
20. Flattened at the poles
22. Beatty and Rorem
24. 23rd Greek letter
25. Cookie containers
27. Quadrennial candidate Harold
29. Guiding light
33. Suffix with fact
34. Any symphony
35. Alimany receivers
37. "Cheers" waitress
41. Bird's beak
42. Boxing ring boundaries
44. Cartoonist Browne
45. Actress Garbo
48. "Uh-uh"
49. Sit in the sun
50. ___ Na Na
52. Ragged
54. Hindu retreats
58. P.O. items
59. Reddish-brown horse
60. Doofus
62. Have more troops than
66. Anatomical passage
68. Land of Esau's descendants
70. Photog's request
71. Baseball's Sandberg
72. Violinists' needs
73. Afternoon: Sp.
74. Sideless cart
75. "You can say that again!"
76. High-hat

DOWN

1. Eight, in Spain
2. Bacon buy
3. Salute
4. Subjects of wills
5. If nothing changes
6. Brunswick competitor
7. Goatee site
8. Sweethearts
9. Comfortable with
10. Mil. unit
11. Quibbles
12. Bad treatment
13. Greet and seat
21. "Come in!"
23. Uttered
26. The "S" in WASP
28. Star Wars, initially
29. Ping-___
30. 0 on a phone: Abbr.
31. Garage job
32. Move, as a plant
36. Floral leaf
38. Hebrew month
39. "Just do it" sloganeer
40. Barely made, with "out"
43. Bench-clearing incident
46. Dungeons & Dragons game co.
47. "Moby Dick" captain
49. Ring holder
51. One-celled protozoan
53. Has faith in
54. Eat like ___
55. Nymph chaser
56. "Laughing" scavenger
57. Sin city
61. 1992–93 heavyweight champ
63. Dali contemporary
64. A Ray
65. Hair removal brand
67. Juan Carlos, e.g.
69. AOL alternative

Solution on page 335

Mildly Tricky 97

ACROSS
1. Oodles
6. Jack of "Barney Miller"
9. Olympic gymnast Kerri
14. Bicycle part
15. London's ___ Gardens
16. In shape
17. Prince Valiant's wife
18. "Ich bin ___ Berliner"
19. Some tests
20. "Blue" or "White" river
21. Soccer legend
22. Got up
23. Chilling
25. Sandra of "Gidget"
27. Shuteye
30. Italian cheese
35. Select, with "for"
38. Ingratiate
40. High-five sound
41. Buenos ___
43. Subj. for immigrants
44. Knot again
45. Hwys.
46. Beethoven's Third
48. Ill. neighbor
49. Got fresh with
51. Laurel and Musial
53. B&O stop
55. Checks
58. Palm Pilots, e.g., for short
61. Emit coherent light
64. Back muscles, for short
66. Anne of comedy
67. Rapper Dr. ___
68. Poet's concern
69. Impressive display
70. Alias
71. Calendario opener
72. Appears
73. Kazakhstan, once: Abbr.
74. Mends

DOWN
1. Bridge
2. "The Color Purple" role
3. "The Story of ___ H"
4. Library gadgets
5. Hearst kidnap gp.
6. ___-Ball (arcade game)
7. Trompe l'___
8. Had
9. Mall units
10. Bullfight bull
11. Genetic molecules
12. Congo river
13. Mdse.
21. Hammer's end
24. Martinique et Guadeloupe
26. Attention
28. Fulda feeder
29. Mexican coins
31. Honshu bay
32. Height: prefix
33. Put on
34. Newspaper page
35. Boat propellers
36. Falafel bread
37. "___ bien!"
39. Came down
42. Double curve
44. Declaim
46. Buffalo's summer hrs.
47. Big beer buy
50. Lamb's output
52. One-named Tejano singer
54. Actors Robert and Alan
56. Alma ___
57. Back of a boat
58. French father
59. Be bold
60. Composer Khachaturian
62. Synagogue chests
63. Burn
65. B'way hit signs
66. Bell and Barker
68. Club ___

Solution on page 336

Mildly Tricky 98

ACROSS

1. "I'm ___ here!"
5. Physics units
9. Shouts of triumph
14. Alum
15. "On the Waterfront" director Kazan
16. Journalist ___ Rogers St. Johns
17. Actress Virna
18. "Neato!"
19. Preserves, as pork
20. Grovel
22. Be in session
24. Fair-hiring abbr.
25. Bundle up
26. Atlas section
28. Senate spots
31. Tell
35. Poker prize
38. Impassive
40. Of the kidneys
41. High-performance Camaro
43. Nine: Prefix
45. Wedding reception centerpiece
46. "Ditto"
48. Aroma
50. Chest muscle, for short
51. Syrian city
53. Dimethyl sulfate, e.g.
55. Sony competitor
57. Arousing
61. Beefeater product
64. Communication for the deaf: Abbr.
65. Southwestern saloon
66. Bothered
68. The "E" in Q.E.D.
70. Rudiments
71. "Casablanca" actor Peter
72. Nerve network
73. Suckling spot
74. Belt holders
75. Frankfurt's river
76. Celtic language

DOWN

1. Looks at lustfully
2. Dickens's ___ Heep
3. Discrimination
4. Nike rival
5. Make over
6. "Thanks ___!"
7. God, in Roma
8. Chalupa topping
9. More palatable
10. Critic ___ Louise Huxtable
11. Proofreader's notation
12. Choir member
13. Enclosure with a MS.
21. Currier and ___
23. Jerusalem's land: Abbr.
27. A Baldwin
29. Heaps
30. Because
32. Take ___ (doze)
33. Accept uncomplainingly
34. Basic util.
35. Tucson's county
36. Baseball's Hershiser
37. Carry
39. Average grades
42. Nightclub of song
44. Aardvark
47. Tranquilizers
49. Beach bird
52. Cries of pain
54. Spin
56. Olds model
58. Rome's river
59. Ancient Peruvians
60. Hindu social division
61. Chutzpah
62. Langston Hughes poem
63. Roman "fiddler"
65. Actress Blanchett
67. Dadaism founder
69. Bloodshot

Solution on page 336

Mildly Tricky 99

ACROSS

1. Make ___ of (botch)
6. Budding entrepreneurs, for short
10. Captures
14. Tithe portion
15. Dreadful
16. Longfellow bell town
17. Euripides drama
18. Volunteer's words
19. Guide
20. High schoolers
22. Cut off
24. Sleep phenomena
26. ___ Zeppelin
27. ___ culpa
28. Coop group
31. Here, in Le Havre
33. "What's the ___?"
35. Gardner of "On the Beach"
36. Double's doing
38. Nobel-winning poet Nelly
42. Ike's wife
44. Debussy's "La ___"
45. Religious scroll
46. Lend ___ (listen)
47. Tiffs
49. G.I. entertainers
50. "Platoon" setting
52. South-of-the-border uncle
53. Cabinet div.
54. "I" problem
57. Bit of butter
59. Use a keyboard
61. Unlikely protagonist
63. Brazilian dance
66. Spoil, with "on"
67. Trudge
70. Loved ones
72. Brouhahas
73. Mother of Apollo
74. "Love Is a Hurtin' Thing" singer
75. Dosage amts.
76. Carve in stone
77. Furnish with a fund

DOWN

1. $$$ dispenser
2. Assemble
3. "Momo" author Michael
4. Has the wheel
5. Classic Alan Ladd western
6. Start of the 16th century
7. Ballpoint brand
8. Thin as ___
9. Felt
10. Formal dance
11. First-stringers
12. Fireplace frame
13. Cassette half
21. Struck, old-style
23. Keats and others
25. Stagnates, as a pond
28. Syrian city
29. Author Hunter
30. Tom, Dick, or Harry
32. All thumbs
34. ___ Schwarz
36. Colorful wrap
37. Blue eyes or baldness, e.g.
39. Motley ___
40. Door fastener
41. Worn out
43. Holm of "The Fellowship of the Ring"
48. 1992 Robin Williams movie
51. Christie's Miss
53. Abase
54. Conclude by
55. Merchandise
56. Victorious
58. For rent
60. Man with a mission
62. Dame Myra
64. Madam
65. Folk singer Guthrie
68. Like some stocks, for short
69. Homer Simpson outburst
71. Opposite NNE

Solution on page 336

Mildly Tricky 100

ACROSS
1. Box office take
5. ___ acid
10. "Whew!"
13. Aviation pioneer Sikorsky
14. Harness racer
15. 1/500 of the Indianapolis 500
16. Aaron or Raymond
17. "___ at the office"
18. "___ be a cold day . . ."
19. Pooh's pal
21. Dines
23. Scout's mission
25. Lock
26. Irascibility
28. Dict. offering
29. Courted
30. Sponsorship
32. ___ Strauss & Co.
36. Old World herb
37. ___ double take
38. Eatery
39. "The ___ the limit!"
40. Parade spoiler
41. Following
42. "Listen up!"
43. Frisco gridders
45. Old hat
48. Big tops
49. It's another day
51. Mounts
55. "Lemme ___!"
56. Public storehouse
58. 1978 Village People hit
59. Eclectic magazine
60. Actress Braga of "Kiss of the Spider Woman"
61. French novelist Pierre
62. The "S" of CBS: Abbr.
63. "Popeye" creator
64. Even, to Yves

DOWN
1. Barbed remark
2. Chills
3. Canadian Conservative
4. Perfect
5. Each
6. 'Zine
7. Corporate raider Carl
8. St. Petersburg's river
9. Son of Agamemnon
10. Snacks
11. Earthenware pots
12. Cheerleader's bit
15. Charades, essentially
20. Like an oboe's sound
22. Comics bark
24. Sometime
26. Saturate
27. Small horse
28. Sen. Feinstein
29. Lbs. and ozs.
31. "There but for the grace of God ___"
32. Modus vivendi
33. ___'acte
34. Victory signs
35. Sale tag abbr.
38. "Divine Comedy" writer
40. Set right
42. Old what's-___-name
44. Ready to roll
45. Eccentric
46. Words of agreement
47. Volume
48. Nashville sound
49. Greek crosses
50. Ally of the Missouri
52. Pollution problem
53. Eight: Prefix
54. Do perfectly
57. Zadora of "Butterfly"

Solution on page 336

Section 2: Challenging Puzzles

Challenging 1

ACROSS
1. Also-ran's words
6. "Blondie" boy
10. "The Dock of the Bay" singer Redding
14. Made public
15. Stretched out
16. Big tippler
17. "If ___ Would Leave You"
18. Cosecant's reciprocal
19. Wall St. deals
20. Ristorante desserts
22. Enlarge, as a hole
24. Faline's mother, in "Bambi"
25. Apple or pear
27. Rained hard?
29. Free
33. Capt.'s inferiors
34. Addition column
35. Burn a bit
37. Alarm
41. Half brother of Tom Sawyer
42. Comedy intro?
44. Early
45. Geyser output
48. Former Ford models
49. Greenish blue
50. ___ Master's Voice
52. One way to argue
54. Scholars
58. Bygone theaters
59. Motor suffix, commercially
60. "Don Juan DeMarco" actor
62. They're cast
66. Upscale
68. Boater's worry
70. 1978 co-Nobelist
71. Sandwich filler
72. "Dr. Zhivago" heroine
73. Turner autobiography
74. Anita of jazz
75. Beginning drawing class
76. Destitute

DOWN
1. "___ your pardon!"
2. Bathe
3. City founded by Ivan IV
4. Sonora shawls
5. Money manager?
6. 1997 U.S. Open winner
7. Animal shelter
8. They may be shafted
9. Low tie
10. Barn denizen
11. High land
12. ___ fell swoop
13. "Alas"
21. Apple products
23. "Miracle" team of 1969
26. Lucy's friend
28. PC "oops" key
29. Deprivation
30. Monogram ltr.
31. "Venerable" saint
32. Terra firma
36. Bill add-on
38. Dumbfounded
39. "Get ___!"
40. Hard to hold
43. 1970 World's Fair site
46. "Bingo!"
47. Give a darn
49. Having a will
51. Mrs. Kowalski
53. Alarm
54. ___ voce (quietly)
55. One way to pray
56. Woman of letters?
57. Bit of broccoli
61. It's cast
63. Comics canine
64. Cape Town cash
65. Collar insert
67. "Whoopee!"
69. Trombonist Winding

Solution on page 337

Challenging 2

ACROSS

1. Skating event
6. ___ the finish
10. 1990s Indian P.M.
13. Cruel sorts
14. Local theater, slangily
15. Party mtg.
16. Actress Patricia et al.
17. Jordanian queen
18. Autobahn auto
19. Crossword worker?
20. Ambition
21. Strapped
23. Even though
26. Hostelries
27. Round lot's 100
30. Classroom drudgery
32. "Deed I Do" singer
33. Go-getter
35. ___-Pei (wrinkly dog)
39. Curved Alaskan knife
40. Save for a rainy day
43. "Die Meistersinger" heroine
44. Uses a shuttle
46. Peat sources
47. Divination deck
49. Boris Godunov, for one
51. Baseball's Hank and Tommie
52. Baccarat alternative
54. Thinly spread
57. Breakfast fare
59. "Aladdin" prince
60. Auto pioneer
64. Had debts
65. Dickens clerk
67. Catch some Z's
68. "___ of the Thousand Days" (1969 film)

69. Cole Porter's "Well, Did You ___?"
70. Boxer Ali
71. D-Day vessel
72. Suvari of "American Beauty"
73. Allude

DOWN

1. Cornmeal bread
2. A long, long time
3. 1979 revolution site
4. Brush up on
5. "Greetings" org.
6. Bellybutton type
7. A Judd
8. Blood letters
9. Garr of "Mr. Mom"
10. Where Joan of Arc died
11. Much of Chile
12. "Ars amatoria" poet
15. Film festival site
20. Belly muscles
22. Coll. hoops competition
24. Bottom of the barrel
25. Corners
27. Boarded up
28. Granada greeting
29. Stuck, after "in"
31. Sch. in Tulsa
33. Opportunities, so to speak
34. Assn.
36. Deli order
37. Bard's river
38. "Darn it!"
41. TV schedule abbr.
42. Fund-raising grps.
45. Bit of progress

48. Biological rings
50. "My boy"
51. "Exodus" hero ___ Ben Canaan
52. Babes in the woods
53. "___ you glad you did?"
55. Song of joy
56. Beginning
57. Young Arab
58. "Beg pardon . . ."
61. Viking Ericson
62. Edit out
63. Bandy words
66. "The Three Faces of ___"
67. Camera type, briefly

Solution on page 337

Challenging 3

ACROSS
1. Actress Best
5. Ram
9. Common URL ender
12. "___, right!"
13. Against a thing, legally
15. "Curses!"
16. "___ homo"
17. Freak out
18. Former poet laureate Dove
19. Diplomat Deane
21. Cartoon collectible
22. Clickable symbol
23. Conceal, in a way
26. Sultry Sommer
28. ___ au vin
31. Gangsters
33. Summing up
37. Eggs, biologically
38. Hot issue?
39. Postwar prime minister
40. "Don't look at me!"
42. Jeter of the Yankees
44. Leo, for one
45. Grammy winner Morissette
47. Like a 911 call: Abbr.
49. Good, in the 'hood
50. "WarGames" org.
51. Lilted syllables
52. "Well, ___ be!"
53. First-grader's attention-getter
55. Pinup's legs
57. Bank deal: Abbr.
60. Planet, poetically
62. Dance in Rio
66. "___ not to reason why": Tennyson
67. Examine, slangily, with "out"

70. Showy trinket
71. CEOs' degrees
72. Gave a darn?
73. Burns title starter
74. "Casablanca" pianist
75. Salacious
76. Pen points

DOWN
1. Goats make them
2. Metric prefix
3. Salt, symbolically
4. Lots
5. 1988 Hanks movie
6. 108-card game
7. ___ II razor
8. Plain homes
9. Smart
10. "___ victory!"
11. "Oh, my aching head!," e.g.
14. Cartoonist Lazarus
15. Positions
20. Mordant Mort
24. Oodles
25. "Hop to it!"
27. Emergency ___
28. First name in late-night TV
29. Convex molding
30. Gulf state
32. Risk taker
34. Out, of sorts
35. Corporate department
36. U.S. Open champ, 1985–87
39. Cub Scout pack leader
41. Topsy-turvy
43. Online periodical, for short

46. Chemical suffix
48. Namath's last team
51. Old Toyota
54. Trunk growth
56. "Cosmos" creator Carl
57. Soccer ___
58. Big brass
59. Ending with cable or candy
61. Boxer Riddick
63. Kahului's island
64. Gardener's purchase
65. Annexes
68. Chapel fixture
69. Announcer Hall

Solution on page 337

Challenging 4

ACROSS

1. Off base, in a way
5. Middle: prefix
9. Clothes line
12. Hindu music
13. Eye: prefix
15. Golf's Ballesteros
16. Fingerboard feature
17. Charger
18. Salem's st.
19. Address
21. Playwright Akins
22. "I forgot the words" syllables
23. Rejections
25. Sing the praises of
27. Actress Van Devere
30. "___ your imagination!"
32. Bedevil
36. Churchill's "so few": Abbr.
37. Eye rakishly
39. Xerxes ruled it
40. Lone Star State sch.
42. 16 drams
44. Screen
45. Rugged range
47. Jemima, for one
49. Balance provider, for short
50. Like a shoe
51. Sot's symptoms, for short
52. Medieval merchants' guild
54. Flimsy, as an excuse
56. Cowboy singer Wooley
58. "Chiquitita" quartet
61. Big lug
63. Boot part
67. Dugout, for one
68. Arson, e.g.
70. Baseball's Blue Moon
71. Brain section
72. "Norwegian Wood" instrument
73. Brioche
74. Peruvian-born Sumac
75. Hockey great Phil, familiarly
76. Act like an ass?

DOWN

1. Pound sounds
2. "Star Trek" speed
3. Arch type
4. Gets darker
5. Israeli statesman Dayan
6. Outer: prefix
7. Egyptian port
8. World Cup chant
9. Daughter of Cronus
10. First name in daredeviltry
11. Prefix with phone
14. Ancient Greek concert halls
15. Joins, in a way
20. Silver salmon
24. "Star Trek" helmsman
26. Sporty truck, for short
27. Tie up
28. Pi, e.g.
29. Sondheim's "___ Pretty"
31. French assembly
33. From the East
34. Examines carefully
35. Message on a Wonderland cake
38. ___ few rounds
39. Flair, e.g.
41. Church dignitary
43. Swear
46. Cereal box abbr.
48. At that time
51. Hon
53. Take in
55. Soft shoes
57. Sacred: Prefix
58. Well
59. Prosperous time
60. Ali ___
62. Partner of starts
64. ___-Eaters
65. "Damn Yankees" role
66. "Little" girl in "David Copperfield"
69. Glove compartment item

Solution on page 337

Challenging 5

ACROSS

1. Vintner's prefix
4. Rhein port
8. Easy ___
13. Tire
15. Outback critters
16. Biblical prophet
17. See red
18. Country venue, for short
19. Doing battle
20. Like paradise
22. Compass heading
24. Call to Fido
25. Tree exudation
26. Turned into
28. Far from certain
30. Drive-in worker
34. Dr. Frankenstein's workplace
37. Aquatic mammal
40. Ache
41. Black gold
42. France's Oscar
44. Mr. ___ (old whodunit board game)
45. Sea
48. Enjoy
50. E. Lansing school
51. Saw
53. Looks over
55. Plots
58. Dallas suburb
62. Bio
65. Hootchy-___
66. They're rarely hits
67. Vast, in verse
69. Average
71. Astronomical sighting
72. Take ___ (travel)
73. Open carriage
74. Cyclist LeMond
75. Boxer's bane
76. Listeners
77. "___ pales in Heaven the morning star": Lowell

DOWN

1. Put forward
2. Duck
3. Celebrities
4. McDonald's founder
5. "Alley ___!"
6. Actor Greene
7. Justin Timberlake's band
8. "But of course!"
9. Defiant remark
10. Life ___ know it
11. Symbol on California's flag
12. Kind of package
14. Guardian spirits
21. Stats, e.g.
23. GI Jane
26. Storage units
27. Kentucky Derby time
29. Antitrust org.
31. Do damage to
32. Assayers' stuff
33. French tire
34. Lung section
35. Superciliousness
36. Radar signal
38. Tikkanen of hockey
39. All-night parties
43. Cowboy Rogers
46. Neighbor of Cameroon
47. "___ out!"
49. Lifting units
52. Former U.S. terr.
54. Armrest?
56. Oater group
57. Fuss
59. Be mad about
60. Not even once
61. ___ orange
62. Page (through)
63. Like LAX
64. Driver's warning
66. Word before and after "will be"
68. Army cops
70. Mediterranean isl.

Solution on page 337

Challenging 6

ACROSS

1. Kind of market
5. Bingo relative
9. "The Wizard of Oz" studio
12. Carry on
13. Toothbrush handle?
15. Spelling of "Beverly Hills 90210"
16. Betwixt and between
17. Fertilizer ingredient
18. "___ Brockovich"
19. It's a stunner
21. "7 Faces of Dr. ___"
22. "The King ___"
23. "Note to ___ . . ."
26. Cough syrup amts.
28. Add-ons: abbr.
31. Pod items, old-style
33. ___-Bismol
37. Addis Ababa's land: Abbr.
38. Another, in Andalusia
39. Backward
40. "Can't argue with that"
42. Scarlett O'Hara, e.g.
44. Fast-moving card game
45. Take turns
47. Friend of Masterson
49. Actress Merkel
50. "Lulu," e.g.
51. "Ah, Wilderness!" mother
52. Domino spot
53. Roll
55. Make well
57. Barracks site
60. Spotted, to Tweety
62. Native Israeli
66. Inning sextet
67. Chosen ones
70. "No ___!"
71. Platte River people
72. Like some keys
73. Edible pocket
74. Haul
75. Mason, e.g.: Abbr.
76. Sunnis, e.g.

DOWN

1. Greek group, for short
2. Priest of the East
3. Auspices
4. Dangerous mosquito
5. ___-Tiki
6. Verdi's "___ tu"
7. One of the major leagues: Abbr.
8. Pharmaceutical ointment
9. Eve's opposite
10. Electrical network
11. Certain iPod
14. Abbr. in a closely held business
15. Service groups
20. Auction vehicle, often
24. Leave alone
25. Hack's customer
27. Letter abbr.
28. Prefix with dollars
29. Barber's need
30. "On the Beach" author
32. They're underfoot
34. Animate
35. Lopez of pop
36. Available
39. Cliffside dwelling
41. Like harp seals
43. Pirate's punishment
46. ___ chi
48. Exemplars of twinship
51. List shortener
54. Champagne glass part
56. Reindeer herders
57. Heave-ho
58. Golf, for one
59. Tuck away
61. Hit the road
63. Cheese with a rind
64. Campus mil. org.
65. Like ___ out of hell
68. Barracks bed
69. "Don't give up!"

Solution on page 337

Challenging 7

ACROSS

1. Behave
4. Super's set
8. Door pivot
13. Large cask
14. Sire
15. Brunch selection
16. Fight ender, for short
17. ___-Saxon
18. "Death of a Salesman" salesman
19. Paper money
21. Tyler of "The Lord of the Rings"
23. Like a yenta
24. Bar order
27. Bud
29. Thrash
31. Accelerated
35. P.D. alerts
38. Highway safety org.
40. Big mess
41. "___ is me!"
42. Closet item
44. Diddley and Derek
45. Dalai Lama's city
48. Energetic
49. Big cheese
50. Floodgate
52. Air passenger's request
54. Rolaids rival
56. "Hogan's Heroes" setting
59. Comics possum
62. Superquiet, musically
64. Lost color
66. Desktop items
68. Dumas adventurer
71. Moviedom's Myrna
72. Online marketing
73. Urbane
74. Harem chamber
75. Not all there
76. Certain skirt
77. Small cyst

DOWN

1. Abbr. on an envelope
2. "My Fair Lady" director
3. U.S. security
4. Barbie's ex-beau
5. Cackleberry
6. Cheer
7. Zeno, notably
8. Strong acid, chemically
9. Tireless ones
10. "Little" comics fellow
11. Transcript figs.
12. Chooser's opening
14. "Sweet" herb
20. Two of fifty?
22. Letters on tapes
25. Follower of Mary
26. Fabricators
28. FedEx alternative
30. Parkinson's treatment
32. Actress Maryam
33. Eerie sightings, briefly
34. Kisser
35. Leather stickers
36. Sci-fi writer Frederik
37. Bridges of Hollywood
39. Author Lessing
43. Computer adventure game
46. "Go fly a kite!"
47. Prefix with pressure
49. Gymnastics coach Karolyi
51. Akihito, e.g.: Abbr.
53. Backslide
55. Tic
57. Let
58. Crystal-lined rock
59. Dappled
60. Twice tetra-
61. Satyr, in part
63. Spitting sound
65. Cannon of film
67. Arch
69. Conned
70. Prefix meaning "egg"

Solution on page 338

Challenging 8

ACROSS

1. More competent
6. Handel oratorio
10. Resort town near Santa Barbara
14. Painter Uccello
15. "In that case . . ."
16. ___ erectus
17. Blow
18. Alone
19. It's outstanding
20. Takes away
22. Paesano's land
24. "A Hard Road to Glory" author
25. 1930s heavyweight champ Max
26. "Dragnet" org.
29. "___ I'm told"
31. Adams of Yosemite
35. Parcels out
37. One of the Cartwrights
39. Marseille Mrs.
40. She played Hannah in "Hannah and Her Sisters"
41. Attendants
43. ___-Locka, Florida
44. N.C. State is in it
45. Knowing, as a secret
46. Official decrees
48. Volleyballer/model Gabrielle
50. Tim of "Sister, Sister"
52. Actress Ione
53. ___ brat
55. Art follower
57. Last car?
60. Unwavering
64. Capstone
65. Iris's place
67. Eye surgery procedure
68. Popular fast-food chain, informally
69. Yielding
70. "Who's there?" reply
71. Pandora's release
72. Massachusetts motto starter
73. First known asteroid

DOWN

1. Did a sendup of
2. Au naturel
3. Lummox
4. Where Goyas hang
5. Rosters
6. Many a bridesmaid
7. Siesta times: abbr.
8. "La Femme Nikita" network
9. Religious maxims
10. "Shoot!"
11. Book after Hosea
12. Prefix with dexterity
13. Itty bit
21. Picked
23. Razzed
25. Timely benefit
26. Texas university
27. Carroll girl
28. Come in second
30. Stand out
32. Painter's protector
33. Recycled item
34. Buy alternative
36. Judges and juries
38. Jacket materials
42. Disraeli, for one
47. Quarantine
49. Stroke
51. Conceive
54. Verdun's river
56. Infant's woe
57. Last name in spydom
58. Biol. branch
59. Form of nitrite
60. Makes calls
61. "Back in the ___" (Beatles song)
62. Ump's call
63. Barely gets, with "out"
66. Name part meaning "from"

Solution on page 338

Challenging 9

ACROSS

1. Believers
5. First-floor apartment
9. Rumsfeld's predecessor
14. Salon service
15. Common mixer
16. Clued in
17. Samoan port
18. Egyptian solar deity
19. Poem
20. Pursues
22. 1978 Triple Crown winner
24. Military assaults
26. Air safety org.
27. Eyelid inflammations
29. Turning point
34. Abandon
37. Chipper
39. Vincent Lopez theme song
40. "Dance On Little Girl" singer
41. Adjutants
42. "Jeopardy!" ans.
43. One of the major leagues: Abbr.
44. Half a leaf
45. Pervasive qualities
46. Initiations
48. Duck
50. TV adjustment: Abbr.
52. It's not pretty
56. Introduces gradually
61. Snare
62. Athena's shield
63. Copier company
65. Neil Diamond's "___ Said"
66. Oscar winner for "The Cider House Rules"
67. Lay eyes on
68. Pertaining to the ear
69. Birds at sea
70. Flood guard
71. 1987 Costner role

DOWN

1. "No bid"
2. Nasal partitions
3. Court activity
4. Modest
5. Abbey Theatre playwright
6. "___ so fast!"
7. Zeno's home
8. Alberta park
9. Expensive spread
10. One in the red
11. Damage
12. European language
13. Call for
21. Kin's partner
23. Friday's request
25. Old photo
28. Bulrush, e.g.
30. Unsettled
31. Become disenchanted
32. Intestinal parts
33. Cheek
34. Linda of soaps
35. ___ uproar
36. Times Square sign
38. "Still Me" autobiographer Christopher
41. Lhasa ___ (small dogs)
45. Gulf capital
47. Requirements for some degrees
49. Deck assent
51. Frost-covered
53. Hold the floor
54. "Groundhog Day" director
55. Heroic tales
56. Dueler's distance
57. Get from the grapevine
58. Opposed, in Dogpatch
59. Math ratio
60. Not yet final, in law
64. Toll rd.

Solution on page 338

Challenging 10

ACROSS

1. Swimmer's routine
5. "Road" destination
9. "All My Children" role
14. Caesar's "vidi"
15. An OK city
16. Attach, as a patch
17. Julia's ex
18. Actress Talbot
19. "Fun, Fun, Fun" car
20. Air
22. Bantu language
23. Buster's pet
24. Chesterfield or ulster
25. ___ Zee Bridge
28. Nobelist, e.g.
32. Shakespearean sprite
33. Hotsy-___
34. Sportscaster Scully
35. 1492 vessel
36. River in Hades
37. 1/100 of a euro
38. Sun ___-sen
39. Goes the distance
40. Intrude, with "in"
41. Dining option
43. Egg roll time
44. Reed and Rawls
45. City areas, informally
46. Paternal relative
49. Sort of
53. Hub-to-rim lines
54. Parentheses, essentially
55. Ratted
56. "The Nutcracker" girl
57. Mouselike animal
58. H.S. math
59. Like some buckets
60. Breezed through
61. Tube trophy

DOWN

1. Buoyant tune
2. "___ sow, so shall . . ."
3. Grow tiresome
4. Flowering climber
5. Harmless
6. Absinthe flavor
7. Dietary, in ads
8. Author Tarbell
9. River's end
10. Buyer's incentive
11. Victor's shout
12. Part of a parachute
13. "Shave ___ haircut"
21. Clinic container
22. Stir
24. Many churchgoers: Abbr.
25. Singer Tucker
26. Windows typeface
27. One of Columbus's three
28. Soprano Lehmann
29. Deflect
30. Bit of color
31. "The door's open!"
33. Checks out
36. Lash of oaters
37. Tape holder
39. Kip spender
40. Barbara, to friends
42. Actress Danes
43. Cleared
45. Cry of surrender
46. Bowed, in music
47. Blowout
48. Fargo's st.
49. ___-Z: Camaro model
50. "Cheers" barfly
51. Common cowboy nickname
52. Avant-garde
54. Clark's "Mogambo" costar

Solution on page 338

Challenging 11

ACROSS

1. Macho type
6. Patrick's "Ghost" costar
10. "___ next?"
14. Fragrant resin
15. "___ Kampf"
16. Org. for boomers, now
17. Spartan serf
18. Joe Millionaire picked her
19. "The Immoralist" author
20. Danger signal
22. One on a board
24. Match
26. Fifth-century warrior
27. Like some vbs.
28. Film rating org.
31. Levy
33. Uncle, in Uruguay
35. Vintner's prefix
36. In accordance with
38. Light up
42. Had in mind
44. Ariz.-to-Kan. dir.
45. Not at full power
46. Horrify
47. Athenian lawgiver who introduced trial by jury
49. Bass, for one
50. Tail motion
52. Give a thumbs-down to
53. From a great distance
54. Gang
57. Measly amount
59. Kind of phone
61. Electrical gizmo
63. "Of course"
66. Italian painter Guido
67. Clothing
70. Swift brute
72. Sweet-talk
73. Bar in the kitchen
74. Fabricators
75. Just
76. Anthem opener
77. Rich tapestry

DOWN

1. Snickering syllable
2. Zeno of ___
3. Cartoonist Lazarus
4. Microscopic critter
5. Explosion maker
6. Noncombat area, for short
7. Fair-hiring letters
8. Hilarity
9. Bound by routine
10. Jokers
11. Half of Hispaniola
12. "The usual," maybe
13. Hitler's architect
21. Sounds of disapproval
23. Accord
25. Nixon's undoing
28. NYC cultural center
29. Hatchery sound
30. Take ___ (snooze)
32. Tube gas
34. Every, on an Rx
36. After much delay
37. Antique item
39. Minnesota's St. ___ College
40. Stimulating nut
41. Basin partner
43. Slangy refusal
48. Big bovines
51. Kind of eyes
53. Star in Aquila
54. ___ Island, Fla.
55. Ancient Greek theater
56. Far from fresh
58. Europe/Asia divider
60. Clapton classic
62. Sprite
64. Singe
65. Lively dance
68. "In Dreams" actor
69. Lad
71. CIA's forerunner

Solution on page 338

Challenging 12

ACROSS
1. Mail org.
5. Chad neighbor
10. Date with a dr.
14. Disregard
15. Senator who wrote "Dreams From My Father"
16. Be too rich
17. Hockey feint
18. Enter, as data
19. Time of day
20. Operatives
22. Part-time player
24. Pungent green
27. Greyhound stop: Abbr.
28. Up ___ (cornered)
31. "The Hustler" prop
33. Food thickeners
37. Ltd., in Paris
38. Is of use
41. Dizzy's jazz
42. Brain test, for short
43. Golden, in France
44. Abet
46. "___ Town"
47. George Sand's "Elle et ___"
48. "On Language" columnist
50. "Agnus ___"
51. Disassembled
54. "Son of," in names
55. In other words
57. It may have a window: Abbr.
59. Hardly Mensa material
61. "Billy Budd" director
65. Slanted
69. Jar
70. Composes
73. Church tribunal
74. Avian mimic
75. Legend maker
76. Fall preceder, perhaps
77. X and Y, on a graph
78. "Alice" star
79. Blow off steam?

DOWN
1. Food stamp agcy.
2. Keel extension
3. Expressway
4. British architect Sir Basil
5. Hubbub
6. Arab name part
7. Breach
8. Avian sources of red meat
9. Hotel posting
10. Sore
11. Drop heavily
12. Decant
13. Rookie
21. Radial pattern
23. 1959 Kingston Trio hit
25. Sacred beetle of ancient Egypt
26. ___ generis (unique)
28. Amtrak speedster
29. Highway headache
30. Aqua ___ (gold dissolver)
32. "Seinfeld" gal
34. Digs
35. Rakes
36. Sail extender
39. Marilyn ___ Savant
40. "Dear" one
45. Thomas Jefferson, religiously
49. G-man
52. Spanish royalty
53. Old cable TV inits.
56. Scarcity
58. Not shy
60. Month after Adar
61. West Point inits.
62. Charon's waterway
63. Whistler's whistle
64. Explorer Cabeza de ___
66. Actress Petty
67. Reply to "That so?"
68. Limits
71. Murray Schisgal play
72. Hosp. picture

Solution on page 338

Challenging 13

ACROSS
1. "Paradise Lost" figure
6. Did laps, say
10. Craft's men
14. "Home ___"
15. Use a surgical beam
16. "Star Wars" dancing girl
17. "Crazy" singer Patsy
18. Deuce follower
19. "A Prayer for ___ Meany"
20. "Krazy ___"
21. Rackets
23. Leblanc's Lupin
25. Drunk
26. "Nova" subj.
27. "Awesome!"
28. Common sense
32. Flew
33. Barbecue spot
34. G.I.'s mail drop
35. Big gulps
40. "A likely story!"
41. Convened
42. Award bestowed by "The Village Voice"
43. Angle symbol
45. Alts.
46. Crack
47. Scottish refusals
49. Sow anew
50. Franken and Gore
53. Coupon amt.
54. Shindigs
55. Roofer, at times
57. Bring (out)
58. Escort's offering
61. 11,000-foot Italian peak
62. Golfer Aoki
64. "Terminal Bliss" actress Chandler
66. Whole lot
67. Skiing mecca
68. Of pitch
69. None of that?
70. Bonny one
71. Show off

DOWN
1. Fire
2. ___ breve (music marking)
3. "Hop ___!"
4. "sex, lies, & videotape" heroine
5. Must
6. Handwriting feature
7. Bankrolls
8. "___ recall . . ."
9. Growl at
10. Cote calls
11. Crew member
12. "Mefistofele" soprano
13. Tapered off
22. Cyclades island
24. Clears (of)
26. Ocelot features
28. Brief quarrel
29. Prepare potatoes
30. Play to ___
31. Break in relations
32. Fop's footwear
34. "Angela's ___"
36. Romances
37. Suffix with corrupt
38. "Out with it!"
39. Induce rain from
44. Ending to avoid?
46. Sonnet endings
48. Of a heart part
49. "Winnie-the-Pooh" baby
50. "___ of robins . . .": Kilmer
51. Glom (onto)
52. 1956 invasion site
54. Waste matter
56. Youngsters
57. Last call?
58. "___ extra cost!"
59. Area away from the battle
60. Go soft
63. Hearst kidnap grp.
65. Bribe

Solution on page 339

Challenging 14

ACROSS

1. Can't stand
5. A heap
10. Center of a ball?
13. Far from ruddy
14. Hooded snake
15. Burt's ex
16. ___-Ball
17. Kind of treatment
18. "Are you some kind of ___?"
19. Grease, of sorts
21. Brandy cocktails
23. John and Paul
25. "Long time ___!"
26. First game
28. Bill
29. Weight lifter
30. Makes accessible, old-style
32. Barbershop sound
36. Silas Marner, e.g.
37. Org. founded in 1890
38. Veep after Hubert
39. Borodin's "Prince ___"
40. Hems, say
41. Island west of Maui
42. They, in Tours
43. Habituates
45. Model wood
48. "___ Jacques"
49. Sweetie
51. Best suited
55. 1924 Darrow client
56. Bright
58. Not well
59. Raggedy dolls
60. Davis of "King"
61. Start another hitch
62. Came down with
63. Off
64. One-named supermodel

DOWN

1. Fastening device
2. "___ silly question . . ."
3. Those people
4. Revelation
5. Tough spot
6. Bill's partner
7. Chasm
8. "Curses!"
9. Steinbeck's birthplace
10. Charity, e.g.
11. Accustom: Var.
12. Morsels
15. Dawdles
20. Not the glad-handing sort
22. Head, slangily
24. Washes away
26. Not a dup.
27. ___ doble (Spanish dance)
28. Less verbose
29. Early 10th-century year
31. Hairy hand
32. Middle weight?
33. Diamond complement
34. Investment options, for short
35. Luau dish
38. Drink impolitely
40. Applies haphazardly
42. Country est. in 1948
44. Put in order
45. Actor Victor
46. Bond, for one
47. Bell ___
48. Sumptuous spread
49. Refinery refuse
50. The Pointer Sisters' "___ Excited"
52. K–6: abbr.
53. Squalid digs
54. Category
57. "Road" destination

Solution on page 339

Challenging 15

ACROSS

1. Terrible twos, e.g.
6. Battery type
9. Kate's TV roommate
14. Enthusiastic
15. Rental ad abbr.
16. "El Capitan" composer
17. Preferred course of action
18. Hosp. units
19. Destroyer detector
20. 90 degrees
21. Freelancer's enc.
22. Beehive State natives
23. Reject
25. Barnacle Bill, for one
27. Gets naked
30. Ribs
35. Attention getters
38. "Get lost!"
40. Bunny tail
41. "___ Gold"
43. "Scram!"
44. Flat replacement
45. Have in mind
46. Ring master?
48. Submit
49. Blood lines
51. Sleep sound
53. 1960s radical grp.
55. Better balanced
58. U.K. honors
61. Egyptian slitherers
64. No neatnik
66. River to the Rhone
67. Kid's cry
68. Move laterally
69. Elbows
70. ". . .___ quit!" (ultimatum)
71. Staff leaders
72. "Green ___"
73. Cause of inflation?
74. Toast opener

DOWN

1. ___ Le Pew
2. NFL pioneer George
3. Visibly shocked
4. Lampooned
5. Gay Nineties, e.g.
6. Medieval chest
7. Gremlins, Pacers, etc.
8. Black ink item
9. Give confidence to
10. Boodle
11. Crescent
12. "A miss ___ good . . ."
13. Dumbo's "wing"
21. Cut with a knife, old-style
24. Lee's men, for short
26. A.B.A. member
28. Titicaca, por ejemplo
29. Moves a muscle
31. Death on the Nile cause, perhaps
32. Picket line crosser
33. 100 cents
34. Hasenpfeffer, e.g.
35. Colorado River city
36. Promise, e.g.
37. Brand, in a way
39. Major Calif.-to-Fla. route
42. Tolkien's Treebeard, for one
44. Short-billed rail
46. "Hazel" cartoonist Key
47. "ER" doctor
50. Evaluate
52. Store on the farm
54. Margaret Mead topic
56. Church leader
57. John of Jamestown
58. Playwright Connelly
59. Rude person
60. "The Neverending Story" author
62. Calcutta coverup
63. Brace
65. 1940s first lady
66. Vichy, e.g.
68. Educ. institution

Solution on page 339

Challenging 16

ACROSS

1. Bodybuilder's pride
4. Apocalypse
8. Inner connection?
13. Anti-fur org.
15. View from Chamonix
16. ___ Lodge (motel chain)
17. Sunbeams
18. Klinger player
19. Wyoming's ___ Range
20. Without a break
22. Franklin's 1936 foe
24. Lickety-split
25. Emphatic turndown
26. Aussie lassie
28. Finn's transport
30. French
34. Priestly vestment
37. ___ Island, Fla.
40. Wooer of Olive
41. Bazooka, e.g.
42. Spanish hors d'oeuvres
44. Roast hosts, for short
45. Broncos great John
48. Rube
50. Frat letter
51. Country
53. Place for an iris
55. Stuck
58. 1964 title role for Tony Randall
62. B'way postings
65. "Rushmore" director Anderson
66. Baseball's Hank and Tommie
67. Draconian
69. Q-Tip, for one
71. Peak in Greek myth
72. Ho-hum feeling
73. "Slaves of New York" author Janowitz
74. Time span
75. Kind of shooting
76. ___ appeal
77. Patty Hearst's kidnap grp.

DOWN

1. Splatter catcher
2. Game of chance
3. Eyelid woes
4. Bonkers
5. Bribery suffix
6. Big name in book clubs
7. Actress Oberon
8. Collector's goal
9. Glacial matter
10. ___ bene
11. Baseballer Slaughter
12. Habit
14. Light ___
21. Fill fully
23. Cookie fruit
26. Leave the flock
27. Family dog, for short
29. ___ Tuesday (Mardi Gras)
31. Coal unit
32. Cast wearer's problem
33. "___ fan tutte"
34. "Happy Days Are Here Again" composer Milton
35. Corker
36. Yuppies' wheels
38. Navy noncom
39. Caulking material
43. A few: Abbr.
46. Up for debate
47. Yang's opposite
49. Moon of Jupiter
52. Bird call
54. Traffic director
56. Speaks facetiously
57. ___ High Dam
59. Takes it on the chin
60. Adams of Yosemite
61. Honshu city
62. Cows and sows
63. File's partner
64. Caen's river
66. Quatrain scheme
68. Best seller
70. Latin 101 verb

Solution on page 339

Challenging 17

ACROSS

1. Resell illegally
6. Las Vegas figures
10. Standard setting at 0 degrees long.
13. Ends of the earth
14. Animal stomach
15. When repeated, a fish
16. __ once
17. "Funny!"
18. "Dilbert" intern
19. Giant great
20. '80s Peppard costar
21. Chiang Kai-shek's capital
23. Most senior
26. Extorted money from
27. Glacial formations
30. Philosopher David
32. Grounded birds
33. Flowerless plant
35. Kind of store
39. Netflix offering
40. Entered surreptitiously
43. Bit of hope?
44. Big part
46. Furnace fuel
47. Agreeing (with)
49. Whomp
51. Kicked off
52. Dean of "Lois and Clark"
54. Satisfies
57. Drive recklessly
59. Ambulance abbr.
60. Bayonet
64. Old flatboats
65. Son of Judah
67. In itself
68. Open, as an envelope
69. Prefix with sphere
70. Eleniak of "Baywatch"
71. Babe
72. "Norma Rae" director
73. Blue Ribbon maker

DOWN

1. E-mail nuisance
2. RC, e.g.
3. Comrade in arms
4. Charge for using
5. L.A. hours
6. Earthy color
7. Mild oaths
8. Morse T
9. Belt
10. Quebec peninsula
11. Did a blacksmith's job
12. "Kon-__"
15. Sent off
20. Hosp. workers
22. Rocket killer, briefly
24. More, in a maxim
25. Midafternoon
27. Extra: Abbr.
28. Be itinerant
29. Old Norse collection
31. Commercial prefix with vision
33. Pays for
34. __ Grove Village, Ill.
36. Mashie, e.g.
37. Lioness's lack
38. Looked over
41. Horned Frogs' sch.
42. Puppy pickup point
45. Least sweet
48. Mosaic square
50. "__ moment"
51. Authorizes
52. Monte __
53. Actor Alan
55. Was biased
56. "Are so!" retort
57. Carry's partner
58. Roulette bet
61. Lou Grant's paper, for short
62. Says "When?"
63. Ready for the sack
66. "__ won't be afraid" ("Stand by Me" lyric)
67. Cheerleader's asset

Solution on page 339

Challenging 18

ACROSS

1. Winter pear
5. Word of contempt
9. U.K. fliers
12. Et ___
13. Nice notions
15. Eight furlongs
16. "The Mod Squad" role
17. Ma's instrument
18. Armchair quarterback's channel
19. Ali's trainer Dundee
21. Beau Brummell
22. Refs' decisions
23. Sandberg of baseball
25. Bangkok resident
27. Wyoming's ___ Range
30. Golfs, e.g.
32. Bordeaux wine
36. Ancient greeting
37. Inside shot?
39. Goddess of the dawn
40. Categorical imperative philosopher
42. Time and ___
44. Phoenix team
45. Salad green
47. Bit of folklore
49. Feathery accessory
50. Japanese immigrant
51. Cigarette pkg.
52. Power units
54. Ratchet part
56. Top Tatar
58. Where Samson defeated the Philistines
61. Head lines, for short
63. "___ Farm"
67. "___ giorno!"
68. Pigtail, e.g.
70. Intro to marketing?
71. Wall St. pros
72. Nonsense
73. Ocho ___, Jamaica
74. Aussie jumper
75. Corporate VIPs
76. Dada collectibles

DOWN

1. ___ Cynwyd, Pa.
2. "thirtysomething" star
3. Be a rat
4. "De oratore" author
5. Molly of Yiddish theater
6. Chemical suffix
7. Narcissist's love
8. Spartan serfs
9. Insurer's calculation
10. Gravy Train competitor
11. Marshlands
14. Jayvee athlete, perhaps
15. Occupations
20. Cat with tufted ears
24. Cole Porter's "Well, Did You ___?"
26. ___ Darya (Asian river)
27. Sulu portrayer, in "Star Trek"
28. "Dynasty" actress
29. Is disposed
31. Lawman Earp
33. Question
34. "Believe it ___!"
35. Some adobe abodes
38. Arctic explorer John
39. Pt. of a 1955 merger
41. Cravat adornments
43. Gaunt
46. ___ Veneto
48. McGregor of movies
51. White-collar worker?
53. "Peer Gynt" dancer
55. Friday on TV
57. Styx setting
58. Angle iron
59. Continental capital
60. Drifter
62. Big blow
64. Former Israeli prime minister
65. Cockeyed
66. Diminished by
69. Billy Joel's "___ to Extremes"

Solution on page 339

Challenging 19

ACROSS

1. Atl. crosser
4. Eva's husband
8. Camera setting
13. Collar victim
15. ___ jure (by law)
16. Mislead
17. Mil. truant
18. But, in Bordeaux
19. Composer Bruckner
20. Kathmandu native
22. M.D.'s wall hanging
24. Turned right
25. Swedish money
26. Passover celebrations
28. Forehead
30. Amazon, e.g.
34. Animal pouch
37. 1993 Sinatra album
40. Dutch treat
41. Sch. founded by Jefferson
42. Lake near Carson City
44. It's to jump for
45. Yclept
48. Actress Winona
50. Mouths, in zoology
51. 8 x 10, often
53. "Fine by me"
55. Garlicky dish
58. Davis of "Commander in Chief"
62. Came to
65. Golf phenom Michelle
66. Protons' places
67. Kitchen appliance brand
69. Rock's Motley ___
71. Secretive sort
72. Around
73. Orange cover
74. "Women and Love" author
75. Siouan tribesmen
76. Bullfight bravos
77. ___-crab soup

DOWN

1. Paddle
2. Ratty place
3. Prefix with sphere
4. First name at Woodstock
5. ___ tree
6. "All kidding ___ . . ."
7. Beat (out)
8. It has many keys: Abbr.
9. Serenades
10. French noodle?
11. Native Nebraskan
12. Polliwog's place
14. Fallback option
21. Enrich, in a way
23. Dropout's doc.
26. Say "#@$%!"
27. Baseball's Maris, to pals
29. Away from the office
31. Stephen King canine
32. Air freshener target
33. Yucatec speaker
34. Like some telegrams
35. Of grandparents
36. GI wear, for short
38. Your, of yore
39. "Me too"
43. "A mouse!"
46. Core
47. Mil. decoration
49. Prego competitor
52. Fishtail
54. "Ugh!"
56. Brewery opening?
57. Jeopardy
59. Designer Perry
60. Poet's "below"
61. "La Dolce Vita" star
62. 1993 standoff site
63. Fail to do
64. Popular syrup
66. Composer Rorem and others
68. Some batteries
70. Arles article

Solution on page 340

Challenging 20

ACROSS
1. Cologne cries
5. "Ocupado"
10. "The Flintstones" pet
14. Sappho, e.g.
15. Defeated, in a way
16. Tony winner Judith
17. Vaulted area, perhaps
18. Breathing problem
19. Poetic dusks
20. Bowling alley button
22. Together
24. Carry on
27. Digital communication?: Abbr.
28. Baby food
31. Rifles
33. Building support
37. "Where did ___ wrong?"
38. Albuquerque student
39. Relatives of Tahitians
41. Feminizing suffix
43. Sealy rival
45. "Not to mention . . ."
46. Living-room piece
48. Dance partner?
50. Unagi, at a sushi bar
51. Close up
52. Singer Luft
53. "Full," on B'way
54. Shirt size (abbr.)
56. Sea dogs
58. Cut
62. Actress Hayek
66. "___ Three Lives"
67. Subtitle of many biographies
70. Aim
71. Driver's warning
72. Break off
73. Friendly femme
74. "Nana" star Anna
75. "___ evil"
76. Hong Kong's Hang ___ Index

DOWN
1. On ___ with
2. Handle adversity
3. Dame of the piano
4. Take the conn
5. "___ Believer"
6. Day break?
7. ___ Reader (magazine)
8. Regarded to be
9. Dutch exports
10. Mint hardware
11. "A Little Bitty Tear" singer
12. Endangered state bird
13. Sounds of woe
21. Coffee size
23. Et ___
25. Choker
26. Hamlet option
28. Bakers' wares
29. De Mille of dance
30. Italian bridge
32. Body of art?
34. Fancy neckwear
35. Rhone delta city
36. Part of a step
39. Heavenly gift
40. Helpless?
42. H, to Herodotus
44. Cause for a lawsuit
47. "Enchanted" girl in a 2004 film
49. Long-jawed fishes
52. Actress Sobieski
55. Not Astroturf
57. Epic tales
58. Gumball machine feature
59. "Take one!"
60. "I Dream of Jeannie" star
61. Joint
63. Capital of Togo
64. Central
65. "Break ___!"
66. Hypotheticals
68. Boggy area
69. Mancinelli opera "___ e Leandro"

Solution on page 340

Challenging 21

ACROSS

1. ___ Minor
5. Proof goof
9. Locomotive part
12. Loamy deposit
14. Jeer
15. Ballot
16. Not out
17. Lauders
19. Cornhusker State: Abbr.
20. Mr. Kostelanetz
22. Bone of contention
23. Borrowed
25. Not yet actualized
26. Neutered
28. Be charitable
29. Brought on board
30. Swells
32. Airport abbr.
33. Be in charge
34. Diploma word
37. King's issue
39. Hip to, with "of"
41. 1974 Medicine Nobelist George ___
43. Let off
44. Easter event
45. Mock
47. Vinegar: comb. form
48. Three-reeler, e.g.
49. Cooler
52. Bugbear
54. 1911 chemistry Nobelist
56. "Dianetics" author ___ Hubbard
57. Sketch out
58. Correct
59. Barcelona bear
60. Stumpers?
61. Hoses down

DOWN

1. ___ Bator
2. Poet laureate Nicholas
3. Coastal region
4. "Don't ___!"
5. Bara of old films
6. Backwoods possessive
7. John Paul II, e.g.
8. Ear: prefix
9. Pamper
10. Bring into harmony
11. Attack from all sides
13. Shut tight
15. Outlooks
18. Elephantine
21. Affirmative action?
24. "Bill ___, the Science Guy"
25. Credit union offering
26. "Ain't ___ Sweet"
27. Casino area
28. Venetian magistrate
30. Part of n.b.
31. Form of I.D.: Abbr.
33. Tilt-A-Whirl, for one
34. Happy-go-lucky
35. Mary of "Where Eagles Dare"
36. Club ___ (resort chain)
37. Typewriter roller
38. Hazardous gas
39. Individually
40. Bunch of bills
41. Sulky pullers
42. Playground retort
43. Delhi title
44. Poet Neruda
45. Golf's ___-Ryder Open
46. Levels
48. Actor O'Shea
50. "If it ___ broke . . ."
51. Beatty and Buntline
53. Antonym: Abbr.
55. Underground org.

Solution on page 340

Challenging 22

ACROSS
1. Union inits.
4. Scale down
8. Mar. honoree
13. Battery contents
15. Notorious Idi
16. Khomeini, for one
17. Barn bundle
18. Like gazpacho
19. Quiche Lorraine ingredient
20. Reply to "Am too!"
22. Journey part
24. Disney dog
25. Deceived
26. "Calendar Girl" singer
28. Talk up
30. Deli item
34. "Dirty" Cajun dish
37. Nobelist Walesa
40. Indian melodies
41. Coverage co.
42. Repetitive
44. Canyon edge
45. Beauts
47. 24-karat
48. Hipsters' homes
49. Handel bars?
51. Fast feline
53. To a greater extent
56. Caper
60. Hamburg's river
63. Mop & ___ (floor cleaner)
64. Capital on the Missouri
65. Chow line?
67. Together, musically
69. "Aloha" accompaniments
70. Makes holes
71. "Huh-uh"
72. DOS part: abbr.
73. "Halt!" to a salt
74. Radio feature
75. Doo-wop syllable

DOWN
1. Plot
2. "As if ___!"
3. Stinko
4. Formal agreement
5. "___, amas, I love . . ."
6. Moon valley
7. Finito
8. Sis, e.g.
9. Singsong sounds
10. Spotted cavy
11. "And giving ___, up the chimney . . ."
12. Infinitesimal
14. Stand for
21. "Double Fantasy" artist
23. Neon, e.g.
26. Brew
27. Miniature racer
29. Maximum: abbr.
31. City east of Jaipur
32. Motel employee
33. Theories
34. Pi followers
35. Mae West's "___ Angel"
36. "The Big Lebowski" director
38. Wine bottle word
39. Marx with a horn
42. :, in analogies
43. Opposite of alt
46. "The Ten Commandments" role
48. Discussion groups
50. Cape Tres Puntas locale: Abbr.
52. Avril follower
54. Spiral-horned grazer
55. "Me too"
57. Low cards
58. Kind of coffee
59. Pelota catcher
60. Island near Corsica
61. 10th-century pope
62. Vamp Theda
64. Drink garnish
66. "The buck stops here" monogram
68. ___ tree

Solution on page 340

Challenging 23

ACROSS

1. "Beowulf," e.g.
5. Cribbage marker
8. "Socrate" composer
13. Reddish-brown gem
14. "Let 'er ___!"
15. Grandparents, often
16. Like a tundra
18. Delights
19. Strauss's "___ Heldenleben"
20. Artist's asset
21. Put away
22. Yuletide, e.g.
24. Beatle follower?
25. AOL rival
26. Tres y tres
27. Access, with "into"
30. 1966 movie or song hit
33. "___ cost you"
34. Guns the engine
35. Transported
36. First word of Dante's "Inferno"
37. "Soap" family
38. Algonquian Indian
39. Caterer's carrier
40. Dead to the world
41. "Get the picture?"
42. Did a smith's job
43. Air-testing org.
44. Pepe of cartoons
46. Act the snitch
49. Dialect
50. "___ Beso" (1962 hit)
51. "Is that ___?"
53. "The Freshmaker" candy
54. Plan on it
56. Trigonometry ratio
57. "Zip-A-Dee-___-Dah"
58. Cockeyed
59. Snake, to Medusa
60. B & B
61. Kind of pool

DOWN

1. Punta del ___, Uruguay
2. Helen's abductor
3. Papas of "Z"
4. Alphabetic trio
5. Victimize
6. ESPN anchor Rich
7. Some M.D.s
8. Lawgivers
9. Arcade name
10. Private
11. Really steamed
12. Curve shape
15. Micromanager's concern
17. Flat dweller
21. Rank
23. Nitrogen compound
26. Stand in good ___
28. Affirm with confidence
29. "Hey you!"
30. Basics
31. Body of knowledge
32. Like many writers
33. How corn is planted
34. Attacked
37. Move with stealth
39. Believer
42. Impromptu percussion
43. Home of Lafayette College
45. Singers James and Jones
46. Dovetail part
47. It may be in a stew
48. First name in rock
49. Earl, for one
52. Bound along
53. Colo. clock setting
54. ___ Amin
55. Faultfinder

Solution on page 340

Challenging 24

ACROSS
1. [not my error]
4. Five-time Wimbledon champ
8. It's pulled on a farm
13. Auditors
15. "Aren't ___ lucky one?"
16. "___ beaucoup"
17. Lost, in a way
18. Pest control brand
19. Huffs and puffs
20. Strip
22. Sheriff's asst.
24. Corner piece
25. Hotel crew
26. Lulls
28. Explorer Vasco da ___
30. Mediterranean capital
34. Totally gross
37. F.B.I. agent
40. Dry, in a way
41. Thor Heyerdahl craft
42. Edy's competitor
44. 16th-century start
45. Shade of green
47. Sturdy cart
48. From
49. High-hat
51. Push-ups strengthen them
53. "Speed" star
56. Getaway spots
60. See red
63. It can't be helped
64. Tennessee Williams title critter
65. ___ fours
67. Curtain holders
69. Navy noncoms
70. Landed
71. Puddinglike serving
72. Bar sounds
73. Song thrush
74. Smarmy
75. Reserved

DOWN
1. Rugby formation
2. Classic toothpaste
3. Pants style
4. Linger
5. Non-Rx
6. ___ Island red
7. "The Balcony" playwright
8. Diamond authority
9. Letter opener
10. Bond foe
11. Prefix with morph
12. Insurer's calculation
14. Old-fogyish
21. Eagles' org.
23. Place for a pint
26. Limping, maybe
27. Sunday seats
29. Team VIP: Abbr.
31. Lens holders
32. Bring to ruin
33. Cry of relief
34. Ticks off
35. City near Le Havre
36. Two pounds, plus
38. Firth of Clyde port
39. Semimonthly tides
42. Computer unit
43. Bar order
46. Dangerous siren
48. Per se
50. In addition
52. Smoke
54. Sign of summer
55. Common bacillus
57. Blue shade
58. Methuselah's father
59. Flippant
60. Froth
61. Donald, to Dewey
62. Basketball Hall-of-Famer Harshman
64. 2002 Eddie Murphy film
66. Mormons: Abbr.
68. Can. money

Solution on page 340

Challenging 25

ACROSS

1. Recorded deeds
5. "It's a Wonderful Life" director
10. "___ silly question . . ."
14. Reagan cabinet member
15. "Little Darlings" actress
16. Cowboy singer Wooley
17. Author/illustrator Silverstein
18. "Psycho" setting
19. Handle adversity
20. Discounted
22. Nimble
24. Grating
27. TV's "___ Haw"
28. Olympic racers
31. Ukr. neighbor
33. Lions' prides?
37. Clean Air Act org.
38. Slender
41. Biblical gift-givers
42. Gridiron org.
43. Buffoon
44. "Frasier" character
46. Audrey's "My Fair Lady" costar
47. Cost to cross
49. Gully
51. Iowa hrs.
52. Canadian skater Brian
54. Marceau's everyman
55. Toothsome
57. Astronaut Grissom
59. Attar source
61. Drink
64. Sea spots
68. "The Censor" of Rome
69. Weighed down
73. Cordon ___

74. Give ___ for one's money
75. Cursor mover
76. Letters on a B-2
77. Capone's nemesis
78. Blotter entry
79. Garr of "Tootsie"

DOWN

1. Facetious "I see"
2. "All the Way" lyricist Sammy
3. Lashes
4. Blazing
5. Shows up
6. "It's ___-win situation!"
7. Fido or Fluffy
8. ___ Dawn Chong
9. Islamic deity
10. Really funny
11. "Buzz off!"
12. French military cap
13. "Not on ___!"
21. Dogie catcher
23. Like L.B.J.
25. Home built in a day?
26. Brynner of "The King and I"
28. Slow, to Salieri
29. Excited about
30. Exasperates
32. Credit card feature
34. Busters?
35. Cast out
36. A mile a minute
39. Dictionary abbr.
40. Big time
45. Some sorority women
48. Multitudes

50. Big shot
53. Obstacle
56. Very nearly
58. 1965 march site
60. Points at the dinner table
61. Words of confidence
62. Lunar plain
63. HVAC measures
65. "Do it, or ___!"
66. Floor it
67. Muslim mystic
70. MSN competitor
71. Hwy. offense
72. Tikkanen of hockey

Solution on page 341

Challenging 26

ACROSS

1. Bar __
5. In check
10. Designer Gucci
14. New Mexico artists' colony
15. Oregon Trail city
16. Protein bean
17. Start of a Web address
18. Top mark
19. Swim's alternative
20. Badger
22. Wipes out
24. British verb ending
25. Second-generation Japanese
27. Back muscles, in gym lingo
29. Ukr. neighbor
30. Journalist Stewart
34. Geometric fig.
35. 1986 self-titled soul album
38. "No problem"
39. "2001" mainframe
40. Lambda followers
41. A prime
43. P.O. box item
44. "The __ Love" (R.E.M. hit)
46. Balkan capital
48. Chop (off)
49. Tubular pasta
51. __ Bingle (Crosby)
52. One of the Lennons
54. Bamboozled
56. Degree div.
57. Obliquely
60. Surgical tools
63. Electrical units
64. Ventriloquist Bergen
67. Move, in Realtor lingo
69. Order
70. Baseball manager Joe
71. Maja painter
72. Broadway Auntie
73. Goes after
74. 1914 battle line

DOWN

1. Advanced degree?
2. "@#$%!," e.g.
3. "__ chance!"
4. Verve
5. Bring down
6. The best
7. "The Family Circus" cartoonist Keane
8. Pac-10 sch.
9. Green lights
10. Besets
11. Clark's love
12. Force unit
13. Thousand __, Calif.
21. Indian state
23. "Danny Boy" actor
25. Crackpot
26. Beatty bomb of 1987
27. Tropical vine
28. "Stormy Weather" composer
29. Live
31. Roman dictator, 82–79 B.C.
32. "What the Butler Saw" playwright
33. Collar victim
34. Karate move
36. Same old, same old
37. Barley bristle
42. Fertile spot
45. Rashly
47. Cabernet, e.g.
50. Ages
53. Zip
55. Keeps in
56. Some bays
57. Kind of radio
58. Some Muslims
59. Good earth
60. Escapade
61. Antique autos
62. Roy Rogers's real last name
65. Anonymous one
66. Coll. senior's test
68. Propel, in a way

Solution on page 341

Challenging 27

ACROSS
1. Dow figures
6. Silo occupant
10. Like a neat lawn
14. Birdbrain
15. Russian assembly
16. Galba's successor
17. Difficulty
18. Footnote abbreviation
19. Stimulate
20. ___ Friday's (restaurant chain)
21. "O" in old radio lingo
23. Stands for sittings
25. "Batman" sound
26. Russian fighter
27. "King Kong" studio
28. Belfast's province
32. Lot
33. Twin of myth
34. Dim ___
35. Flushed
40. Entre ___
41. Native: Suffix
42. 1960s–70s Italian P.M.
43. They may be heaved
45. "i" completer
46. Floral display
47. Hammer end
49. Attempts, with "at"
50. Jazz violinist Jean-___ Ponty
53. Charlottesville inst.
54. Grog ingredient
55. Wagnerian heroine
57. Conn of "Benson"
58. Flit about
61. Miles of "Psycho"
62. Stat start
64. One in a black suit
66. "Mockingbird" singer Foxx
67. Feeder filler
68. "My Fair Lady" character
69. Scale start
70. Resistance measures
71. Made mention of

DOWN
1. "Java" trumpeter Al
2. "Gotcha"
3. Best Picture of 1958
4. Sob syllable
5. Disco fixtures
6. "Eat crow" or "talk turkey"
7. 27, to 3
8. ASCAP counterpart
9. Succeeded
10. Cuts blades
11. Catchall category
12. Marine snail
13. "That's a lie!"
22. Exclude
24. "Ain't She Sweet?" composer
26. "Oleanna" playwright
28. Buffet table items
29. Sainted fifth-century pope
30. Puffed up
31. Keister
32. Sleep on it
34. Top of a platter
36. Strike callers
37. "David Copperfield" wife
38. Bummer
39. Cellist Ma
44. Carb source
46. Japanese stringed instrument
48. Extremely
49. Cabinet dept. since 1965
50. Hopping mad
51. "___ hooks"
52. Apple gizmo
54. Laughfests
56. Veg out
57. Adjudge
58. Amble or shamble
59. Cooper's tool
60. Out of juice
63. "Come again?"
65. Gaza force, for short

Solution on page 341

Challenging 28

ACROSS

1. Beyond tipsy
4. Charles barker
8. Infield cover
12. Assayers' samples
14. Checked out
15. Blackthorn fruit
16. Home, informally
17. Other: Fr.
18. Airline launched in 1948
19. Dimethyl sulfate and others
21. "Fear Street" series author
23. Trencherman
26. Aliens, briefly
27. Daytime fare
30. Brooks of "Blazing Saddles"
32. Barn dances
36. Prepare, as a salad
37. Opening word
39. Hawaii's Mauna ___
40. "Baloney!"
41. Fold, spindle or mutilate
42. 50 Cent piece
43. Bother
44. Bass, e.g.
45. Comes to mind
47. Heart
48. Takes a chance
50. Blazed a trail
51. Carryalls
52. The law, to Mr. Bumble
54. Words repeated at the start of the "Sailor's Song"
56. Former Greek P.M. Papandreou
60. Singer Brewer
64. Have a bias
65. What's here
68. Dribble
69. Highway division
70. Lessens
71. Gen. Robt. ___
72. Go downhill fast?
73. Counterfeit
74. A.A.R.P. members

DOWN

1. Hermitic
2. Cholers
3. Makeup, e.g.
4. Track-and-field org.
5. Concorde, e.g.
6. Guam, e.g.: abbr.
7. An Astaire
8. African bloodsucker
9. Sheryl Crow's "___ Wanna Do"
10. Colorful horse
11. Brazilian soccer legend
13. Brews
14. Play group
20. Dorm VIPs
22. Sore throat cause, briefly
24. Food Network name
25. ___ gestae
27. Prized violin, briefly
28. Alley Oop's girl
29. Autumn bloomer
31. Rio Grande city
33. "Adam Bede" author
34. Mr. Moto portrayer
35. Benefits
37. Mediterranean isl.
38. More, in Madrid
41. En ___ (all together)
46. Band performance
47. Unrefined
49. Took in
51. "Fore" site
53. Fills up
55. Jeanne d'Arc et al.
56. "___ well that ends well"
57. "Hud" Oscar winner
58. Hamlet, e.g.
59. Bygone ruler
61. Congers and kin
62. Amphilochus, in Greek myth
63. Bronx Zoo houseful
66. Tikkanen of hockey
67. Theological sch.

Solution on page 341

Challenging 29

ACROSS
1. Fuji competitor
5. Like a designated driver
10. "The Nazarene" novelist
14. Berth place
15. Battery part
16. 1953 Leslie Caron role
17. Linear
18. Kentucky college
19. Victoria's Secret selections
20. Article lead-in
22. Most like a wallflower
24. Prefix meaning "one-billionth"
25. Scoundrel
26. Golfer's concern
29. OB-GYN job
30. Pumice features
31. "Doe, ___ . . ." (song lyric)
32. Barely beat
35. Breakfast staple
36. Unmistakable
37. ___ Alto, California
38. "Face/Off" director John
39. Form-related
40. Cheech of Cheech and Chong
41. Mountain air
42. Family members
43. Noted gatekeeper
46. Catches some rays
47. Attaches, in a way
48. Pocket Books logo
52. Footnote word
53. Go with the flow
55. "High" time
56. Church part
57. Scrap
58. Prefix meaning "all"
59. Campbell of country
60. Water jugs
61. Cross

DOWN
1. Snake, for one
2. Actress Gershon
3. Stocking stuffers
4. Battle of the Bulge locale
5. Texas-Louisiana border river
6. Brief bid
7. Drill
8. Dutch city
9. Logician
10. White rat, e.g.
11. Begot
12. Reunion group
13. Prefix meaning "tissue"
21. Insect exudates
23. It grows on you
25. Feminist Eleanor
26. Belch forth
27. Ghana neighbor
28. 50-oared ship
29. "What ___!"
31. Birch family member
32. Bust maker
33. 1973 French Open winner Nastase
34. Diva Lily
36. Secret identity
37. Fellow countrymen
39. Marquand sleuth
40. Art-conscious dynasty
41. Sycophants
42. 1598 edict city
43. Overcharge
44. ___ wave
45. Annoy
46. Get to the point?
48. Hardy cabbage
49. Cakewalk
50. A Chaplin
51. "Come ___"
54. Drops on the grass

Solution on page 341

Challenging 30

ACROSS
1. Jag
6. Grasslands
10. "Cast Away" setting
14. End of ___
15. Gimlet flavoring
16. Warm, in a sense
17. Hanging tapestry
18. Work without ___
19. Have ___ with
20. Chairpersons?
22. Lith. and Lat., once
23. Numerical prefix
24. Bear witness
26. Skill
29. Stars, in Kansas' motto
31. Bonus NFL periods
32. Novelist Ephron
34. Trac II alternatives
38. Sled dogs, as a group
40. Shoulder muscles, briefly
42. Allay
43. Attacked
45. Permeates
47. Coal storage
48. Assigned stars to
50. Take umbrage at
52. Heir's concern
55. Carnival sight
56. First-rate, slangily
57. Bottom line
63. Breaks down
64. View from Sandusky, Ohio
65. Left at sea
66. Come-on
67. "Voila!"
68. Carried
69. Madrid Mmes.
70. "Keep it" notation
71. Some deco works

DOWN
1. Canaanite deity
2. Calvary inscription
3. "I, Claudius" role
4. Starbucks size
5. Area of London
6. Alpaca's cousin
7. Article in Der Spiegel
8. From the U.S.
9. Attacks
10. Really perturbed
11. Taste, e.g.
12. Retreats
13. "Ninotchka" director Lubitsch
21. Didn't wait
25. "La la" preceder
26. Little ones
27. Done to ___
28. Aspiring J.D.'s exam
29. Had a bug
30. Fill beyond full
33. ___ majeste
35. "Streamers" playwright David
36. Alphabet book phrase
37. Wired, e.g.
39. Quagmires
41. Bender
44. D.C. baseballer
46. Having feeling
49. Beliefs
51. Drunken daze
52. British nobles
53. Search thoroughly
54. Prefix with fluoride
55. Be generous
58. "Was to be," in Latin
59. All alternative
60. Frist's predecessor
61. Locust, e.g.
62. Norms: abbr.

Solution on page 341

Challenging 31

ACROSS

1. Combo gear
5. Put ___ on (limit)
9. Of a region
14. Mother of the Titans
15. Kind of palm
16. Miss Hawkins of Dogpatch
17. Enterprise counselor
18. Advantages
19. Rimes of country music
20. Founder of the Shakers in America
22. Ode title starter
24. Really bad coffee
25. Hardly windy
27. "Not ___ bet!"
29. Takes it on the chin
31. 1972 Nixon host
33. 1988 Grand Slam winner
37. Twice
38. Held another session
40. Tropical palm
41. Bluffer's ploy
43. "Rosemary's Baby" author Levin
44. Something to talk about
45. I, to historians
46. Citadel student
48. "Intimations of Immortality," e.g.
49. City district
50. ___ Poly
51. Loo sign
53. Ike's command, once: Abbr.
55. Speak monotonously
57. It may be up
60. "___ Como Va" (1971 Santana hit)
62. You can get down from them
65. "And thereby hangs ___": Shak.
67. Chocolate factory sights
69. Honoree's spot
71. Pinker in the middle
72. Give off, as light
73. It can be a stretch
74. More artful
75. Bar offerings
76. Film director Petri

DOWN

1. Ten-percenter: Abbr.
2. Wilson of "Matilda"
3. Drudge
4. Superdome team
5. Malign
6. Gives a rap
7. "Give it ___!"
8. Assignment
9. Narnia lion
10. Charlotte of "Bananas"
11. Cheese burg
12. Hokkaido native
13. Do banker's work
21. Looked like a wolf
23. "Hollywood Squares" win
26. May birthstone
28. Prefix meaning "soil"
29. Tropical vine
30. Basketry twig
32. Just slightly
34. Transplant
35. Litmus reddeners
36. Stand up to
37. Forehead
39. Easily split stuff
40. Come to
42. "No Ordinary Love" singer
47. They're legends in their own minds
50. Demure
52. Razz
54. It's human
56. Adjust, as laces
57. Some are jam-packed
58. Emphatic type: Abbr.
59. Lake Michigan city
61. "How can I ___ thank you?"
63. Air alternative
64. ___ Valley, Calif.
66. "Clockers" director
68. One of the "Little Women"
70. "Wellll . . . ?"

Solution on page 342

Challenging 32

ACROSS

1. Blood type, briefly
5. Dudley Do-Right's org.
9. Harsh cries
14. Wine or hair quality
15. Suffix with smack
16. Coincide
17. Hardly rosy
18. Go yachting
19. Qantas critter
20. Pac-10 school
21. "Little" girl in "David Copperfield"
22. Deli breads
23. Bugs
26. Sunscreen additive
29. Apt. feature
30. Deem appropriate
34. Tower site
37. Elliptical path
40. German pronoun
41. Proper partner
42. Has a hunch
43. Avoid a crash
44. Suffix with ball
45. Failed to
46. Bungle
47. Evasive maneuver
49. French soul
50. White hat wearer
52. Cold one
56. H. Rap Brown's org.
59. Laine of jazz
61. Mazel ___
62. Russian ballet company
64. Oner
65. Abysmal test score
66. ___ Gay (WWII plane)
67. Actress Moran
68. Phone button
69. Window sticker
70. Oats, e.g.
71. Anthem opener

DOWN

1. Shooter
2. Like Odin
3. Pronouncement
4. High school class
5. Look for again
6. Pulls an all-nighter
7. Work hard
8. Hydra, for one
9. Gab
10. Hellenic hangouts
11. "King Kong" star
12. Soccer great
13. Salty septet
24. Abound (with)
25. Diminutive, in Dogpatch
27. Closeout caveat
28. Track action
31. Cries of disgust
32. Clinched
33. By way of, old-style
34. Lodge letters
35. Elvis Presley's middle name
36. Tough spot
37. Brit. lexicon
38. Cartoon chihuahua
39. Club alternative
42. Hunky-dory
43. Penthouse feature
45. "How obvious!"
46. Tussaud's title: Abbr.
48. Pepsi rival
49. Roughly
51. Bass notation
52. Refute
53. Way up
54. "M*A*S*H" setting
55. Key material
56. Short agenda?
57. Mudville count
58. "Peter Pan" critter
60. Drawing card
63. Kilmer of "Batman Forever"
65. Bronx attraction

Solution on page 342

Challenging 33

ACROSS

1. Awaken
5. Declines
9. Bird's sound
14. Main Web page
15. 6,272,640 square inches
16. Loggers' contest
17. Asian nursemaid
18. Hoops nickname
19. Really bothered
20. Late
22. Indians play them
23. Laid up
24. Lot of loot
25. Cordwood measures
28. Woo, in a way
32. Boorish
33. Out-and-out
34. Clinton, e.g.: Abbr.
35. French river
36. Fixed look
37. IRS data
38. Expose, in verse
39. Composer Camille Saint-
___
40. Alliance created in 1954
41. Prevaricate
43. Transmitter
44. "Absolutely!"
45. Chill, so to speak
46. Numbers games
49. Wagner's final opera
53. "West Side Story" girl
54. Ruination
55. "The Lion King" lioness
56. "Funny Face" director
Stanley
57. Middle name of "the
King"
58. A util.

59. Shift, e.g.
60. French door feature
61. Go the distance

DOWN

1. Herring kin
2. Big book
3. Apple product
4. Run through
5. Mouths off to
6. Felt (for)
7. Mortarboard wearer
8. Et ___ (footnote abbr.)
9. Movie promo
10. Spoiled
11. Intestinal parts
12. Cordelia's father
13. Plenty
21. Lincoln and others

22. Yes or no follower
24. Jury members
25. Dart
26. Drivel
27. Art supporter
28. Alan Ladd classic
29. Bashar of Syria
30. Al ___
31. David of CNN
33. Lager holder
36. Corporate division
37. Guard
39. Mead subjects
40. Cong. meeting
42. Starbucks orders
43. Chilled out
45. Wouldn't stop
46. "Shane" star
47. ___ about

48. Antler feature
49. Chutist, briefly
50. FDR's Scottie
51. Brews
52. Milk: prefix
54. Protestant denom.

Solution on page 342

Challenging 34

ACROSS

1. Tartan-wearing group
5. Electric guitar effect
9. City council rep.
12. Spot of relief
14. Calculating types
15. Craft's men
16. Slender woman
17. Hindu honorifics
18. To ___
19. Prickly plant
21. "___ were you . . ."
22. "The ___ From Ipanema"
23. Son of Prince Valiant
24. Chain's partner
26. Least ingenuous
28. First name in Communism
29. Playground marble
30. ___ song
33. Club in a Manilow song
35. Resistance-related
40. Butcher's offering
41. Serengeti scavenger
43. Saragossa's river
44. Reporting to
46. Blah
47. Moneyed one
48. Asner and Begley
50. A bunch
52. Like farmland
56. Saunders of jazz
57. Child advocacy org.
60. Energetic
61. 1977 double-platinum
    Steely Dan album
63. Electronics whiz
65. Not very much
66. Cape Town cash
68. Replay option
69. Microwaves
70. Soy-based soup
71. Gown material
72. Compass point
73. Sch. type
74. Miniature sci-fi vehicles

DOWN

1. ___ del Sol
2. Stratum
3. Narnia lion
4. Cheese ___
5. Loos
6. Patriots' Day month
7. Stray animal
8. St. Francis's birthplace
9. "The Sopranos" restaurateur
10. Dirty looks
11. Resided
13. Biblical queendom
15. Shrewd
20. Pine cousin
25. Big name in insurance
27. Corp. takeover
28. Classic Welles role
29. Run
30. Winter woe
31. Suffix with ball
32. Divest
34. A pop
36. Sneaky laughs
37. Wharton grad
38. Sportscaster Cross
39. Speedy Sebastian
42. Cut short
45. CSA monogram
49. "Goodness!"
51. Glorify
52. Staring intently
53. Rosters
54. Slack-jawed
55. Physiques, slangily
56. Parson's place
57. I.D. item
58. Retiring
59. Long times
62. Clink
64. Give a hand
67. Benedictine title

Solution on page 342

Challenging 35

ACROSS

1. Kitchen counter?
6. Accomplished
10. At the peak of
14. Febrero preceder
15. Caught in the act
16. Off-white
17. Guam's capital, old-style
18. Fly, e.g.
19. "Got two fives for ___?"
20. One on a force
22. Platforms
24. Suffix with hip
25. Actress Daly
26. Bed support
29. Contents of some banks
31. "A Passage to India" heroine
35. Medal winners
37. Crimson rivals
39. A Bobbsey
40. Prefix with fauna
41. Strong and proud
43. Baseball's Master Melvin
44. Mr. ___ (old whodunit board game)
45. Fourth rock from the sun
46. Excoriate
48. Marinara alternative
50. Numero uno
52. Angry, with "off"
53. Cupid, to the Greeks
55. Kind of package
57. Tricky problem
60. Lets go
64. Abbr. at the bottom of a business letter
65. Actor Alda
67. O'Connor successor
68. Caesar's sidekick
69. Performer in whiteface
70. Very, to Verdi
71. Boom producers
72. PC programs, for short
73. Thickset

DOWN

1. Afternoon gatherings
2. TV's Swenson
3. Brunch, e.g.
4. Automaker Maserati
5. Cook on a spit
6. Kansas motto word
7. Page
8. "___ Girls"
9. Contest submission
10. Humbled
11. Big bag
12. Rara avis
13. Signature pieces?
21. Suez Canal terminus
23. Momentarily
25. Ankle bones
26. On the dot
27. Flood barrier
28. A fire sign
30. High-strung
32. Cybermemo
33. Shaping machine
34. Fed the kitty
36. "Get Shorty" novelist Leonard
38. Hook up: Var.
42. Emblems of power
47. Pigged out
49. Magnetic induction units
51. They're in the act
54. Advertising suffix
56. Lots and lots
57. Gumshoes
58. "The Dukes of Hazzard" deputy
59. Bank statement no.
60. Alternative to steps
61. Farm structure
62. Accusatory words
63. It's found in stacks
66. Insolence

Solution on page 342

Challenging 36

ACROSS

1. Marine shade
5. Merry old times
10. ___-night doubleheader
13. Brusque
14. Elevate
15. Greek queen of heaven
16. Padlock piece
17. More cunning
18. "Excuse me . . ."
19. Royal toppers
21. Uncalled for
23. "Them"
25. Apartment sign
26. Bearish
28. "___ du lieber!"
29. The Joads, e.g.
30. Georgia ___
32. Joint
36. Tubular pasta
37. Little newt
38. Pep (up)
39. An NCO
40. Duds
41. Chimp's cousin
42. Combat
43. Silvery
45. Fat cat
48. Asimov or Stern
49. Tip off
51. Around, so to speak
55. Medieval chest
56. Africa's largest country
58. Charter
59. Revenuers, for short
60. Say "tsk!" to
61. Monogram pt.
62. Bummed
63. Nymph
64. Times Square sign

DOWN

1. Eight, in Essen
2. Paris's ___ d'Orsay
3. Bear up?
4. Now
5. Let up
6. Rose of rock
7. Monsoonal
8. "Twittering Machine" artist
9. Duration
10. Little laugh
11. Take forcibly
12. Alpo rival
15. Campus location
20. Biscotto flavoring
22. "Stupid me!"
24. Falling star
26. Luau instruments
27. Cabal
28. Takes the role of
29. Photo ___ (camera sessions)
31. Alphabet trio
32. Bull's-eye
33. Director Reitman
34. Air outlet
35. Chang's Siamese twin
38. Canada's highest peak
40. Hot stuff
42. Amaze
44. Came down
45. Bellini heroine
46. Curved
47. Pinto, e.g.
48. Private filmmaker, informally
49. Saturated substances
50. Essen's river
52. Sty cry
53. Habeas corpus, for one
54. Is left with
57. Seat of Pontotoc County, Oklahoma

Solution on page 342

Challenging 37

ACROSS
1. Bagel choice
6. Deg. issuer
10. "___ y plata"
13. Up ___ (stuck)
14. "Me neither"
15. Feds
16. Lullaby syllables
17. Disney goldfish
18. "Streamers" playwright David
19. Gas company known for its toy trucks
20. Yes, in Yokohama
21. Advanced
23. Works
26. Money guarantor, for short
27. Take a break
30. Bistro
32. New York city
33. Sedona and Sorento
35. Shells, e.g.
39. Long of "Boyz N the Hood"
40. Loses it
43. Detroit org.
44. Shaggy oxen
46. Code bits
47. "South Pacific" role
49. Short-lived particle
51. Heads off
52. Scott Turow work
54. Outcome
57. Skin softeners
59. Verbal stumbles
60. "Carmina Burana" composer
64. Time of day
65. Other, to Ortega
67. Work unit
68. Professor 'iggins
69. Rows
70. Hands over
71. Animal house?
72. Keister
73. Grab the tab

DOWN
1. Hiker's route
2. Nebraska City's county
3. Mavens
4. Public image
5. "___, though I walk . . ."
6. "The Last of the Mohicans" Mohican
7. "It's true!"
8. Boiling blood
9. Instrument played with a bow
10. Gulf State resident
11. Renaissance instrument
12. Linear
15. First-class
20. March sound
22. Mistaken
24. Twinge
25. Frauds
27. Rabbit fur
28. Et ___
29. Deck wood
31. Film box letters
33. Sandra's "Speed" costar
34. "Kinda" suffix
36. Sierra Club founder John
37. Many a beer
38. Has a tab
41. "Deep Space Nine" role
42. "Whip It" band
45. Like wet ink
48. Copycat
50. City on the Danube
51. Massage table sounds
52. Home of the Black Bears
53. Prefix with transmitter
55. Runs smoothly
56. Flop's opposite
57. Bistro awning word
58. Santa soiler
61. Uncouth
62. Kind of market
63. Song ending?
66. ___ cross
67. RR crossing

Solution on page 343

Challenging 38

ACROSS

1. "Wheel of Fortune" buy
4. Fundraiser suffix
8. Seconds: Abbr.
13. Jump out of one's skin?
15. Vintner's prefix
16. Kind of print
17. "Legally Blonde" girl
18. Teacher's deg.
19. Not as bright
20. They serve dictators
22. Brit. lexicon
24. Castle feature
25. Medicinal shrub
26. Like some inspections
28. "What ___ now?"
30. Sonnet ender
34. Woolen caps
37. Cheer
40. "Keen!"
41. "Life ___ beach"
42. Sibyl
44. Put out, in a way
45. Saltpeter, to a Brit
47. Country singer Evans
48. Part of a casa
49. Most of Libya
51. Geom. shape
53. Adulterate
56. Takes wing
60. Neil Diamond's "___ Said"
63. ___-rock (music genre)
64. Stephen King's first novel
65. Be a busybody
67. Ward of "Once and Again"
69. Suffix with persist
70. Bone: prefix
71. All the time
72. "The King and I" setting
73. Can't do without
74. Commanded
75. 67.5 deg.

DOWN

1. "Don't make ___!"
2. "Cape Fear" actor
3. "Zelig" director
4. Thumb and others
5. "For ___ a jolly good . . ."
6. Tie ___ (tipple)
7. Meeting points
8. Eiger, e.g.
9. Like Anna's students
10. Capital of Manche
11. "___-Team"
12. Class
14. It has its faults
21. Treaty gp. since 1948
23. Belittle, slangily
26. Siouan tribesmen
27. Addition column
29. Blind rage
31. "Bye!"
32. And more
33. "Animal House" party wear
34. Cans
35. ___ Minor
36. Subject that gives students lots of problems
38. Mouths, anatomically
39. ___ Haute, IN
42. Desertlike
43. Oil can letters
46. Acted the ham?
48. Puts away
50. "The ___ Daba Honeymoon"
52. J.E.B. Stuart's country
54. 1942 Preakness winner
55. Carved pillar
57. "L.A. Law" lawyer
58. Costa ___
59. Terse summons
60. "The heat ___!"
61. "As I Lay Dying" father
62. Bit of dust
64. Blanchett of "Elizabeth"
66. Not neg.
68. Ben-Gurion Airport city

Solution on page 343

Challenging 39

ACROSS

1. Grade enhancer
5. Legend's locale
10. Word with market or collar
14. No-goodnik
15. Lilac, e.g.
16. Crew members
17. Chip's chum
18. Aristotle, to Alexander the Great
19. Sitcom station
20. Swimsuit brand
22. Medium settings?
24. Engine sound
26. Hole maker
27. Collar inserts
30. Diving bird
32. Creep
36. Flanders of "The Simpsons"
37. On the disabled list
39. Corkscrew
41. Language of Lahore
43. Jazz (up)
45. Veg out
46. Covers with crumbs
48. Indolent
50. -y, pluralized
51. BART part
52. ___ canto (singing style)
53. American symbol
55. When repeated, a Gabor
57. Give a hand
59. Trials
63. Familiar with
67. Norse peace god
68. Circus employee
70. Social reformer Jacob
71. Feudal worker
72. Chopin composition
73. Hustles
74. Barely managed, with "out"
75. Old-fashioned
76. "Do ___ others . . ."

DOWN

1. Professors' degs.
2. Ballet move
3. River to the Ubangi
4. Happy colleague
5. ___ Martin (classic auto)
6. Horned Frogs' sch.
7. Jared of "Panic Room"
8. Hooded jacket
9. Glass sipper
10. Drumstick source
11. Cottage site
12. Drops a pop
13. Cleopatra biter
21. Rooftop fixture
23. Fast pace
25. Irving hero
27. Give the cold shoulder to
28. ___ incognita
29. Abacus user
31. Handy
33. Big fat zero
34. Food writer Claiborne
35. Eye shade
38. ___ Constitution
39. "___ who?!"
40. ___ majesty
42. Abu Dhabi is its cap.
44. Math class, for short
47. Moonstruck state
49. Congressional assents
52. Golf ball material
54. Short summary
56. Filled up
58. Drew in
59. Ural River city
60. Russo of "Get Shorty"
61. Turned blue, maybe
62. Blue books?
64. "Runaround Sue" singer
65. Salon job
66. Bologna bone
67. Charge for services
69. Dutch city

Solution on page 343

Challenging 40

ACROSS

1. Onetime tadpole
5. Minn. neighbor
9. Surrealist Joan
13. Rich kid in "Nancy" comics
15. Circuit protector
16. Surefooted goat
17. Actor Quinn
18. Get shot, maybe
19. "What ___ say?"
20. Invoice abbr.
22. Steamed
24. "A merry heart ___ good like a medicine": Proverbs
26. Babi ___: historical WWII site
27. Nor. neighbor
28. Hoad of tennis
29. Blow gently
32. Apprehend
34. Diamonds, to hoods
35. Lowest deck on a ship
37. Downstairs, to a salt
41. Frontier nickname
43. Had the nerve
45. NFL Hall of Famer Marchetti
46. Game show announcer Johnny
48. Cut back
50. ATM maker
51. Post-WWII gp.
53. Hawaiian dance
54. Pester for payment
55. Persian's plaint
58. Exiled Cambodian Lon ___
60. Aquarium problem
62. Sign of a slip
64. Nabors role
65. In shape
66. ___ Hari
68. Pricing phrase
72. Printing process, for short
73. In need of liniment
74. Kind of eclipse
75. Couturier Cassini
76. In this way
77. Light

DOWN

1. Brother's title
2. Lyon king
3. Dated
4. Driving hazard
5. Dirty Harry's org.
6. The Everly Brothers, e.g.
7. Evaluate
8. Wynn of "Dr. Strangelove"
9. Cursor controllers
10. Building supports
11. Extend, in a way
12. Deuterium ___ (heavy water)
14. Powerful combination
21. Beet variety
23. Take rudely
24. Window sticker
25. 1936 Olympics hero
28. Italian resort
30. Book jacket part
31. Pentateuch
33. Panhandle
36. Big copper exporter
38. Hunt in Hollywood
39. At the right time
40. Dog-eared
42. Moo
44. Postpone
47. Part of Mork's goodbye
49. Trinity River city
52. Layout
55. ___-Goldwyn-Mayer
56. "My Wicked, Wicked Ways" author Flynn
57. Ralph of "The Waltons"
59. Percolate
61. Columbus's birthplace
63. Industrial-strength air?
64. Compensates
67. Thanksgiving, e.g.: Abbr.
69. Mid-6th-century date
70. Former Mideast alliance
71. Be a Nosy Parker

Solution on page 343

Challenging 41

ACROSS

1. "Wham!"
6. Allegheny Mts. state
9. Ear related
14. Nitrogen compound
15. Hotel annex?
16. Area of land
17. Fabricators
18. Insurrectionist Turner
19. Like lions
20. Sicilian city
21. Aptly named fruit
22. Builder of the Reo
23. Pizazz
25. Conscription org.
27. Spring bloom
30. In conflict
35. U.S.S.R. successor
38. It's broken at mixers
40. Uplift
41. Intense
43. "Suspicion" studio
44. David's verse
45. TV's Griffin
46. Put the pressure on
48. ___ Plaines
49. Black Sea city
51. Go around
53. Triangle part: Abbr.
55. Layers
58. "Crouching Tiger, Hidden Dragon" setting
61. Cousin of a mandolin
64. Porter topper
66. Swamp thing
67. AP rival
68. Sheikdom of song
69. Upholstery fabric
70. Start of Julius III's papacy
71. Polished off
72. "___ Dream" ("Lohengrin" piece)
73. Ante body?
74. Booby trap

DOWN

1. Long green
2. PABA part
3. Bench site
4. Cloverleaf part
5. Bentley of "American Beauty"
6. Hockey position
7. Wiener schnitzel meat
8. Cager Gilmore
9. No more than
10. Orenburg's river
11. Cape Town cash
12. Air force heroes
13. Inc., in Ipswich
21. "Looks like trouble!"
24. Fountain of jazz
26. Oil can letters
28. "Quo Vadis" role
29. "Omigosh!"
31. Delivery docs
32. Couple
33. Welfare, with "the"
34. Sylvia of "The World of Suzie Wong"
35. GI wear, for short
36. Bumped off
37. "Of course!"
39. Stopper
42. Remote targets
44. "Frasier" actress Gilpin
46. Islet
47. Give as an example
50. English counties
52. Mideast capital
54. Roly-poly
56. Lariat
57. Civil War weapon
58. Dickens's pen?
59. Big name in elevators
60. Gaucho's gadget
62. Beehive, e.g.
63. Feature of the earth
65. Force unit
66. Co. that merged with Bell Atlantic
68. JFK's UN ambassador

Solution on page 343

Challenging 42

ACROSS

1. Little fight
6. Edible root
10. "Nova" network
13. Aerodynamic
14. Not "fer"
15. Mars: prefix
16. Interminably
17. Breakfast area
18. New Jersey city
19. Does wrong
20. Team VIP: Abbr.
21. Sideshow spiel
23. Female spider's creation
26. Indian Ocean vessel
27. Prison in a Johnny Cash song
30. Skyline obscurer
32. Boors
33. A la King?
35. Fundamentals
39. Auto loan letters
40. Winter expense
43. Bumper sticker letters
44. Tut's kin?
46. Smooch
47. Scottish estate owner
49. Burg
51. Second smallest of seven
52. Cassandra, e.g.
54. Gelcap alternative
57. Sportscaster Dick
59. Cool, in slang
60. Group of prayers
64. Earth sci.
65. Car bar
67. Name in wines
68. Not well
69. Become frayed
70. ___ nothing
71. Hearst kidnap grp.
72. Barbra's "A Star is Born" costar
73. 1944 battle site

DOWN

1. IRS I.D.s
2. Race in "The Time Machine"
3. Harry Potter, e.g.
4. Stretched to the limit
5. Gave the go-ahead
6. Distinctive flavors
7. Ancient assembly area
8. Brazilian city, familiarly
9. Working in a mess
10. Prefix with type
11. Moisten
12. Evening, to Yves
15. Gibson of tennis
20. "The Wizard of Oz" studio
22. Cutting tool
24. "Gee whiz!"
25. Comedian Rock
27. Out of fizz
28. "My bad!"
29. Hide in the shadows
31. "Atlas Shrugged" author Rand
33. Ill-fed
34. Extra NBA periods
36. Scott of "Happy Days"
37. Complain
38. "Smooth Operator" singer
41. "Charlotte's Web" monogram
42. Collagist's need
45. Hard
48. Gallery event
50. Hart Trophy winner, 1970–72
51. Brownie
52. Fishhook fastener
53. African virus
55. He lost to Dwight
56. Round units
57. Protection: Var.
58. Rubberneck
61. ___ May Clampett
62. Flow stopper
63. Shredded
66. Gen ___
67. "For Me and My ___"

Solution on page 343

Challenging 43

ACROSS
1. Battle of Britain grp.
4. With the bow, to a violinist
8. Tombstone brothers
13. Silent auction site
15. Snort
16. Peace Nobelist Root
17. Rhine tributary
18. Lodge letters
19. Went ballistic
20. Cold spell
22. Populous area
24. Big mouths
25. Central point
26. Butt of jokes
28. Brit's "Baloney!"
30. Good-for-nothing
34. Pass
37. Test the weight of
40. Massenet opera
41. Tiny Tim's instrument, for short
42. Blatant deception
44. "___ rang?"
45. Bring up the rear
47. Let go
48. Shrill barks
49. Pan-fries
51. John or Paul
53. "Three's Company" actress
56. "Cheers" barmaid
60. Medieval chest
63. Emma player in "The Avengers"
64. Fishing spot
65. Empire
67. Melville novel set in Tahiti
69. "Cheers" regular
70. At full speed
71. Stats for Alex Rodriguez
72. Part of the Hindu trinity
73. Sal of "Giant"
74. Sci-fi sage
75. PC linkup

DOWN
1. Focus again
2. Old adders
3. Made out
4. Novelist Prevost
5. Good name, briefly
6. Pull
7. New Mexico county
8. Eternally, in poetry
9. City on San Francisco Bay
10. Baltic port
11. "Thank goodness!"
12. Brewski
14. Likely to rise?
21. 1964 Ronny & the Daytonas hit
23. Short cut
26. Bundle
27. Monopoly, e.g.
29. "Quiet down!"
31. "Only Time" singer
32. Gunk
33. Serengeti herd
34. Fortitude
35. Creole vegetable
36. Sweetheart
38. Calendar abbr.
39. Infield protectors
42. Laine of jazz
43. ___ gratias
46. "I've been framed!"
48. Pines
50. Home of the Mustangs
52. Agt.'s cut
54. Atlanta university
55. Sly guy?
57. Lubricate anew
58. Caterpillar, for one
59. Mideast capital
60. Saroyan's "My Name is ___"
61. Do followers
62. "The Godfather" actor
64. Cub with a club
66. 6, on a phone
68. Suffix with human

Solution on page 344

Challenging 44

ACROSS
1. 1989 Literature Nobelist
5. Peddle
9. Put forward
14. Of grandparents
15. Ruthless boss
16. Cremona artisan
17. Cold coating
18. VHS alternative, once
19. Any "Seinfeld," now
20. Nonstop
22. Brilliant finish?
24. Sephia maker
25. Clan cloth
26. ___ oil (varnish ingredient)
28. Tuscan city
31. Interference
35. Bump
38. Body build
40. Incredible bargain
41. Egg
43. Whiskey chaser?
45. Mrs. Peel of "The Avengers"
46. Old Apple computers
48. Line of cliffs
50. Bobby's wife on "Dallas"
51. Japanese mat
53. Intense hatred
55. Approach, with "for"
57. Conundrum
61. Chow mein additive
64. Cath., e.g.
65. Menu heading
66. Young hog
68. Political suffix
70. "Leave ___ Beaver"
71. Pig out
72. Atahualpa, for one
73. Gazillions
74. Go over the limit?
75. Wonka's creator
76. Synthesizer man

DOWN
1. Proofreader's mark
2. 1980 Tony winner
3. Debussy work
4. They may be red
5. "Carmen" highlight
6. Leap for Lipinski
7. Dewy
8. Deadly snake
9. Brings up
10. Cockney's abode
11. Cutty ___
12. Needle holder
13. Merrill of "Butterfield 8"
21. Babe in the woods
23. Fraternity letters
27. Golden ___
29. Bothers
30. Exxon rival
32. Fill-in
33. Paul Simon's "___ Rock"
34. Chowder chunk
35. Shake up
36. Converse competitor
37. Fall shade
39. "Crikey!"
42. "Just the facts, ___"
44. Monopoly avenue
47. Hurt
49. Fourth down option
52. "I like ___"
54. Sister of Moses
56. 1961 Charlton Heston role
58. Irk
59. Copycat's words
60. "With ___ in My Heart"
61. E-mail: Abbr.
62. Galleria unit
63. "An Inconvenient Truth" star
65. "___ Dawn I Die" (Cagney/Raft flick)
67. Bronze, for one
69. Biology class abbr.

Solution on page 344

Challenging 45

ACROSS

1. Kind of ray
6. Italian port
10. Baby bouncer
14. Construction girder
15. "___ a traveler from an antique land": "Ozymandias"
16. Crossing point
17. Glove fabric
18. Short cuts
19. Mass. neighbor
20. Close by
22. Sharp as a tack
24. Actress Vardalos of "My Big Fat Greek Wedding"
25. April 13, e.g.
27. Contract parts
29. "Min and Bill" Oscar winner
33. Cone bearer
34. In the flesh
35. Nonclerical
37. Fix firmly
41. "Rocky ___"
42. Intensified, as sound
44. Soccer phenom Freddy
45. Muslim faith
48. Log-burning time
49. M.I.T. grad: Abbr.
50. Compensation
52. Like the Owl and the Pussycat's boat
54. Not so dense
58. Sound of an exploding cigar
59. Fireplace shelf
60. Salon creation
62. MASH procedure
66. Norse saint
68. Go bad, in a way
70. Inflame
71. "Little Caesar" role
72. Forever's partner
73. Physicist Ohm
74. Work like a dog
75. Tidings
76. Barely beats

DOWN

1. River to the Colorado
2. "This won't hurt ___!"
3. Come together
4. The blahs
5. Makes right
6. Layette item
7. Frenziedly
8. Renaissance instrument
9. What "ipso" means
10. Fast-food inits.
11. High times?
12. "My Three Sons" son
13. Author Ferber and others
21. Perry's secretary
23. Depilatory name
26. Sordid
28. Altdorf's canton
29. Sixth-century date
30. Social reformer Jacob
31. Axis of ___
32. Tear to shreds
36. VIP
38. Wind indicator
39. Add a fringe to
40. Go sour
43. Handed out
46. 0% ___
47. Like some Fr. nouns
49. Regally attired
51. Navy clerk
53. Mustang holder
54. Easily provoked
55. Salk's conquest
56. Old adders
57. ___ Janeiro
61. Diamond defect
63. Awestruck
64. "Breathless" star
65. There are 10 million in a joule
67. Tennessee athlete
69. Bad start?

Solution on page 344

Challenging 46

ACROSS
1. Sing, so to speak
5. Had a bawl
9. Dance, slangily
13. "Dream Children" essayist
14. ___ breve (music marking)
15. Blabbermouth
16. The Crimson Tide
17. Four-time Indy 500 winner
18. "Cats" poet
19. Ragtime dance
21. Actress Dahl
23. Bean holder
24. Small songbird
26. "America's Next Top Model" airer
27. Fraternity letters
28. Aachen article
30. River in Spain
34. Summits
37. Retirement plan name
39. Way over there
40. Fowl pole
41. E-mail address ending
42. Register
44. City in Kyrgyzstan
45. Some hospital procedures
47. McDowall of "Planet of the Apes"
48. Puff
50. "That's ___-brainer"
51. Fresh
52. Embassy fig.
54. Rare bills
56. "Fat chance!"
59. Most artful
62. Nowadays
64. Handwriting feature
65. Hangover?
67. Saintly
68. Aggressive, personalitywise
69. Small merganser
70. "Coming of Age in Samoa" author
71. Funny Foxx
72. ___ de combat
73. Supermodel Banks

DOWN
1. Jazz genre
2. The plain in Spain
3. Intended
4. Meadow sounds
5. Thin treats
6. Bolt to bond
7. Layer
8. "Bye-bye!"
9. Moon of Saturn
10. "Come ___"
11. Native Oklahoman
12. ___ Tuesday (Mardi Gras)
15. Canine cry
20. Parts of some plots
22. Crosspiece
25. Is unobliged to
27. Ballot marks
29. Chits
31. Polar explorer
32. Large cross
33. One's partner
34. Get one's ducks in ___
35. "___ fan tutte"
36. Kind of scale
37. Shakespearean actor Edmund
38. Unorthodox thinking
43. "On the double!"
46. Semi parts
49. In distress
51. "Haven't heard a word"
53. Intro to physics?
55. Hesitate
56. Bunk
57. Bellowing
58. Ibsen's Gabler
59. Roy Rogers's real last name
60. "Dragnet" org.
61. New Age composer John
63. Bus. heads
64. The Bosporus, e.g.: Abbr.
66. Latin lover's word

Solution on page 344

Challenging 47

ACROSS

1. Shirt brand
5. "Nah!"
9. Stowe character
14. Hailer's cry
15. El ___ (weather phenomenon)
16. Draw out
17. Got a move on
18. Augustus' god
19. Absorb
20. Suffix with direct
21. Minn. neighbor
22. Four of a kind
24. Tube
26. Ms. alternative
27. Apollo's creator
29. A.C. measure
30. Pa. nuke plant
33. Bridge authority Charles
36. A sib
38. Like some situations
40. Board member, for short
41. Barnyard sound
42. Milieu for Lemieux
43. Is offensive, in a way
45. Breakfast drinks, for short
46. Crackers
47. Having one flat, musically
48. Place
50. Rock's Jethro ___
52. Diamond great Hodges
53. "Forget about it!"
57. Scheduled
60. Bird's beak
61. Fu-___ (legendary Chinese sage)
62. Scarlett's third
63. Concerto, e.g.
65. Bomb
66. "Taras Bulba" author
67. Sham
68. Itchy feet, say
69. Talked a blue streak?
70. Bend
71. Sew up

DOWN

1. "Some Like ___"
2. Mobutu's land
3. Daisy variety
4. Carried out
5. Drawers
6. Hastens
7. Burma's first prime minister
8. Parasite's home
9. Trial
10. Air freshener targets
11. Metamorphosis stage
12. Move quickly, as clouds
13. Slangy affirmative
21. Detach, in a way
23. 911 respondent
25. Sweater style
28. Head monk
29. Toot one's own horn
30. Tease
31. In perfect condition
32. Black
33. Spice Girl Halliwell
34. Beasts of burden
35. Natural barrier
37. Rule, in India
39. Face-to-face exams
44. Saliva
46. Amorphous mass
49. Glob add-on
51. Like some salons
52. Swamp thing
54. Midway alternative
55. "It's ___ of the times"
56. In heaps
57. Come in third
58. Block brand
59. Tip, as a hat
60. Microwave
62. Some NFLers
64. Bud
65. Giant word

Solution on page 344

Challenging 48

ACROSS
1. "Try this!"
6. "And ___ thou slain the Jabberwock?"
10. Chesterfield, e.g.
14. Aspirin targets
15. Ottoman bigwig
16. Take ___ (snooze)
17. Zagreb native
18. Cambodian capital
19. Catches
20. Smarts
22. Game piece
23. Some are slippery
24. Some drums
26. Calif. barrio locale
29. Long operatic solo
31. "Monty Python" airer
32. Old comic actress ___ Janis
34. Pass
38. Fiber source
40. Emits coherent light
42. Half court game?
43. Suppressed
45. Butter up?
47. Clothing tag abbr.
48. Runway walker
50. Philippine port
52. Like federal tax laws
55. Bring in
56. Actor Frobe
57. Physical part
63. Art school subj.
64. Chain with stacks
65. Clemson athlete
66. "Must be something ___"
67. Bubbly drink
68. Japanese porcelain
69. D'back, e.g.
70. Parker of "South Park"
71. Poem division

DOWN
1. Dash gauge
2. Phobia starter
3. Toots in a restaurant
4. Afternoon service
5. Parsons of "Bonnie and Clyde"
6. Fast runners
7. Not "fer"
8. The Beatles' "___ Leaving Home"
9. "Honor Thy Father" author
10. Hot wind
11. Live, in a TV studio
12. It ends in a point
13. Basilica parts
21. Like some talk
25. Austin-to-Dallas dir.
26. Fades away
27. Magician's start
28. "Beat it!"
29. Agave fiber
30. So-so grades
33. Kemo ___
35. Others, to Ovid
36. Director Reiner
37. Novice: Var.
39. "Don't sweat it"
41. Farm enclosures
44. "Smoking or ___?"
46. Flexible
49. Cease
51. Ideals
52. "Not ___!"
53. Kidney-related
54. Bucket of bolts
55. Make good on
58. God with a hammer
59. Depended (on)
60. Richard of "A Summer Place"
61. Spanish muralist
62. Blink-182, e.g.

Solution on page 344

Challenging 49

ACROSS
1. Clear
4. Recipe amount
8. Supermarket section
13. Times to call, in ads
15. Capital of Samoa
16. Carpi connectors
17. Yachter's woe
18. Field of honor event
19. Sink
20. Iroquoian tribe
22. Pampering, briefly
24. Gets into
25. Foul
26. Hit the roof
28. Lend a hand
30. Chinese discipline
34. "Wait a ___!"
37. Rips off
40. Emasculate
41. Nigerian tribesman
42. Pesky fliers
44. Leftover bit
45. Spin doctor
48. Single-masted vessel
50. "Car Talk" airer
51. Cornhusker rival
53. Birds in barns
55. Approached
58. Seat of Marion County, Fla.
62. Go on the lam
65. Brooder?
66. Less fresh
67. Holiday visitors
69. Frog spit, for example
71. Bit of Frost?
72. Formal rulings
73. Paint crudely
74. Automaker Ferrari

75. Chelmsford's county
76. In ___ (as found)
77. Long-jawed fish

DOWN
1. Spy work, for short
2. A former Mrs. Trump
3. Strikes out
4. Arp's art movement
5. Kwik-E-Mart proprietor on "The Simpsons"
6. Luis's lucky number
7. Actress Berry
8. Name
9. Legendary rubber
10. Preceder of many words?
11. Come down
12. Deep desires
14. Common alias

21. Colors
23. PC component
26. Reaches over
27. ___ Claire, Wis.
29. Cabin component
31. "Follow me!"
32. Kind of seal
33. Foreword: Abbr.
34. Drinks a little
35. Rain in Spain collector
36. "It's Impossible" crooner
38. Carrier to Seoul
39. Got up
43. Piglet's mother
46. One of the original Mouseketeers
47. Born, in bios
49. Garden area
52. "Go, team!"

54. Suffix with land or sea
56. Interprets
57. Chou ___
59. Beside
60. Gibbons of TV
61. Cause of knight sweats?
62. Screenplay direction
63. Pitcher Tiant
64. Env. contents
66. "Elephant Boy" star
68. Kenny G's instrument
70. Kind of instinct

Solution on page 345

Challenging 50

ACROSS
1. Panama and porkpie
5. Addis ___
10. Helgenberger of "CSI"
14. Seuss's "Horton Hears ___"
15. Fray
16. "Aba ___ Honeymoon"
17. Catch but good
18. Hobbit's home
19. Leveler
20. Go-getter
22. Lower
24. Armed forces VIP
26. Govt. lender
27. Fashions
30. Panama, e.g.
32. Manchurian border river
36. Even if, briefly
37. Compared to
39. Presidential middle name
41. Dict. offerings
43. "SNL" alum Cheri
45. Burst of wind
46. Lessee
48. Sisters
50. Like Gen. Powell
51. Plant with bell-shaped flowers
52. ___ Croix, Que.
53. A long time
55. "The Simpsons" bartender
57. Bears' lairs
59. Is faithful
63. "___ Weapon"
67. Athens's home
68. Hokey
70. Prefix with spherical
71. Inside info
72. Jam ingredients
73. Final, e.g.

74. Phoenician port
75. Oater transport
76. Big Indian

DOWN
1. Bridge holding
2. Off
3. Watered down
4. Comfort giver
5. Bad lighting?
6. "Humph!"
7. Dedicated
8. Forlorn
9. First Hebrew letter
10. Store stock: Abbr.
11. Sighs of relief
12. Stadium stats
13. School of whales
21. Atomizer's output

23. "Big Mouth" Martha
25. Chew the fat
27. ___ Helens
28. "Now I remember!"
29. "Holy Sonnets" poet
31. With regard to
33. Calc. prerequisite
34. 1944 Preminger classic
35. Big name at Indy
38. All the rage
39. Cacophony
40. Baseball's Ed and Mel
42. Give in to gravity
44. Had second thoughts about
47. Iditarod destination
49. New Year's Eve word
52. Show to the door
54. Purim honoree

56. SeaWorld attractions
58. "Family Ties" mother
59. Call to a mate
60. New Look designer
61. Clinton's birthplace
62. Lady of Sp.
64. Prefix with -gon
65. Key of Beethoven's Symphony No. 7: Abbr.
66. Bean town?
67. Go with, with "for"
69. Creamy quaff

Solution on page 345

Challenging 51

ACROSS
1. They may provide relief
5. Skins
10. "Hamlet" has five
14. Shrek, e.g.
15. Bar, at the bar
16. "Later!"
17. Den din
18. ___ incognita
19. "Handy" one
20. Lead on
22. Breaks away
24. Rhine feeder
26. 1950s political inits.
27. In a fitting way
30. Check fig.
32. Two-___ sloth
36. Calendar abbr.
37. Except for
39. Woman's shoe style
41. "Twittering Machine" artist
43. "The Second Coming" poet
45. ___ Cynwyd, Pa.
46. Virgil hero
48. Plane, e.g.
50. Private eye, slangily
51. Blowgun missile
52. "Atlas Shrugged" author Rand
53. Notched, as a leaf
55. Sales slip: abbr.
57. "Anything ___?"
59. Former capital of Kazakhstan
63. In addition
67. Racer Luyendyk
68. Perfumer Nina
70. ___-tat
71. Is prone

72. Detective Pinkerton
73. "___ out?"
74. Hires competition
75. Hose shade
76. Lunar plain

DOWN
1. "Encore!"
2. Stravinsky ballet
3. Backside, slangily
4. Kind of number
5. Fizzle, with "out"
6. "-speak"
7. U.S.PS pieces
8. Pawed
9. Elbowroom
10. Sch.
11. French film
12. Smidgens

13. ___ sauce
21. Islets
23. Garage figs.
25. Gutter location
27. Aleutian island
28. Whimpered
29. Singer ___ Marie
31. Substantial
33. Gambling site, briefly
34. Bard's inspiration
35. Valleys
38. Cries of regret
39. Chinese menu general
40. Act the expectant father
42. Bard's "always"
44. Muscular fitness
47. Blade brand
49. Out of concern that
52. "Scourge of God"

54. Cut over
56. Diamond measure
58. Frankie who sang "Moonlight Gambler"
59. "Mi chiamano Mimi," e.g.
60. Wasn't straight
61. Bungle, with "up"
62. Legal rights org.
64. Tennis star Mandlikova
65. Suffix with fabric
66. Gross minus net, to a trucker
67. City council rep.
69. Ceiling

Solution on page 345

Challenging 52

ACROSS

1. North Sea feeder
5. Figure skater Thomas
9. "The Rum ___ Tugger" ("Cats" tune)
12. Some spies
14. Biblical name meaning "hairy"
15. First-class
16. Cousin of a raccoon
17. Utmost extent
19. Blank filler: abbr.
20. Some brews
22. Districts
23. Shop worker
25. Wrinkle
26. "Beats me"
28. Expunge
29. Put through a sieve
30. Gave birth in a stable
32. D.J.'s stack
33. Bullwinkle foe
34. Horror director Craven
37. Touches up
39. Sparkle
41. Fervid
43. Symbol of discipline
44. Undertakes
45. Lazy
47. Rainbowlike
48. Works the land
49. The Crystals' "___ a Rebel"
52. Draw on a board
54. Miss America topper
56. Spare parts?
57. The Untouchables, e.g.
58. Descendant
59. Outer: prefix
60. Hawk
61. Bear with us at night

DOWN

1. Disco standard
2. Anon
3. Some bands
4. Like Gen. Schwarzkopf
5. Al ___ (firm)
6. $C_4H_8O_2$, e.g.
7. Scornful cries
8. Birth control option, briefly
9. Pawed
10. Discomfort
11. Reagan attorney general
13. Stored, as fodder
15. Concurred
18. Country/rock singer Steve
21. Pier grp.
24. "To Autumn," e.g.
25. Animation frames
26. AEC successor
27. Suffix with human
28. Oration station
30. Helvetica, for one
31. Old California fort
33. Propensity
34. Terrier type
35. Ambient music pioneer
36. Benchmark: Abbr.
37. Detroit duds
38. Gettysburg general
39. Some trick-or-treaters
40. "___ Liaisons Dangereuses"
41. Of a main line
42. Take back
43. Allen of "Home Improvement"
44. Quebec peninsula
45. Grainy, in a way
46. Vogue
48. Notability
50. Oscar Wilde poem "The Garden of ___"
51. Yemen's capital
53. "Punk'd" airer
55. Hosp. area

Solution on page 345

Challenging 53

ACROSS

1. White oak
6. Sean Connery, e.g.
10. Closing passage
14. Harvard, Yale, Brown, etc.
15. Bowser's bowlful
16. Crew equipment
17. Test versions
18. Clubs, e.g.
19. "SNL" offering
20. Look for again
22. Not so nice
24. 8 x 10, say: abbr.
25. Oscar ___ Hoya
26. Tokyo, once
27. Convenes
30. Kramden laugh syllable
32. Dine
34. The ___-i-noor diamond
35. Seeing red
37. Author Lofts
41. Send, in a way
43. Wray of "King Kong"
44. "Be-Bop-___" (Gene Vincent hit)
45. Sees socially
46. "1776" role
48. "Rugrats" dad
49. Small island
51. Child-care writer LeShan
52. Marker
53. Hospital unit
56. Remarked
58. "___-ching!"
60. "Friends" actress
62. Raised
65. Apple's apple, e.g.
66. Personal prefix
68. It won't keep you up
70. "A Chapter on Ears" essayist
71. Prefix meaning "Chinese"
72. Start a point
73. File's partner
74. Cripple
75. More faithful

DOWN

1. Chest protector?
2. "Back to you"
3. Angler's hope
4. Charters
5. Big Bertha's birthplace
6. N. Dak. neighbor
7. Billy the Kid portrayer Gulager
8. Imagine
9. Comes to
10. How much to pay
11. Comic actor Jack
12. Cut's partner
13. Nolan Ryan, notably
21. Designed for all grades
23. Steamy spots
25. Was terrified by
27. Agenda, informally
28. Seat of Allen County, Kansas
29. "Take ___!"
31. Italian sports car, briefly
33. Campaigner, for short
35. Put up a fight
36. Couple
38. Hurry
39. Prefix with meter
40. ___ monde (high society)
42. 1773 jetsam
47. Defensive spray
50. Lao-tzu's system
52. Calling
53. Farm bundler
54. ___ Gay
55. Cook's exhortation
57. Home to more than a billion
59. Biblical verb
61. Drench
62. Capacity
63. Alternative to nude
64. Humorist Barry
67. Ristorante suffix
69. Chemin de ___

Solution on page 345

Challenging 54

ACROSS

1. Thesis defense, often
5. Smell ___
9. Haile Selassie worshiper
14. Grabber's cry
15. Crunchy munchie
16. "Save me ___"
17. Barbara of "Mission: Impossible"
18. Service expert?
19. Too much, in music
20. "Entertaining Mr. ___" (Joe Orton play)
22. French soul
24. Turn down, as lights
25. Wetland flora
27. Surgery ctrs.
29. "Private Parts" author
31. "___ a pity"
33. First Hebrew letter: var.
37. "Am ___ believe . . . ?"
38. Some pitchers
40. Attack ad, maybe
41. "Now you ___, now . . ."
43. Airport abbr.
44. Break off
45. Draw ___ in the sand
46. "Touched by an Angel" co-star
48. Avg.
49. Clark of the Daily Planet
50. ___-mo (instant replay feature)
51. Schools for engrs.
53. Carry-___ (small pieces of luggage)
55. Nick name?
57. Little shaver
60. ___ grass
62. Dog star
65. The last Oldsmobile made
67. ___ were
69. "Eh"
71. Where to see "The Last Supper"
72. "Song of the South" title
73. Not exo-
74. English Channel feeder
75. Arab capital
76. Heedless

DOWN

1. Fed. fiscal agency
2. Narrow inlets
3. Deep blue
4. "The Raven" maiden
5. Finished
6. Fought the clock
7. The Red Baron, for one
8. When said three times, a WW II film
9. Critic, at times
10. ___ rule
11. E-mail, say
12. Jacques of "Mon Oncle"
13. Bit to split
21. Freshen
23. Criminal patterns, for short
26. Sound investments?
28. "___ difference!"
29. Inscribed stone
30. Front wheel alignment
32. Apropos of
34. Most trifling
35. Positions for Goren
36. Mr. Rogers
37. Writer Dinesen
39. Clayey deposit
40. Gets wind of
42. A fan of
47. "Ol' Blue Eyes"
50. F.I.C.A. funds it
52. Dissed, in a way
54. Everybody's opposite
56. "Star Trek" extra
57. Skedaddles
58. What George couldn't tell
59. Hero's place
61. Notebook projections
63. "The Last Days of Pompeii" heroine
64. Are, in Argentina
66. Appeared in print
68. Mme., in Madrid
70. Gut reaction?

Solution on page 345

Challenging 55

ACROSS

1. Do nothing
5. Q-U connection
8. Hosiery mishaps
13. "I get it now"
14. Sympathetic sounds
15. Perfectly
16. Drop off
18. Ultimate goal
19. Charlemagne's realm: Abbr.
20. Quite a hgt.
21. Oil, in a way
22. Hosts
24. Contrite
25. Make sense, with "up"
26. Cajun staple
27. Tach letters
30. Blue-pencils
33. Spacewalks, to NASA
34. Astronomical effect
35. IQ test pioneer
36. "1-2-3" singer Barry
37. Yankovic parody
38. ___-deucy
39. Clue
40. Strike zone boundary
41. "Close to the Edge" band
42. Feedbag feed
43. "Gloria in excelsis ___"
44. Black
46. Beethoven's Symphony No. 3
49. Some are free
50. Debtor's letters
51. Naval VIP
53. Chars
54. Feeler
56. Waylay
57. Quiche, e.g.
58. "A Boy Named Sue" writer Silverstein
59. Hammer parts
60. Floors, briefly
61. Bovine bunch

DOWN

1. It may get plastered
2. "Butterfield 8" author
3. Inquisitive one
4. Adversary
5. Mouthed off
6. Some trumpeters
7. 1/6 fl. oz.
8. State bordering Arizona
9. Lowest point
10. Be that as it may
11. Cabbage
12. Partner of poivre
15. Choir section
17. Surrounded by
21. Obliquely
23. Pirate's pal
26. Pizza places
28. Ballerina's bend
29. Bits of wit
30. Auction site
31. They're spotted in casinos
32. Basically
33. Aristocrats
34. Le Duc Tho's capital
37. Scrape together
39. Most strapping
42. Haunt
43. They don't work
45. About 1% of the atmosphere
46. Kids' song refrain
47. Secret store
48. Freud contemporary Alfred
49. Gambling, e.g.
52. Canasta combo
53. Chucklehead
54. Toll rd.
55. Bat material

Solution on page 346

Challenging 56

ACROSS

1. Big pig
5. Start of a prayer
9. "His Master's Voice" initials
12. Bond trader's phrase
14. ___ Mawr
15. Declined
16. Dewy-eyed
17. Amontillado holder
18. Common rhyme scheme
19. "Gunsmoke" actor
21. Hit CBS drama
22. Author Grey
23. Blockhead
24. Cry of eagerness
26. Come out
28. Identical
29. Capote, briefly
30. Final Four gp.
33. Bk. after Nehemiah
35. Checks out the stars
40. Frau's partner
41. Torn apart
43. "To Renew America" author Gingrich
44. Places to paint
46. "The Persistence of Memory" painter
47. Hang on to
48. Co. that merged with Bell Atlantic
50. Kind of engr.
52. Shape up
56. Phone
57. Get-up-and-go
60. Jotted reminder
61. ET craft
63. Exotic vacation
65. ___ arms
66. Not busy
68. German wine valley
69. Pealed
70. Dirty look
71. The Trojans, for short
72. "Alice" spin-off
73. Current event?
74. Rich deposit

DOWN

1. Far from fresh
2. Hokkaido port
3. Mimicry
4. **** review
5. "ER" network
6. Spinachlike plant
7. "Swiss Family Robinson" author
8. Blacker
9. Concrete reinforcer
10. Trolley sound
11. "A Delicate Balance" playwright
13. Plant anew
15. Discomfit
20. Less forward
25. Like some kicks
27. Kisser
28. Lip-puckering
29. Louise's partner
30. Blues group, for short
31. Biz biggie
32. Declaration of puppy love?
34. Dam-building agcy.
36. Symbol of life
37. #26 of 26
38. "Concentration" pronoun
39. 500 letters?
42. Physicist Bohr
45. Pepper, for one
49. Muss up
51. Shuts (up)
52. Blue cartoon character
53. Sherpa's home
54. Acid in proteins
55. Pioneering video game
56. Whispered sweet nothings
57. Explorer Balboa
58. "___ you loud and clear!"
59. ___ Lacs, Minn.
62. Skedaddled
64. April honoree
67. Like some humor

Solution on page 346

Challenging 57

ACROSS

1. Play thing
5. Impulses
10. Iodine source
14. Akebono's sport
15. Avignon's river
16. Of the hipbone: Prefix
17. Sacred bird of Egypt
18. Actor Michael
19. Apply spin to
20. Take hold
22. Hires
24. 1 on the Mohs scale
27. Burns role
28. Diamond honor
31. Booze
33. Like LAX
37. Crude, e.g.
38. Cast
39. Looked searchingly
41. Brightly colored fish
43. Say "Li'l Abner," say
45. Fuss over, with "on"
46. "La Loge" painter
48. Ho Chi ___
50. "Israfel" writer
51. Comedian Foxx
52. Drop off
53. 30, in the newsroom
54. Circus cries
56. Teen hangout
58. Own
62. Spiritual leaders
66. Vincent Lopez theme song
67. Flea-bitten
70. Copier company
71. Caramel-topped dessert
72. Sp. misses
73. Totally botch
74. "Metropolis" director Fritz
75. ___ alcohol
76. Largest human organ

DOWN

1. Penultimate Greek letters
2. Bumpkin
3. Cut out
4. Propose
5. Ashes holder
6. Campus letter
7. Joint problem
8. Tee off
9. Omega rival
10. Lip service?
11. Nevada city
12. Mortgage, e.g.
13. "Batman" sound effect
21. Rambler maker
23. She plays Carmela on "The Sopranos"
25. Popular a.m. host
26. Weights rep
28. Drop anchor
29. Malicious one
30. Smoother
32. Scale
34. Beatty of "Deliverance"
35. Figure of speech
36. Acknowledge
39. Tetra- plus one
40. Home paper
42. Coal carrier
44. Circle meas.
47. Altar exchanges
49. War, to Sherman
52. Put forward
55. "Siddhartha" author
57. Innocent ones
58. Negri of silents
59. "The Good Earth" heroine
60. Caroled
61. Fourth man
63. Draw out
64. French possessive
65. Cut
66. Eagles' org.
68. Calendar box
69. Designer inits.

Solution on page 346

Challenging 58

ACROSS

1. Cold War threat
6. Joker, e.g.
10. Fairbanks-to-Anchorage dir.
13. "Family Matters" nerd
14. Chinese gelatin
15. "___ boy!"
16. Blockade
17. Ancient alphabetic symbol
18. Hip
19. Today, in Tijuana
20. Absent from
22. Best Actor of 2000
23. "Each Dawn ___" (Cagney film)
24. Browns, now
26. Brit's exam
29. Driller's deg.
30. Importunes
31. Wise old heads
35. Friday et al.: Abbr.
39. Life story, for short
40. Play a kazoo
41. Writer Santha Rama ___
42. "___ does it"
44. "This ___ a drill!"
46. Karaoke need
47. "Think" sloganeer
49. Keynoted
51. Minimally
55. Cel character
56. Hunky-dory
57. Shills for, e.g.
59. G.I. rank
62. Hang fire
63. Turner and Eisenhower
64. 10 on a scale of 1 to 10
66. Sea birds
67. Ernie's pal
68. Actress Lords
69. Napoleonic marshal
70. "Cope Book" aunt
71. Give an invitation for

DOWN

1. Quiet
2. Pizazz
3. ___-doke
4. Actress Tilly
5. Zinc sulfide
6. Bill of fare
7. Iago contents
8. Cost
9. Dr. of rap
10. Barfly's perch
11. Legree's creator
12. Dylan Thomas's home
15. Transversely
21. Olive and linseed products
22. El ___ (Heston role)
23. Hosp. hookups
25. Map lines: Abbr.
26. French clergyman
27. "Star Wars" role
28. Hollywood giants?
32. Checkup sounds
33. Rev
34. Funny Philips
36. Backbone
37. Bit of filming
38. Sought damages from
43. Rates of return
44. AOL exchanges
45. Bender
46. "Holy smokes!"
48. Passbook fig.
50. Bilingual Muppet
51. Forest quaker
52. Shakespearean contraction
53. Comic Bruce
54. Selfish sort
55. Seed coating
58. Road shoulder
59. Reach a high
60. It's the truth
61. Pitcher's prize?
63. "When Will ___ Loved"
65. ER figures

Solution on page 346

Challenging 59

ACROSS

1. Molecule builders
6. "Peter Pan" role
10. Give ___ on the back
14. Suit fabric
15. Runners
16. Drone, e.g.
17. Some like it hot
18. Flaps
19. Court records
20. Montemezzi's "L'amore dei ___ re"
21. Fall guys
23. Charm
25. Mantra sounds
26. "Wheel of Fortune" buy
27. Like some humor
28. They fix locks
32. Fishing, perhaps
33. Drops
34. Ararat lander
35. Half a '60s foursome
40. Jaywalking, e.g.
41. Bonn pronoun
42. Coatrack parts
43. Down provider
45. Adage
46. Mark up, maybe
47. Poet Juana ___ de la Cruz
49. Most miffed
50. "The Joy Luck Club" author
53. "Help!"
54. Whitney and others: Abbr.
55. Some terminals
57. Mason's work
58. It may be direct or indirect: Abbr.
61. Brief moments
62. ". . . to skin ___"
64. "Maybe" musical
66. Green Hornet's sidekick
67. Kind of screen
68. Labors
69. Hindu honorifics
70. Being, to Brutus
71. Rob of "Melrose Place"

DOWN

1. ___ prof.
2. Eye drop?
3. Heraldic border
4. British sports cars
5. Annual foursome
6. High-fives
7. Some are OTC
8. I, to Claudius
9. Dead Sea Scrolls scribe
10. In ___ rush
11. Walked nervously
12. Place of worship
13. Like some goodbyes
22. Early times, for short
24. Half-moon tide
26. Crooked
28. Loudness unit
29. Mine, on the Marne
30. Soprano Jenny
31. Early Nebraskan
32. Met highlights
34. Boobs
36. Rich Little, e.g.
37. Baseball's Rose
38. Turkish generals
39. An NCO
44. Court order?
46. Pink-colored
48. Register button
49. A and B, in D.C.
50. Duties
51. Close by, once
52. Night: Prefix
54. Glossy alternative
56. Brit. decorations
57. Fires
58. "Step ___!"
59. Ill humor
60. Boxer Willard
63. U.S.S.R. successor
65. Dissenting votes

Solution on page 346

Challenging 60

ACROSS

1. Wrigley Field player
4. They may be checked
8. Cashless deal
12. Car loan figs.
14. Former FBI chief
15. Like some traffic
16. Bit of choreography
17. Dweeb
18. Nectar flavor
19. 1976 uprising site
21. Diplomat's quest
23. Give info to
26. Dorothy Parker quality
27. DNA half
30. Poet laureate before Southey
32. Plot again
36. Fit to ___
37. Break away
39. She was June in "Henry & June"
40. Ewe, for one
41. Violinist Jean-___ Ponty
42. Ben-Gurion Airport city
43. Loire laugh
44. Atmospheric prefix
45. Like our numerals
47. Stereo knob
48. Clandestine meeting
50. Runner Sebastian
51. Like some alarms
52. Prefix with flop or plop
54. Reaction to bad news
56. Crown
60. Properly
64. Boxer Oscar de la ___
65. Nape drape
68. Go to and fro
69. Scott Turow title
70. Lies against
71. Prince, e.g.
72. Bridge option
73. "Swiss Family Robinson" author
74. Big D.C. lobby

DOWN

1. Singing Mama
2. As many as
3. Cook up
4. A sib
5. D.D.E. opponent
6. Turned right
7. Nag
8. Fla. vacation spot
9. A question of timing
10. Smell ___
11. Chaste
13. Mintage
14. Arctic ice
20. Formal wear, informally
22. Bushed
24. Medicinal syrup
25. First U.S. capital
27. Laces into
28. Aromatic solvent
29. Cautious
31. Harder to grasp
33. Piece of cave art
34. Not quite right
35. No longer in
37. Big ___
38. "What's up, ___?"
41. Grow dark
46. Fen
47. Cast out
49. Toasts
51. "___ out!"
53. Further shorten, maybe
55. Bozos
56. Karate move
57. Geraldine Chaplin's mother
58. Dark loaves
59. National frozen dessert chain
61. Singer Stefani
62. Minuscule margin
63. Supermodel Banks
66. Danube locale: Abbr.
67. Amendments 1–10 subj.

Solution on page 346

Challenging 61

ACROSS

1. Close with
6. Latin 101 verb
10. Literary collections
14. TV executive Arledge
15. Clematis, for one
16. Come across
17. Cravings
18. Departed
19. Loafer, for one
20. Below, poetically
22. Fats Domino's real first name
24. Prep exam, for short
26. Celtic sea god
27. Application datum: Abbr.
28. Bird shelter
31. Floral ring
33. Rocker Ocasek
35. Assayer's specimen
36. Nixon commerce secretary Maurice
38. Activate
42. Arm of the sea
44. Canterbury can
45. Kite's weapon
46. "Ally McBeal" role
47. Burn a bit
49. "___ Love You"
50. 1040 org.
52. Become prone
53. ___ greens
54. Blocker of "Bonanza"
57. "Apocalypse Now" setting
59. Was present
61. Mined find
63. Realizes
66. Turn over
67. Canticles
70. Simmers
72. This, in Tijuana
73. Saint Philip ___
74. Exhausted
75. Outback critters
76. [I'm shocked!]
77. Little fight

DOWN

1. Schubert's "The ___-King"
2. "Verb," for one
3. Teaspoonful, maybe
4. Not live
5. Rooks' homes
6. Batting stat.
7. Italian possessive
8. Record of one year
9. High schooler
10. Schoolyard retort
11. Some soft drinks
12. Long times
13. "Merry Company" artist
21. Word before "Who goes there?"
23. "Valse ___"
25. Dabbling ducks
28. Mint product
29. Author Sarah ___ Jewett
30. Recount
32. How sardines are often packed
34. Tax preparer, for short
36. Caterer's heater
37. Seattle athlete, for short
39. View from Chamonix
40. "Titanic" heroine
41. Heal, in a way
43. "Y" wearer
48. Duffel filler
51. It's a wrap
53. John or Paul
54. Kitchen gizmo
55. Playground retort
56. Signal, in a way
58. Euripides tragedy
60. Tablelands
62. Modernists
64. Bombard
65. Loretta of "M*A*S*H"
68. Ambulance sites, briefly
69. Nurse
71. ___-Caps (candy brand)

Solution on page 347

Challenging 62

ACROSS

1. "If ___ be so bold . . ."
5. Short snort
9. Garfield feature
14. British title
15. Wool: prefix
16. Companion of Kukla
17. Closely related
18. "Up and ___!"
19. Barbecue offering
20. Daughter of Loki, in Norse myth
21. Cast opening?
22. U.S.SR news agency
23. Euripides tragedy
26. Turn about
29. The Beatles' "And I Love ___"
30. Peace Nobelist Sakharov
34. Innocent ones
37. In-box filler
40. Equi- kin
41. Stewpot, or its contents
42. Lions' prides?
43. Campus VIP
44. Tiny, in Troon
45. Boca ___, Florida
46. Skull cavity
47. Black currant liqueur
49. Liq. measures
50. Chow
52. Seedless raisin
56. Begin a hand
59. Gift-wrapping need
61. Delivery vehicle
62. Discount rack abbr.
64. Colleges, to Aussies
65. South American monkey
66. Actors Hale Sr. and Jr.
67. Confined, with "up"
68. Jack of oaters
69. Temple of Zeus site
70. Flock members
71. Brown rival

DOWN

1. Admission of 1890
2. Meet one's ___ (die)
3. "I'd walk ___ for . . ."
4. Kobe cabbage
5. Roofing specialist
6. Can't stand
7. Scott Turow book
8. x
9. ___ choy
10. Jubilant
11. Goya's "Duchess of ___"
12. Ocho ___, Jamaica
13. Ball girls
24. 1973 World Series stadium
25. Your, to Yves
27. Golden Triangle country
28. Young ___ (tykes)
31. Nothing, in Nice
32. "I saw ___ sawing wood . . ."
33. Cyclotron bits
34. Pear type
35. Heroine of Tennessee Williams's "Summer and Smoke"
36. "Gil ___"
37. Framer's need
38. "Another Green World" composer
39. Chaps
42. Sail support
43. Kind of atty.
45. Coastline feature
46. Cardinal letters
48. Moon goddess
49. Searches
51. Dimwit
52. Coward's lack
53. St. Teresa of ___
54. Brazilian port
55. Cartoon art
56. Naturalist Fossey
57. Agatha contemporary
58. Saroyan's "My Name is ___"
60. From scratch
63. Fed. property manager
65. "Brat Farrar" author

Solution on page 347

Challenging 63

ACROSS
1. New newts
5. Certain Prot.
9. "Nova" network
12. "Hercules" spinoff
13. Alphabetizes, e.g.
15. Basketballer's target
16. Epistle writer
17. Actress Marisa
18. Air France destination
19. Senators' home
21. Off-roader's purchase, for short
22. 11/11 honorees
23. Small amounts
25. Burglar's booty
27. Start of a holy name
30. Kung ___ chicken
32. Ryan's daughter
36. River to the Volga
37. Hood
39. Eyetooth
40. All-knowing
42. Genius
44. Abbr. on a cornerstone
45. Sailors' safekeeper
47. Punch
49. LI doubled
50. Dog-___ (well-worn)
51. "Everybody Hurts" band
52. Milo of "Barbarella"
54. Mid-2nd-century date
56. Stain
58. Dart
61. May honoree
63. Cyberhandle
67. Yorkshire river
68. Bikini, e.g.
70. Aftermath
71. Highlands hillside

72. Calyx component
73. B-school subj.
74. Blue shade
75. Radiation measures
76. Fashion initials

DOWN
1. World's fair
2. Accomplishment
3. Bolt holder
4. Lipton rival
5. Business sign abbr.
6. Cutesy-___
7. "The Joy of Cooking" author Rombauer
8. Chest: prefix
9. Dermal opening
10. Make a break for it

11. 1974 Gould/Sutherland spoof
14. Part of the Hindu trinity
15. Rush-hour traffic facilitator
20. Cool one's heels
24. Stud poker?
26. "Respect for Acting" author Hagen
27. Search for water
28. Wakayama woofer
29. DVD reader
31. Banded stone
33. Former CBS chairman Laurence
34. Disentangle
35. Press
38. "Oz" network
39. Atlanta's ___ Center
41. In

43. Prosodic foot
46. Start of Julius III's papacy
48. Sticky substances
51. Water cannon target
53. Blotto
55. "___ corny as Kansas . . ."
57. Slow times
58. Palms (off)
59. Hide in the shadows
60. "My word!"
62. Have the blues
64. Pinion's partner
65. Religious image: Var.
66. Declare untrue
69. Flight

Solution on page 347

Challenging 64

ACROSS

1. Hail Mary, e.g.
5. Archaeological find
9. "Not on ___!" ("No way!")
13. ___ O's (Post cereal)
14. Plaintiff
15. City on the Aire
16. Manor man
17. Charter
18. Do-___
19. "To reiterate . . ."
21. Lao-tzu follower
23. Call, as a game
24. Fat, in France
26. Chain letters?
27. Be-bopper
28. Not just "a"
30. Canner's supply
34. Diamond corners
37. Chutzpah
39. Never, in Nuremberg
40. Some native New Yorkers
41. Actor Alejandro
42. Auto option
44. "Go on . . ."
45. Nice notions
47. Diamond groups
48. Some deer
50. D.C. setting
51. Bear lair
52. Antiquity, in antiquity
54. Petitions
56. Amaze
59. Toots
62. Ballerina Makarova
64. Done in
65. Expressionist Nolde
67. Miniature sci-fi vehicles
68. Cartoon mirages
69. Dispense, with "out"
70. First president of South Korea
71. 100-lb. units
72. Brain passage
73. Beach, basically

DOWN

1. Kind of bear
2. Came into being
3. Line of type
4. Poor blokes
5. Concert souvenir
6. "A Dog of Flanders" author
7. Debussy subject
8. Cy Young winner Saberhagen
9. Forward pass
10. Resting places
11. Cut, maybe
12. "The Waste Land" poet's monogram
15. Minnesota's state bird
20. 1999 U.S. Open champ
22. Citrus quaffs
25. D and C, in D.C.
27. Average grade
29. "Airplane!" star Robert
31. "Back ___ hour" (shop sign)
32. Awful
33. Theological schools: Abbr.
34. Den denizen
35. Florence flooder
36. Competing team
37. Engendered
38. Most rational
43. Architect Maya ___
46. "___ Dinah" (Frankie Avalon hit)
49. One thing after another
51. He'll give you a hand
53. Contact, e.g.
55. Band together
56. Hi from Ho
57. Spread
58. Let up
59. Beanery side
60. Future's opposite
61. Circular opening?
63. Car loan figs.
64. Assn.
66. Big Apple attraction, with "the"

Solution on page 347

Challenging 65

ACROSS
1. Suffix with corrupt
5. Little rascal
10. So-so grades
14. City near Le Havre
15. Smidgen
16. Sheryl Crow's "__ _ Wanna Do"
17. Kin of -ess or -trix
18. Played over
19. Cattail, e.g.
20. "Gangs of New York" director
22. Subtle shade
24. Expansive
25. Bach work
26. Go around
29. "The Stranger" author Albert
30. Rifles
31. "Arabian Nights" group
32. "China Beach" setting
35. Yorkshire river
36. Beach sights
37. Artful dodge
38. PC monitor
39. Very cold
40. Chekhov title character
41. In-box filler
42. It's attractive
43. Gentle pace
46. Lemon peel
47. Nimble
48. Bear
52. Cask dregs
53. Dry as __
55. Stick __ in the water
56. Draft choices
57. City in a Porter song title
58. It's in a jamb

59. Chase of "Now, Voyager"
60. Old oath
61. "Little" girl in "David Copperfield"

DOWN
1. Cool treats
2. French bench
3. Carson successor
4. Sap
5. Underscore
6. High point
7. Swiss river
8. Record biz initials
9. Lewis Carroll and others
10. Ring figures
11. "Uncle Vanya" role
12. Go for
13. Top of a platter

21. Cheekiness
23. "E pluribus __"
25. Gave a fig
26. Group
27. Part of BYOB
28. Assignment
29. __ Major (southern constellation)
31. Mr. __ (Tati role)
32. Former Georgia senator
33. "__ sow, so shall . . ."
34. Spam, e.g.
36. Record company receipt
37. Fashion industry, slangily
39. Spice Girl Halliwell
40. Arrangement holder
41. Greek peak
42. Free-for-alls
43. Start of a holy name

44. Children's author Scott
45. Rosetta stone language
46. Spaced (out)
48. When said three times, a WWII movie
49. Bohr study
50. Cat's-paw
51. Like a King novel: Var.
54. Groceries holder

Solution on page 347

Challenging 66

ACROSS

1. Crooner Jerry
5. Message board?
10. Having no depth
14. Critical hosp. areas
15. Smith's block
16. Where to find interstates H1, H2, and H3
17. Elbow-bender
18. It's a steal
19. Evening, in adspeak
20. Tack on
22. Leopardlike cat
24. Martini partner
27. Word part: Abbr.
28. Caught some z's
31. Holy animal?
33. Lorna of literature
37. Calculus bound: Abbr.
38. Expiator
41. Drain bane
42. Like Shostakovich's Symphony No. 2
43. Mother Teresa, for one
44. Big jerk
46. "The Ice Storm" director Lee
47. Esoteric
49. Not so nice
51. Cpl., e.g.
52. Break up
54. Calypso cousin
55. John on the Mayflower
57. Bon ___
59. Earth Day's month
61. Purport
64. Even
68. Bankruptcy
69. Fleeced
73. Red-hot one?

74. "___ Rhythm"
75. Danny's "Taxi" role
76. "___ plaisir!"
77. Paradoxical Greek
78. Still in contention
79. Titillating

DOWN

1. "Home Again" host Bob
2. ___ above
3. Strong desire
4. F equivalent
5. Scouts take them
6. Durham sch.
7. "___ been had!"
8. Peter Pan rival
9. Choir group
10. "Wild Thing" rapper
11. Sound like a siren
12. "___ be in England"
13. Music for two
21. Trig function
23. Charisse of "Singin' in the Rain"
25. Light biscuits
26. Carbonium, e.g.
28. Playground fixture
29. Sheets and stuff
30. Plant firmly
32. Moist towelette
34. Chan portrayer
35. Present
36. Encourage
39. "The Rum ___ Tugger" ("Cats" tune)
40. Feel bad about
45. Wood pattern
48. Vivid red

50. Alias initials
53. ___ up (dress)
56. Alpaca cousins
58. Edison contemporary
60. Actress Blakley
61. Mex. neighbor
62. Downhill racer
63. Aslan, e.g.
65. Do road work
66. Financial page acronym
67. Off-color
70. Jan.1, e.g.
71. Arles affirmative
72. Columbia, e.g.: Abbr.

Solution on page 347

Challenging 67

ACROSS

1. Yeats and Keats
6. Did away with
10. ___ Solo of "Star Wars"
13. NFL Hall-of-Famer Hirsch
14. Port opening
15. Colombian city
16. Extension
17. Soon, to a bard
18. Expectant
19. Country dance
20. 11th-century date
21. Way out
23. Foreigners
26. Emporium
27. Main lines
30. M.I.T. part: Abbr.
32. Hitler's architect
33. Josip Broz, familiarly
35. Artsy NYC area
39. Suffix with human
40. "Puh-leeze!"
43. Some univ. degrees
44. Dodge model
46. Code sounds
47. Jungian principle
49. Algerian port
51. Lush, in a way
52. Brook
54. Most docile
57. "I swear!"
59. Bela contemporary
60. Admit openly
64. Egyptian deity
65. Prayers to Mary
67. Spanish silver
68. "Why don't we?"
69. Bog down
70. Salon colorings
71. Cobb and others
72. Absolute worst, with "the"
73. "Belling the Cat" author

DOWN

1. Bosc
2. Shoppe sign word
3. Earth, to Mahler
4. "You missed it"
5. Antonym's antonym: Abbr.
6. Synfuel source
7. Red head
8. "Eldorado" rock grp.
9. Press release?
10. Bigot
11. Preferred group
12. Cheese ___
15. Ring figures
20. Bad start?
22. Baseball VIP's
24. Metallica drummer Ulrich
25. Web spots
27. ". . . unto us ___ is given"
28. '60s TV boy
29. Change the decor
31. ___ de guerre
33. Slangy denial
34. NYC line
36. Eastern sashes
37. Scenery chewers
38. Anthem opener
41. Palm Pilot, e.g.
42. All ___
45. Surprisingly
48. Merchant of music
50. "Dr. Jekyll and Mr. Hyde" monogram
51. ___-X
52. Grid great Grier
53. JFK, e.g.: abbr.
55. Whistle, maybe
56. Noted Charlton Heston role
57. Sword part
58. Pat down
61. U-Haul rentals
62. "Beetle Bailey" bulldog
63. Slender-waisted insect
66. "QB ___"
67. Bake sale grp.

Solution on page 348

Challenging 68

ACROSS

1. Disney goldfish
5. Bakery workers
10. Book after Proverbs: Abbr.
14. Cannabis
15. Clunky shoe
16. "Mission: Impossible" theme composer Schifrin
17. Frozen confection brand
18. Color of honey
19. Figurehead's place
20. Tell tales
22. Lorre's "Casablanca" role
24. Early invader of the Punjab
25. Some sorority women
28. Mogul
30. Like oak leaves
34. Brouhaha
37. Art subject
39. Dutch oven feature
40. Aspersion
41. Our land, informally
43. Large green moth
44. Director Browning
45. ___ John
46. Inferior
48. Annually
50. Parrot
52. Inadequate
54. Roman household spirits
58. Rial spenders
61. "Wonderful Town" song
63. "Hook" producer Fayed
64. Conical home
67. Big tournament
68. ___-European
69. "No bid"
70. Bully's target
71. Some humor
72. Beethoven's last symphony
73. "Grand" brand

DOWN

1. Fine dinnerware
2. Old Renault
3. File material
4. Numbers person?
5. "Time ___ a premium"
6. Regained consciousness
7. "Cabaret" lyricist
8. Anonymous Richard
9. Pompous walk
10. Rio Grande city
11. Mystery writer John Dickson ___
12. Flow stopper
13. "The Lyon's Den" star
21. Author Seton
23. Beaufort scale word
26. One might be roasted
27. Plenty, slangily
29. Rock's Motley ___
31. Depressed
32. One overseas
33. "Saving Private Ryan" event
34. Ashe Stadium org.
35. Maneuver
36. Uncivil
38. Freshwater fish
42. Marionette maker Tony
43. Not to mention
45. Eins + zwei
47. "The Laughing Cavalier" artist
49. Embryonic sac
51. One doing clerical work
53. John of "The Addams Family"
55. Caught, in a way
56. EGBDF part
57. Thrills
58. Exaltedly poetic
59. Like early LP's
60. Env. info
62. Former "Entertainment Tonight" host John
65. Center starter
66. Broadway flier

Solution on page 348

Challenging 69

ACROSS

1. Eve's opposite
5. Gang's domain
9. Answers an invitation
14. ___-Ball
15. Golfer Aoki
16. Tooth remover?
17. Blue shade
18. "Silent Running" star Bruce
19. Backless sofa
20. "Ciao!"
21. Raised
22. Capitol cap
23. "The Screwtape Letters" writer
26. Israeli submachine guns
29. Goon's gun
30. Is histrionic
34. Rank above maj.
37. Freeze
40. "I told you so!"
41. Fish story
42. Long ___
43. Had on
44. Manhattan sch.
45. Charged, in a way
46. Animals
47. "You ___ worry"
49. Entrepreneur-aiding org.
50. Halloween purchase
52. Toned
56. "Return of the ___"
59. De ___ (again)
61. Cold and wet
62. Extract with a solvent
64. Potpourri
65. Composer Thomas
66. Roebuck's partner
67. Work in the garden
68. Scottish Highlander

69. Sylvester's co-star in "Rocky"
70. Go-aheads
71. Rock's Jethro ___

DOWN

1. "Hardball" broadcaster
2. Approves
3. Make merry
4. Napoleonic marshal
5. Choice morsel
6. Netizens
7. Hard to find
8. Ballet leg bend
9. "Mayberry ___"
10. Gave the O.K.
11. In ___ (occurring naturally)
12. British baby buggy
13. New Year's Eve word
24. Painter Schiele
25. Retail store opening?
27. Hera's husband
28. Babysitter's handful
31. Biblical pronoun
32. Bring home
33. 1973 World Series stadium
34. City between Boston and Salem
35. Diggs of "Rent"
36. Rock's Motley ___
37. H+, e.g.
38. X, to Xanthippe
39. Env. extra
42. Writes rapidly
43. Cry from a crib
45. ___ manner of speaking
46. Some NFL ball carriers

48. Composer Shostakovich
49. Hair nets
51. Famous
52. Like Wrigley Field's walls
53. Pianist Claudio
54. Jury
55. "The Seven Year Itch" actor
56. "Surely you ___!"
57. Zeno's home
58. Like some controls
60. Blue Bonnet product
63. Tikkanen of hockey
65. Ten-percenter: Abbr.

Solution on page 348

Challenging 70

ACROSS

1. Metric wts.
4. Crawling (with)
8. Show's partner
12. Zeno of ___
14. With everything counted
15. Racer Luyendyk
16. Penitent one
17. Brief appearance
18. "Eat ___ eaten"
19. African antelope
21. German auto pioneer
23. Mork's home planet
24. Interfere with
26. Gumbo vegetables
28. Qualify
31. Bender
32. Geisel's pen name
33. Chinese poet of the eighth century
36. Part of n.b.
40. Core
41. Way back
44. Ob-___
45. Formerly, formerly
47. Quarry
48. Egged on
50. Univ. dorm supervisors
52. As you like it
54. Sir, in old India
57. Beloved of Aphrodite
59. Outer: prefix
60. Alternative magazine founder Eric
62. School assignment
66. City north of Carson City
68. With fervor
70. Watchful one
71. Go smoothly
72. "It's ___!" ("See you then!")
73. Figure skater Thomas
74. Ukr. and Lat., once
75. Moistens
76. Veer suddenly

DOWN

1. "Felicity" star Russell
2. Down
3. Exude
4. Cell constituent
5. Shakespeare's feet
6. Admiral's command
7. Carolina college
8. Chinese principle
9. Overthrow, e.g.
10. Scales up?
11. Vichyssoise vegetables
13. A Musketeer
14. Poker phrase
20. Mucho
22. Animals: Suffix
25. Sniggler
27. Cold War org.
28. Crossword worker?
29. Prefix with -itis
30. Clumsy boats
31. Nudge
34. Expert finish?
35. Check words
37. Quiche ingredients
38. Nikita's "no"
39. "The Neverending Story" author
42. Some M.D.s
43. Navel type
46. Pod opener?
49. Irritated
51. ___ Dhabi
53. Deli request
54. Lowly workers
55. Lipinski leaps
56. Pay tribute to
57. Battery pole
58. Coup follower
61. Melt
63. Court call
64. 1988 country album
65. Math course
67. Cutting remarks?
69. Shavetails: abbr.

Solution on page 348

Challenging 71

ACROSS

1. Unsubstantial
5. Some laptops
9. Prepare for surgery
14. Placed
15. Beam
16. Mistreat
17. WWW facilitators
18. Zip
19. Examine again, as a patient
20. Muscle: Prefix
21. Fad disk of the '90s
22. Stood out
24. City on the Penobscot
26. It turns out lts.
27. Big name in home furnishings
29. Deserved
30. Away from the bow
33. Minute plant structure
36. Reply to a captain
38. "Well, I __!"
40. Proceed
41. Queen of the fairies
42. Soy-based soup
43. Pioneering 1940s computer
45. Aussie bird
46. Hardly a he-man
47. Rush-hour hour
48. Pinafore letters
50. Lady's partner
52. Pres. of the U.S.
53. __ in (redeems)
57. Skulls
60. WWII general Arnold
61. Request to a switchboard oper.
62. Rap

63. Angle iron
65. Paycheck deduction
66. Gads about
67. Snort
68. Sick as __
69. Heaps
70. Call at first
71. Storage spots

DOWN

1. Out on __
2. Cushy course
3. Bad-mouth
4. Drapers' meas.
5. Snub, in a way
6. Toot one's own horn
7. Central
8. Hose woe
9. Crusader's foe
10. Good buddies on the road
11. Trojan horse, e.g.
12. Drew on
13. Worker, perhaps
21. Nudge
23. Mary's boss on "The Mary Tyler Moore Show"
25. Cohort of Chevy and Laraine
28. Willie of "Eight Is Enough"
29. Remove errors from
30. Budget rival
31. Admit, with "up"
32. "Iliad" city
33. Has a mortgage
34. Start of a Latin boast
35. Popular computer operating system

37. Candied vegetable
39. Broadcasts
44. Takeout option
46. Button alternative
49. AT&T rival
51. Card game for two
52. Caravan beast
54. Alpine heroine
55. Record holder?
56. Bucks
57. Hoofbeat
58. First name in sitar playing
59. Mass robes
60. Game division
62. Grille cover
64. "Luck __ Lady"
65. Groovy

Solution on page 348

Challenging 72

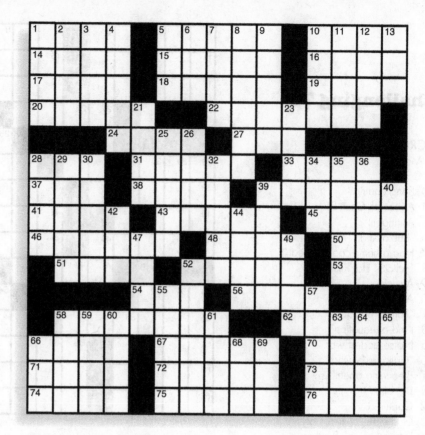

ACROSS
1. Whopper juniors?
5. Gardener's aid
10. Hearty hello
14. Actress Petty
15. Upholstery fabric
16. "Z" actor Montand
17. Bare-bones subj.?
18. Circles overhead
19. Tabloid fodder
20. Deejay Casey
22. Bishop's domain
24. Falls off
27. '80s defense prog.
28. Record biz initials
31. Fields of comedy
33. Dadaist collection
37. Offshoot
38. Headed for overtime
39. Stirred up
41. Carpe ___
43. Dictator's aide
45. Madly in love
46. Fillet
48. Deaden
50. Beach acquisition
51. Carpentry groove
52. Army base near
    Petersburg, Va.
53. A little work
54. Mail HQ
56. They may be cast
58. Like tactile hair
62. Cabbies
66. Moist
67. Nutty as a fruitcake
70. "Believe" singer
71. "Famous" cookie maker
72. 1973 #1 Rolling Stones
    hit

73. Soprano Te Kanawa
74. Karaoke need
75. Do a double take, e.g.
76. ___ souci

DOWN
1. Antiaircraft fire
2. Isle of Mull neighbor
3. Victoria's Secret selections
4. Put in place
5. Archaic verb ending
6. 1950 film noir classic
7. Richly adorn
8. Kay Thompson creation
9. Fix, as a golf green
10. Stevenson fiend
11. National competitor
12. "Able was ___ . . ."
13. D-Day vessel

21. Diamond target
23. "See ya!"
25. Sang-froid
26. Let it be, editorially
28. Highway safety org.
29. Reacted to a tearjerker
30. Amorphous creature
32. Birth cert., e.g.
34. Fix, as a fight
35. Word with hot or home
36. Popeye's creator
39. "Arise, fair sun, and
    kill the envious moon"
    speaker
40. "Drat!"
42. Stylish, in the '60s
44. Empty, in math
47. Egg drinks

49. One of Alcott's "little
    women"
52. As an example
55. Kind of bear
57. Gridiron stat
58. Final Four game
59. "Star Wars" creature
60. Big Board abbr.
61. Eastern discipline
63. ___ Pet (novelty item)
64. "Show Boat" composer
65. Hindu honorifics
66. Hoover, e.g.
68. Snap
69. So far

Solution on page 348

Challenging 73

ACROSS
1. Madams
6. Cooties
10. Song ending?
14. Agnes, to Cecil B.
15. Astringent
16. "Kubla Khan" river
17. Had a home-cooked meal
18. "Felicity" star Russell
19. Artifice
20. AOL, e.g.
21. "Family Ties" role
23. Kind of equation
25. Norse god of war
26. "Collages" author
27. Bleaching agent
28. Big bills
32. Captured
33. Garfield's predecessor
34. Herbert of Pink Panther films
35. Goes it alone
40. Uppermost point
41. Cutting remarks?
42. Noah of "ER"
43. Vader of "Star Wars"
45. Coffee order: Abbr.
46. Boot camp boss, informally
47. Phone abbr.
49. Barely move?
50. Some batters, for short
53. Seek a seat
54. Cry's partner
55. Fret
57. Drop off
58. Gossip
61. Not orig.
62. Fan sounds
64. Polite Italian word
66. Competes
67. Mouth, in slang
68. "___ pray"
69. Professor 'iggins
70. Withdraws, with "out"
71. "Barnaby Jones" star

DOWN
1. ___ B'rith
2. Small islands
3. Break down
4. Seventh-century date
5. Governing bodies
6. Staples Center player
7. Holm oak
8. Blackguard
9. Designer Pucci
10. Babe in the woods
11. Architect Saarinen
12. Spread out
13. "Ta-da!"
22. Fleur-de-___
24. Puts one's John Hancock on
26. Chinese menu phrase
28. Niger neighbor
29. Big name in auto parts
30. ___ and terminer
31. It is written
32. Illegal parker's worry
34. "Two Women" Oscar winner
36. Man-___ bird
37. Apollo's instrument
38. "Three Sisters" sister
39. Be "it"
44. Honker
46. Jack's workplace?
48. ___ Vallarta, Mexico
49. Catch some rays
50. Shot from a tee
51. Encircle
52. Peeping Tom
54. Door fasteners
56. Bitsy beginning
57. "Come again?"
58. Comes down with
59. Fluish feeling
60. Cap'n's underling
63. "Mustache Hat" artist
65. Fighter in gray

Solution on page 349

Challenging 74

ACROSS

1. Chase of "Now, Voyager"
5. ___ friends
10. British baby buggy
14. Rumor generator?
15. More urgent
16. Points
17. Supplicate
18. It may be golden
19. Eight, in Essen
20. Motion detector
22. "Hmmm . . ."
24. Furtive fellow
27. CD follower
28. Patronize, in a way
31. ___ Xing (street sign)
33. Blacksmiths' tools
37. Arg. neighbor
38. 1998 Masters champion
41. Take the cake
42. Robot drama
43. Snaps
44. Calendar spans: Abbr.
46. Here, in Brest
47. Broad sash
48. Aptly named flight
50. Brake part
51. Annie's dog
54. For example
55. Skein formers
57. Burgle
59. Blood component
61. Be afraid to
65. Bank jobs
69. Old flames
70. Maynard G.'s pal
73. Healthy look
74. Barflies
75. Patsy's pal on "Absolutely Fabulous"
76. "___ Lama Ding Dong" (1961 hit)
77. 500 spot
78. Punches
79. "The Blackboard Jungle" author Hunter

DOWN

1. Little rascals
2. Euros replaced them
3. Hate group
4. Milano of "Charmed"
5. Be gaga over
6. Bag thickness
7. Former California fort
8. A Bush brother
9. "The Female Eunuch" author
10. Red Cross supply
11. Fabled fliers
12. Lumbago, e.g.
13. Arachnid
21. Dominant
23. Anderson's "High ___"
25. Summits
26. New Zealand parrot
28. Mark replacements
29. Its capital is Oranjestad
30. City on the Po
32. "Not a ___ in the house"
34. Filch
35. Type measures
36. Like some remarks
39. Atlantis docked with it
40. It may finish second
45. Smooth transition
49. "___ Boot"
52. Smart
53. Hither's opposite
56. Asylum seeker
58. Portends
60. Ostrichlike birds
61. Ricky, really
62. Neural transmitter
63. Emeritus: abbr.
64. ___ list
66. Serb, e.g.
67. 1970s Tony Musante series
68. Park lake denizen
71. Lighter brand
72. Publicity, slangily

Solution on page 349

Challenging 75

ACROSS

1. Celtic tongue
5. Twangy, as a voice
10. "Ah, me!"
14. Little lice
15. Mountain crest
16. Do followers
17. Work shift
18. More than unpopular
19. Exactly
20. Driving hazard
22. Glossy fabrics
24. "Any day now"
27. Grass transplant
28. Suffix with dull or drunk
31. Degauss, e.g.
33. Hot times abroad
37. Drink, so to speak
38. Yahoo.com, e.g.
39. Decreased?
41. Der ___ (Adenauer)
43. Canadian physician Sir William ___
45. Closeout
46. Read the catcher's sign
48. Seed cover
50. Blair's house number
51. Very, in Versailles
52. Author Alexander
53. "C'___ la vie!"
54. Back muscle, familiarly
56. ___ souci
58. To the extent that
62. Addled
66. "Guilty," e.g.
67. Nymph
70. Hgts.
71. ___ impasse
72. Stiller's comedy partner
73. $200 per hour, e.g.
74. Pre-coll. exams
75. Partner of dangerous
76. Luxurious resorts

DOWN

1. Breaks off
2. 100 dinars
3. Eye problem
4. Lots of sass?
5. "Ixnay"
6. Altar constellation
7. Gets hard
8. "Relax!"
9. Caused
10. "Vissi d'___"
11. Novelist Uris
12. Latin 101 word
13. Order to Fido
21. Low digits
23. Linda of "Jekyll & Hyde"
25. Hunter of myth
26. Ex-D.C. baseballers
28. "Fast!" on a memo
29. Found a new tenant for
30. Office stamp
32. Psalms interjection
34. Lean-___ (sheds)
35. Growing outward
36. 1991–92 U.S. Open champ
39. "Three Sisters" sister
40. Mar, in a way
42. ". . .___ I saw Elba"
44. "-zoic" things
47. Madonna's "La _ _ Bonita"
49. "Sweater Girl" Turner
52. Rude observer
55. Bakery beckoner
57. Great balls of fire
58. Calgary's prov.
59. Candidate's goal
60. Rooters
61. A-line line
63. "Fresh!" follow-up
64. "At Last" singer James
65. "___ Death" (Grieg work)
66. Audio systems, for short
68. "___ you getting this?"
69. Family member

Solution on page 349

Challenging 76

ACROSS

1. Unit of capacitance
6. Alternatives to iMacs
9. Glowing piece
14. Angelou's "And Still __"
15. Martinique, par exemple
16. France's longest river
17. Balkan capital
18. Periodical, for short
19. Hersey locale
20. Phone button
21. "Etc.," when tripled
22. 100 centavos
23. Ed of the Reagan cabinet
25. Platters, briefly
27. Leaves rolling in the aisles
30. Play time
35. Third-century date
38. Digs
40. Deep laugh
41. Food chain?
43. Canada's smallest prov.
44. Neighbor of Togo
45. Se Ri Pak's org.
46. Simple shed
48. Bond, for one
49. Weak
51. Russian retreat
53. Part of E.U.: Abbr.
55. Pickle juice
58. Takes most of
61. "Dear" one
64. Loaded
66. Pigeon shelters
67. "You stink!"
68. Arum lily
69. Heavens: prefix
70. Dickens alias
71. Indian, e.g.
72. Six-Day War hero

73. NYSE debut
74. Trumps

DOWN

1. Drop a line?
2. Woolf's "___ of One's Own"
3. M-1, for one
4. Digressions
5. Justice Dept. division
6. Arizona Indian
7. Covered
8. "Love Story" author Erich
9. Go by
10. Statistics calculation
11. Civil rights concern
12. Cosmetics maker __ _ Laszlo
13. Alternative to a Maxwell

21. Congressional assents
24. Berth place
26. Country club figure
28. "Holy cow!"
29. "Golf Begins at Forty" author
31. "Evita" character
32. A long, long, long time
33. Cutter or clipper
34. Betamax creator
35. Baby whale
36. Bull baiter
37. "Bus Stop" playwright
39. "Pride's Crossing" playwright Howe
42. Brylcreem amount
44. Nobel physicist Niels
46. Romanian currency

47. National frozen dessert chain
50. Parable feature
52. Rickenbacker, e.g.
54. Browning's Ben Ezra, e.g.
56. Frasier's brother
57. Fanfare
58. Circle dance
59. Our Gang affirmative
60. Rowlands of "Gloria"
62. Betty __
63. Classic clown
65. Geiger with a counter
66. Jersey chew
68. Corn site

Solution on page 349

Challenging 77

ACROSS
1. Literally, "baked"
6. Keglers' org.
9. Sitar accompaniment
14. Pianist Claudio
15. "Dig in!"
16. Right Guard rival
17. Midsection
18. 20-20, e.g.
19. Depends (on)
20. "ER" order
21. Believers
22. Subject to a fine, maybe
23. Heavenly abodes
25. ___ Bo (exercise system)
27. Fortunetellers
30. Noah's landfall
35. Cleveland cager, for short
38. Move unsteadily
40. Herb in stuffing
41. Stews
43. Bring home
44. Taylor of "The Nanny"
45. Rock's Lofgren
46. Always, in a poem
48. -y, pluralized
49. Brosnan TV role
51. Helmsley of hotels
53. "Star Trek" rank: Abbr.
55. Wrapping weights
58. Bowls over
61. "Soap" family name
64. Mer sights
66. Gets ready, with "up"
67. ___ king
68. Steven Bochco series
69. Rich treat
70. Thrice, in prescriptions
71. Give extreme unction to, old-style
72. Contemptuous look
73. Fair-hiring letters
74. Hindu princess

DOWN
1. Cornfield cacophony
2. Be bombastic
3. Simple chord
4. Tries
5. Self: Prefix
6. Favorites
7. Worms, sometimes
8. Alamogordo event
9. More fanciful
10. Atlas stat
11. Little terror
12. Field of work
13. Infomercials, e.g.
21. "Amazing Grace" ending
24. Brings home
26. Berne's river
28. "Seasons of Love" musical
29. Kind of wool or drum
31. Peer Gynt's mother
32. Asian royal
33. "Let Us Now Praise Famous Men" author James
34. Caddie's bagful
35. Hustles
36. Came to rest
37. Repellent
39. To be, at the Sorbonne
42. Sugary suffix
44. Soap actress Sofer
46. Dusk, to Donne
47. Do, e.g.
50. Second-rate
52. ___ Afghan Airlines
54. Cabinet department
56. Actress Barkin
57. "A Lonely Rage" autobiographer Bobby
58. Ages and ages
59. Pottery
60. Romain de Tirtoff, familiarly
62. Downwind, at sea
63. Poi, essentially
65. ___' Pea
66. Sporty cars
68. Roman household spirit

Solution on page 349

Challenging 78

ACROSS
1. Little dent
5. Whipped cream serving
9. Ices
13. Audio effect
14. "The Wizard of Oz" actor
15. Forty-niner's filing
16. Not sharp
17. Emerald City princess
18. "Farewell, mon ami"
19. Pseudo fat
21. Comes out with
23. Isr. neighbor
24. Booby, e.g.
26. Oz. and mg.
27. Model Carangi
28. Court gp.
30. Minor quarrel
34. More reserved
37. Magnetic induction unit
39. Neckline shape
40. Stash away
41. "The Addams Family" cousin
42. Big bill
44. Belief
45. Begets
47. Round dances
48. Waistcoat
50. NBA stats
51. ___ Luthor, of "Superman"
52. Birds-feather connector
54. The others
56. Tour organizer, for short
59. Newspaper section
62. Was humiliated
64. "Twelfth Night" role
65. Male swans
67. Bindle bearer
68. Back way
69. Part of a nest
70. Lionel track layout, maybe
71. Doofus
72. Literally, "I forbid"
73. Gets hitched

DOWN
1. Audition tapes
2. Without warmth
3. NY Ranger, e.g.
4. Neptune and Pluto
5. Praise from a choir
6. Agent Swifty
7. Bit of resistance
8. Meister ___ (beer brand)
9. Guinness adjective
10. Evenhanded
11. Cries of disgust
12. Texas Mustangs, for short
15. Suffragist Carrie Chapman ___
20. Ford classics, familiarly
22. "___ the night before . . ."
25. Crime lab job
27. Neth. neighbor
29. Reservations
31. Actor Novello
32. Greek cheese
33. Club income
34. Hood's blade
35. Argyles, e.g.
36. Thanksgiving dish
37. Encircled
38. Plot
43. Night, to Nero
46. "___ first you don't . . ."
49. Drove (around)
51. Releases
53. Donnybrook
55. Wont
56. Turn out
57. Turn
58. They're off-base
59. Place for a cooling pie
60. Game of chukkers
61. John Candy's debut show
63. Eats
64. Little sucker?
66. "I ___ you one"

Solution on page 349

Challenging 79

ACROSS

1. Antitank weapons, for short
5. "Misery" costar
9. HBO rival
12. River to the Ubangi
13. Flowed back
15. Bull: Prefix
16. 32-card game
17. Loewe output
18. Broadway opening?
19. Family auto
21. Archery bow wood
22. A.A.A. suggestions
23. Break, in a way
26. "___ that special?!"
28. Lotion letters
31. Explorer Amundsen
33. Philippine island
37. Comic Margaret
38. Auld lang syne
39. Zimbabwe's capital
40. ___ Hashana
42. Drudge
44. "The Little Mermaid" prince
45. Nuts
47. Phnom ___, Cambodia
49. Fighting Tigers' sch.
50. "The Old Wives' Tale" dramatist
51. Rhone feeder
52. "___ the glad waters of the dark blue sea": Byron
53. Wart cause, in folklore
55. Spare parts?
57. Bat Masterson's weapon
60. Boom box button
62. Drag one's feet
66. Teacher of Heifetz
67. Seine feeder
70. Nichols hero
71. Salon stock
72. "Wake of the Ferry" painter
73. Feudal drudge
74. Wing, of sorts
75. Job detail, for short
76. Passion

DOWN

1. Actor Tamblyn
2. Silky-coated dog, briefly
3. Garden bloom, informally
4. Attack
5. Hwy. designers
6. "20/20" network
7. "___ Named Sue"
8. Sea nymph
9. Boor's lack
10. Remote control button
11. NFL analyst Collinsworth
14. Moistens, in a way
15. Rarer than rare
20. ___ a soul
24. Fraternal fellow
25. Banjoist Scruggs
27. Code-breaking org.
28. Makeshift money
29. Get on the horn
30. "All That Jazz" director
32. Abrupt transitions
34. Danny's daughter
35. Begin
36. Come again
39. Artist Toulouse-Lautrec
41. They hold your horses
43. Prez's backup
46. "The Matrix" hero
48. Female lobsters
51. Exemplars
54. Cache contents
56. Secret supply
57. Lion tamer's workplace
58. "The Clan of the Cave Bear" author Jean
59. Carter of "Gimme a Break!"
61. Cut short
63. ". . . sting like ___"
64. Former capital of Italy?
65. Departed
68. Not, to a Scot
69. SASE, e.g.

Solution on page 350

Challenging 80

ACROSS
1. Samantha of "The Collector"
6. Tarot suit
10. ___ buco (veal dish)
14. Dry white wine
15. Introduction to culture?
16. Crack, in a way
17. Beeper calls
18. It may be pitched
19. "Pal Joey" lyricist
20. France's patron saint
22. Singer?
24. Complex dwelling
26. Common Market: Abbr.
27. Acid, so to speak
28. Talk up
31. G, in the key of C
33. Remote button
35. Proverb ending?
36. Business biggie
38. Bubbling over
42. Fountain name
44. "The Island of the Day Before" author
45. John ___ Garner
46. "Frasier" dog
47. Board
49. Part of U.S.N.A.: Abbr.
50. Pinch hitter
52. "___ 'nuff!"
53. "Beloved" writer Morrison
54. Sportscaster Cross
57. Asta, to Nick and Nora
59. Benefit
61. Kind of diver
63. Vast extents
66. Ballet attire
67. "The Untouchables" extras
70. Time and ___
72. Halley's sci.
73. Go for
74. Andrea Bocelli, for one
75. Will of "Jeremiah Johnson"
76. Ht.
77. "Ready, ___!"

DOWN
1. Dubious "gift"
2. Egg on
3. "Eleni" author Nicholas
4. Means of access
5. Plant exudation
6. "Wheels"
7. Actor Tognazzi
8. Plain writing
9. Kitchen gizmo
10. ___ Rios, Jamaica
11. "We ___ Overcome"
12. Agra attire
13. Withdrew, with "out"
21. Spanish ayes
23. Vast amounts
25. Clan carving
28. "Women and Love" author
29. Sale site
30. Entreated
32. Spikes
34. Pugilists' org.
36. Commuters' woes
37. ___ Ark
39. ___ account (never)
40. Words of confidence
41. Dolly ___ of "Hello, Dolly!"
43. Baron's superior: abbr.
48. Darks or whites
51. Retro car
53. Snicker
54. Lapel label
55. Don't waste
56. Sporty Chevy
58. Indian tongue
60. "Endymion" poet
62. Contented sound
64. Gasp
65. Toil wearily
68. Just make, with "out"
69. It's east of Calif.
71. Not to

Solution on page 350

Challenging 81

ACROSS
1. Actress Sorvino
5. Albanian currency
8. Alliance acronym
12. Giant screen format
13. Pickle
14. Dry out, informally
15. H. H. Munro's pseudonym
16. Dudley Do-Right's org.
17. Best
18. Be suspicious
20. Wall upright
21. Gets clean
22. Comparative suffix
23. In the recent past
26. Thug
30. Contend
31. As a whole
34. Seagoing: Abbr.
35. Perfume
37. Award bestowed by Queen Eliz.
38. Welsh breed
39. Life partner
40. Landlord
42. Do goo
43. Court wear
45. Verbal zinger
47. Pro ___
48. More inclined
50. Big do
52. Imbued with
56. Access the Web
57. Put up
58. Air port?
59. Longhorn rival
60. Arm part
61. "Power Lunch" network
62. "Son of Frankenstein" role
63. A TV Tarzan
64. Bit of yarn

DOWN
1. Hit alternative
2. Islamic holy man
3. Autumn tool
4. Armpit, anatomically
5. Monetary gain
6. Bombeck and others
7. Had in stock
8. Elementary particle
9. Farthest of the Near Islands
10. Mrs. Lincoln's maiden name
11. Kitchen gadget company
13. Lily-livered
14. Doctor, at times
19. "See ya"
22. Games gp.
23. Some tracks
24. Belong
25. Words of assistance
26. Takes off
27. "Key ___"
28. Winter Olympian
29. Inclined
32. 1899–1902 war participant
33. Barbell abbr.
36. Slaughterhouse
38. Weirdo
40. "Solaris" author Stanislaw
41. Sandinista Daniel
44. Nancy Drew creator
46. Ditch
48. Even a bit
49. Small change
50. Verne's circumnavigator
51. Toaster Swirlz brand
52. Cage's "Leaving Las Vegas" co-star
53. Lady of Lisbon
54. Novel I.D.
55. Guitar part
56. Ballad

Solution on page 350

Challenging 82

ACROSS

1. Milo of "Ulysses"
6. Crowds into
10. Pool division
14. Not these
15. Take ___ (snooze)
16. "Pardon . . ."
17. Durable woods
18. Himalayan legend
19. Ford product, briefly
20. Melodic piece
22. Off base, perhaps
24. Dashboard inits.
25. Complimentary
26. Wallace of "E.T."
27. "Make ___!" (Picard's order)
30. www.yahoo.com, e.g.
32. "Ed Wood" director Burton
34. Cow, for one
35. Late-ish bedtime
37. Spiral shell
41. Like some eclipses
43. Joanne of "Abie's Irish Rose"
44. The end of ___
45. Discombobulate
46. Office furniture
48. Suffix with Caesar
49. Peke squeak
51. JFK was in it
52. Units of energy
53. El ___ (Heston role)
56. Like many a cellar
58. Beerfest mo.
60. Plastered?
62. Reb Jeb
65. Mentor
66. Spick-and-span
68. Exult maliciously
70. Seed cover
71. One-eyed Norse god
72. Garlicky sauce
73. 1996 Tony-winning musical
74. Level
75. x

DOWN

1. Giant in Cooperstown
2. Flushing stadium
3. Frozen dew
4. Nunavut native
5. Fable fellow
6. Deli jarful
7. "A Chorus Line" number
8. Ulan ___
9. It's smaller than a grand
10. Fabric with metallic threads
11. Forward
12. Audacity
13. Mike holder
21. Blackball
23. Expensive cameras
25. Sudden outburst
27. Mallorca, e.g.
28. Fall sound
29. Radio, e.g.
31. Comic Foxx
33. Back-to-work time: Abbr.
35. Tater Tots maker
36. Rumple, with "up"
38. At no time, in poetry
39. Mountain climber's obstacle
40. Geiger with a counter
42. One of the Khans
47. Granny, e.g.
50. Church leader
52. List ender
53. Post-delivery handout
54. Habituate
55. "Splish Splash" singer Bobby
57. Crete's highest elev.
59. Bandleader Xavier
61. Kind of film
62. New Year's Eve word
63. Part of a Clue accusation
64. Account
67. Gillespie, to fans
69. "___ folly to be wise"

Solution on page 350

Challenging 83

ACROSS
1. Constant complainer
5. Social reformer Jacob
9. Wall Street pessimist
13. Ruination
15. "Jarhead" org.
16. Sphere starter
17. Stevens of "The Farmer's Daughter"
18. Hoodwink
19. Caprice
20. Tear apart
22. Surround
24. Easy stroll
26. Movement word
27. "___ 'nuff!"
28. Cartridge holder
29. Fixes, in a way
32. Disney collectible
34. Symbol of might
35. Candidate list
37. Boxer's stat
41. Shield border
43. "Like me"
45. Source of relief
46. Topps rival
48. Academy freshman
50. Brazilian hot spot, briefly
51. "The Company"
53. Fearsome dino
54. Come-___ (marketing ploys)
55. Cutting remarks?
58. "It's c-c-c-cold!"
60. Peter, Paul, or Mary
62. Beseeches
64. Come together
65. Five-star
66. Toaster waffle
68. Touch of color

72. Short ways to go?
73. Hose woes
74. Cook in a wok, perhaps
75. Glossary entry
76. Slangy approvals
77. Hubs: abbr.

DOWN
1. Phi follower
2. Bled
3. Batting stat.
4. Transvaal settlers
5. Uncivil
6. Pocatello sch.
7. Motivate
8. Picturesque
9. Blubber
10. Cultural credo
11. Modern-day horse-and-buggy travelers
12. 1996 Leonardo DiCaprio role
14. Newsmen of yore
21. "Ta-da!"
23. One with a handle
24. Diver's find
25. Bracelet site
28. Vanishing sound
30. [I'm shocked!]
31. Long-legged bird
33. Neighbor of Syr.
36. Linda of Broadway's "Jekyll & Hyde"
38. All-time RBI leader
39. Singer Black
40. Managed care grps.
42. Common Market: Abbr.

44. Plump, plus
47. Barbecue fare
49. Glorifies
52. Angioplasty target
55. Bridget Riley's genre
56. Penned
57. Less loco
59. Elephant gone amok
61. Kind of artery
63. Polite reply from a ranch hand
64. ___ stick (incense)
67. Econ. measure
69. Eccentric
70. HQ
71. Your, to Yves

Solution on page 350

Challenging 84

ACROSS

1. ___ Grande, Fla.
5. Big 'do
9. African grazer
12. MP3 player
13. Bull: Prefix
15. "D"
16. Like a worn tire
17. "Roots" Emmy winner
18. ___ vez (again, in Spanish)
19. [expletive deleted]
21. Abe Lincoln's son
22. "Murphy Brown" bar owner
23. 45, e.g.
26. "Go ahead!"
28. ___ favor
31. Binges
33. The second Mrs. Trump
37. Pier grp.
38. Kachina doll maker
39. Some like it hot
40. Salinger girl
42. Idaho, e.g.
44. Baseballer Martinez
45. Microscopic
47. Caustic alkalis
49. ___ Dinh Diem
50. Boutros-Ghali's successor
51. Saw things
52. WWI army: Abbr.
53. Far from exciting
55. Crack the books
57. Belgian songwriter Jacques
60. Snickering syllable
62. Reach
66. Assistant on the Hill
67. Bedouins, e.g.
70. Augur
71. Don of morning radio
72. Fergie, formally
73. At some distance
74. Fond du ___, Wisconsin
75. Beanery handout
76. Behind

DOWN

1. Lettuce variety
2. Girasol, e.g.
3. "Unforgettable" singer
4. Included
5. ___ premium
6. Scale notes
7. Littlest of the litter
8. Mountain nymphs
9. Teutonic invader
10. "Me neither"
11. Caspian feeder
14. Mass booklet
15. Toaster treat
20. Nitty-gritty
24. Like a chimney sweep
25. Club in a Manilow song
27. The Beatles' "___ Mine"
28. Michelangelo work
29. Sportscaster Merlin
30. Japanese noodle dish
32. Ownership
34. Isabella, por ejemplo
35. Oscar winner Jessica
36. Distant
39. El Greco's birthplace
41. Gives power to
43. Ogler
46. Belushi's old show, for short
48. Carpet type
51. Sign of spring
54. Epiphanies
56. Keep out
57. Release money
58. Terza ___ (Italian verse form)
59. Cabinet dept. since 1979
61. Fabled braggart
63. Meat substitute
64. A Ponderosa son
65. Maryland athlete
68. Embargo
69. Moo ___ chicken

Solution on page 350

Challenging 85

ACROSS
1. Yes-___ question
5. Part of A.A.R.P.: Abbr.
9. Flat topper
12. "The ___ have it"
13. Brunch fruit
15. Slangy suffix
16. Agitation
17. Witchy woman
18. "Look ___ hands!"
19. Basic principle
21. ___ Dee river
22. "Daniel Boone" actor
23. Mature
26. Berkshire school
28. 6-pointers
31. Fished for congers
33. Deposes
37. Act the fink
38. Matches, as a wager
39. Lacking vitality
40. French articles
42. Native of the Steppes
44. Glen Gray's "Casa ___ Stomp"
45. Online brokerage
47. Start of a Cockney toast
49. Small songbird
50. Caterpillar competitor
51. Rice-___
52. Masthead contents, briefly
53. "It's ___ state of affairs!"
55. "Two Years Before the Mast" writer
57. ___ Sea (Amu Darya's outlet)
60. Classic Japanese theater
62. Backpack part
66. Aswan's river
67. Judge
70. Actress Kedrova
71. Appoint
72. Exodus commemoration
73. "There ought to be ___!"
74. Small batteries
75. Rick who sang "Disco Duck"
76. Sun. speeches

DOWN
1. Brewer's kiln
2. Sandberg of baseball
3. Ja's opposite
4. Blender brand
5. Cable choice
6. Rev.'s talk
7. Sty fare
8. "Don't bother"
9. Way around London, once
10. Bang-up
11. Dairy airs?
14. Hair remover brand
15. Common temple name
20. Lashes
24. Quarterback Rodney
25. Zeno of ___
27. Suffix with ball
28. Made level
29. "Paradiso" poet
30. Cordwood measure
32. Banana oil, for one
34. Struck
35. Retiring
36. Beats it
39. Hippodrome, e.g.
41. Big name in cakes
43. Yankee nickname
46. "Der Ring __ _ Nibelungen"
48. Does wrong
51. Went gaga over
54. "The Naked Jungle" menace
56. Book with legends
57. Magnani of "The Rose Tattoo"
58. Anti-piracy org.
59. Handouts
61. Camouflage
63. Irritate
64. Apple application, once
65. Dog's "dogs"
68. A foot wide?
69. $200 Monopoly props.

Solution on page 351

Challenging 86

ACROSS
1. NYSE debuts
5. Handled
10. Ogee, e.g.
14. Jargon
15. Merger
16. Hawaii County's seat
17. Elbe tributary
18. Capone contemporary
19. Pained look
20. Like some Christians
22. Conceal
24. "Hopalong Cassidy" actor
26. "Cry ___ River"
27. Jazzy Chick
30. Codgers' queries
32. Like the Citadel, now
36. Lacto-___ vegetarian
37. Chip's cartoon chum
39. Fright
41. ___ Verde National Park
43. Aristotle's teacher
45. Italian painter Guido
46. Ring of color
48. Filmmaker Riefenstahl
50. Green target
51. Tut's kin?
52. Pocatello sch.
53. Dillon and Damon
55. Cable giant
57. Of two minds
59. Poet's pause
63. Food writer Ruth
67. Pencil-and-paper game
68. Scope
70. Feng ___
71. Alpo rival
72. Like Art Deco, today
73. Lines of thought?
74. "Lohengrin" heroine
75. Dairy section selections
76. "Enough!"

DOWN
1. Message writer, at times
2. Beep
3. First-floor apartment
4. Disco flasher
5. Cheerful
6. "I'd like to buy ___"
7. Mental faculties
8. Clan emblems
9. Chilled
10. "Alas!"
11. Barrel of laughs
12. Hint
13. Break ground?
21. Way to go
23. Triathlon, e.g.
25. Compaq competitor
27. Robin Cook thriller
28. For all to see
29. Kentucky Derby prize
31. Makes better
33. "Catch-22" pilot
34. At attention
35. Toroidal treat
38. Shrinks' org.
39. Elephant's weight, maybe
40. Saws with the grain
42. Fine, informally
44. Ger.
47. D-Day transports
49. Nagy of Hungary
52. David, "the sweet psalmist of ___"
54. Aromatic herbs
56. Pack animal
58. Layered treats
59. Scuttle filler
60. P.I.N requesters
61. She, in Salerno
62. Handful of chips, maybe
64. Atkins of the Opry
65. Quasimodo's creator
66. Talk like Daffy
67. Give out
69. A doz. doz.

Solution on page 351

Challenging 87

ACROSS

1. Baltic capital
5. "That's nice!"
8. Agnew's plea, for short
12. "Psst! Pass ___!"
13. Type of type
14. Galloping
15. Subatomic bit
16. "Walkabout" director Nicolas
17. Alter
18. Academy site
20. Wallop
21. Admit
22. Holed up
23. "___ Pointe Blank" (John Cusack film)
26. Apportion, as costs
30. Increase, with "up"
31. Some sorority women
34. Workplace regulator, for short
35. Disney's middle name
37. Gen ___
38. Capsize
39. Forbids
40. Vitamin C source
42. "___ Blue?"
43. View
45. Sudan's ___ Desert
47. Summer mo.
48. In ___ (unborn)
50. Big name in power tools
52. Low blow
56. Girl rescued by Don Juan
57. Hose woes
58. Verboten: var.
59. Gawks at
60. Chichi
61. Microwave, e.g.
62. Group of players
63. Clean tables
64. Some floor votes

DOWN

1. Philbin's co-host
2. Put ___ writing
3. "Tell me more"
4. History
5. Garlic mayonnaise
6. ___ the hole
7. Caldron stirrers
8. Try to impress, in a way
9. Cartel letters
10. Connect
11. "That's ___ . . ."
13. President ___ (acting head)
14. Ham's need
19. Mexican beans?
22. Billable bits: Abbr.
23. Cousin of a loon
24. Track event
25. Like Bo-Peep's charges
26. Henry's sixth
27. Very, to Verdi
28. Recurring melody
29. Dine at home
32. Door sign
33. Acquire
36. Went after
38. Take forcibly
40. Gear tooth
41. On pins and needles
44. Island dances
46. Fenway Park locale
48. Ruark novel
49. Circus sights
50. Arcade name
51. Place for a firing
52. Complain
53. "___ Nagila"
54. Heed
55. Port vessels
56. High ball?

Solution on page 351

Challenging 88

ACROSS

1. "Arrivederci ___"
5. Meat loaf serving
9. "How to Murder Your Wife" star Virna
13. Bearded bloom
14. Baum barker
15. Foofaraws
16. Bubblehead
17. A Guthrie
18. Clumsy
19. The least bit
21. War horses
23. In lieu of
24. Elizabeth of "La Bamba"
26. Blunder
27. "Oysters ___ season"
28. Geometry suffix
30. Aerobic bit
34. CD store section
37. Canasta plays
39. G.I. dinner
40. Boiling
41. "Bravo!"
42. Hotpoint competitor
44. ". . . ___ a lender be"
45. Blackthorns
47. "Olympia" artist
48. Dairy Queen order
50. "___ bodkins!"
51. Earthlink competitor
52. Hosts, briefly
54. Some cameras: abbr.
56. Drink from a dish
59. Gym wear
62. Come out
64. Meltdown sites
65. "Now, about . . ."
67. "Every ___ winner!"
68. Bradley and Sharif

69. Whaler's adverb
70. "The Lion King" villain
71. Is off-guard
72. Leftovers
73. Towel embroidery

DOWN

1. Free from
2. City near Bangor
3. Track athlete
4. Bubbly source
5. New York's ___ Island
6. Navigation acronym
7. The Braves, on scoreboards
8. Hecklers' chorus
9. Solitary sorts
10. Put the finger on
11. Absorbs, with "up"
12. Adherent's suffix
15. Amphitheater section
20. Guesses
22. Keep an eye on
25. Undying
27. Slowing, in mus.
29. Arena yells
31. Counterfeiter catcher
32. Coastal raptor
33. Bog stuff
34. "The Mod Squad" role
35. Buck suffix
36. Mountain lake
37. General feeling
38. Indian turnover
43. Bad start?
46. Bewildered
49. Foreign dignitaries
51. Puts in the mail?
53. Big Mama

55. Sic on
56. Cyclist Armstrong
57. On ___ (carousing)
58. Compote fruit
59. Body of an organism
60. Trendy sandwich
61. 1974 Peace Nobelist Eisaku
63. Raid the fridge
64. Debate side
66. NYSE unit

Solution on page 351

Challenging 89

ACROSS
1. Elephant of children's books
6. Nos. on checks
10. Perry Como's "___ Loves Mambo"
14. Beyond's partner
15. Hurting
16. Hydroxyl compound
17. Cameos, e.g.
18. Tibia
19. Bickering, say
20. Pistol, slangily
21. A lot
23. Like some solutions
25. CIA forerunner
26. A head
27. Bering, e.g.: Abbr.
28. Eritrea's capital
32. Passport endorsement
33. Dusting, say
34. Afflict
35. NATO and SEATO
40. Sup
41. Grand ___, Nova Scotia
42. Docile
43. Pandemonium
45. Danube locale: Abbr.
46. Conductor Georg
47. Tolkien monsters
49. Broke up
50. Fondue, for one
53. Author Rita ___ Brown
54. The "S" of R.S.V.P.
55. Gadabout
57. "___ Rebel" (Crystals hit)
58. Pronoun for Miss Piggy
61. Sicilian city
62. "L'___ c'est moi"
64. Airborne
66. Lends a hand

67. Bagel topping
68. Pine Tree State
69. "Serpico" author Peter
70. Lacquered metalware
71. Storage sites

DOWN
1. Roseanne, formerly
2. Peek follower
3. Stressed, in a way
4. "Hail, Caesar!"
5. Give back
6. Grps.
7. Kind of scale
8. Part of TNT
9. Feels
10. Burst of laughter
11. They're not pros
12. Exact moment

13. Let down, say
22. Explorer Johnson
24. Give ___ (care)
26. A ton
28. "Dirty Deeds Done Dirt Cheap" band
29. ___ Tzu (toy dog)
30. Pulitzer poet Van Duyn
31. Mars: prefix
32. Bug
34. Abreast (of)
36. Love, in Lima
37. Knick rival
38. Cabeza, across the Pyrenees
39. Lose traction
44. A bit
46. Bows
48. Hardest to find

49. TV's Magnum and others
50. Night vision?
51. Ancient region of Asia Minor
52. ___ bear
54. Otto's preceder
56. Physics calculation
57. Campus building
58. Work hard
59. ___ consequence
60. Residents: Suffix
63. Eastern "way"
65. "Love Story" composer Francis

Solution on page 351

Challenging 90

ACROSS

1. Tabula ___ (blank slate)
5. Arctic native
9. E'en if
14. Life ___ know it
15. Cork's country
16. Show again
17. "The Cosby Show" kid
18. Give ___ for one's money
19. Elegance
20. Shipping route
22. "Tarzan" extra
24. "Nightmare" street
25. Punctual
26. "Stormy Weather" singer Horne
28. Check books
31. Strait of Dover port
35. PC program
38. Valium manufacturer
40. Slow, to Mozart
41. Cartoonist Addams
43. Football Hall-of-Famer Greasy ___
45. "___ fan tutte"
46. Sylvester's co-star in "Rocky"
48. Defeat decisively
50. Danny's "Do the Right Thing" role
51. 1887 Verdi opera
53. Comics canine
55. Rewards for waiting
57. Brush up on
61. Envy, e.g.
64. Nova Scotia hrs.
65. Philadelphia university
66. Surgery souvenirs
68. "___ in Calico"
70. Family group
71. Bristles
72. Split apart
73. Glasses option
74. Holds back
75. 1990 World Series champs
76. Salty septet

DOWN

1. Joe Buck's pal
2. Beyond the pale?
3. Worry about
4. Asia Minor region
5. Pressured
6. Billion add-on
7. Boston skyscraper, informally, with "the"
8. Kind of colony
9. Magazine
10. Do-over, in tennis
11. Diggs of "Rent"
12. Rise
13. Beehive State city
21. Tatar Strait feeder
23. Ab neighbor
27. "The Black Stallion" boy
29. Clinches
30. "___ life!"
32. Years abroad
33. "___ boy!"
34. Dirty
35. Part of a Spanish play
36. "Cool," updated
37. Far from ruddy
39. Carolina college
42. Bank deposit?
44. Spring birthstones
47. Rap sheet list
49. C in C
52. Photo ___
54. Plots
56. Belle or Bart
58. "Dallas" matriarch
59. Rod Stewart's ex
60. Bad impressions?
61. Flat sound
62. "New Jack City" costar
63. Cager Archibald
65. Reel in
67. Gate crasher?
69. "How about that?!"

Solution on page 351

Challenging 91

ACROSS

1. Gullet
4. Gossips
8. Under way
13. When quintupled, a 1976 Abba hit
14. Marketing ploy
15. Writer Calvino
16. Fate
17. "___ jolly swagman . . ." ("Waltzing Matilda" start)
18. Recorded
19. Sternward
21. Wellness org.
23. Turns right
24. Wholly absorbed
27. Add kick to
29. Dr. Alzheimer
31. In cubbyholes
35. Second word of "The Raven"
38. Albatross, figuratively
40. Singer Bryson
41. Margarine container
42. No-goodniks
44. Elephant grp.
45. Rainbow: Prefix
48. Go down
49. Carter's sch.
50. Up-to-the-minute
52. Spooks
54. Groaners
56. The Supreme Court, e.g.
59. Generic pooch
62. "Tic ___ Dough"
64. "Nuthin' But a 'G' Thang" rapper
66. Relaxed
68. Actress Christine
71. Hang back
72. Deed holder
73. "Henry & June" character
74. Having one sharp, musically
75. Easy mark
76. Rhett's last word
77. Lad

DOWN

1. Leon Uris's "___ 18"
2. Clay + straw + water
3. Odin, to the Germans
4. Card player's cry
5. Former nuclear agcy.
6. "Tres ___"
7. Slug's kin
8. Comic shtick
9. Tchotchke holder
10. Be slack-jawed
11. 1997 title role for Peter Fonda
12. Agrees, in a way
14. General Mills brand
20. Friend of Kukla and Ollie
22. Gives birth to
25. Pal of Piglet
26. Like a trident
28. ___ a plea
30. Court figures
32. Puts out, in a way
33. Black, in verse
34. L-___ (Parkinsonism treatment)
35. Elec., e.g.
36. Aqua ___
37. Life lines?
39. Incline
43. Political slant
46. Kicks out
47. The Buckeyes, briefly
49. Mouse manipulator
51. Big bang cause
53. "The ___ near!"
55. First course, maybe
57. Go off script
58. Pipe cleaner
59. Bomb
60. "Field of Dreams" setting
61. "Cut it out!"
63. Scene of Jesus' first miracle
65. Like custard
67. Mock or crock ending
69. Prosciutto
70. Bolivian export

Solution on page 352

Challenging 92

ACROSS

1. Make even deeper
6. Empty spaces
10. Figure skater Kulik
14. Gas in a layer
15. Bridge toll unit
16. New Jersey city
17. Earth layer
18. Bridle part
19. Auctioneer's shout
20. More bohemian
22. One on the run
24. "Blah, blah . . ."
25. Flash, of sorts
26. Georgia, once: abbr.
27. Attend Choate, e.g.
30. New Deal agcy.
32. Last mo.
34. Guy Fawkes Day mo.
35. "Air Music" composer Ned
37. Place to curl up and dye?
41. Graff of "Mr. Belvedere"
43. Mozart's "L'___ del Cairo"
44. Love, in Livorno
45. Largish combo
46. Crayola choice
48. Den device
49. Some appliances
51. "Shanghai Noon" actress Lucy
52. Flip (through)
53. Printer ad abbr.
56. Used a firehouse pole
58. Entrepreneur-aiding org.
60. One with lots to offer
62. Was rude, in a way
65. Goofing off
66. Anti-fur org.
68. Wheels for big wheels
70. Drudge of the Internet
71. Sufficient, old-style
72. Early American crop
73. Land map
74. Pronounces
75. Toss about

DOWN

1. "Arabian Nights" creature
2. Pound of literature
3. Hardly upbeat
4. Foot part
5. "See?"
6. Teri of "After Hours"
7. Can
8. Practiced
9. Had a hunch
10. "As Time Goes By" requester
11. Cloverleaf parts
12. Runs without moving
13. Support person
21. Big name in shoes
23. Kind of salad
25. Freezing
27. Nabokov novel
28. Hershey brand
29. Flush
31. "Peter Pan" critter
33. Video maker, for short
35. Student's second chance
36. Bamako's land
38. It's all you need
39. "Free Willy" creature
40. Soft ball
42. Photog's item
47. Boot
50. Pitches
52. Rodeo rope
53. Preen
54. Organ part
55. Valletta's land
57. "The Faerie Queene" character
59. Soothers
61. Riga native
62. Lumberyard equipment
63. Abu Dhabi dignitary
64. Drop off
67. Shih Tzu, e.g.
69. Clinch, with "up"

Solution on page 352

Challenging 93

ACROSS
1. Halloween decorations
5. Playground retort
10. Dada collectibles
14. A succulent
15. Made public
16. "Beat it!"
17. Gull kin
18. Nehi flavor
19. Word repeated after "Que"
20. Brand of candy pieces
22. Halloween bagful
24. Comic Bill, briefly
25. Bricklayer
27. Emulate Icarus
29. ___ offensive
30. Bikini experiment, for short
34. Amtrak stop: Abbr.
35. 1974 Mocedades hit
38. Bristle
39. "A jealous mistress": Emerson
40. Boom preceder?
41. Bank acct. entry
43. Noisy quarrel
44. Limit one's intake
46. Dorm room staple
48. Elected officials
49. Golden calf's maker, in Exodus
51. Help wanted abbr.
52. WWI German admiral
54. Furniture designer Charles
56. ___ Maria
57. Threat ender
60. Tasty fungi
63. Spy on the inside
64. Frome of fiction
67. Neeson of "Kinsey"
69. "Take it or leave it"
70. Upholstery fabric
71. PC linkups
72. Actress Charlotte et al.
73. Factions
74. Mars, to the Greeks

DOWN
1. Be up
2. D-Ray, e.g.
3. Rushed
4. Iroquoian language
5. Batting-practice areas
6. Snobs put them on
7. Anti-Brady bill org.
8. 30-day mo.
9. "Golden Boy" dramatist
10. Yeses
11. She played Carla on "Cheers"
12. After-dinner drink
13. With the intent
21. Painful spots
23. Palillo of "Welcome Back, Kotter"
25. ___ amis
26. Clothes
27. Narrow furrow
28. Cowboy film
29. Proctor's charge
31. A la King?
32. Rolling musician?
33. Shooters
34. Thompson of "Pollock"
36. Loire laugh
37. A, in Ardennes
42. "___ With Love"
45. Like sandals
47. Aurora's counterpart
50. "Illmatic" rapper
53. Dish made with saffron
55. Athletic events
56. Color wheel display
57. "A jug of wine . . ." poet
58. Parks in 1955 news
59. "The Missile Crisis" author Abel
60. Fountain order
61. When repeated, a 1997 Jim Carrey comedy
62. Balanced
65. Corn site
66. Sot's sound
68. Ed.'s pile

Solution on page 352

Challenging 94

ACROSS

1. Word on a biblical wall
5. Fill with cargo
9. 1969 Peace Prize grp.
12. "Saving Private ___"
13. WW II vessel
15. Agenda part
16. ". . . which ___ was irksome to me": "As You Like It"
17. "The Gondoliers" flower girl
18. "Peter Pan" pooch
19. Can't abide
21. ___ Avivian
22. Sci-fi film of 1982
23. Poll answerer: Abbr.
25. "Able was ___ . . ."
27. Diagram, in a way
30. Son of Prince Valiant
32. Rhino relative
36. Downed a sub, say
37. Aussie buddy
39. Williams of tennis
40. Alpine transport
42. Comes close
44. Glance over
45. Cafeteria-goers
47. Harts' mates
49. One of "Them!"
50. Days-old
51. Vintner's prefix
52. Descartes and Magritte
54. Hydrocarbon endings
56. "A Perfect Peace" author Oz
58. Hombre's home
61. "Shop ___ you drop"
63. Kind of projection
67. Living units: Abbr.
68. Loud, like fans
70. A Saarinen
71. Don Juan
72. Frat letter
73. Tolkien forest creatures
74. LAPD alert
75. Back-to-school mo.
76. Jazzman Allison

DOWN

1. TV palomino
2. Australia's largest lake
3. Boss Tweed skewerer
4. Punches in
5. Riga residents
6. Marge's father-in-law on "The Simpsons"
7. Verb with thou
8. Enter cautiously
9. ___-Tass news agency
10. "Leading with My Chin" author
11. Arab League member
14. "A ___ of Two Cities"
15. Sobbing
20. Come across as
24. Bean, so to speak
26. 66, e.g.: Abbr.
27. Cracker toppers
28. Chance for a hit
29. Lariat
31. Aptly named English novelist
33. Praline nut
34. Cockeyed
35. Harangues
38. T or F, e.g.
39. Abilene-to-San Antonio dir.
41. Free
43. "Class Reunion" author Jaffe
46. Cartoon canine
48. B'way postings
51. Egyptian underworld god
53. High regard
55. Greek H's
57. Charlotte Corday's victim
58. "Fame" singer Irene
59. Each, informally
60. Rain check, e.g.
62. Balcony box
64. City near Sparks
65. Song and dance, e.g.
66. Ditch
69. Band blaster

Solution on page 352

Challenging 95

ACROSS

1. Triple Crown stat
5. Centers
9. Hwy. designers
12. "___ Dream" ("Lohengrin" piece)
14. "The ___ Love" (R.E.M. hit)
15. Mural site
16. Bay sound
17. Kind of package
18. Hip dance?
19. Erodes
21. "ER" extras
22. Egyptian deity
23. Schuss, e.g.
24. ⅛ of a fluid ounce
26. Beat the wheat
28. Small dam
29. "Don't make me laugh!"
30. Mrs. Dithers
33. Kind of nut
35. Welcome words to a hitchhiker
40. Cashmere, e.g.
41. Some is spam
43. Director Wertmuller
44. Fence supplier
46. Haywire
47. "Peanuts" girl
48. -y, pluralized
50. Qatar's capital
52. Plying with pills
56. Rabbit fur
57. Extreme
60. Certain Prot.
61. Literary monogram
63. Batten down
65. Subject to penalties, perhaps
66. "Li'l Abner" creator
68. Composer Boulanger
69. Chimney channel
70. Its motto is "Industry"
71. Insider's vocabulary
72. Equal amt.
73. Hang fire
74. Musician John

DOWN

1. Descartes and Magritte
2. Unpromising
3. Last Supper query
4. Slumps
5. Ad follower
6. Render harmless
7. Swiss capital
8. Reason to close up shop
9. Zealot's pursuit
10. Island of immigrants
11. Reduce drastically
13. Little bit
15. Blender sound
20. Tot's wheels
25. Bouquets
27. Loser to R.M.N. in '68
28. Whip mark
29. Bob, e.g.
30. 100 lbs.
31. "How exciting!"
32. Yield fig.
34. Police, with "the"
36. Spicy stew
37. More, in music
38. "Monsters, ___"
39. Floor call
42. Rhone city
45. Half a sawbuck
49. Breakfast dish
51. Laughing beast
52. Dutch pottery city
53. Iridescent gems
54. Exercise unit
55. "Gotcha!"
56. House shower
57. Attention getter
58. Small bands
59. Moor
62. Restrain
64. Golfer's vehicle
67. Advanced deg.

Solution on page 352

Challenging 96

ACROSS

1. Wall St. figure
4. ___ Park, Queens
8. Yesterday, to Yves
12. Engine part, for short
14. Practices boxing
15. Christiania, now
16. Industry big shot
17. Takes on
18. Invoice stamp
19. Calm
21. Act of faith?
23. "Is ___, Lord?"
24. Skier's spot
26. "As You Like It" forest
28. Dessert wine
31. "Ain't ___ shame?"
32. Squirreled-away item
33. The Crimson Tide
36. Attendee
40. Ballot abbr.
41. Classy
44. Knave
45. Some summer babies
47. ___ vital
48. The "I" in IV
50. "For the Boys" gp.
52. City liberated by Joan of Arc
54. "___ at the Bat" (Mudville nine poem)
57. Confetti
59. Reporter's query
60. Anniversary, e.g.
62. Becomes established
66. Get one's ducks in ___
68. Poet Doolittle
70. Faulkner character ___ Varner
71. Covered walkway
72. Sealskin wearer, maybe
73. Take down ___
74. "Death in Venice" author
75. Give a little
76. Dirty digs

DOWN

1. Bkprs.' records
2. Bring down
3. Thin fastener
4. Troy, NY, sch.
5. Baseball Hall-of-Famer Combs
6. Nod to, maybe
7. Olympus neighbor
8. Quick trip
9. "To repeat . . ."
10. "Who's Who" group
11. "The Gates of Hell" sculptor
13. Stiff drink
14. Wind ___ (flying hazard)
20. Yours, once
22. Frisk, with "down"
25. Tag
27. Dusting cloth
28. Letters
29. High school breakout
30. Dummy
31. "At Seventeen" singer Janis
34. Turkish for "lord"
35. Estate
37. Hepta- plus one
38. Be worthy of
39. Nutritional figs.
42. "Seinfeld" uncle
43. Spanish mark
46. "Peggy ___ Got Married"
49. Lipton rival
51. Barrett of Pink Floyd
53. Convened again
54. Abyss
55. Arterial trunk
56. Pass out
57. Steps over a fence
58. Euripides play
61. 1956 Peck role
63. Has a late meal
64. "___ a Song Go Out of My Heart"
65. Hungary's Imre
67. Far from ruddy
69. Fizzler

Solution on page 352

Challenging 97

ACROSS

1. Hardly rosy
5. Wanders aimlessly
9. Univ. figure
12. First name in TV talk
14. Words of agreement
15. Bone to pick
16. Loafed
17. Evening, to Yves
18. Voting "no"
19. Fishing nets
21. Can. province
22. "Cold one"
23. Blouse, e.g.
24. Lion's share
26. Actually existing
28. Ex-lax?
29. "Gidget" star
30. Hit the bottle
33. "And ___ bed"
35. Oscars' org.
40. "Battle Cry" author
41. "___ Gantry"
43. "Hair" producer
44. A goner, slangily
46. "Happy motoring" brand
47. Pituitary hormone
48. Apt. coolers
50. "Roots," e.g.
52. Pacer's place
56. Unit of pressure
57. Aunt Polly's nephew
60. Courtney Love's band
61. Big fuss
63. "Dreaming of You" singer
65. Nice notion
66. Phoenix team
68. Copier need
69. D.C. fundraisers
70. "Cogito, ___ sum"
71. When Macbeth gives his dagger soliloquy
72. Part of S.S.S.: Abbr.
73. 9–5 carmaker
74. Put an edge on

DOWN

1. Future flour
2. Bulldogger's place
3. Long Island town
4. Deportment
5. Dogfaces
6. On ___ (carousing)
7. Off
8. Combat mission
9. Chromosome components
10. Rose and Rozelle
11. Burning up
13. Plant swelling
15. Innocent
20. Lush
25. Some minks
27. Cultural org.
28. Trueheart of "Dick Tracy"
29. Playground retort
30. "Tsk!"
31. "___ y plata" (Montana's motto)
32. Zadora of "Hairspray"
34. Logos, e.g.: abbr.
36. Film rating org.
37. D.C. donor
38. Disposed
39. Geom. solid
42. Bellows
45. 1960s chess champ
49. Breaks off
51. "On the Record" host Van Susteren
52. They're rigged
53. Morning show
54. Guinness et al.
55. Apiary residents
56. Island nation east of Fiji
57. Nearing the hour
58. "There's ___ every crowd!"
59. Donny's sister
62. ___ mater (brain membrane)
64. Ness, for one
67. Bawl

Solution on page 353

Challenging 98

ACROSS
1. BB's, e.g.
5. Start to cure?
9. Buffalo
14. Phobos, to Mars
15. ___ of Evil
16. Prohibited
17. Western tie
18. Robt. E. Lee, e.g.
19. Blunted blades
20. Playground retort
22. Event for Alice
24. Clothes, slangily
26. Tout's offering
27. Do lutzes, e.g.
29. Go back to the drawing board
34. Goes limp
37. "My treat"
39. "Othello" schemer
40. Logical start?
41. Composer heard at graduations
42. Basin accompanier
43. Went off the board
44. Stand at a wake
45. Fish in a John Cleese film
46. Paris palace
48. Kind of suit
50. Pound sound
52. Bubbly
56. Dash part
61. Reserved
62. Snacks in shells
63. Drone's home
65. Former Swedish P.M. Palme
66. ___ water
67. Three or four
68. Prank
69. Goes for
70. Track action
71. Blunted weapon

DOWN
1. Sphere of influence
2. Sponge
3. Back biter
4. Alert
5. Multiroofed structure
6. Computer file name extension
7. Effort
8. ___ of Langerhans
9. Grassy plain
10. Spanish tidbit
11. Over in Germany
12. Big name in champagne
13. Floral arrangement
21. Fifth Avenue store
23. Network, e.g.
25. Russian export, familiarly
28. Georgia of "The Mary Tyler Moore Show"
30. Double dessert
31. Bowling green
32. Got mellower
33. "Sleepless in Seattle" director Ephron
34. Off the mark
35. "American ___"
36. Impose
38. "West Side Story" song
41. Critic Roger
45. "___ #1!"
47. Casts out
49. Moistens, in a way
51. "28 Days" subject
53. Cup-shaped flower
54. Chip away at
55. Friday's creator
56. Auditory
57. Linda of soaps
58. Phil of folk
59. Like some points
60. Abundant
64. Boxer doc

Solution on page 353

Challenging 99

ACROSS

1. Scale notes
4. Love handles, essentially
8. "Eight Bells" painter Winslow
13. K–6: abbr.
15. "Streamers" playwright David
16. Harden
17. Italian resort
18. "Dancing Queen" pop group
19. Bush or Kerry
20. Found out
22. Type
24. Carnival performer
25. Christie and Karenina
26. Longing
28. Garbage hauler
30. Mason of "The Goodbye Girl"
34. Keyboardist Myra
37. Jalopy
40. Program offerer
41. ___ snail's pace
42. It may be polished
44. Band box
45. Hon
47. Polar explorer
48. Rare bills
49. Some bar fixtures
51. Evil Norse god
53. Combat
56. Adult insect
60. Guitarist Atkins
63. Pharm. watchdog
64. Nike competitor
65. Menotti hero
67. Batik artisan
69. Naldi of the Ziegfeld Follies
70. "Long time ___!"
71. Atty.-to-be's exam
72. Icky stuff
73. Rhone tributary
74. Days of ___
75. Lady of Sp.

DOWN

1. Chap
2. Roswell crash victim, supposedly
3. Family car
4. Sig Chi, e.g.
5. Golden alternative
6. Yippie Hoffman
7. Jennifer of "Flashdance"
8. Attention-getter
9. Wild asses
10. Pack animal
11. 1813 battle site
12. Exude
14. Entanglement
21. Iran-Contra grp.
23. Kipling classic
26. Nerd
27. Julia of "Kiss of the Spider Woman"
29. "I guessed it!"
31. "Candida" playwright
32. Blood: prefix
33. Dadaist collection
34. Fastening device
35. Pincushion alternative
36. "Roots," for one
38. "___ questions?"
39. "Ici on ___ fran+ais"
42. De ___ (excessive)
43. Altar answer
46. Bar request
48. Comic's concern
50. Lotion letters
52. Fool
54. To everyone's surprise
55. Approval
57. "Later"
58. Swamp thing
59. 1970 World's Fair site
60. "What ___ say?"
61. Managed care gps.
62. Contentment
64. Puccini's "Vissi d'___"
66. "Crooklyn" director
68. Pencil holder, at times

Solution on page 353

Challenging 100

ACROSS

1. Copy
6. Pigeon drop, e.g.
10. Crude abode
13. Alvin of dance
14. Fire starter?
15. Gaunt
16. Prepare for winter takeoff
17. "Ignorance ___ excuse"
18. Estrada of "CHiPs"
19. It's about 350 miles NW of LAX
20. Starbucks offering
22. Brahman, e.g.
23. Goddess of youth
24. Den mother
26. Come up with
29. '50s monogram
30. Move like the Blob
31. Encumbrances
35. Mil. medals
39. Keydets' sch.
40. "___ cool!"
41. Cry of disbelief
42. Discrimination watchdog: Abbr.
44. Ramadan, e.g.
46. Hoisted, nautically
47. "Deep Space Nine" role
49. Died down
51. Worthless pile
55. Kill
56. Bunk
57. Healing plants
59. Mustard, e.g.: Abbr.
62. Bryn ___
63. Jab
64. Froth
66. ". . . baked in ___"
67. Panhandle loc.
68. Packed away
69. Batiking need
70. Cronies
71. E. C. Bentley detective

DOWN

1. Heels
2. Willingly
3. Medley
4. Japanese computer giant
5. Lace place
6. Ill will
7. Closed sac
8. Textile trademark
9. ___ juice (milk)
10. Buggy power
11. Hand and foot
12. Small fry
15. Conked
21. Biblical brother
22. New England catch
23. Possess, to Burns
25. Fingers, briefly
26. Sheltered bay
27. "Gladiator" setting
28. Singer Pinza
32. 1945 battle site, for short
33. Suffix with Caesar
34. Big Apple paper, initially
36. Good name for a Dalmatian
37. Give in
38. Get rid of
43. Hold fast
44. Extinct bird of New Zealand
45. Fit as a fiddle
46. What "that" ain't
48. "L.A. Law" actress Susan
50. Short-legged dog
51. Sportscaster Rashad
52. In a lather?
53. Actor Mandel
54. Winter wear
55. They're jerked
58. Act the couch potato
59. Adorable
60. Black cat, maybe
61. Advanced
63. Dad
65. Good thing to break

Solution on page 353

Challenging 101

ACROSS

1. Get steamy
6. ___ Pet (novelty item)
10. Engine parts
14. "___ Fly Now"
15. Ice cream purchase
16. "___ old cowhand . . ."
17. Decalogue word
18. Jared of "Panic Room"
19. "The Immoralist" author
20. "60 Minutes" reporter since 1991
22. Poor rating
24. Corporate VIPs
26. Came in first
27. Since Jan. 1
28. Dark purple
31. Inflation meas.
33. Furbys, once
35. First person in Berlin
36. City ESE of Bombay
38. Spring sound
42. Lotus car model
44. Delivery docs
45. Big voting bloc
46. Spanish hors d'oeuvres
47. Deli pancake
49. Record label inits.
50. Fivescore yrs.
52. Morse tap
53. Moonroof alternative
54. Certain theater, for short
57. "My mama done ___ ___ me . . ."
59. "Fancy" singer McEntire
61. Film material
63. Walks awkwardly
66. Joe Millionaire picked her
67. Wyle of "ER"
70. Kramden or Nader

72. BPOE part
73. "Eat ___ eaten"
74. "Time in a Bottle" singer
75. Escritoire
76. On one's guard
77. Tore into

DOWN

1. NFL scores
2. Circus cries
3. Black fly, e.g.
4. Loosen, in a way
5. Newsreel pioneer Charles
6. Pfc.'s superior
7. Get a move on
8. Following
9. Many
10. Butts
11. Accord

12. Cross with
13. Bergen spoke for him
21. Bananas
23. Give power to
25. Kite flier's aid
28. Painter Mondrian
29. Bruins' home
30. Flake
32. Out of favor
34. ___ good deed
36. Barcelona buck
37. Buzzing
39. "A likely story!"
40. Pitcher Hideo
41. Film crew member
43. Amniotic ___
48. Big name in music compilations
51. Later

53. Ballerina Karsavina
54. Demolished
55. Sorbonne, e.g.
56. Job extras
58. Arrowsmith's wife
60. Canoe material
62. Assignment
64. Drudge
65. Humane org.
68. Like pocket dicts.
69. "You, there!"
71. Worked (up)

Solution on page 353

Challenging 102

ACROSS

1. Build up
6. "Jake's Thing" author
10. Dear ones?
14. Oscar de la ___
15. Have the gumption
16. Simile center
17. Ear part
18. Arabian Sea gulf
19. Longfellow's bell town
20. Medicinal amounts
22. Hollywood hopeful
24. CPR pros
26. Kid
27. Some M.I.T. grads
28. Wall St. pros
31. Priestly vestment
33. Old video game inits.
35. N.J. neighbor
36. Bailiwicks
38. Action
42. Chips in?
44. Not dis
45. "Pagliacci" role
46. Breaks
47. Has space for
49. Alternative to dial-up, briefly
50. Grafton's "___ for Evidence"
52. Foundation exec.
53. Constrictors
54. Blue
57. Airline to Oslo
59. Confirmation, e.g.
61. Gorge crosser
63. Swedish imports
66. Air: prefix
67. Auction off
70. Sober, in a way
72. Chucklehead
73. Stick ___ in the water
74. Roebuck's partner
75. "___ and Lovers"
76. 2000 homer king
77. Attack

DOWN

1. Parenthesis, essentially
2. "Beowulf" quaff
3. The "A" in A.D.
4. Equilibria
5. Capital on the Willamette River
6. Holly Hunter in "The Piano"
7. Like a wet hen
8. Start of a legal conclusion
9. Forwarded
10. Coal-rich German region
11. Carpet fiber
12. Carnival show
13. Foul moods
21. "Shining ___" (Earth, Wind and Fire hit)
23. Bikini events
25. Flexible Flyers
28. Month after Shebat
29. Mel's "Ransom" costar
30. Diner orders
32. Bleated
34. Pou ___: vantage point
36. Rink stat
37. Flight segment
39. Prefix with -morph
40. City on the Arno
41. Answers, for short
43. Berlioz's "Les nuits d'___"
48. Speaker in Cooperstown
51. Dips for chips
53. Licked
54. Tries
55. ___ Detoo ("Star Wars" android)
56. Exorcist's target
58. Make sure of
60. Italian poet Torquato ___
62. Has a bawl
64. Meadow sounds
65. "Your majesty"
68. ___ Altos, Calif.
69. Salonga of "Miss Saigon"
71. Summer clock setting: Abbr.

Solution on page 353

Challenging 103

ACROSS
1. Mild smoke
6. Bean concoction?
10. "Happy motoring" company
14. Femme fatale
15. At the front of the line
16. Sail a zigzag course
17. "Time is money," e.g.
18. Kin's partner
19. French possessive
20. Mean
22. It's nothing new
24. 16th-century start
25. Street fixture
26. Old video game inits.
27. Wear a long face
30. Scoreboard letters
32. "The Name of the Rose" writer
34. Ristorante suffix
35. Head of costume design
37. Shady place
41. ___ Picchu
43. Seminoles' sch.
44. Spine-tingling
45. Lay to rest
46. ___ ease
48. Size abbr.
49. Doo-___
51. Dr. Seuss's Sam ___
52. Tanners catch them
53. Watch pocket
56. Partner of circumstance
58. Chemical suffix
60. Milan attraction
62. ___ Berry Farm
65. Tom Joad, for one
66. Coupler
68. Iranian money
70. Deputy
71. Stuffed shirt
72. Simple chord
73. Golf gadgets
74. Does wrong
75. Pitches in

DOWN
1. Jefferson Davis was its pres.
2. Canner's supply
3. Smell ___
4. Powers that be
5. Ceaselessly
6. Like a moonless night
7. "Agnus ___"
8. Superfluous
9. Not out
10. South Dakota, to Pierre
11. Lustrous fabric
12. Teacake
13. The Joads, e.g.
21. Encircle
23. Directed skyward
25. Reveal inadvertently
27. Puccini heroine
28. Son of Judah
29. Ancient Brit
31. LP player
33. Dungeons & Dragons monster
35. Mother of Minos
36. Hippy dance
38. ___ Cynwyd, Pa.
39. Bacchanalian bash
40. Some whiskeys
42. Chop down
47. Notorious Idi
50. Sea anemones, e.g.
52. Stop working
53. Seaplane part
54. Comic actor Jack
55. Half a 45
57. New Zealander
59. Needle point?
61. So-so grades
62. They're tapped
63. Party game pin-on
64. High-five, e.g.
67. Blood, so to speak
69. '60s demonstrators

Solution on page 354

Challenging 104

ACROSS
1. Wings
5. Bridge feat
9. Battle site of 1836
14. Burns and Allen: Abbr.
15. Without ___ (broke)
16. Rose up, in dialect
17. Spring feature
18. Cross shapes
19. Bag
20. "It's ___-brainer!"
21. Cigar end?
22. Many a trucker
23. Roman household gods
26. Movie extra, in brief
29. PC linkup
30. Underscore
34. Blind parts
37. Scrabble pieces
40. Start of many Brazilian
    city names
41. Sleek, for short
42. Greek vowels
43. Follow
44. ___ Andreas fault
45. Thrown for ___
46. Lover's suffix
47. Actress North
49. Beverage suffix
50. Blunders
52. Bears witness
56. Grps.
59. Actor Benicio del ___
61. Sylvester, to Tweety
62. Gives sparingly
64. Columnists' page
65. Finito
66. Coeur d'___, I.D.
67. Bassoon, e.g.
68. "Havana" actress
69. Origins
70. Pipe bends
71. "Cool!"

DOWN
1. Songwriters' org.
2. '70s Italian president
3. Charged particle
4. Immigrant's subj.
5. Shiny fabric
6. Exams for would-be attys.
7. Juillet's follower
8. Sources of inspiration
9. Horace's "___ poetica"
10. Cavalry member
11. Kuwaiti, e.g.
12. ___ mortals
13. Baltic feeder
24. A chorus line
25. Brits' thank-yous
27. Brings to bear
28. Goals, e.g.: Abbr.
31. Morales of "NYPD Blue"
32. Spanker, e.g.
33. Pump part
34. Be rude to
35. Judah's mother
36. "Alfred" composer
37. Excessively
38. "___ a deal!"
39. Much of "Deck the Halls"
42. Actor Robert of "The
    Sopranos"
43. Quaker's "you"
45. ___ Lingus (Irish carrier)
46. L.A. hrs.
48. Forward
49. Disagreeing
51. Cache
52. Staggering
53. Lifted, so to speak
54. Patty Hearst's name in the
    S.L.A.
55. Blockage reliever
56. Harem quarters
57. Lady Macbeth, for one
58. Exultation
60. Autobahn auto
63. French pronoun
65. Mafia boss

Solution on page 354

Challenging 105

ACROSS

1. "The Grapes of Wrath" figure
5. Propeller type
10. Wet forecast
14. Have a yen for
15. Beef cut
16. "O patria mia" singer
17. Delineate
18. Humane org.
19. Water sport gear
20. Try again
22. Made of clay
24. Enthusiasts
26. Endangered whale
27. Devonshire dad
30. Abu Dhabi is its cap.
32. Make a call
36. At bat stat
37. Intends
39. Lady of la casa
41. A hundred sawbucks
43. Future fungus
45. "Blue Velvet" star
46. Rockies range
48. Canceled, to NASA
50. Hitched
51. Boxer's wear
52. "The Princess and the ___"
53. 1936 Cooper role
55. Brandy letters
57. Faucet brand
59. Satisfy
63. Experts
67. Down Under greeting
68. Capital of Morocco
70. Daytime TV fare
71. Accounting period
72. "There Is Nothin' Like ___"
73. Julius Dithers's wife, in "Blondie"
74. Member of la famille
75. Grannies
76. Skin care brand

DOWN

1. One in the red
2. Bard's shrew
3. Barely move
4. Anesthetic gas
5. Genesis
6. "CSI" network
7. 1948 Hitchcock thriller
8. Protect, in a way
9. "___ not amused"
10. Obi
11. Winged goddess
12. Husband of Frigg
13. Functioned as
21. Halo, e.g.
23. Spare, maybe
25. Cesspool
27. Bapt. or Meth.
28. Capp lad
29. Associate with
31. All together
33. Sturm ___ Drang
34. "My Fair Lady" composer
35. Blew it
38. Mag. edition
39. Part: abbr.
40. "No ifs, ___ . . ."
42. Hunk
44. Go from pillar to post
47. Campbell of "Party of Five"
49. Had too much, briefly
52. Yankees catcher Jorge
54. Romanian composer Georges
56. Foil alternative
58. "Them" author
59. "Song of the South" syllables
60. Carson's predecessor
61. Combustible pile
62. "Voice of Israel" author
64. "Dirty" activity
65. "Gone With the Wind" setting
66. Alter, in a way
67. Swindle
69. Anti-smoking org.

Solution on page 354

Challenging 106

ACROSS

1. Fuzzy fruit
5. Hit a low note?
10. Farrier's tool
14. Exam for a doc-to-be
15. Slalom champ Phil
16. Morlocks' victims in "The Time Machine"
17. Afflicts
18. Short jackets
19. Scattered, as seed
20. Setback
22. Excite
24. Buy and sell
25. Imp
28. Breaks up
30. Get strong again
34. Gas rating
37. Earned
39. "Mud"
40. Advent song
41. 1985 Kate Nelligan film
43. Bookie's worry
44. Iowa college
45. Bone-dry
46. Channel crosser of 1926
48. Bunsen burner relatives
50. Flip-flop, e.g.
52. Interact
54. Man of many words
58. Glass ingredient
61. Destroyers, slangily
63. Sequel to "Typee"
64. Egyptian god of wisdom
67. "Betsy's Wedding" actor
68. "Gentlemen Prefer Blondes" author
69. Eucalyptivore
70. It may be grand
71. "I haven't got it ___!"
72. Sought answers
73. Omar of "Scream 2"

DOWN

1. It first opened in 1962
2. Less friendly
3. When doubled, a Washington city
4. "You're on!"
5. Tussaud, et al.
6. Horse operas
7. "Eureka!"
8. Coastal bird
9. Cul-___
10. Fix, as a pump
11. 1966 NL batting champ
12. Farm females
13. Emulate Echo
21. Brown foe
23. Coin rating
26. Targeted
27. "South Park" boy
29. Bambi, for one
31. Admitting a draft
32. Churn
33. Ancient Persian
34. First word of "The Raven"
35. Crotchety sort
36. Freshman, probably
38. Conked out
42. Actress Kudrow
43. Move
45. "Just ___!"
47. "Phooey!"
49. Melodious
51. Bug
53. Andy's "Taxi" role
55. Lively round dance
56. Eventually become
57. Peter and Paul, but not Mary
58. Arias, e.g.
59. Springsteen's "___ Fire"
60. Hang over one's head
62. "___ no idea!"
65. Sounds from Santa
66. Furniture wood

Solution on page 354

Section 3: Perplexing Puzzles

Perplexing 1

ACROSS
1. 1960s civil rights org.
5. Extinct Slavic language
10. Catapult
14. Ham's father
15. Key material
16. Parmenides' home
17. Culture starter
18. Sealy competitor
19. Dam
20. Having little talent for
22. Lowered oneself
24. Starting
26. Script ending
27. "The Temptation of St. Anthony" painter
30. Software program, briefly
32. Year in reign of Eugene III
36. Detroit-based org.
37. Carol time
39. Whence the line "Thy word is a lamp unto my feet"
41. A.A.A. recommendations
43. Satisfy
45. California county or its seat
46. Took its toll?
48. Fleming hero
50. Modern: Ger.
51. River whose name means "hateful"
52. "Rock and Roll, Hoochie ___" (1974 hit)
53. ___ as the hills
55. Opposite of dep.
57. En passant capture
59. Bribe
63. Buy in a hurry
67. Bok ___ (Chinese cabbage)
68. Make ___ of
70. Popular caramel candy
71. In a ___ (stuck)

72. Giuseppe's wife in "The Gondoliers"
73. K-P connection
74. Barrie buccaneer
75. Dilettantish
76. "Awright!"

DOWN
1. Break
2. Inoperative
3. Beloved, in "Rigoletto"
4. French Prime Minister: 1986–88
5. Green sauce
6. U.K. award
7. House member
8. Pay
9. Quickly, mailwise
10. Carved
11. Beekeeper in a 1997 film
12. Journalist Whitelaw ___
13. Malay gibbon
21. Gray, in a way
23. Masterpieces
25. Eden event
27. Pat on the back?
28. "Bellefleur" author
29. Hard work
31. R & B singer Bryson
33. Ax
34. Gaucho's turf
35. Drive
38. Currency exchange board abbr.
39. Signature piece?
40. Mideast royal name

42. Adjective for Brer Fox
44. Surgeon general under Reagan
47. Makeup, e.g.
49. Beginning
52. "Ship of Fools" director
54. Easily irritated
56. Ranch in "Giant"
58. Examination
59. Level
60. Traffic director
61. Murderous alter ego of fiction
62. Catch one's breath
64. Quince, e.g.
65. It parallels a radius
66. "Fiddlesticks!"
67. It keeps an eye on TV
69. Lottery-running org.

Solution on page 355

Perplexing 2

ACROSS

1. Drawled address
5. Certain Fed
9. Australian export
14. "Dark Angel" star Jessica
15. "LOL," vocalized
16. Part of a religious title
17. Elated
18. Produce protection
19. Etched in stone
20. Of the '50s or the '60s
22. They average 100
24. ___-Caps
25. Bad blood
26. Syrian island
28. Inverted "e"
31. Lebanese language
35. Monokini's lack
38. Do schoolwork?
40. Nobelist in physics: 1973
41. Life's partner
43. Computer input
45. Word form of "sacred"
46. Florida's ___ National Forest
48. "Unforgettable" singers
50. Resinous deposit
51. Cling
53. Bob Marley was one
55. Cold war capital
57. Exacting
61. "What's that?"
64. Tognazzi of "La Cage aux Folles"
65. Coleridge character
66. Some spreads
68. Nest part
70. Tennis edge
71. Ballet support
72. Barreled along
73. Plenty
74. Like many movies nowadays
75. Stationery store stock: Abbr.
76. Once (upon a time)

DOWN

1. Zsa Zsa's sister
2. Kind of wrench
3. Early calculators
4. House keepers
5. Clobbered
6. Attire for Galahad
7. "Kung Fu" actor Philip
8. Point of greatest despair
9. "Probably . . ."
10. It may be shot in the open
11. "Sorry to say . . ."
12. Croquet site
13. Prefix with Tibetan
21. Way in or out
23. Between sine and non
27. Line from a book?
29. WWII servicewoman
30. Fox or Coyote
32. Fee to free
33. Furniture giant
34. About: Abbr.
35. Coalition
36. Part of P.R.
37. Nanjing nanny
39. Kind of skirt
42. Blister
44. E-mail
47. Fired up
49. Suffix with game
52. H.S. class
54. Do the Wright thing?
56. Neapolitan night
58. Home of a biblical bewitcher
59. Checks
60. "The Great Forest" painter
61. Down-and-outer
62. It means "red" in Mongolian
63. Buffalo bunch
65. ICBM type
67. One of the Wright brothers, for short
69. Hit the jackpot

Solution on page 355

Perplexing 3

ACROSS
1. "The Garden of ___" (Wilde poem)
5. Long tales
10. Some stay at home
14. Kind of block
15. Rainbow: Comb. form
16. Ding-a-ling
17. Face-off
18. Bedevil
19. Ex-senator Sam
20. Showy bird's mate
22. Just right
24. Corvine call
25. Member of the wedding
27. Act the banshee
29. Kind of deer
30. Book before Nahum
34. Bit
35. Not optional
38. Composed
39. Duracell size
40. Off-road goer, for short
41. Hunk's pride
43. Conservative leader
44. Some diner orders
46. Kick off the throne
48. ___-80 (old computer)
49. Figure skater Cohen
51. Jap. neighbor
52. Certain protest
54. "___ Pretty": 1957 song
56. First name in horror
57. Acquire
60. Celestial being
63. Burglar's take
64. "___ kick out of you"
67. Rain cats and dogs
69. Fruitless
70. Chad toucher
71. "Oh"
72. Georgia et al., once: Abbr.
73. Beaker
74. Ticker locale: Abbr.

DOWN
1. Antiquity
2. Sign on for another tour
3. Pointed arch
4. Give comfort to
5. Muscle power
6. Islands off Galway
7. One-horse carriage
8. 1969 Nabokov novel
9. ___ voce (softly)
10. Forceful
11. August, in Arles
12. Physical force
13. Loudness measure
21. Yogi's co-creator
23. South Africa's ___ Paul Kruger
25. Coin word
26. Nike rival
27. Eucalyptus muncher
28. Divisions politiques
29. Idolize
31. Whines
32. Argus-eyed
33. Med. groups
34. Barbed comments
36. SFO posting
37. Recommendations
42. Table
45. Escutcheons
47. Campaign pro
50. Edwards, for one: abbr.
53. Neat ___
55. Giving the once-over
56. Becomes frayed
57. Chuck alternative
58. "Stop rowing" command
59. "The Ghost and Mrs. ___," 1947 movie
60. Jeanne d'Arc et al.: Abbr.
61. Arrangement item
62. Spectrum bands
65. "Drums Along the Mohawk" hero
66. Kind of CRT
68. Mr. ___ (old whodunit game)

Solution on page 355

Perplexing 4

ACROSS

1. Part of a large envelope
6. Black wildebeest
9. Engender
14. Book of prophecies
15. Suffix with ball or bass
16. Pond growths
17. Oil supporter
18. North of Arg.
19. Circumspect
20. Nutritional info
21. Little one
22. Cooking aid
23. Forger
25. ___ Friday's
27. "Revenge of the ___"
30. Spheres
35. Buffalo-to-Baltimore dir.
38. Shade
40. Brown bagger
41. Coming up
43. ___ Appia
44. Words following "often"
45. 1968 British comedy "Only When I ___"
46. Prepare some leftovers
48. Sharkey's TV rank
49. Ponied up?
51. Rush hour problem
53. Nero, e.g.: abbr.
55. "Grand" hotel
58. Hightail it
61. Cork sources
64. Tudor queen
66. Doughnut-shaped surface
67. Alley org.
68. Eyelashes
69. City west of Daytona Beach
70. "___ a sock in it!"
71. Interminably
72. French greeting
73. ___ clip
74. "The Sound of Music" song

DOWN

1. "Clueless" lead role
2. A heap
3. Tea-growing state
4. Greets and seats
5. Cohort
6. Elapse
7. Breakfast place
8. Empty, as an apartment
9. ___ Mae
10. Fund-raising letter, e.g.
11. Stress, say
12. "Beaver's" dad
13. Napoleon's "bravest of the brave"
21. By way of, briefly
24. Gravitate
26. Educ. test
28. Kevin Kline comedy, 1993
29. Mean moods
31. Jimmy Stewart syllables
32. Hayes of "The Mod Squad"
33. Alphabet quartet
34. ___ speak
35. Large hall
36. 1979 exile
37. Gateway Arch architect Saarinen
39. "Call Me Irresponsible" lyricist
42. Home of the Atlas Mts.
44. Off
46. "Shiny Happy People" band
47. Spa sounds
50. Assails
52. Thin layer
54. Old man
56. Old German coin
57. "Lemon Tree" singer Lopez
58. ___ Raton, Fla.
59. Like some exams
60. Knockout
62. Have an edge against
63. Judo exercises
65. Word usually said in triplicate
66. How-___
68. URL ending

Solution on page 355

Perplexing 5

ACROSS

1. Pickpocket, in slang
4. San ___
8. Moves toward
13. Ranch extension?
14. Per annum
15. Native New Yorkers
16. Canon camera model
17. *Fortune* 500 company based in Moline, Ill.
18. "All clear" signal
19. Cutting
21. Mauna ___, HI
23. "Bill & ___ Excellent Adventure"
24. Barbara of horror films
27. German valley
29. Church chorus
31. Interstice
35. Indian rice
38. First name at the Fed
40. Apprehended
41. "Runaway" singer Shannon
42. Showed fright
44. "First Blood" director Kotcheff
45. Internet marketing
48. "Able was ___ I saw Elba"
49. Adds turf to
50. Book of the Apocrypha
52. Roman sandal
54. Old English letters
56. Begins
59. "By yesterday!"
62. In-flight guesstimate, for short
64. Birch of "American Beauty"
66. Conventions
68. Out of the way
71. Alphabet trio
72. " . . . ___ and hungry look": Shak.
73. Tears to pieces
74. End for serpent or elephant
75. 1955–77 alliance
76. Kit Carson's home
77. Cabin bed

DOWN

1. G.P.A. spoilers
2. "Reversal of Fortune" star
3. Assume as fact
4. Bar staple
5. Bigfoot's shoe width
6. Earthy deposit
7. After-lunch sandwiches
8. ___ Ziyyona, Isr.
9. Asmara is its capital
10. Frigid finish
11. "The Third Man" director
12. I.D.s for the IRS
14. Revoke legally
20. Official with a list
22. Bond rating
25. Act of faith
26. Big name in Chinese history
28. Music sheet abbr.
30. Corporate department
32. Able to see right through
33. Wasn't honest
34. Added details
35. "Song of the South" song syllables
36. 1986 World Series champs
37. "When I was ___ . . ."
39. ___ Circus (where St. Peter was crucified)
43. Strike
46. "Again . . . ."
47. Bucko
49. Obi, e.g.
51. "___ Cried" (1962 hit)
53. Diminutive endings
55. Get cracking
57. Bar mixer
58. Down East college town
59. Latin 101 verb
60. Dover delicacy
61. Acreage
63. Floating, perhaps
65. In ___ (miffed)
67. ___ Balls (Hostess snack food)
69. Rescuer of Odysseus, in myth
70. Drill wielder: Abbr.

Solution on page 355

Perplexing 6

ACROSS

1. Mischievous one
4. ___-American
8. O.T. book
12. Air
14. Glossy
15. "M*A*S*H" actor
16. Gumbo ingredient
17. Form of greeting
18. Virna in "Arabella"
19. What the pot calls "black"
21. Cayuga or Keuka
23. Colo. neighbor
24. Minuscule
26. Brighton bye-byes
28. "Try it!"
31. Fort Worth inst.
32. "Young Man With ___" (1950)
33. Certain bond, informally
36. In the dumps
40. Archipelago unit: Abbr.
41. "West Side Story" song
44. "Boola boola" singer
45. "Zuckerman Unbound" novelist
47. "Mildred Pierce" novelist
48. ___ list
50. Little ___
52. Triumvirates
54. Green spots
57. Grouper group
59. Soccer star Freddy
60. Dog bane
62. Legends
66. Rinehart character
68. Busy
70. Nigerian people
71. "___My Song": 1991 film
72. Eugene of travel guide fame
73. Insect nests
74. Stars
75. Cafeteria item
76. Take in

DOWN

1. Comment after an accident
2. Squeakers
3. Cheeky
4. Eskimo knife
5. Brings down
6. Olympic event
7. "All right already!"
8. Half of a 1955 merger: Abbr.
9. House coat
10. By land ___
11. Plagiarizes
13. Go on
14. "Hear No Evil" star
20. Diva Mitchell
22. "Yadda, yadda, yadda," briefly
25. Mythical lion's home
27. Dog days mo.
28. It'll grow on you
29. "Now I see!"
30. Battery word
31. Behavioral quirk
34. Altdorf is its capital
35. Beethoven's "Choral" Symphony
37. News source, maybe
38. Forearm part
39. Go wide of, say
42. Hosts
43. "For the whining of ___": Donne
46. Clamor
49. Astronaut Collins
51. Bouncing check abbr.
53. "Gotcha"
54. Blue language
55. "Later!"
56. Lazy ___
57. What to call un hombre
58. Part of a polliwog
61. Plagiarize
63. Not worth ___
64. Like some sums
65. Leave out
67. Big hits: Abbr.
69. Kind of flour

Solution on page 355

Perplexing 7

ACROSS

1. Cpls. and sgts.
5. Variety of diving bird
10. Spanish tar
14. Word form meaning "wine"
15. "In & Out" star, 1997
16. Ankh feature
17. College application nos.
18. Cupid's boss
19. Adjust
20. Foreign assembly
22. Starting points
24. "Cannery Row" character
27. A.C.L.U. concerns: Abbr.
28. "___ the fields we go"
31. Flat-topped formations
33. Comparative word
37. Certain southeast Asian
38. Embroiders
39. Exactly
41. English elegist
43. French equivalent of the Oscar
45. Founder of New York's Public Theater
46. Having a handle
48. Suffix with symptom
50. "The Facts of Life" actress
51. "Air" head
52. Patsy's "Absolutely Fabulous" pal
53. Martinique, e.g.
54. Surgery sites, briefly
56. Picks (up)
58. Meter maid?
62. Conk out
66. "Turandot" role
67. Deli display
70. Difference in values
71. Hierarchy level
72. Joint
73. Rifle part
74. Flight data, briefly
75. "Home Alone" actor
76. Editor's veto

DOWN

1. Thick drinks
2. French chef's mushroom
3. Grandson of Leah
4. 1960 Everly Brothers hit
5. Accepts
6. Diminutive suffix
7. "I ___ the Sofa": Cowper
8. Puts in
9. Rested against
10. Some diner orders
11. Bounder
12. A dog's age
13. Big clod
21. Gobblers
23. "___ perpetua" (Idaho motto)
25. Model Gabrielle
26. " . . . mercy on such ___": Kipling
28. "Eugene Onegin" mezzo
29. ___ living (bring home the bacon)
30. Certain tribute
32. Longtime Syrian leader
34. Fortune
35. Arcade pioneer
36. High land
39. Group of three
40. Fleuret's kin
42. Orange tuber
44. Eagerly expectant
47. Barfly's binge
49. Stadium souvenirs
52. Ancient ascetic
55. Make new charts
57. Attempts
58. Grimace
59. "Oliver!" choreographer White
60. Diner menu section
61. "The Odd Couple" director
63. Bust ___
64. For dieters
65. 1990s Senate majority leader
66. Grand ___ ("Evangeline" setting)
68. Mom's specialty, briefly
69. Tre + tre

Solution on page 356

Perplexing 8

ACROSS

1. Inferior
6. Learned
10. Arguing loudly
14. "___ Song Go . . ."
15. Gudrun's victim
16. Shave
17. Pear-shaped instrument
18. Buck passers?
19. Deposer of Obote
20. Irritate
22. Dye stuff
24. Abbr. in a help-wanted ad
25. Like a line, briefly
26. Back muscle, briefly
27. Shooting marbles
30. Literary monogram
32. Essex contemporary
34. Vietnamese coin
35. Gardner and others
37. Chili rating unit?
41. "The results ___"
43. Constellation
44. Playwright Jones
45. Doesn't play
46. "Beowulf," et al.
48. Beetle, e.g.
49. Part of ATM
51. '60s chess champ
52. Traffic ___
53. ___-80 (old computer)
56. Choice
58. Balmoral Castle's river
60. Brimming
62. Devilfish
65. Forerunner of the Sensor, Mach3 and Fusion
66. A Muppet
68. Ornamentation
70. German crowd?
71. Essex contemporaries
72. "Star Wars" droid
73. Got a load of
74. Sch. periods
75. Charteris sleuth

DOWN

1. Ill. neighbor
2. "Hollywood Homicide" actress, 2003
3. Nervous network
4. What some stars stand for
5. Have an ___ the ground
6. "Marat/___"
7. ___ Z
8. Collect slowly
9. Disney head
10. "Be ___!" ("Can you help me here?")
11. Language of India
12. One of Chekhov's "Three Sisters"
13. CIA director under Clinton and Bush
21. Groucho expression
23. Tens, perhaps
25. Be in charge of
27. "___ she blows!"
28. Interlaken's river
29. Bounced checks, hangnails, etc.
31. "Oh, my!"
33. "___ Buttermilk Sky"
35. Cinch
36. Big account
38. "Giovanna d'___" (Verdi opera)
39. Bookbinding leather
40. Entangle
42. "Give ___ whirl"
47. "Crimes and Misdemeanors" actor
50. Home runs, in slang
52. Et ___
53. Business
54. Have another go at
55. Bout of indulgence
57. CSA general
59. "___ a Man" (Calder Willingham novel and play)
61. Installed
62. Terrarium growth
63. Broadway opening
64. Sometime today, say
67. Recipient of many a televised "Hi"
69. "Poppycock!"

Solution on page 356

Perplexing 9

ACROSS

1. Bowl-shaped pan
4. Pubmates
8. Recipe abbr.
12. City in S France
14. Big book
15. Dewey's brother
16. "Ol' Man River" composer
17. It's usually boring
18. Printer's amount
19. Captivated
21. Stops
23. Alter
26. Tyler of "Armageddon"
27. Hung a curve
30. Apparatus
32. Food, shelter, etc.
36. Fridge foray
37. Back out of (an agreement)
39. Eat late
40. Mil. branch
41. Ad ___
42. Eighty-six
43. Cable co. that merged with AT&T
44. Ile ___-H,ISne
45. Good luck charm
47. Alarm
48. Auto selection
50. Unspecified no.
51. "Leave ___ Heaven," 1945 melodrama
52. April 15 payment
54. Asking price
56. Blocks
60. Fortunate
64. Our genus
65. Sip
68. Tony's portrayer on "NYP. D. Blue"
69. Bows
70. Got to
71. Johnny Bench's team
72. Crux
73. ___ effort
74. Run down

DOWN

1. Boat trailer?
2. Author Robert ___ Butler
3. "From Here to Eternity" actress
4. First lady before Eleanor
5. H.S. class
6. Went kaput
7. *New Yorker* cartoonist Edward
8. Do well
9. Pleads
10. Everglades deposit
11. British actress Sylvia
13. Caught
14. Minnesota of pool
20. Pepe le ___, of cartoons
22. Nasal spray brand
24. Darkness personified
25. Carry the day
27. Bridge support
28. Dispatch
29. Frosty
31. League of Nations seat
33. Ethyl acetate, e.g.
34. Ticket on the streets
35. Dick's veep
37. Flange
38. "Skedaddle!"
41. Polynesian porch
46. "My Name Is Asher ___" (Chaim Potok novel)
47. Trial balloon
49. Not more than
51. Marauder
53. Seat of Greene County, Ohio
55. Wasn't honest
56. Great pretender
57. Rent
58. Pool site, maybe
59. Travel the Internet
61. Brought into play
62. Moslem judge
63. Chocolate treat
66. MGM rival, once
67. Father's talk: Abbr.

Solution on page 356

Perplexing 10

ACROSS

1. ___ Na (rock group)
6. "Je ne ___ quoi"
10. New Deal org.
13. "El Cid" actress
14. Mediterranean port of Spain
15. James of "Las Vegas"
16. Eager
17. Songwriter Jacques
18. A4 maker
19. Flashed signs
20. Diner cupful
21. Part of the Louisiana Purchase
23. Workshop of Hephaestus
26. Last name in radar
27. The prince in "The Prince and the Pauper"
30. Former GDR ally
32. Radio host Hansen
33. Dodger pitcher Alejandro
35. Flout
39. Ed.'s in-box filler
40. Unknown element
43. Pulitzer playwright Akins
44. Cuatro doubled
46. Old English letters
47. Cinema name
49. Martha of "Some Came Running"
51. Paper section
52. "Even ___ speak . . ."
54. Attempts
57. Is out
59. Sock sound
60. Gulf of Greece
64. "___ do"
65. Kind of bed
67. "Come ___?"
68. Cover
69. Nick
70. Engender
71. Neighbor of Uru.
72. Marie and others: Abbr.
73. ___ directed

DOWN

1. Moravian, e.g.
2. Give an edge to
3. "Vissi d'___," Puccini aria
4. WKRP news director Les
5. "___ calls?"
6. Clog kin
7. Word form of "kidney"
8. Cause of an explosion
9. He defeated polio
10. Gounod opera
11. Assailed
12. Flavoring for a Cannes cordial
15. False rumor
20. One of the Beverly Hillbillies
22. Cries on seeing a cute baby
24. "The Lost World" menace
25. Em and Bee
27. Dagwood's neighbor
28. Computer insert
29. No-loss, no-gain situation
31. ___ Miguel (largest of the Azores)
33. Sky pilot
34. Command level: Abbr.
36. Israel's Weizman
37. Pump filler
38. Driving needs
41. Honorarium
42. Like some muscles
45. "Them's the breaks"
48. Pharmacists' concerns
50. "Uh-huh"
51. Byword
52. ___ ego
53. Baseball exec Bud
55. Milksop's lack
56. Numbers
57. Destructive Hindu god
58. F.C.C. concerns: Abbr.
61. Have a tantrum
62. "___ yellow ribbon . . ."
63. Lowly workers
66. "Educated insolence," according to Aristotle
67. ___ Dhabi, U.A.E.

Solution on page 356

Perplexing 11

ACROSS

1. Flamboyant fish
5. "Hogwash!"
9. "Gunsmoke" bartender
12. Jimmies
14. Beat, but barely
15. Port prefix
16. Out on a limb?
17. Radiant look
18. Got on
19. Antarctica's ___ Coast
21. Reagan's "Star Wars" prog.
22. Capital of Fiji
23. Bladed tool
24. Chicago trade center
26. Conical abodes
28. Erato's instrument
29. Aquatic shocker
30. It's insurable
33. Month after Ab
35. Old highway name
40. Cup part
41. Hockey great Potvin
43. Concept: Comb. form
44. Flip
46. Actress Foch
47. Field for an engr.
48. Abbr. on an Rx
50. Land on the Strait of Hormuz
52. Like tears
56. ___ Hubbard
57. Article written by Freud
60. Colonial orator
61. Staff sgt., e.g.
63. Acropolis figure
65. Face up to
66. Belted out
68. Sniggled
69. Art Spiegelman's Pulitzer-winning graphic novel
70. ___-deucey
71. Game ragout
72. 911 responder
73. Desolate
74. "The Banana Boat Song"

DOWN

1. Sofia's portrayer in "The Color Purple"
2. Site of some famous hangings
3. Anouk of "Lola"
4. Make sound
5. Med. country
6. In other words, in other words
7. Cry of mock horror
8. Phoenician, e.g.
9. Transition
10. Advil rival
11. Touchy fellow?
13. Like some eels
15. Door fixture
20. Auriculate
25. Soften
27. Babb's girlfriend
28. NASA craft
29. "Sense and Sensibility" sister
30. Units of wt.
31. "Deathtrap" author Levin
32. Hi-___
34. Prefix with cellular
36. Paint
37. Do, re, mi
38. Federal agcy., 1946–75
39. Kabuki kin
42. Mead subject
45. Penn ___, NY
49. Monthly
51. Poker payments
52. Amiens is its capital
53. Elite military unit
54. Capt.'s inferior
55. Adherents
56. Kind of wolf
57. Street of fiction
58. Kind of fire
59. Beachgoer's carry-along
62. Bad: Prefix
64. Stock unit
67. Med. specialty

Solution on page 356

Perplexing 12

ACROSS

1. Filly
5. P.M. times
9. Terse reproof
12. Moundsman Hershiser
13. Inexperienced
15. Small salmon
16. Scold severely
17. Complex unit
18. Difference in values
19. Clan emblem
21. Public works project
22. Alert the host
23. It's often taken
26. Actions at auctions
28. "Make ___ double"
31. Trades
33. Anatomical dividers
37. Big bird
38. Ben's "Meet the Fockers" costar
39. Graduated
40. Name part: Abbr.
42. Beth's preceder
44. It comes in a roll
45. Higher-ranking
47. Box kite's lack
49. "Seduction of the Minotaur" author
50. Bush whacker?
51. Spoilers
52. Chess pc.
53. Where Samson died
55. Unit of fat
57. Air
60. Suffix with planet
62. Like some TV shows
66. Hardly a blabbermouth
67. Branch of knowledge
70. Pickup shtick?
71. Experience
72. "Ditto!"
73. Old Chinese money
74. Chemical suffix
75. Passbook amts.
76. Flight segment

DOWN

1. Room at the top
2. 1968 live folk album
3. Stock exchange membership
4. More devious
5. Radio abbr.
6. Back
7. Minister
8. Lot choices
9. Threads
10. Dagger
11. Surgeon general under Reagan
14. "It Ain't Gonna Rain ___"
15. Baby-shower gift
20. Aerosol output
24. Use four-letter words
25. Auto pioneer Benz
27. Mil. hero's award
28. Maya Angelou's "And Still ___"
29. Not flabby
30. Flying through
32. Michelangelo masterwork
34. Ship board
35. Green gimme
36. Common contraction
39. More likely to retire
41. Draw
43. Hunger sign
46. Mouths, zoologically
48. Hurdle for an atty.-to-be
51. Dealt with a leak, maybe
54. Lens type
56. Fountain fare
57. "___ Breaky Heart"
58. ___-Ude (Trans-Siberian Railroad city)
59. Four-star
61. Be too fond
63. "South Pacific" girl
64. Child support?
65. Painful bark
68. Bushes are in it
69. Attention-getters

Solution on page 356

Perplexing 13

ACROSS

1. Prunes
5. Music lover's collection
10. Callao's land
14. Company founded by Ingvar Kamprad
15. 1960s TV dog
16. Wood sorrels
17. 1856 Stowe novel
18. More genuine
19. Dilute
20. "The Terminator" heroine
22. Spoils
24. Winston Churchill, e.g.
27. Drug at Woodstock
28. Came by
31. Rank above sarge
33. 911 respondents: Abbr.
37. "Exodus" character
38. Blowgun ammo
39. Shade of red
41. Skips commercials, in a way
43. "Gin a body ___ body": Burns
45. Seldon in "Foundation Trilogy"
46. George and others
48. Hardly the pick of the litter
50. Trophy
51. City in the center of Sicily
52. Santa portrayer in "Elf"
53. Fat letters
54. Some chess pieces: Abbr.
56. Key with three sharps: Abbr.
58. Draft choice
62. Agreements
66. Prefix with globin
67. Like some chili
70. ___ room
71. 1951 NL Rookie of the Year
72. August birthstone
73. Parisian peeper
74. "I went into a public-___ to get a pint o' beer": Kipling
75. Recesses
76. Capital of Moravia

DOWN

1. Hats, slangily
2. Gumbo green
3. Duke, e.g.
4. 1978 Camp David visitor
5. "Gimme ___!"
6. Acre's land: abbr.
7. Formal accessory
8. Like jambalaya
9. Breeds
10. Kitties
11. Bounce back, in a way
12. Beatles hit
13. CPO's org.
21. Broker's advice
23. Pulitzer-winning biographer Leon
25. Drifts
26. Days of old
28. See stars, maybe
29. Pope's cape
30. Easy two-pointer
32. Anatomical canals
34. Start of a Chinese game
35. Hint
36. Milk whey
39. Cave ___
40. Good things that come to those who wait
42. Jupiter, to Saturn
44. Charlie, for one
47. Appropriate
49. Ambush
52. Like a somnambulist
55. Bay city
57. John ___ Astor
58. ___ de soie (silk cloth)
59. Tan and others
60. Fail to convince a jury
61. Barbering obstacles
63. "Bang Bang" singer, 1966
64. Mirror backing
65. Capital of France's Manche department
66. Coverage corp.
68. 7-up, e.g.
69. Gridiron gains: Abbr.

Solution on page 357

Perplexing 14

ACROSS

1. In good shape
5. Part of CRT
9. High ___
12. Blue Cross rival
14. Single
15. ___ processor
16. Asperity
17. Lighten
18. Iso- relative
19. "Who ___?"
21. Excite, with "up"
22. Osso ___
23. Starter's need
24. Like an octopus's defense
26. Dodgers' field, once
28. Prefix with -algia
29. Burma's first P.M.
30. Long-snouted fish
33. Gentle stuff
35. As yet
40. Alternative to Windows
41. Silvery salmon
43. Chi follower
44. Siamese fighting fish
46. High notes
47. Mormon State flower
48. Part of N.J.
50. Patton namesake
52. Loafer, e.g.
56. Designer Wang
57. Forum matter
60. Languish
61. Football positions: Abbr.
63. Tintoretto's "The Miracle of ___ Freeing the Slave"
65. London greeting
66. Home of Rubbermaid
68. Camp craft
69. The Kennedys, e.g.
70. Exxon has one
71. ___ cuisine
72. Chief
73. Fontanne's partner
74. Detect

DOWN

1. Good start?
2. Five of a kind
3. Wearer of three stars: Abbr.
4. Abel's nephew
5. Diary abbr.
6. The not operator, e.g.
7. First or third
8. Big roll
9. Chef's hat
10. Burp
11. "Later!"
13. 1970s sitcom
15. Emily of "Our Town"
20. Some bolt holders
25. "Ship of Fools" director
27. "Speed" setting
28. Apple's cousin
29. Burning the midnight oil
30. Where to find porters
31. Like Bruckner's Symphony No. 7
32. Little vixen
34. Tiny particle: Abbr.
36. City on the Om
37. "Bah!"
38. Oscar winner Lee
39. Density symbol, in physics
42. Bygone autocrats
45. Arizona mining town
49. Matriculate
51. "But of course!"
52. Crumb
53. Charles de Gaulle's birthplace
54. Dental work
55. Hacienda hand
56. Triumphant gesture
57. Incurred
58. Word form of "sexy"
59. Sport with traps
62. G
64. Peter who wrote "The Valachi Papers"
67. Salesman's dest.

Solution on page 357

Perplexing 15

ACROSS

1. Shots, for short
5. Big model
9. '50s campaign name
14. Catty remark
15. Eight bells
16. Awaken rudely
17. Couple's word
18. Beethoven's "Archduke ___"
19. Sgt. York
20. "For the Boys" subj.
21. Like some mus. keys
22. San Diego suburb
24. One paying a flat fee
26. "___ Max," 1979 Mel Gibson film
27. A Swiss army knife has lots of them
29. Geol., e.g.
30. Most NPR stations
33. Prince Valiant's lady
36. Code on Hartsfield-bound luggage
38. Addition symbol
40. Play the siren
41. Dubai is part of it: Abbr.
42. Foxx on the box
43. All, in stage directions
45. Heavy-duty cleanser
46. Throws a party for
47. Bull markets
48. "Sesame Street" watcher
50. Cascades lake
52. Mortar beater
53. Shoot over
57. It rises in the Cotswolds
60. An ounce of grass, on the street
61. Artist Shahn
62. "Johnny B. ___": Berry hit
63. Class-conscious grps.?
65. Briny drop
66. "Not without ___": Pope
67. "___ Baby" ("Hair" song)
68. Beloved, in "Rigoletto"
69. They fought the British in 1900
70. "Nuts!"
71. "___ be a cold day in hell . . ."

DOWN

1. Henri's love for Coco
2. North Sea feeder
3. Dolt
4. Pained expressions
5. Total
6. Eve's counterpart
7. How Miss Piggy refers to herself
8. Chemical compound
9. Like the words of Jesus
10. Parceled
11. Pampers rival
12. Flu source
13. BBC rival
21. Acoma is built on one
23. Cable network
25. One in a class by himself
28. Waterfall
29. Unwelcome forecast
30. Agonize
31. Ancient Iranian
32. Benchmarks: Abbr.
33. Jesus, for one
34. Mattress problem
35. Coastal raptors
37. Dundee firth
39. Ain't right?
44. Pollen producers
46. ___ Gailey of "Miracle on 34th Street"
49. Eng. award
51. Gone up
52. "M*A*S*H" character
54. Skip ___
55. Unit of wisdom
56. Join
57. "___ the morning!"
58. Boring result
59. WWI plane
60. Animal house
62. Blah-blah-blah
64. As yet unscheduled: Abbr.
65. Cable co. that merged with AT&T

Solution on page 357

Perplexing 16

ACROSS

1. Drop
4. Al Mundy's boss
8. "The Devil and Daniel Webster" writer
13. Answering-machine prompt
15. Car part
16. Cape ___, WA
17. Farm calls
18. Makes it?
19. Rest stop lineup
20. Ultimate object
22. Clairvoyance, for short
24. "Alice" diner
25. Sherlock Holmes' creator
26. Its one-euro coins depict an owl
28. Prefix with carpal
30. Washington and others
34. Amateur video subject, maybe
37. Dixie drink
40. Musical Waters
41. Caret's key
42. Beersheba locale
44. ___ Darya River
45. Act the advocate
48. Author Marsh
50. ET from the '50s
51. Smelt, e.g.
53. "Children of the Poor" author
55. Some museum pieces
58. German town
62. Bull sheet?
65. Suffix with super
66. Snookums
67. Fatty liquid
69. "Mystic Pizza" actress
71. "___ Old Cowhand"
72. Saki, really
73. Hit the road
74. "___ Blame Me"
75. 1973 resignee
76. "A Loss of Roses" playwright
77. Bowl call

DOWN

1. Declined
2. Gambling game
3. Some eyes are this
4. Abbr. in many org. names
5. Chemical prefix
6. "Luck and Pluck" author
7. "Demian" author
8. Humanities degs.
9. Periodic table member
10. Finger, in a way
11. Base
12. Itar-___
14. Hymn
21. Actor ___ Cobb
23. "Foot" form
26. Physician to Marcus Aurelius
27. Inc., overseas
29. 252 wine gallons
31. Barrymore role in 1930
32. Blood pigment
33. House of a lord?
34. Mail letters
35. Record holder
36. Cart pullers
38. ___ roll
39. Harry & David order
43. "QB ___" (Uris novel)
46. "Top Hat" star
47. "In excelsis ___"
49. Chantilly's department
52. Soft & ___ (deodorant brand)
54. Far from flighty
56. Conductor Sir Georg
57. Lover of Eos
59. Breastplate
60. Rigg of TV's "The Avengers"
61. Extra inning
62. Cook book
63. Chug-___
64. ___ Station
66. Acute
68. "___ what?"
70. Car nut

Solution on page 357

Perplexing 17

ACROSS

1. Pioneer cell phone co.
4. "The Censor"
8. Made-up
13. Quaint sigh
15. Expressed surprise
16. Longtime "All My Children" role
17. Breaks down, in a way
18. Carry the torch for
19. Bowery figures
20. Easy on the eyes
22. Handicapper's hangout, for short
24. Ally McBeal, e.g.: Abbr.
25. Back, in a way
26. Banner
28. Science fiction writer Frederik
30. Alaskan National Park
34. Consequently
37. Affectation
40. Verboten
41. All ___
42. Keats, to Shelley
44. Commotion
45. Tons
47. Magnesium silicate
48. Flood preventer
49. Bacteria-ridden
51. It's money, proverbially
53. Ancient meeting places
56. "Rubber Soul" or "Revolver"
60. Altercation
63. "___ Blu Dipinto Di Blu": 1958 hit
64. Long cigar
65. Get around
67. "East of Eden" girl
69. "The fix ___"
70. Actress Thomas
71. Geometric fig.
72. Eight: Comb. form
73. Brooklyn's ___ Institute
74. Drugs, briefly
75. Neighbor of Turk.

DOWN

1. Canadian peninsula
2. Prickle
3. Surround snugly
4. Ape
5. Yellowfin tuna
6. Mortise's mate
7. "Night Music" playwright
8. Limited number
9. Columnist Huffington
10. Dryer detritus
11. Connery, by birth
12. Lenient
14. Prevents
21. Brace
23. Nod, maybe
26. "Ash Wednesday" poet
27. Comprehends
29. "We've been ___!"
31. Dugout shelter
32. "Over there!"
33. "___ you one!"
34. "Jabberwocky" opener
35. Online giggle
36. Sun Bowl Stadium sch.
38. Code carrier, for short
39. Main men?
42. Eat like ___
43. Here, elsewhere
46. Cocked
48. Texas border city
50. Fleece
52. Autumn Harvest Uprising leader
54. Violate a treaty, perhaps
55. "Seascape" playwright
57. Certain pears
58. Accord
59. Big house
60. Way off
61. Match king Kreuger
62. Public assemblies
64. Skimbleshanks' musical
66. "i" lid
68. Abbr. on a manifest

Solution on page 357

Perplexing 18

ACROSS

1. Bohemian
6. Flake material
10. Beef
14. Death in Venice
15. "The Professional" star
16. Word form of "sacred"
17. Area over a stage
18. x, y, or z
19. Halogen: Comb. form
20. Seers see them
22. Enter quietly
24. Booty
26. Many, many moons
27. Chemical ending
28. The in crowd?
31. Elemental ending
33. Latin 201
35. Four-time Japanese prime minister
36. Band leader Shaw
38. Beat
42. Actress Gray and others
44. Broadway bio of 1989
45. Hot spot
46. Sound units
47. Like "The X-Files"
49. Big pooch
50. U.S. monetary unit
52. June bug
53. "Tom Thumb" star Tamblyn
54. __ de Cologne (perfume)
57. Good name, for short
59. Garden-variety
61. Kind of lineup
63. Snake pit's state
66. First name in gossip
67. Island near Corsica
70. Amor's ammo
72. Asian cuisine
73. Queen who wrote "Leap of Faith"
74. Iterate
75. Word before disk or copy
76. City on the Hudson
77. Essay, say

DOWN

1. Big inits. in bowling
2. Popular caramel candy
3. In good shape
4. Hardens
5. Like some questions
6. Kind of strap
7. "Toy Story" dinosaur
8. Cordial flavoring
9. Star jelly genus
10. Pet plant
11. Garlicky spread
12. Made over
13. Inclined
21. "Bon __"
23. Crate
25. "___ le feste" ("Rigoletto" aria)
28. Baker's dozen?
29. Another, in Madrid
30. Beef buy
32. Stuck in the mud
34. Bantu tongue
36. Catalog
37. New money
39. Dilly
40. Much may follow it
41. Captures
43. James Fenimore Cooper's "___ Myers"
48. ___-Z (Camaro model)
51. Discovered
53. Lion
54. Our "mother"
55. __ shirt (colorful garment)
56. Of an armbone
58. Ranking monastic
60. Quick
62. Aforementioned
64. Estimate follower
65. In order (to)
68. "Bad call!"
69. "Muskrat Ramble" composer
71. Fourth of July?

Solution on page 357

Perplexing 19

ACROSS

1. Dried coconut meat
6. Poet Van Duyn
10. Smack
14. Immature hooter
15. "The company for women"
16. "Come ___!"
17. Academy head
18. No-goodniks
19. Seltzer starter
20. Restricts
22. Scottie, e.g.
24. ___ Tamid (synagogue lamp)
25. CIA worry
26. "That wasn't nice!"
27. Kunis of "That '70s Show"
30. WWII agcy.
32. "Gee whiz!"
34. New Zealand tribe
35. Expressionless
37. Go ___ for
41. "Haystacks" painter
43. "O patria ___" ("Aida" aria)
44. Budget alternative
45. Dry cell part
46. Counts' counterparts
48. Tom Hanks comedy, 1988
49. Wine: Prefix
51. 401, to Marcus
52. Small fry
53. Cosset
56. Podded plants
58. Its capital was Richmond, Va.
60. Rolled by
62. Donnybrooks
65. Facial spasms
66. Boxing's Oscar ___ Hoya
68. Plant suffix
70. "No returns"
71. Like some church matters
72. "Affliction" star, 1998
73. Baryshnikov, by birth
74. Corner pieces
75. "___ Want to Know a Secret?": Beatles

DOWN

1. Booking agent?
2. Hogwarts messengers
3. Surveyor's work
4. Image receiver
5. Observe Yom Kippur, say
6. Apple products
7. Female gametes
8. Acknowledge
9. Saint honored on April 21
10. Adonis's killer
11. Pitch-black
12. "Oliver Twist" villain
13. Carroll prey
21. Canter alternative
23. Ropes on the range
25. Nuts
27. "Oh, ___!"
28. Lay ___ (flatter)
29. London kitchen flooring
31. Quince, e.g.
33. He disposed Sihanouk
35. Imbues
36. Draper's unit
38. The Who's "___ O'Riley"
39. In
40. Garb
42. Tokyo, before 1868
47. Vermin
50. Cleopatra's ___
52. It's only skin-deep
53. Bridal path bit
54. Actress Neal of "The Hughleys"
55. Assumed
57. "You've got ___!"
59. Blackjack option
61. "Hey, buddy!"
62. Bursae
63. Overly suave
64. "And ___ bed": Pepys
67. "___ ol' me?"
69. Modern: Ger.

Solution on page 358

Perplexing 20

ACROSS

1. Lifeline site
5. Invoice word
10. "___ chance"
14. Iris holder
15. Children's refrain
16. Actor-composer Novello
17. Beverage brand
18. "Dallas" Miss
19. Back
20. Columbus discovered it in 1498
22. Emotional pang
24. Sarcastic reply
25. Kind of algebra
26. Erred on
29. "I Can't ___ Satisfaction": Stones hit
30. Perjurer's admission
31. Stupefy
32. Arizona mining town
35. ___ Pahlavi, former shah
36. Not fresh
37. Badlands Natl. Park locale
38. Guitar, familiarly
39. Slaves
40. Rich dessert
41. Double features?
42. Brightened, with "up"
43. Struggling
46. Chief Big Bear, for one
47. ___ land
48. Completely
52. "Baseball Tonight" airer
53. Best
55. Having no force
56. Carpet feature
57. Betting game
58. She outwrestled Thor
59. Four's inferior
60. Tent caterpillar
61. Chancellor of Austria: 1953–1961

DOWN

1. Football play
2. Say so
3. City near Provo
4. Gist
5. Thatched
6. Gulf of Aqaba port
7. Fuse
8. George ___
9. Directly opposed
10. Ex ___ (from nothing)
11. Like Mary's follower
12. Fiji neighbor
13. "As You Like It" setting
21. Abbr. in Bartlett's
23. Accustomed
25. Outdoes
26. Red giant in Cetus
27. Holly genus
28. Giant economy ___
29. Rock's J. ___ Band
31. Pickler's need
32. One of the Aleutians
33. Hunky-dory
34. Endorsed
36. Arduous
37. Airport worker
39. Fund-raising suffix
40. Leave in a hurry, with "out"
41. Star of 1925's "The Phantom of the Opera"
42. Right
43. Oafish
44. Private reply
45. Capacious
46. Smokejumper's need
48. Maleska's predecessor
49. Dance that tells a story
50. Cantina cooker
51. Fast-talking
54. Oft-laced drink

Solution on page 358

Perplexing 21

ACROSS

1. Amoeba, essentially
5. President of France: 1954–1959
9. Cattle feed
13. Narrow way
14. Gelatin substitute
15. Similar: Prefix
16. At the moment when
17. Bungle
18. Bathsheba's husband
19. Transparency
21. Presses, folds and stretches
23. Kind of service
24. Cutter part
26. "Thimble Theater" name
27. Kind of state
28. Adjust a skirt
30. Card catalogue abbr.
34. Accessory
37. Hospital area, informally
39. Sitka souvenir
40. Traveler
41. Atmosphere: Prefix
42. Automaton
44. Berlioz's "Nuit d'___"
45. Bedeck
47. "___ worse than death"
48. Joins
50. A train?
51. Personal ad abbr.
52. Year in Edward the Elder's reign
54. Newspaper space meas.
56. Peggy Lee's "___ a Tramp"
59. Express
62. Like money in the bank
64. Barbaric
65. Direction at sea
67. Word on the Great Seal
68. German philosopher
69. Dither
70. Banker Kahn
71. Kind of column
72. Joule fractions
73. Blockhead

DOWN

1. Puff up
2. Cavalry weapon
3. First words of "Waltzing Matilda"
4. Paragon of redness
5. Beach robe
6. Eyeballs
7. ___ particle
8. H.S. annual
9. Esprit de corps
10. In
11. Red and Black
12. Water, structurally
15. Long in politics
20. Egyptian god of the universe
22. "It Ain't Gonna Rain ___"
25. Duds
27. Pulitzer playwright Akins
29. Haunted: Var.
31. Tubby, for one
32. Quite often
33. Guitar relative
34. Some
35. Prom partner
36. Scott in 1857 news
37. Green spot in Paris
38. Some scampi
43. ___-line (disconnected)
46. Baseball stats
49. Plasterer's tool
51. Source of strength
53. Washington locale, with "the"
55. "The Caine Mutiny" captain
56. "Leave ___ Heaven," 1945 melodrama
57. Put an ___
58. Dog dropping
59. Attend Eton
60. Enormous
61. Moderate
63. "It's gone!"
64. Comedienne Margaret
66. Env. item

Solution on page 358

Perplexing 22

ACROSS

1. Go downhill fast?
5. Cut
10. Antony of antiquity
14. Wharton course, for short
15. Buddy
16. Pet bat on "The Munsters"
17. Apartment
18. Talk, talk, talk
19. Abbr. on a food label
20. Ability
22. Closely connected
24. Reduce a sail
26. "The Simpsons" character Disco ___
27. Dostoyevsky novel, with "The"
30. Decide to leave, with "out"
32. Talk like Sylvester
36. August appliance
37. Word before and after "against"
39. Got soft
41. Brewskis
43. Bagnell Dam river
45. Vermeer's "Woman With a ___"
46. Cloverleaf component
48. Transparent tunicate
50. AEC today
51. Picker-upper
52. Affect, with "to"
53. Pi, for one
55. 100 cts.
57. Grand
59. Sent with a click
63. Obstructed, once
67. Memory: Prefix
68. Grisham's "___ to Kill"
70. Old German duchy name
71. Before maniac or technic
72. Big drawer?
73. Tours with?
74. Fit for sainthood
75. "Smart" ones
76. Green around the gills

DOWN

1. It's just not right
2. Westwood institution, for short
3. Good shot
4. Prefix with bacteria
5. Poker Flat chronicler
6. Bird of the Outback
7. Sports column?
8. Limelight hog
9. "The Magic Box" star
10. Go for the gold?
11. Reps.
12. "Lady Jane Grey" dramatist
13. Computer monitor, for short
21. Belg. neighbor
23. Drug smuggler
25. Swells
27. In case it's true
28. Cow
29. Chief Vedic god
31. "___ porridge hot . . ."
33. "___ say!"
34. Dar Robinson specialty
35. ___ dish
38. Alley ___, of the comics
39. Sharples of "Alice"
40. Chrysler Building style
42. Combo member, maybe
44. Concert take
47. Late-'60s fashion item
49. ___-dieu (kneeling bench)
52. Humperdinck heroine
54. Represents
56. Beast of Bolivia
58. They're entered in court
59. Greek war goddess
60. British blackbird
61. City on Fukien coast
62. "No ___!"
64. Rikki-tikki-___
65. Suit, so to speak
66. Flatten
67. Abbr. on a ticket
69. 1200, to Tiberius

Solution on page 358

Perplexing 23

ACROSS
1. "Goldberg Variations" composer
5. Bout enders, for short
9. Nay sayers
14. ___ d'amore
15. August, in Arles
16. Boxer's asset
17. Dancing girl in "The Return of the Jedi"
18. Crown
19. Onyx piece
20. Gertrude who swam the English Channel
22. Isolate
24. Put in other words
26. Mont Blanc, e.g.
27. Goes over
29. Bounty stop of 1788
34. Great Lakes acronym
37. Former Genoan magistrate
39. "Dream on!"
40. "Caribbean Blue" singer
41. Takes out
42. Windmill blade
43. Source of "It is more blessed to give than to receive"
44. Dietary supplement
45. ___ paradox
46. Tittered
48. Brown shade
50. It docked with "Atlantis"
52. "Take that!"
56. Thief
61. Like wedding cakes
62. 1982 World Cup site
63. ___ Nui (Easter Island)
65. Years in old Rome
66. Drew a bead on
67. Newton, e.g.
68. "Murphy's Romance" director
69. Flip side?
70. Chihuahua child
71. After-dinner selection

DOWN
1. Unhappy spectator
2. Digs, so to speak
3. "Unforgettable" singers
4. Serenity
5. Retina layers
6. Big inits. in camping
7. Diamond data
8. Expensive
9. Secrets
10. Lowest high tide
11. Author Janowitz
12. "Happy Birthday" writer
13. Opportunity
21. Overtakes, in a way
23. Spots for chapeaux
25. Terminator, too
28. Is helpless?
30. Don't be cruel
31. "My life ___ open book"
32. First baseman Martinez
33. Yoruban names
34. Fuzz
35. Enough, for some
36. The Bible, to many
38. Pool contents?
41. Iced
45. Alternative to bow ties
47. Blue-pencils
49. Non-computer chip?
51. It's nothing new
53. Banks in Chicago
54. ___-Wreck
55. Cleans up, in a way
56. Atty.-to-be exam
57. Pacific capital
58. Branches
59. It can be bleu in Bordeaux
60. Asian princess
64. Fasten

Solution on page 358

Perplexing 24

ACROSS

1. It stands where Arbela stood
6. Actress Sofer
10. Beat the pants off
14. Grub
15. Not supporting, slangily
16. Hebrides island
17. Cap sites
18. "Needles & Pins" composer
19. Crack in the cold
20. ___ Friday
21. X's
23. Defiant dare
25. VCR control
26. Chickadee relative
27. Iced, with "in"
28. Woodstock wear
32. Cumming attraction?
33. Certain collars
34. Log Cabin Republican
35. Pulitzer-winning novel of 1925
40. Smallest cont.
41. It began in A.D. 800
42. Equipment for Berra
43. Prepared to propose
45. Human tail?
46. First book of el Nuevo Testamento
47. Weak one
49. Rebounds
50. B.S., e.g.
53. German 101 verb
54. "However . . ."
55. Carol opener
57. Egyptian king
58. Kay Kyser's "___ Reveille"
61. Prospect
62. Laugh ___
64. "Gigi" composer
66. The "kid" in "Here's looking at you, kid"
67. Dirt
68. Italian playwright ___ Fo
69. Hard to grasp
70. Anthropologist Fossey
71. Claude who starred in TV's "Lobo"

DOWN

1. Benevolent order
2. Buzzed
3. One of TV's Mavericks
4. "___ fallen . . ."
5. East Indian sailors
6. Like some fans
7. Inflatable things
8. "Children of the Albatross" author
9. Social breakdown
10. Ilsa's love
11. Voiced admiration
12. Eastern Algonquian language
13. Used a VCR
22. Wickiup, for one
24. Bill producers
26. Fiddled
28. Deck material
29. Beat in an upset
30. Firefighter's need
31. Like JFK Airport: Abbr.
32. Another role for Nimoy
34. "___ Story," by Straub
36. "The Leaves of Life keep falling one by one" poet
37. ___-Honey (candy bar)
38. Checklist unit
39. Old Pontiacs
44. Needle
46. Roald Dahl title character
48. Password preceder
49. Drop from the a-team
50. Patron saint of Wales
51. Ancient Roman magistrate
52. Brants
54. Back at the track
56. Kind of meet
57. Comfy spot
58. Austin of "Knots Landing"
59. "Bingo!"
60. Most August babies
63. Kamoze of reggae
65. Bookshelf wood

Solution on page 358

Perplexing 25

ACROSS

1. Meat, of sorts
5. Etta of comics
9. Bookbinder's tool
12. Sword of yore
14. "Would ___?"
15. Height: prefix
16. More artful
17. Absolute worst
18. Lay up
19. Two-seater
21. IM provider
22. Carry-on
23. Contractor's fig.
24. Annoyance
26. Nitrogen compounds
28. European capital
29. Medicare's org.
30. Greek vowel
33. "Hard Road to Glory" author
35. Music rights org.
40. Bond and Helm
41. Many fake I.D. users
43. Cosmos star
44. Annual report item
46. "Kojak" of TV
47. Italian car, briefly
48. Alliance created in 1948: Abbr.
50. Dot-___
52. Did a double take?
56. "See ya"
57. Co. with a butterfly logo
60. Utter conclusion?
61. Has too much, briefly
63. Prefix with sphere
65. Lows
66. First name in linguistics
68. Subdues, with "down"

69. Native Oklahomans
70. Safekeeping
71. Coco's colleague
72. Budgetary acronym
73. Pisan pronoun
74. Primate feature

DOWN

1. Chanson de ___
2. Mallorca y Menorca
3. Stretch
4. Nailed obliquely
5. Laotian currency unit
6. Cuban boy in 2000 headlines
7. Challenger of Stalin
8. Magnetic flux density units
9. Follow, as a tip
10. Composed

11. Home Depot rival
13. Fancy flapjack
15. Italian wine-growing region
20. Corday victim
25. Maps within a map
27. Calf's cry
28. Contemptible
29. "What fools these mortals be" writer
30. ". . .___ penny earned"
31. Mother of Jupiter
32. Actor Hardin et al.
34. Bit of a chuckle
36. Body shops?
37. Animation supply
38. Gov. Landon
39. Dimwit's brain size
42. Covers with coal dust

45. Additionally
49. In a New York minute
51. Having a dull finish
52. Novarro of "Ben-Hur"
53. Short Internet message
54. Beat everybody to the news story
55. Amerada ___ (Fortune 500 company)
56. Autocrats
57. Underwater ray
58. "Skittle Players" artist
59. Pried
62. "___ I say!"
64. Hebrew for "beginning"
67. "Peel ___ grape"

Solution on page 359

Perplexing 26

ACROSS

1. It'll help you up
5. Keynoter's spot
9. China's ___ Piao
12. "Das Lied von der ___"
13. Big duck
15. Celebratory dance
16. Field protector
17. "A Passage to India" woman
18. John-Boy's sister
19. ___ shrdlu
21. Present time, for short
22. Kudrow of "Friends"
23. Become unhinged
25. "The Day the Earth Stood Still" star
27. Ceremonial staffs
30. Carbohydrate ending
32. Calyx leaf
36. Biographer Winslow
37. Slander, e.g.
39. Legislative assembly
40. Eaten up
42. Ranch in "Giant"
44. Brio
45. Disquiet
47. "___ yellow ribbon . . ."
49. Antiquity, quaintly
50. Collar attachment
51. Still, in poetry
52. Household gods
54. Bolts down
56. "___ happens . . ."
58. High notes
61. Fourth qtr. followers
63. Show instability
67. Yesterday, in Italy
68. Artful Dodger
70. Wing: Fr.
71. Indian bread
72. "Let's have a dance ___ are married": Shak.
73. Auction cry
74. Fig. in identity theft
75. Earned a citation?
76. 1961 chimp in space

DOWN

1. French bean?
2. Small sausage, for short
3. Mediterranean port of Spain
4. Rest
5. Country singer Carter
6. A hand
7. Fingered
8. Sister of Helios
9. Loughlin of "Full House"
10. Blue flag, e.g.
11. Barrie barker
14. Dash
15. Greek
20. Acad.
24. Go (over)
26. "Peer Gynt" character
27. Big shot
28. Admiral Byrd book
29. City in Crete
31. Assert
33. Less ruddy
34. Start of a Dickens work
35. Advances
38. Assayed material
39. Cover letter letters
41. Starts gently
43. Fey of "30 Rock"
46. Doo-wop's ___ Na Na
48. Sam Shepard's "___ of the Mind"
51. Aromatic compounds
53. Lolling
55. Barreled along
57. Charger, e.g.
58. Oberhausen one
59. Grazing sites
60. Islands off Galway
62. Penetrate slowly
64. Noun suffix
65. London greeting
66. Colors
69. Winter Olympics powerhouse: Abbr.

Solution on page 359

Perplexing 27

ACROSS

1. Singer Manilow
6. Arezzo's river
10. Some savings accts.
13. Poe family
14. "Barton Fink" director
15. Kind of gin
16. Some winds
17. Santa said it
18. Bills, e.g.
19. Some DVD players
20. The 21st, e.g.: Abbr.
21. Parent, e.g.
23. Thistlelike plant
26. Crushed
27. Revolt
30. French wave
32. Bad looks
33. Soup with sushi
35. Cotton ball applications
39. Frame in a frame
40. Public park
43. "___ TURN" (road sign)
44. Certain hockey shot
46. Supermodel Sastre
47. You can see right through them
49. ". . . blackbirds, baked in ___"
51. Copier supplies
52. Blanch
54. Fleet
57. Ceremonial dinners
59. American ___
60. Hasty
64. Retina cells
65. Bring on board
67. Monthly bill
68. "Get ___!" (boss's order)
69. One of the "Ghostbusters"
70. On ___ (rampaging)
71. Procedure: Abbr.
72. Spanish lady
73. Judges

DOWN

1. Raymond or Aaron
2. "Wait ___!"
3. American ostrich
4. Betelgeuse, for one
5. Age abbr.
6. Tylenol targets
7. Longtime first name at ABC News
8. Book after Ezra: Abbr.
9. "___ off?"
10. Humidor item
11. Gave medicine to
12. Very: Ger.
15. One way to run
20. "East of Eden" brother
22. SFO posting
24. Adamson's cat
25. Gets licked
27. Donations
28. Clap
29. "Fur is dead" org.
31. Affirmative action
33. Bison features
34. "___ Mine" (Beatles song)
36. Charles' sister
37. ___ War
38. Figure (out)
41. Flavius' 52
42. Footless
45. Most like a ghost
48. At ___ (nevertheless)
50. ___ annum
51. Pro follower
52. Showy flower
53. Start of an African capital
55. LuPone stage role
56. "Mefistofele" role
57. Cheap digs: Abbr.
58. Cast off
61. ". . . sting like ___"
62. Criticize
63. Half a matched set
66. "___ Pogo": Kelly
67. Dirty dog

Solution on page 359

Perplexing 28

ACROSS
1. Crumbs
5. Agronomist's concern
9. PC feature
12. "Dream Along with Me" singer Perry
13. IM user, perhaps
15. "Cleopatra" before Taylor
16. Alexis, e.g.
17. "All ___" (1967 Temptations hit)
18. Hindu land grant
19. Epic poem by Vergil
21. Mrs., abroad
22. Popular ice cream brand
23. Petal perfume
25. No. 2
27. Clobber
30. Dot on the Rhine
32. Tony of baseball
36. French collagist
37. "Friends" role
39. ___ march (one-up)
40. "The Waltons" actor
42. They touch people's hearts
44. Call up
45. The Muses, e.g.
47. Explorer John and others
49. Long of "Third Watch"
50. In disrepair
51. '50s monogram
52. Better
54. Like some verbs: Abbr.
56. Beach bird
58. On ___ (equipotent)
61. Egg warmer
63. Enron Field team
67. "Six Feet Under" son
68. Saved on supper, perhaps
70. Crier's place
71. Appointment
72. Mississippi's ___ State University
73. Betting odds
74. Form letters?
75. Buttonhole, e.g.
76. "Anything ___" (Woody Allen film)

DOWN
1. Eight: Comb. form
2. "The ___ Tattoo," 1955 movie
3. Eliot Ness, for one
4. Cross with
5. "You ___ mouthful!"
6. Bass tail?
7. L'eau lands?
8. Eye lasciviously
9. Smooth, in a way
10. Supercomputer inventor
11. Runs into
14. Intake optima: Abbr.
15. Obviously embarrassed
20. Aqueduct of Sylvius, e.g.
24. Croak
26. Collected dust
27. Cell alternative
28. The Palestra, e.g.
29. All in
31. Grenoble's department
33. Its motto is "Dirigo"
34. Delon in "Borsalino"
35. Before bar or dressing
38. Library ref.
39. Birmingham-to-Montgomery dir.
41. Many a Floridian
43. Carefree quality
46. "We the Living" author Rand
48. ___ serif
51. Products of glaciation
53. Pluck
55. Mississippi senator Cochran
57. Charged toward
58. "___ Love Her": Beatles
59. "I kid you not" speaker
60. Bar assn. members
62. 1994 film based on the play "Idioglossia"
64. Muddy
65. Has power over
66. Bygone blade
69. "Lord, is ___?": Matthew

Solution on page 359

Perplexing 29

ACROSS
1. Punt, for one
5. Blueprint detail
9. Relinquish
14. Breakfast brand
15. Cousin of an agouti
16. Kharg Island resident
17. "Knowledge can split ___ of light": Dickens
18. Billing abbr.
19. Kind of jar
20. Unspecified no.
21. Slicer site
22. Georgia and others, once: Abbr.
23. African pests
26. Chignon setting
29. "And I Love ___"
30. Unwanted buildup
34. Clean up, in a way
37. Anne of fashion
40. Hitter's stat
41. Count
42. What "shalom" means
43. Brilliant victory
44. Old letter
45. Big name in infomercials
46. Tony winner Rivera
47. Ups
49. BlackBerry, e.g.
50. AC or DC
52. Minimally worded
56. A following?
59. Altar exchange
61. Gulager of "The Virginian"
62. Onward
64. Like many a centerfold
65. Bullwinkle, for one
66. "Il Convivio" author
67. Suffix with Dixie
68. "Lay it ___!"
69. Keep an ___
70. Georgetown hoopster
71. Tries to win

DOWN
1. Beauty's admirer
2. Baddies
3. Mojave plant
4. Pekingese, e.g.
5. Gardener, at times
6. Treasure map distances
7. Book after Prov.
8. "The ___ the Hat"
9. Lower, in a way
10. Desk item
11. Gravity target
12. "___ out?" (dealer's query)
13. Anchovy containers
24. He and she
25. Alternative to a Keogh acct.
27. Even, after "in"
28. Goat-legged god
31. Sirtis' role in "Star Trek"
32. Be up against
33. Philbin cohort
34. Joel Chandler Harris title
35. Castor's mother
36. Grade school, for short
37. Cognizance
38. Anita Brookner's "Hotel du ___"
39. "A Theory of Semiotics" author
42. Ask
43. Alternative to Chuck
45. Bill of Rights subj.
46. Spock, e.g.: Abbr.
48. Handled
49. Euro preceder
51. Breeze
52. Now
53. ___-Car
54. It helps you see plays
55. Strains
56. Enjoined
57. Kaolin
58. Cooked
60. Spanish peso
63. Col.'s boss
65. Drag along

Solution on page 359

Perplexing 30

ACROSS

1. Bookstore section
6. Big show
10. April forecast
14. Cub reporter on "The Daily Planet"
15. Finish off
16. Advertiser's award
17. Durango dough
18. Like some track meets
19. Nick
20. Harbor barge
21. "___ soup yet?"
23. "They chose atheism as an ___": Bentley
25. Directly
26. "Love Story" composer
27. Songwriter Coleman and others
28. Breeding ground
32. Impression
33. Bouquets
34. "Andy Capp" cartoonist Smythe
35. Do a butler's job
40. Musical with the song "The Night They Invented Champagne"
41. A.C.C. member
42. Baylor's home
43. English variety
45. Dance: Fr.
46. Buggy places?
47. Big name in chips
49. Put right
50. Bit
53. Old-style low notes
54. Big belts
55. Einstein, e.g.
57. Green hue
58. Cowardly fellow
61. Word form of "recent"
62. "Happy Days Are Here Again" composer
64. Congo charger
66. Mythical craft
67. Jazz pianist Allison
68. Art of jazz
69. Cow chow
70. Bellow in the library
71. Stooge Howard

DOWN

1. JV player, perhaps
2. Geppetto's goldfish
3. Paris suburb on the Seine
4. Rock music's ___ Fighters
5. Guts
6. "Frasier" pooch
7. Strike
8. "Lo's Diary" author ___ Pera
9. Like some museum paintings
10. Start of the 15th century
11. ___ artery
12. Full of fluff
13. Olden magistrates
22. Afrique du ___
24. ___ bread
26. Copier setting
28. Monopolizes
29. Lyrical
30. Fast-food option
31. Falklands war participant
32. Hindu deities
34. Keeler and Dee
36. Did the breaststroke
37. Batman's creator
38. Like some coffee
39. Curious
44. Cast aspersions on
46. Strands
48. Special forces units
49. Colleague of Paddy
50. Joltless joe
51. "Honor is ___ scutcheon": Shak.
52. Pig out
54. Playwright Capek
56. In bounds
57. Proper name in Masses
58. Adduce
59. "One" on a one
60. Gambol
63. Indian state
65. "That'll show you!"

Solution on page 359

Perplexing 31

ACROSS

1. It has two shoulders but no head
5. Do one's part?
9. First bed
13. Before dollar or farmer
14. #1 spot
15. Plumed headgear
16. Housecat's perch
17. 1969 Oates novel
18. Great Western Forum player
19. Sweet girl of song
21. Observes Yom Kippur
23. Blanched
24. Links transport
26. Have a mortgage, perhaps
27. Bit of a draft
28. Man from Mars
30. Holy man
34. Confound
37. Flings
39. Bar topic
40. Backs
41. "Antony and Cleopatra" prop
42. "Goodnight" girl
44. Seat, slangily
45. Mah-jongg pieces
47. Some sneaks
48. Arizona river
50. AT&T acquisition of 1991
51. Rx instruction
52. Audience
54. "Je ne ___ quoi"
56. Shaker ___, O.
59. Syndicate
62. Delegating command
64. Curtain fabric
65. In ___ way
67. De Gaulle alternative
68. Modern workout system
69. Chevalier song
70. Alpha ___
71. British general in the American Revolution
72. "Wheel of Fortune" choice
73. "I Loves You, Porgy" singer

DOWN

1. Further shorten
2. "A Dog of Flanders" writer
3. "I Love a Parade" composer
4. Barbie or baby
5. Doze
6. Yellow earth
7. Sra., across the Pyrenees
8. Synagogue platform
9. She made "No. 5" famous
10. Don Juan
11. Turner and others
12. NYC division
15. Boring
20. Least cordial
22. "Nothing ___!"
25. Some TV spots
27. 35mm camera
29. Dosage abbr.
31. Fashion model Wek
32. Encolure
33. Blows away
34. Cut ___
35. Early sitcom name
36. "James and the Giant Peach" author
37. It may follow trig
38. "CSI: NY" star
43. Cleanse
46. Dictator's phrase
49. Oxygen-dependent bacterium
51. Connected
53. ___ point (never)
55. "Same here"
56. Dike, Eunomia and Irene
57. Bread boxes?
58. Eyelid maladies
59. "Bye!"
60. De novo
61. Hightails it
63. Pyramid, e.g.
64. ___ degree
66. Heart monitor sound

Solution on page 360

Perplexing 32

ACROSS

1. Indian bean sauce
4. Mineralogist Friedrich
8. Velociraptor's repast
13. "Wide Sargasso Sea" author
15. Sign in the dark
16. City on the Yamuna River
17. "Ouch!"
18. Malay parrot
19. Croupiers' tools
20. Cyclotron inventor ___ Lawrence
22. Keebler's Ernie, e.g.
24. Airhead
25. 1953 AL M.V.P.
26. Heebie-jeebies
28. Good source of protein
30. "Zip-a-Dee-___"
34. Clothier's concern
37. Zingers
40. Vacant, in a way
41. Wildcats' sch.
42. Counters
44. "Grand Hotel" studio
45. Frontier trophy
48. Exhibits
50. Citrus seed
51. "Fiddler on the Roof" setting
53. Cracked
55. Like Mt. Kilimanjaro
58. Attorney follower
62. Rubs out
65. Cambodia's ___ Nol
66. "The Stunt Man" star
67. Minded
69. "Moving ___" ("Jeffersons" theme)
71. Unstable particle
72. Atlantic lead-in
73. Island do
74. Apple product
75. Children's doctor?
76. "Dear" ones
77. Lizard, old-style

DOWN

1. Bounce setting
2. "No man is ___ to his valet"
3. Rhone's capital
4. Change states, in a way
5. Tic-tac-toe failure
6. Personnel director
7. Bodoni or Helvetica
8. Yalta monogram
9. Entices
10. Nevada's second-largest county
11. Cartoonist Silverstein
12. School subj.
14. Like dessert wines
21. Name-dropper, perhaps
23. Disobeyed a zoo sign?
26. Reins in
27. Dish of roasted roots
29. JFK regulators
31. Extinguish
32. Vessel: Comb. form
33. Burlap source
34. Act the mother hen
35. Mark of a ruler
36. The "id" in "id est"
38. "Nuts!"
39. Upbraid
43. WW II battle site, for short
46. Goes down
47. ___ Club of old TV
49. "Git!"
52. Chat room abbr.
54. Mexican tribe
56. Combines
57. Blah feeling
59. Jeweler's eyepiece
60. Cold fish–like
61. George of "Cheers"
62. Fall times: Abbr.
63. Diet
64. Lady of the haus
66. Sonata, e.g.
68. Welfare chief
70. Neighbor of Isr., once

Solution on page 360

Perplexing 33

ACROSS
1. Eat like ___
5. Witchy women
9. Guitar forerunner
13. Bari bubble
15. "Yow!"
16. Supermodel Sastre
17. Parody
18. Hybrid fruit
19. Refreshers
20. A long way off
22. Bay State symbol
24. In motion
26. "Them"
27. South of Ariz.
28. Be in a cast
29. Loaded
32. Mag magnate
34. Little chow
35. Day before Mercredi
37. "One Flew Over the Cuckoo's Nest" author
41. Bluster
43. Biblical sin city
45. Novelist Grey
46. Just watched
48. Balls
50. Amsterdam-based financial co.
51. Long-faced
53. Pink-slip
54. Archaeological site
55. Quick shot?
58. "Fiasco" novelist
60. ___ del Sur, Phil.
62. By and large
64. Kill, in a way
65. Affluent, in Acapulco
66. Dance move
68. Hinder
72. "Do I dare to ___ peach?": Eliot
73. Least bit of concern
74. Hard stuff
75. Nose: Prefix
76. Halfway houses
77. Makes blue, perhaps

DOWN
1. Exerciser's target
2. Short report
3. UN agcy. for workers
4. Lord it over
5. Appointed time
6. Dog days mo.
7. Staff leader?
8. Civil War battle site
9. Fuzz
10. Render defenseless
11. Crow's home
12. Colchester's county
14. Ratify
21. Met pieces
23. Yielding
24. Legend, e.g.
25. Parade honoree, for short
28. Some alerts, for short
30. Biology class staple
31. Icelandic literary works
33. Shriner's cap
36. Kansas town
38. "You ___ mouthful!"
39. "The Untouchables" composer Morricone
40. Burglar
42. Literary inits.
44. Twin crystal
47. Korea Bay feeder
49. Emulates Sarah Hughes
52. Site of the ancient Pythian Games
55. Kitchen implement
56. Thomas of the NBA
57. Plants in a dry place
59. Casaba, e.g.
61. Rover
63. Flecked steed
64. November honorees
67. Accelerator bit
69. Good deal
70. Big heart?
71. Hi-___

Solution on page 360

Perplexing 34

ACROSS

1. Philippine plant
6. Delicate
10. Excellent, slangily
14. "Good Times" star
15. Banned spray
16. Bickerer in the "Iliad"
17. Run like ___
18. Kind of test
19. Good fellers
20. Race part
21. "___ well"
23. Fondle
25. ___-Bo
26. Dick
27. "Flower Drum Song" actor
28. Bully, often
32. After hard or soft
33. ___ boy
34. Scots yearling
35. One born on a kibbutz
40. Embarkation location
41. "Wheel of Fortune" request
42. One who waits
43. Blip maker
45. Her, to Henri
46. Comics sound
47. Burns up
49. Grayish green
50. Coolers, briefly
53. But, to Brutus
54. Cal. divisions
55. Carried on
57. Damage, so to speak
58. Frequent Powell co-star
61. In line
62. Ancient colonnade
64. ___ des Beaux-Arts
66. King mackerel
67. Clear
68. Skater Lipinski and others
69. Farm females
70. Forever, seemingly
71. Surgical tube

DOWN

1. Asian sea name
2. Be a sign of
3. Shake it or break it
4. Diminutive suffix
5. Freshens, in a way
6. Deep black
7. Cheers
8. Like Falstaff
9. Shipping inquiry
10. "___ Lap" (1983 film)
11. Spells
12. Joe Cocker's "You __ _Beautiful"
13. "Jerusalem Delivered" poet
22. Choreographer Lubovitch
24. First-rate
26. Ancient city of Lower Egypt
28. Intensifies, with "up"
29. "Charles in Charge" star
30. "Right on, brother!"
31. "___ Smile" (1976 hit)
32. Flags
34. Slackened
36. Challenge for Hannibal
37. Digestion aid
38. Admonish
39. Gulf of Greece
44. Acclivity
46. Some stanzas
48. View from Jidda
49. Bandleader Edmundo
50. "It's ___ against time"
51. Rod of Cooperstown
52. [How boring!]
54. Haunted house sounds
56. Ark embarkments
57. Reactor part
58. Anecdotal knowledge
59. "The Good Earth" wife
60. Recently: Abbr.
63. Child's play?
65. Manx, for one

Solution on page 360

Perplexing 35

ACROSS

1. Emulate Bing Crosby
6. Abbey area
10. Clerical garment
13. Polymnia's home
14. Place for portraits
15. Fix
16. Heavy hammers
17. First-year Harvard law student
18. Capital paper
19. U.K. leaders
20. French nobleman
22. Brahmans, e.g.
23. Punish, in a way
24. Lady, e.g.
26. Down the gangplank
29. Angry
30. Mettle
31. They're sometimes stripped
35. Interjects
39. ___ up (irate)
40. Indian writer
41. Debt memo
42. Deadly biters
44. Starts of some pranks
46. Same: Fr.
47. Break off
49. Analyzed
51. Some theater
55. Hubs
56. Massey of "Balalaika"
57. Rinse, as with a solvent
59. Mortgage org.
62. Genealogical abbr.
63. Cardinal
64. Ark contents
66. "Look!" to Livy
67. Asian secret society
68. Appliance brand
69. MGM rival, once
70. Sacred chests
71. Some Balts

DOWN

1. David or Pendleton
2. "Where the buffalo ___ . . ."
3. ___ probandi
4. Drilling goal
5. Winston Cup org.
6. "Oh, give me ___ . . ."
7. Puff
8. "The sweetest gift of heaven": Virgil
9. Angled pipe
10. Strike ___
11. Holds up
12. Memory units
15. Ancient military hub
21. Blood type, briefly
22. Big suit
23. Caesar-salad lettuce
25. Codgers' replies
26. Muslim honorific
27. Hires an ambulance chaser
28. Start of many addresses
32. Ballpark figure, for short
33. Interlaken river
34. Morgue, for one
36. Goes out
37. Buckminster Fuller invention
38. Went after
43. Medium setting
44. 34th U.S. pres.
45. Advance, slangily
46. 3-D exam
48. "We Do Our Part" org.
50. Perfume ingredient
51. Hot or cold drink
52. Smart one
53. Nesquik alternative
54. "___ coffee?"
55. Bronchi termini
58. Weakest part of a chain
59. Brothers' keeper?
60. Spook in Dogpatch
61. Cries of discovery
63. Boston subway insignia
65. Cockney residence

Solution on page 360

Perplexing 36

ACROSS

1. Have down
5. Blue shade
9. El-operating agcy.
12. Charged
14. Hardly Herculean
15. Send
16. Tammany tsar
17. Rend
19. Beginning of Virginia's motto
20. Honors
22. Big picture
23. Like clocks with hands
25. Takeoff
26. On the line
28. Knee-slapper
29. Set up
30. Bring under control
32. Loc. ___
33. Did part of a triathlon
34. Accepted
37. Tolerates
39. Had
41. Attraction
43. Attack
44. Less original
45. Constitution writer
47. "___ your life!"
48. Buckwheat pancakes
49. Light bark
52. "A Girl Like I" autobiographer
54. Area of South Africa
56. Bogs
57. Bottle stopper
58. "___ Lucy"
59. Tail: Prefix
60. Heavy cart
61. Crossword component

DOWN

1. Hobby shop inventory
2. "___ get it!"
3. Like some engagement rings
4. Golfer Michelle
5. Probably gonna, more formally
6. "The Caine Mutiny" captain
7. Actress Merkel and others
8. SW Scotland burgh
9. Styx ferryman
10. Diatribe
11. Well
13. Music box?
15. Encourage
18. High-end viola
21. Class
24. Game with matchsticks
25. Reservoir
26. Patriots' grp.
27. Angle lead-in
28. Goes quickly
30. Depend (on)
31. Barely get, with "out"
33. Vigor
34. Wheeler-dealer
35. Mauna ___ (Hawaii's highest peak)
36. Banned bug-spray
37. Sets apart
38. ___ Park, Calif.
39. Anno ___
40. Japanese apricot
41. Sorry sort?
42. Bodega patron
43. ___ of worms
44. Muddle
45. "La Traviata" mezzo
46. "___ Business" (1983)
48. Lout
50. Shankar of the sitar
51. Hightailed it
53. CRT alternative
55. Dept. of mathematics

Solution on page 360

Perplexing 37

ACROSS

1. Doubtable
5. Domino's fixtures
10. Some alerts, for short
14. Lead
15. Barely bite
16. Catch a glimpse of
17. Hindu god of the underworld
18. Apocopate
19. Prefix with cab
20. Dress down
22. Tony winner Worth and others
24. Cyclades isle
25. Frenzy
27. Opie's answer to Aunt Bee
29. Clothing chain, with "the"
30. Bench activity
34. Inguri or Swift
35. Passes
38. Offed
39. Sixth-century date
40. Farm butter
41. Heart chart: Abbr.
43. Eastern title
44. Ethereal
46. Qajar dynasty's domain
48. Computer key
49. Some R.S.V.P.s
51. "We know drama" sloganeer
52. 1922 physics Nobelist
54. Recoils
56. Progress by leaps and bounds
57. Full-scale
60. Family subdivisions
63. Depilatory brand
64. Cut
67. Legal defendant: Abbr.
69. Orang-___ (ape)
70. Work out
71. "Moses" novelist
72. "___ the perilous fight . . ."
73. "For sure!"
74. In mules, say

DOWN

1. Distant
2. Exercise target
3. Get steamed up
4. Longs (for)
5. ___ a customer!
6. Foul
7. Center opening?
8. Cellular coenzyme, briefly
9. Bock holder
10. Shows up
11. Hammer head
12. Eliot hero
13. Emulates Tomba
21. Archer, at times
23. Grave letters
25. Bit of raingear
26. Most pertinent
27. Bulldog
28. Dubai dignitaries
29. Ovum, e.g.
31. Gulf of Aqaba port
32. Stogie: Var.
33. Q-Tip
34. Attack time
36. Brief time out?
37. Make tracks?
42. Where Libreville is
45. "Don't evade the question!"
47. ER staffers
50. ___ mai (dim sum dish)
53. Met requirements?
55. "___ Easy": Holly hit
56. Toast start
57. "Sometimes you feel like ___ . . ."
58. It gets plastered
59. Baloney producer
60. Crumpled
61. Hebrew consonant
62. Sac: Comb. form
65. Water, structurally
66. Seat of White Pine County, Nev.
68. Third degree, often

Solution on page 361

Perplexing 38

ACROSS

1. "Yo te ___"
4. Hindu titles
8. Yoga position
13. Cogitate
15. "Judge Dredd" actress
16. Filleted
17. Abecedary link
18. Yours, to Yvette
19. Follow ___ (do detective work)
20. Go up and down
22. 22.5 degrees
24. "___ way!"
25. Small finch
26. Sowing machine
28. Clytemnestra's mother
30. Richards of "Jurassic Park"
34. Der ___ (Adenauer nickname)
37. "Hoc ___ in votis"
40. Done less?
41. "Comprende?"
42. Parents, e.g.
44. Business letters
45. About 1.3 cubic yards
47. Commonsensical
48. Brewpub fare
49. Less taxing
51. Astin of "Lord of the Rings"
53. Start of a Jean Kerr title
56. Bambino watcher
60. Eight-time Lorre role
63. High, in music
64. Adventitious roots, often
65. Perplexed, after "at"
67. "Zaza" star
69. Oater sound
70. Doesn't own
71. Parmenides' home
72. "Catch!"
73. Ms. accompaniers
74. Ask for
75. Fraction of a sen

DOWN

1. Conglomerate
2. Louvre, par exemple
3. Wickerwork wood
4. Cabbage dish
5. Backstabber
6. Combined
7. Angler's gear
8. Arab garment
9. Sun parlors
10. Turn ___ profit
11. Kempt
12. Po tributary
14. Store, as corn
21. "Wheel of Fortune" request
23. "The Conspiracy Against Childhood" writer LeShan
26. Long wraps
27. Acts human
29. Grant source: Abbr.
31. Nutmeg skin
32. Aloha State bird
33. Parentheses, e.g.
34. River in Provence
35. "___ Smile Be Your Umbrella"
36. Ball-bearing items
38. Gray of "Gray's Manual of Botany"
39. Perfect, e.g.
42. Fishing tackle
43. Female ruff
46. Counterstroke
48. Old-style revolutionary
50. "Bad Behavior" star, 1993
52. Rosemary Clooney's "Botch-___"
54. Everything, in Ems
55. Hackneyed
57. Track competitor
58. Language akin to Tahitian
59. Before stock or glow
60. "The War of the Worlds" base
61. Olive genus
62. Oceans
64. East Indian liquor
66. Barbecue sound
68. Half a bray

Solution on page 361

Perplexing 39

ACROSS

1. French shooting match
4. When repeated, a vitamin B deficiency
8. "Alfie" actress, 2004
13. Except
15. Chopped
16. Prayer starter
17. Familia members
18. Hull attachment
19. "Aladdin" character
20. American Shakers founder
22. Chaired
24. Calls upon
25. Divulge
26. Give out
28. Sporty car roof
30. Some Met stars
34. Water __
37. Play, in a way
40. Lash of westerns
41. Duct opening?
42. __ Island, NY
44. Breathalyzer attachment
45. Paws
48. Extremely
50. __ Red (apple variety)
51. Fume
53. Native of Novi Sad
55. The Pleistocene Epoch, familiarly
58. Acoustic
62. "Oxford Blues" star, 1984
65. Gov. Bush's state
66. Dress
67. Dander
69. Bore
71. Adoptee of Claudius I
72. Columbian vessel
73. Bldg. planner
74. Antarctica's Prince __ Coast
75. Some moldings
76. Naldi of old films
77. __ juris

DOWN

1. Absolute
2. Ammonia derivative
3. Mirthful
4. Tan too long
5. It's at the end of a program?
6. Staggers
7. Doesn't work
8. Dress fancily, with "out"
9. 1992 David Mamet play
10. City in Belgium
11. Tenor in "The Flying Dutchman"
12. Bad time in the Senate
14. Letter-shaped opening
21. Tolkien tree-men
23. Morse minimum
26. Part of a stage
27. Hair holder
29. Like Nasdaq trades
31. Urbi et __
32. Syrian island
33. Big name in games
34. Short dogs, for short
35. Jazz singer Anderson
36. March flyer
38. Game with Skip, Reverse and Draw Two cards
39. 1980s attorney general
43. Chemical suffix
46. Adriatic port
47. Flash
49. "Blast!"
52. Absolutely, in slang
54. "Give it an understanding __ tongue": Shak.
56. Mayflower Compact signer
57. Bouquet __
59. Cambodian currency
60. Pianist Claudio from Chile
61. Pope after John X
62. Certain surgery, for short
63. At first: Abbr.
64. Bouquet source
66. Akbar's capital
68. Boasts
70. Contract negotiator: Abbr.

Solution on page 361

Perplexing 40

ACROSS

1. Fat or wax
6. Campus marchers, for short
10. Office PC hookup
13. "___ Ben Jonson!"
14. Shawkat of "Arrested Development"
15. Words before tab or temp.
16. Big Brave
17. Cong. period
18. Beau Brummell's alma mater
19. Bell curve figure
20. "Come ___?" (Italian greeting)
21. Stands for things
23. A whole lot
26. Dry
27. Genesis locale
30. "Laugh-In" name
32. Functions
33. Game-ending word
35. Passbook amts.
39. Equal, in combinations
40. Over
43. Genealogy chart word
44. Floor votes
46. Newspaper section, with "the"
47. Martin song subject
49. Feudal domestic
51. Not impressed
52. A lot, maybe
54. Smart one
57. "Seinfeld" character
59. Capt.'s subordinates
60. Computer picture
64. "A Doll's House" wife
65. "___ to leap tall buildings . . ."
67. It joins the Rhone at Lyon
68. Big name in computers
69. New driver, often
70. Cheer
71. That, in Toledo
72. Fruit drinks
73. Agrippina, to Nero

DOWN

1. Farm soil
2. Dies ___
3. Chute opener?
4. Magnetite, e.g.
5. Cave
6. Bob Marley was one
7. City on the Allegheny
8. Sequel to "Angela's Ashes"
9. Beer buy
10. "See ya!"
11. Chameleon
12. Tandoor-baked breads
15. Patch up a worn lawn
20. Collector's dream
22. Halifax clock setting: Abbr.
24. ___ Grande, Ariz.
25. Fills to the gills
27. Cantatrice's offering
28. Looking up
29. African lily
31. "In the Good Old Summertime" lyricist Shields
33. Stable mates
34. Carpenter, e.g.
36. "Wilderness were Paradise ___": Khayyam
37. "Le ___ Goriot"
38. Distribute
41. Browning work?
42. Niels Bohr, e.g.
45. "___ Mom": 1994 film
48. Sweet, dark wine
50. Clinton, for one: Abbr.
51. Constitution lead-in
52. Fugard's "A Lesson From ___"
53. Sophia's husband
55. Berlin avenue
56. Antique guns
57. "The Neverending Story" author Michael
58. "Do I dare to ___ peach?": Eliot
61. Checked item
62. A chip, maybe
63. At no time, poetically
66. Night spot
67. Place for a father-to-be: Abbr.

Solution on page 361

Perplexing 41

ACROSS

1. Daughter of Mnemosyne
6. Farm prefix
10. ___ Arnold's Balsam (old patent medicine)
14. Carried a torch (for)
15. Contender
16. New Zealand isle
17. Stock up
18. "Jurassic Park" place
19. "Don't forget about me"
20. Tears
22. Stress, in a way
24. Suffix with mock
25. "6 'N the Mornin'" rapper
26. Art Ross Trophy org.
27. Order in the court
30. A, overseas
32. Scooby-___
34. Sue Grafton's "___ for Evidence"
35. "Don't be ___ loser!"
37. Jots
41. Big splash
43. "___ a chance"
44. Irish lullaby syllables
45. Biblical verb
46. Health, in Le Havre
48. Shorten, in a way
49. "___ for Innocent": Grafton
51. 1957 Physics Nobelist Tsung-___ Lee
52. Certain column
53. Home-buyer's opt.
56. British tax
58. When it's broken, that's good
60. Impetuously, maybe
62. Leans (on)
65. Big name in construction
66. Suffix with sock
68. Express alternative
70. Goes down swinging
71. "In the Still of the ___" (Boyz II Men hit)
72. Dig deeply
73. Brothers
74. Little red critters
75. Prefix with centric

DOWN

1. N.T. book
2. Grande and Hondo
3. Take ___ (rest)
4. Harness ring
5. More outre
6. Dollar competitor
7. APO recipients
8. Holdover
9. Spieled
10. Go to great heights
11. "___ Frome"
12. Choppers
13. "Hill Street Blues" actress
21. Focus group?
23. Paris's Arc de Triomphe de l'___
25. Forays
27. Do a gardening job
28. "Little Caesar" gangster
29. Ait
31. Cyclotron particles
33. Hugs, symbolically
35. Ancient Greek state
36. "Empedocles on ___" (Matthew Arnold poem)
38. Weighty book
39. "East of Eden" twin
40. Makes the cut?
42. "___ Lay Me Down" (1995 hit)
47. Hit the sauce
50. Collected
52. Old TV part
53. Author Tobias
54. Imminent, old-style
55. Diploma word
57. Block letter's lack
59. Abu Dhabi deity
61. Cockney flop
62. Nimble deer
63. "Silent Spring" subj.
64. Bollywood costume
67. Baseball's "Little Giant"
69. Adman Burnett

Solution on page 361

Perplexing 42

ACROSS

1. Drink, doggie-style
6. Winnebago owner
10. Shoe strengthener
14. Prince Valiant's lady
15. "Industry" is its motto
16. Locks
17. Up
18. Jean Renoir film "La ___ Humaine"
19. Game designer Rubik
20. In unison
22. Hot
24. Louver piece
25. All-inclusive
26. Seldon in "Foundation Trilogy"
29. Fund investor's charge
31. West of Lisbon
35. "Ave Maria" opera
37. Mets, Jets, or Nets
39. Handle clumsily
40. ___'wester
41. Tick off
43. Termination, figuratively
44. Year in Justinian I's reign
45. Escort
46. Wall Street figure
48. Pool problem
50. Railroad siding
52. Lower
53. Critical words
55. Mai ___
57. Hostile
60. Refuses to deal with
64. French chef's mushroom
65. Permeate
67. Backward
68. Spa sounds
69. "Dedicated to the ___ Love"
70. Underwater ray
71. Hardly thrilling
72. "Que ___?"
73. "___ a Man" (Calder Willingham novel and play)

DOWN

1. Boris Pasternak heroine
2. MacGraw et al.
3. Mexican mint product
4. Tool of the trade
5. Cartoon part
6. With freedom of tempo
7. Powerful engine
8. Fill the bill?
9. Butler of fiction
10. Old joke
11. Have coming
12. Soprano from Stockholm
13. Hudson River city
21. Jazz star
23. The Invisible Man, at first
25. Port of Yemen
26. Odyssey maker
27. Castaway's site
28. Hoist again, as a sail
30. Depleted
32. Part of a suit
33. Result of the 16th Amendment
34. Some painted vessels
36. Smears
38. Lead ___
42. Port container
47. One out of the money
49. Over
51. More work
54. "The Boy Who Cried Wolf" writer
56. Words from Caesar
57. Hail ___
58. Saltimbocca ingredient
59. Hebrew bushel
60. Quilters' gatherings
61. Lean
62. "Toodles!"
63. Span. matrons
66. "Bambi" character

Solution on page 361

Perplexing 43

ACROSS

1. "Amscray!"
5. Hitching post?
10. Take ___ (swing hard)
14. ___ in the U.S.A.
15. European capital, in song
16. ___-tiller
17. Sporty trucks, briefly
18. Drawing
19. Injure badly
20. Seed covering
22. Ushers
24. Drake in "Cheers"
27. Gasteyer of "Mean Girls"
28. Mantric syllables
31. TV's "___ Smith and Jones"
33. He fanned 5,714
37. You, abroad
38. Doesn't keep
39. Traveled (along)
41. Too stylish, perhaps
43. Medical prefix
45. Basilica part
46. Hold
48. Evangelist Roberts
50. Bullock thriller, with "The"
51. Pen mothers
52. Appeared
53. ___ Nova
54. "Happy Days" diner
56. RR stops
58. Needle-shaped
62. ___ coil
66. 401(k), e.g.
67. Louisiana's ___ Cajuns
70. "Famous" name
71. ___ advantage
72. Calf catcher
73. Fix
74. Fourier series function

75. Sitcom originally named "These Friends of Mine"
76. Caught, in a way

DOWN

1. It's not clean
2. "Unimaginable as ___ in Heav'n": Milton
3. Confucius's "Book of ___"
4. West of Lisbon
5. Clever
6. Nonclerical
7. Cooperstown nickname
8. Lover of Dido, in myth
9. Sister of Goneril
10. French weapon
11. Big laugh
12. "Really?"
13. Little dog, for short
21. Early invader from Pannonia
23. Edible tuber
25. Crazy as ___
26. They may be picked
28. Glacial ridges
29. Entangles
30. Fracas
32. Famed furrier
34. "Silent Night" adjective
35. "32 Flavors" singer Davis
36. "When hell freezes over!"
39. A goner
40. LAPD investigators
42. Pilot's problem
44. "Aeneid" figure
47. Munich's river
49. Carnival follower
52. Lash out at
55. "Casablanca" actor
57. Company that launched the Discover card
58. Some choir members
59. "Misery" star
60. Female suffix
61. Alike: Fr.
63. "Jolly Roger" crewman
64. Mother ___
65. "I'll be ___ of a gun!"
66. ___ seul (dance solo)
68. Believer
69. Grey in "Three Smart Girls"

Solution on page 362

Perplexing 44

ACROSS

1. "Hound Dog" was one
4. Hermit or horseshoe
8. Move furtively
13. "Let's just leave ___ that"
15. Man ___
16. Atlas, e.g.
17. Eastern music
18. ___ cava
19. A to Z, for one
20. Kay Thompson character
22. Passbook abbr.
24. One teaspoon, maybe
25. Reed or Mills
26. Letter abbr.
28. Drag
30. Fasten
34. Garden decorations
37. Alpo alternative
40. WWI soldier
41. It's a snap
42. Lurches
44. Attention-getters
45. Be of service to
47. Off
48. Hold on
49. Some mattresses
51. "La Belle et la ___"
53. Tangles
56. Cooper hero
60. "Major" animal
63. "You don't say!"
64. 1962 John Wayne film
65. Camelot, to Arthur
67. Aloha State port
69. Deejay Don
70. Obstetric test, for short
71. Have ___ (freak out)
72. Gists
73. Enjoyed
74. More than tear up
75. Approximately

DOWN

1. Took on
2. "Cosmicomics" author Calvino
3. Append
4. Place to moor
5. Literary monogram
6. "Cold Case Files" carrier
7. Highland hillsides
8. Stock unit: Abbr.
9. Results in
10. "___ Angel": West movie
11. Bettors bet on them
12. Cap locale
14. Besmirches
21. ___ Miguel (Azores island)
23. L.A. sked abbr.
26. Funny Anne
27. Gym set
29. Rio automaker
31. "Yo!"
32. Morlocks' prey in "The Time Machine"
33. Pipe problem
34. Arrow poison
35. Bank of Paris
36. Va. neighbor
38. Cat call
39. Certain Europeans
42. "Braveheart" group
43. "The Steve Allen Show" regular
46. "Not true!"
48. Entered
50. Decline
52. Philippine tree
54. Doctor's order
55. Olympus alternative
57. "Caligula" playwright
58. Caribbean getaway
59. Pantywaist
60. ___-Altaic languages
61. Scale sequence
62. Dropped
64. Ginsberg poem
66. John Lennon, once
68. Blue

Solution on page 362

Perplexing 45

ACROSS

1. Polynesian food fish, for short
5. Some pens
9. Word form of "ten"
13. Give approval
14. Streep's "___ in the Dark"
15. Loser to Obama in 2004
16. The Destroyer, in Hinduism
17. "The ___ Sleeps Tonight," 1961 hit
18. Hoover rival
19. Aseptic
21. Danes of "My So-Called Life"
23. Appetite
24. Roseanne's last name
26. NYC subway
27. Little butter?
28. "Disgusting!"
30. Book after Neh.
34. Santa's reindeer, e.g.
37. In pretty good shape
39. Nod, maybe
40. Part of Tafari Makonnen's adopted name
41. City, informally
42. Huge, old-style
44. "Delicious!"
45. Strains
47. They can be taken en passant
48. Sammy Davis Jr.'s "___ _Can"
50. All-natural food no-no
51. First half of a donkey's bray
52. Line score letters
54. Winston Churchill's "___ _Country"
56. Coin of Kabul
59. Electrician's need
62. Excite
64. Mazda roadster
65. "Cats" director Trevor
67. Bavarian river
68. Open, in a way
69. Packinghouse stamp
70. Word form of "partial"
71. Darkens, maybe
72. Cut
73. Tiny, informally

DOWN

1. Antiquated
2. "Go fly ___!"
3. Safety zone
4. Month after Nisan
5. Sentimental song
6. More aloof
7. ___-Magnon
8. In ___ (harmonious)
9. Thumb one's nose at
10. Peeping Tom, e.g.
11. Gospel singer Winans
12. "Don't ___"
15. Zen question
20. Footnote word
22. Parallel to
25. 1942 Abbott and Costello film
27. ___ Kan
29. "On the Money" network
31. Barge on Boston Bay
32. Go bad
33. Bottom lines?
34. "Good heavens!"
35. Made the scene
36. Curry and Rice
37. Rear end
38. Sally forth
43. Rural refusal
46. "Deutschland ___ alles"
49. Eye problem
51. "The Human Condition" author Arendt
53. Bucket of bolts
55. Wards (off)
56. Sound of the Northwest
57. ___ manual
58. Croce's Brown
59. Like some air fresheners
60. Do little
61. Cozy
63. Half in front?
64. Disgraced one's name?
66. G-8 member

Solution on page 362

Perplexing 46

ACROSS

1. 1972 treaty subj.
4. Craving
8. Derby site
13. Kind of crime
15. Toon Le Pew
16. Start
17. "The Seven Year ___": 1955 film
18. Circular course
19. Parrots
20. Mezzo Berganza
22. Geom. measure
24. Small barracuda
25. Destroy by degrees
26. Bibliographical phrase
28. Casing
30. Available
34. Nudge, as memory
37. Cry from the bench
40. "Let's Dance" singer
41. Medical suffix
42. Seven-time NL home run champ
44. Letters at sea
45. "___ we various passions find": Pope
48. Cut the cheese
50. Delivery people, briefly
51. Guenon monkey
53. Discovery maker
55. Rap sheet data
58. "The Bell Jar" writer
62. Brain area
65. Where the deer and the antelope play
66. Evening event
67. Several czars
69. Bell-shaped lily
71. "The X-Files" extra
72. Flock
73. Priory of ___, group in "The Da Vinci Code"
74. Italian saint
75. Kind of wrench
76. "Men always hate most what they ___ most": Mencken
77. Turn black, maybe

DOWN

1. Grab ___
2. Bad dog
3. Large-scale
4. Kraft Nabisco Championship org.
5. One-eighty
6. Lover of lean cuisine
7. "Lovergirl" singer ___ Marie
8. Kind of CRT
9. Frito-Lay's parent
10. "Watch your ___!"
11. Cruel fellow
12. The bulk
14. Loses
21. Zaire's Mobuto Sese ___
23. Shine, in adspeak
26. "The ___ near"
27. Having five sharps
29. Get to
31. "Horton Hears ___"
32. Life partner?
33. Lacking
34. Make one
35. It means everything
36. Pinup's pins
38. Blow up, for short
39. Control, symbolically
43. Color TV introducer
46. Compact
47. "Bad idea"
49. Orr teammate, familiarly
52. States, informally
54. Cast one's lot (with)
56. "Cabaret" director
57. Wheel alignment
59. Holding one's piece
60. Lachrimose
61. "Iceland" star
62. Country singer McCann
63. Cameo shape
64. Can opener?
66. Big name in electronics
68. Dict. listing
70. Part of GNMA

Solution on page 362

Perplexing 47

ACROSS
1. Cause for a handshake
5. Brew goo
9. Met or Card
13. Ref. work
14. Present opener?
15. Cumberland Gap trailblazer
16. Untouched
17. It may be out on a limb
18. "Matter of Fact" columnist
19. Board member
21. Violent struggle
23. Spell
24. Smart
26. Police blotter abbr.
27. Kind of gun
28. Lay low
30. Losing proposition
34. Principle of conduct
37. Patronage
39. Lao-___
40. Small African antelope
41. Pearl Bailey's middle name
42. Churchill's "___ Finest Hour"
44. Not quite XL
45. Call off
47. Ireland's de Valera
48. North Sea feeder
50. Animation
51. Mean: Abbr.
52. Mail abbr.
54. Doctor Zhivago
56. Interrogate
59. On the other side of
62. Like some fishing
64. Actor Stevens of "Peter Gunn"
65. Orang-___ (ape)
67. Farmer in Delhi
68. Great wealth
69. ___ Alto, CA
70. His: Fr.
71. "Shoot!"
72. Dredger's target
73. Raconteur's offering

DOWN
1. Profundity
2. Habituate: var.
3. Star in the Southern Cross
4. Strong cleaners
5. Study
6. Muslim commander
7. IV league?
8. Paw
9. Kind of mutual fund
10. Get rid of
11. Book of the Book of Mormon
12. Gym unit
15. Canine sound
20. Sister of Clio
22. "___ but known!"
25. A fighting force
27. Semi section
29. "And this is the thanks ___?"
31. Couple
32. Pinza of Broadway
33. Revolution
34. Drop down?
35. Binge
36. Tout's opposite
37. French possessive
38. Singer Nicks
43. Beldam
46. Certain briefs
49. Astray
51. Playground retort
53. Obscures
55. Secretary of the Interior: 1961–1969
56. Refuges
57. Korean city
58. Bright-eyed Couric
59. Flooring calculation
60. James of "Thief"
61. Banquets
63. Duff
64. REN or DIR, in a way
66. ___ chi (martial art)

Solution on page 362

Perplexing 48

ACROSS

1. Alien's subj.
4. Indian drum beat
8. Butler's quarters?
12. Half of doce
14. High nest
15. Barker
16. Like cranberries
17. Supreme Court justice: 1911–1916
18. "Symphony in Black" artist
19. Cordwood units
21. Dog-food comparison
23. A way to think
26. Old spy grp.
27. Tobacco kilns
30. Paul McCartney, for one
32. Fix, as a road
36. ___Loma, Calif.
37. Cracker seed
39. Keats's "___ on Indolence"
40. Cereal box no.
41. ___school
42. 100 ergs
43. Abbr. next to a telephone number
44. Always, in odes
45. More chichi
47. "An Essay on Criticism" writer
48. Code subject
50. "Up" positions
51. Elegance
52. Cap
54. Beef source
56. Facing charges
60. Transport on treads
64. Lunar "sea"
65. Pops
68. ___Fyne, Scotland
69. Discordia's Greek counterpart
70. Boosted
71. Robert ___Prewitt ("From Here to Eternity" soldier)
72. Drops off
73. Salinger gal
74. "The Sultan of Sulu" writer

DOWN

1. Attendance figs., often
2. Spot in the Senate
3. Italian bread?
4. "Like a ___-tray in the sky": Carroll
5. Chair part
6. Jodie's "Nell" co-star
7. Correo ___(airmail)
8. ___fly
9. Flying prefix
10. Bank posting
11. Yank, e.g.
13. Geological formations
14. "Besides . . ."
20. 1997 U.S. Open champ
22. Comparable to a lobster
24. In the habit of
25. Knock, slangily
27. Like galleys
28. Wood used for bridge pilings
29. It can be icy
31. Most uncommon
33. Fiesta de ___(bullfight)
34. Crack
35. Visit again
37. To be, in Barcelona
38. Blight
41. Kenyan tribesman
46. Connections
47. Convict's objective
49. Cause of burnout
51. It's an honor
53. Billiard shot
55. "___quam videri" (North Carolina's motto)
56. Peck film (with "The")
57. Japan's first capital
58. Drop acid
59. They're drawn
61. Contract's escalator clause, for short
62. More than passed
63. "Of ___I sing"
66. Monk's title
67. A pint, maybe

Solution on page 362

Perplexing 49

ACROSS
1. Language that gives us "whiskey"
5. Farm workers?
9. Model material
14. Bankrupt
15. Composer Siegmeister
16. Cacophonous
17. "Smart" one
18. Duff
19. Feed fuel to
20. Kennedy or Clinton
22. Back covers, often
24. Pitcher Fernandez
25. "My Cup Runneth Over" singer
26. Middling marks
28. Minor, in law
31. Balance
35. Bonehead
38. Bess's successor
40. Backgammon piece
41. Cathy ___, "East of Eden" wife
43. Earth, in sci-fi
45. "Last Essays of ___," 1833
46. Informal evenings
48. Camp sights
50. Dutch measure
51. Ledger column
53. They're tender
55. Rockefeller Center muralist
57. Cossack chief
61. CEO wannabe
64. That, in Oaxaca
65. Catch
66. Supermarket chain
68. "We the Living" author
70. "Boola Boola" singers
71. Need a bib
72. Outside opening?
73. Crate component
74. Doltish
75. Arise (from)
76. "Working Girl" girl

DOWN
1. DVR option
2. Like some notepaper
3. Historic rival of Florence
4. Bivouac
5. Balloon or dirigible
6. D-back, for one
7. Argentine aunt
8. Glacial ice formation
9. Hounds
10. Dance, e.g.
11. Lorelei Lee's creator
12. "Reginald" author
13. "O, my Luve is like ___. . ."
21. Be prolific
23. ___ Arc, Ark.
27. Fill
29. "___ a man who wasn't there"
30. Exhausts
32. Alone: Stage direction
33. Cetacean genus
34. Clothes line
35. Arabian capital
36. "Money" writer Martin
37. Guinea pigs, maybe
39. Cubemaker Rubik
42. Attends
44. Haphazardly
47. Bell site
49. Fixes
52. G.R.E. takers
54. Least wild
56. Shipping weights
58. "Damage" director
59. Divas' deliveries
60. Egg holders
61. Anti-DUI group
62. In the buff
63. At another time
65. Duck: Ger.
67. Affairs
69. "___ now!"

Solution on page 363

Perplexing 50

ACROSS

1. Sets (on)
5. Supports
10. Sidi ___, Morocco
14. Medicine cabinet item
15. Midwest transfer point
16. ___-Wade
17. Catalan painter Joan
18. Most important
19. Barbra's "A Star Is Born" co-star
20. Disguised, for short
22. Kind of rating
24. Western wolf
27. "Red River" actress
28. Dungeons & Dragons beast
31. Coastal Brazilian state
33. Boys in the 'hood
37. Batman after Michael
38. "The heat ___"
39. Masters
41. Big name in sport shirts
43. "___ on you!"
45. Given by
46. "You Bet Your Life" sponsor
48. The "I" of I. M. Pei
50. "How Can ___ Sure" (1967 hit)
51. ___-eyed
52. Fictional Italian town
53. MA-to-PA heading
54. Boombox button
56. Burrows
58. Rummy variety
62. "From Here to Eternity" wife
66. Golfer Isao
67. Like a shower wall
70. Quick, in trade names
71. Zest
72. Hang
73. "Back in Black" band
74. Gives the heave-ho
75. Wind
76. Bismarck loc.

DOWN

1. 640 acres: Abbr.
2. Have ___ for
3. About: Abbr.
4. Ribbon holder
5. Games grp.
6. "Put a lid on it!"
7. Gladly
8. Frozen food brand
9. Direct
10. Bugs
11. "Watch out!"
12. Ruhr refusal
13. O.R. lines
21. Home to some Mongolian nomads
23. Do a garage job
25. Boito's Mefistofele, e.g.
26. "We're in trouble!"
28. "Amores" poet
29. Leveled
30. Hard to call
32. Grant-___
34. Luftwaffe battler
35. Gold braid
36. High-hats
39. Director Sergio
40. Fish-eating duck
42. Average name
44. Honey liquor
47. Banks on the runway
49. Skein sound
52. Film genre
55. Tallinn natives
57. Wrap choice
58. "Blondie" character
59. Blood-related
60. Cameroon lake
61. Menlo Park name
63. In-basket stamp: Abbr.
64. Ancient work including the Skalda
65. Cutlet?
66. "Desperate Housewives" airer
68. Comic shriek
69. "___ Day" (1993 rap hit)

Solution on page 363

Perplexing 51

ACROSS

1. Pulls
5. "It's only __!"
10. Singer with the 2001 hit "Thank You"
14. Pennsylvanie, e.g.
15. Engine unit
16. Adah's husband
17. Boxer's attire
18. "Tales of the Trail" author
19. Boosts
20. Start of a tryster's message
22. Claws
24. Artist Rousseau
27. Virtual person in a computer game
28. Trail left by an animal
31. Alphabetical trio
33. Ballet practice
37. Breeziness
38. Soon
41. Denial
42. "Aloha Oe" accompaniment
43. Jerk
44. __ cit.
46. End for cash or court
47. "__ iron bars a cage"
48. "The English Patient" setting
50. After April in Paris
51. "Ode to Psyche" poet
54. Fiend
55. Climbing vine
57. "Get __!"
59. Cubes
61. Magazine store?
65. Fat Man and Little Boy, e.g.
69. Author Jorge __ Borges
70. Lending figures
73. Adriatic port
74. Actor Jared
75. Dazzled
76. Run up __
77. She was abducted by the giant Thjazi
78. Tacked on
79. Skates in water

DOWN

1. Expression
2. Missouri's ally, once
3. Where to "gyre and gimble"
4. Prefix with scope
5. Sigourney Weaver sci-fi film, 1979
6. Game winner's cry
7. Store convenience, for short
8. Cold cuts, e.g.
9. Cousins of ospreys
10. Worrywart's words
11. Cow-horned goddess
12. Arp art
13. Dethrone
21. Brownie point
23. Be indisposed
25. National airport name
26. Possibilities
28. Precious mettle?
29. Orange __
30. "Wozzeck," e.g.
32. Desserts at Luigi's
34. Persona's opposite
35. Joyous hymn
36. Over Jordan, on a map
39. NNN
40. __ anglais (English horn)
45. "The Alienist" author Carr
49. Paul Newman film
52. Trinity part
53. Anger, e.g.
56. Map line
58. "The Sound of Music" heroine
60. Scoped out
61. "__ Wanna Do": Sheryl Crow
62. Felt sorry
63. In __
64. Polaroid's inventor
66. First name in spydom
67. Act like an ass
68. They're all in the family
71. Little 'un
72. Dolly, for one

Solution on page 363

Perplexing 52

ACROSS

1. Nasty
5. The Fighting Tigers, for short
8. At the home of
12. Bond
13. "It's gone!"
14. TV's "Evening ___"
15. Numerical prefix
16. River from the Cantabrian Mountains
17. Go at it
18. Experiences dizziness
20. State treasury
21. Screenwriter Southern
22. "O.K."
23. Rent payer
26. Computer command
30. Addams cousin
31. Flat
34. Bidding site
35. Decorative pitchers
37. Singer Scaggs
38. Criticize
39. "Scream" star Campbell
40. Put down
42. Air show formation
43. Bristles
45. Deep sleeps
47. "Brat Farrar" mystery writer
48. Makes sound
50. Sydney salutation
52. Kind of moustache
56. Start of an oath
57. Court grp.
58. Indic language
59. Orchestra section
60. Never, before
61. Bewilder
62. R.N.'s boss?
63. Chester White's home
64. European border river

DOWN

1. Cries of aversion
2. Delight
3. Sumptuousness
4. Fermenting agents
5. Like a grebe's foot
6. Classic board game
7. Eerie sightings
8. Name
9. Witchy women
10. Cabinet dept.
11. End of a series
13. Tube-nosed seabird
14. Hotel amenities
19. Percolates
22. "___ darn tootin'!"
23. Borrower's worries
24. Needle case: Var.
25. McQueen or Martin
26. Bring down to earth?
27. From the beginning
28. Indy 500 contestant
29. Squirts
32. Lying, maybe
33. Nancy, in Nancy
36. Pull-off
38. Hillock
40. "L.A. Law" actress
41. "What is so rare ___ in June": Lowell
44. California's Point ___
46. Ersatz
48. Assails
49. Contest effort
50. Goes on and on
51. Big name in pest control
52. Vandals
53. Pitt in "Seven"
54. Cutting tool
55. One having second thoughts
56. ___ story

Solution on page 363

Perplexing 53

ACROSS

1. "Mule Train" singer
6. Available
10. Bite
14. Painful ending?
15. Follower of the news
16. ESPN's Hershiser
17. How-to listings
18. Connecticut senator Christopher
19. ___ Phraya, Thai.
20. Good judgment
22. Ripken, Jr. and Sr.
23. Game point situation
24. Small types
26. "For shame!"
29. Key of Beethoven's "Eroica"
31. Barbecue residue
32. Go by tandem
34. Abrades
38. Attention
40. Some lilies
42. Essence
43. Ask for more Time
45. Doll up
47. Terre Haute sch.
48. Robert of Broadway's "My Fair Lady"
50. "___ season . . ."
52. Warehouse worker
55. Frequently
56. Before love or blue
57. O.K.
63. "La Dolce Vita" composer
64. McQueen in "Jimmy Hollywood"
65. "Coming to America" prince
66. Times to call, in classifieds
67. Bound
68. Breviloquent
69. "The Way We ___," 1973 film
70. "The Mod Squad" actor
71. All agog

DOWN

1. Mascara target
2. Marian Anderson, for one
3. Disney head Robert
4. Tries to bite
5. Abated
6. Bygone
7. Hacienda hand, maybe
8. Bread leftovers
9. "Forget it!"
10. Some Bach pieces
11. Buddhist who has attained Nirvana
12. Author Zora ___ Hurston
13. Lip cover
21. Loci
25. Predatory fish
26. Himalayan goat
27. Certain plaintiff, at law
28. "In that case . . . ."
29. Tidal flood
30. Arctic sight
33. Co. division
35. "___ goes"
36. Word on a door
37. Turn, as a mast
39. Cut
41. Frame
44. Bad news
46. Wink: Var.
49. Ancient medium
51. ___ leg (hurry)
52. Sprinkle
53. Valuable find
54. TV's "The ___ Limits"
55. Old Persians
58. ___ Suey
59. Smythe strip surname
60. "Lulu" composer
61. Literally, "injured"
62. Like some profs.

Solution on page 363

Perplexing 54

ACROSS
1. Burp
6. Future atty.'s challenge
10. Anna May of "Shanghai Express"
14. ___-guided
15. Hebrides isle
16. It's almost pointless
17. Suggest
18. Tae ___ do
19. Pampers rival
20. Charges
22. Bothers
24. A/C output
25. Rite site
26. "How ___!"
29. Norse god of discord
31. Actor Welles
35. Quick round of tennis
37. Near Islands island
39. Genuine article
40. Friend of Frodo
41. Ophelia's brother
43. Gossip
44. Wall St. event
45. Memo header
46. Saratoga Springs, e.g.
48. Cone-shaped heaters
50. Affixes one's John Hancock to
52. Course requirements
53. ___ attack
55. "Able was ___ I saw Elba"
57. Surveyor's assistant
60. Assailed
64. Compass
65. Transcript stats
67. "For want of ___ . . ."
68. Bills
69. Fortune
70. Resembling a parrot's beak
71. "How ___ the little crocodile": Carroll
72. Elects
73. Bridge support

DOWN
1. "London Magazine" essayist
2. Trans World Dome team
3. Mail letters
4. Former name of Sulawesi
5. Lovers' meeting
6. In this way
7. Plants
8. "Is that ___?"
9. Chief Justice after Marshall
10. Certain boxer, informally
11. Symphony, e.g.
12. Gulf of Finland feeder
13. Exploit
21. Mideast VIP
23. Fire up
25. The Panthers of the Big East
26. First name in talk shows
27. Not fitting
28. Imp
30. Silkwood of "Silkwood"
32. Missouri city, briefly
33. Midwest transfer point
34. Salamanders
36. Cook in "The Killing"
38. Less wordy
42. "ER" actor La Salle
47. "Casablanca" composer
49. Quite the hit
51. Selling points?
54. White, informally
56. Change, chemically
57. Big name in mapmaking
58. New "biscuit" of 1912
59. Pound of flesh, e.g.
60. Delicacy, of sorts
61. Island in Goto Archipelago
62. Connections
63. Automotive pioneer
66. Pluto or Snoopy, once

Solution on page 363

Perplexing 55

ACROSS
1. Oar pin
6. Dept. store stuff
9. Short pants
14. More sound
15. Ability to hit a target
16. Fall fruit
17. Deprive of courage
18. Nanki-___ ("The Mikado" character)
19. Shoot
20. Instigate
21. Buttinsky
22. Case for an ophthalmologist
23. Like a couch potato
25. Uncle: Scot.
27. Circus noises
30. Screwdriver hue
35. Black bird
38. It's often loose
40. Screwball
41. Awards since 1956
43. Supermodel Carangi
44. Serve, in a way
45. Cookbook abbr.
46. Kvetch
48. Actor Byrnes
49. Handles
51. Way up?
53. Part of H.R.H.
55. Designer Mizrahi
58. Andrews of "The Mod Squad"
61. Sherman's word for war
64. Powder, e.g.
66. Airport worry
67. Ethan's "Gattaca" co-star
68. Extended operatic solo
69. Geological ridge
70. Boundary: abbr.
71. Guatemalan native
72. Thrash
73. Jungfrau, for one
74. Suffix with corp or fraud

DOWN
1. Goon
2. City with 1,300 people per hectare
3. "___ River"
4. Chief
5. Coastal flier
6. Be wide open
7. God: Sp.
8. Whacked, Bible-style
9. Knee-slapper
10. Date with an M.D.
11. Active
12. Balletic bend
13. Line part: Abbr.
21. Chief god of ancient Egypt
24. Big birds
26. Curly companion
28. Blow up
29. Barbershop sounds
31. Alias lead-in
32. Goose egg
33. First-place
34. ___ out (barely managed)
35. These are often followed
36. French friar
37. Chip maker
39. Way to go
42. Some dance records, for short
44. Island rings
46. Charles, e.g.
47. Brad, e.g.
50. "___ playing our song"
52. Scapegrace
54. Legendary grid coach Don
56. Keep ___ on (monitor)
57. He follows Jay
58. New Ager John
59. Chase in "The Animal Kingdom"
60. Scottish Celt
62. Biographer Ludwig
63. Desk accouterment
65. Requirement
66. Drops on blades
68. Laura Bush's alma mater, for short

Solution on page 364

Perplexing 56

ACROSS

1. Massenet opera
6. Hannibal's hurdle
10. Corp. bigwig
14. ___ living (bring home the bacon)
15. Lugosi, of thrillers
16. "___ we forget . . ."
17. "Enchanted April" setting
18. Brother of Fidel
19. "I've had it ___ here!"
20. Docket
22. More impertinent
24. Dutch painter Gerard ___ Borch
25. "___ gives?"
26. "Penguin" of baseball
27. Lines of thought, for short?
30. Arizona mining town
32. Riffraff
34. Airline monogram
35. Tower over
37. Musk maker
41. From Bergen
43. Big Ten inits.
44. Semblance
45. Canton neighbor
46. Conductor Koussevitzky
48. Anti-smog org.
49. Destroy the interior of
51. Greenwich Village sch.
52. Tennyson work
53. Junk bond rating
56. Pops
58. Disk space, in a way
60. Spartan
62. Queen's home
65. Hitchcock title
66. Footnote note
68. Occupy
70. Latin trio part
71. Shake up
72. Wonderland message
73. Plenty
74. Off the hook
75. Flightless birds

DOWN

1. Gift of flowers
2. "I can't ___ thing"
3. Mountaineer's challenge
4. Entrances
5. Singer Taylor ___
6. "East of Eden" heroine
7. Open tract
8. Deeply piled
9. Respectful greeting
10. Furthermore
11. Get 30 points in piquet
12. Compact name
13. Level
21. TV's "Quick ___ McGraw"
23. Larry, for one
25. Goes downhill
27. Explosive Italian landmark
28. "Star Wars" critter
29. "Good Advice" star
31. Fixes
33. A.C. letters
35. Bare
36. Wrath
38. Seven up, e.g.
39. Catch a glimpse of
40. Honest
42. Saturate, in dialect
47. Oscar role for Hanks
50. Duty
52. "Four Essays on Liberty" author Berlin
53. 200 milligrams
54. Clinton cabinet member
55. TV from D.C.
57. Exclude
59. Bad dog
61. 1979 Roman Polanski film
62. "Zip-___ Doo-Dah"
63. Nervous network
64. Role for Nick Adams
67. Winter end
69. Anatomical foot

Solution on page 364

Perplexing 57

ACROSS

1. Lath
5. Impromptu
10. Like the Ger. "der"
14. Part of Kb
15. Do well
16. "C'mon, be ___"
17. Islamic leader
18. First strategy
19. Atlantic City game
20. Butterfly, e.g.
22. Black-tie
24. Dawdle
27. Bottom line
28. Org.'s kin
31. Plural suffix
33. Restrained
37. Narc's find
38. Some wool
41. Rat Pack name
42. NL West team, on scoreboards
43. Like a bairn
44. Corduroy feature
46. Sweetie, across the pond
47. Low-___
49. New York lake
51. "___ on my bed my limbs I lay": Coleridge
52. Arab leader
54. Fill-in
55. More likely
57. Coxcomb
59. Amber, e.g.
61. How railroads try to run
64. Put away, in a way
68. Coconut fiber
69. Result
73. Prefix for stat
74. Calendar abbr.
75. Run off
76. 1952 Winter Olympics setting
77. Dept.
78. A lot
79. Banish to Hades

DOWN

1. Take illegally
2. Butter bean
3. "When I was ___ . . ."
4. Better Boy or Early Girl
5. Memo opener
6. "Lady Chatterley" initials
7. Debussy's "Air de ___"
8. Days ___
9. Rosary
10. Incense
11. Boulle's citizenry
12. ___ serif
13. Be too sweet
21. Cousin of a cockatoo
23. Buff
25. Ages
26. Formal vote
28. At full gallop
29. "Out!"
30. Skyline feature
32. Penman
34. Home subcontractor
35. Habituate: var.
36. Sole provider?
39. Papal name
40. A helping hand
45. Washing spot
48. Lead
50. Benelux loc.
53. Data storage site
56. Virgin
58. Henhouse sounds
60. School mos.
61. Sept. 30 follower
62. Subject, usually
63. Draws
65. Very
66. Prefix with drama
67. Spar
70. Reactor-monitoring agcy.
71. Domingo, e.g.
72. German link

Solution on page 364

Perplexing 58

ACROSS

1. Bit of inspiration
6. Erythrocyte: Abbr.
9. Turkish coins
14. Plain ___
15. UN arm
16. Assume
17. On drugs
18. ___ Cayes, Haiti
19. Tastiness
20. 1972 Wimbledon winner Smith
21. Grant
22. Bandleader Fields
23. Curlew's cousin
25. Ballerina's pivot
27. Ameliorates
30. Expunges
35. Behind
38. Flow
40. "HouseSitter" star
41. "___ Gold" (Peter Fonda film)
43. Beauty
44. "___ Thief" (1950 movie)
45. Colorful salamander
46. Cheese made from ewe's milk
48. Domain name suffix
49. Dipsacus: Var.
51. Glistened
53. ". . . through the frosty ___ . . ."
55. Food in Exodus 16
58. Early pulpit
61. Boiardo's patron
64. Give a free pass
66. Hail
67. "The Bourne Supremacy" org.
68. "Honest"
69. Whines
70. Pres. appointee
71. Cameroon coin
72. Outlet
73. Greek letters
74. Some change

DOWN

1. Actor Erwin et al.
2. Assignments
3. ___-American
4. "The Day the Earth Stood Still" star Michael
5. Bud holder?
6. Agitate
7. Oozed
8. Mathematical subgroup
9. QB, at times
10. Wife of Esau
11. Clue weapon
12. For one
13. Atlas abbr.
21. "___ la guerre"
24. Avoid summer school
26. Corp. that makes the parts
28. Accordingly
29. Looks
31. "Kung Fu" actor Philip
32. Maine river
33. The America's Cup trophy, e.g.
34. Angler's woe
35. Polly, to Tom
36. Absquatulate
37. New Mexican pueblo-dweller
39. Chinese nurse
42. Space invaders, for short
44. A Mrs. Chaplin
46. King, in Portugal
47. Iditarod terminus
50. Tao teacher
52. "More!"
54. Digest
56. "A Tree Grows in Brooklyn" family name
57. Make ___ (get rich)
58. In ___ (going nowhere)
59. Dramatic opening?
60. It has a head and hops
62. ___ Valley (Reagan library site)
63. Running things in a bar
65. Bench presser's pride
66. A.M.A. members
68. Pro Bowl side

Solution on page 364

Perplexing 59

ACROSS

1. Football Hall-of-Famer Marchetti
5. Part of the CIA
9. Modern workout system
14. Brand of daminozide
15. So
16. Wisconsin college town
17. Novelist ___Mae Brown
18. Greek goddess
19. Kipling's wolf pack leader
20. The eyes have it
22. Hearst's San ___
23. Wine prefix
24. Arabian peninsula city
25. Zoomed
28. Put off
32. Gold braid
33. Kind of fertilizer
34. Mel Gibson role
35. Crosby, Stills and Nash, e.g.
36. Pack carrier
37. Neighbor of Mauritania
38. Laid low
39. Round of four
40. Stirs
41. Rating range
43. "Sanford and Son" son
44. Shellacking
45. Wedding reception sight
46. Grippers
49. Protected, in a way
53. Dik-dik kin
54. Flat fee
55. Home in a 1936 novel
56. Store selection
57. Naive person
58. Part of A.A.U.W.: Abbr.
59. Final word
60. Turner and others
61. Gershwin's "The ___ Love"

DOWN

1. Vestments, e.g.
2. Word form of "hipbone"
3. Brussels-based org.
4. Handel bars
5. Within reach
6. El ___
7. Smoke, say
8. Roll-call call
9. Apprentice
10. 1993 Super Bowl M.V.P.
11. Sword
12. Machete
13. Put ___ act
21. Notable Virginia family
22. "You ___ mouthful!"
24. Diets
25. Bantu tongue
26. Hatch in the Senate
27. Bad thing to be taken for
28. At full throttle
29. "Gabriela, Clove and Cinnamon" author
30. Curved nail
31. Are
33. Cairo crooner
36. Some Balts
37. Campaign asset
39. No-goodnik
40. Profits
42. Chophouse choices
43. Coffeehouse orders
45. "Now it ___ told"
46. 1994 Shirley MacLaine title role
47. Inter ___ (among others)
48. Slow-moving
49. Top out
50. Lake ___ (Blue Nile source)
51. Name for an Irish lass
52. Winfield of baseball
54. Slugger's stat.

Solution on page 364

Perplexing 60

ACROSS
1. ___ girl
6. Maladies
10. Alliance
14. Buzz
15. Mattress part
16. Grant Wood's home
17. Earth protector
18. De Gaulle's hat
19. Hike
20. Minor player
21. Discharge
23. Bring to life
25. "Dinner and a Movie" channel
26. Can. province
27. Israeli city
28. Marks in Spanish class
32. Helgenberger of "C.S.I."
33. Ship-to-ship calls
34. Check for accuracy
35. Ear canal
40. Animal house
41. Avoirdupois unit: Abbr.
42. Son of Telamon
43. Milk container
45. "Get your hands off me!"
46. Critical
47. "What ___ for Love" ("A Chorus Line" song)
49. Skin-related
50. A season: Abbr.
53. Bit of booze
54. Sch. on the Charles
55. "Wild Thing" group, with "the"
57. Silences
58. "___ Pete's sake!"
61. Alitalia destination
62. Idaho product, slangily

64. Alley pickup
66. "A Little Bitty Tear" singer, 1962
67. Wildcat
68. 1964 role for Audrey
69. Info
70. It takes a beating
71. Innsbruck is its capital

DOWN
1. Marsh critter
2. Colorless liqueur
3. E.P.A. concern
4. "___ dieu!"
5. Clytemnestra's killer
6. FDR's Interior secretary
7. MGM founder Marcus
8. Collagen target
9. Deli need

10. Dentist's request
11. Major defense contractor
12. Have a loan from
13. Encrusted
22. "Zoboomafoo" network
24. Fixes
26. Actress Duke
28. "The forbidden fragrance"
29. "If ___ a Hammer"
30. "Hawaii Five-O" star
31. Fraction of a newton
32. Called for Friskies
34. Screening device
36. "The Alienist" author Caleb
37. In ___ (stuck)
38. Basalt source
39. Jump in the rink
44. Bilbo Baggins' find

46. Gears up
48. Put down, slangily
49. Archaeological site
50. Landing place
51. 2002 Olympics venue
52. "Thus with a kiss I die" speaker
54. "Call Me ___"
56. ["Oh, no!"]
57. Ashram figure
58. C-worthy?
59. Italian soup ingredient
60. "It's been ___!"
63. Structure with triangular faces: abbr.
65. Carry on

Solution on page 364

Perplexing 61

ACROSS
1. Concertedly
6. Dwell
10. Biblical shepherd
14. Doll
15. Last of a Latin trio
16. Food sticker
17. Handle
18. Singular, to Caesar
19. Essay page
20. Rags
22. South American cowboy
24. Pitcher Robb ___
25. Spinnaker, e.g.
26. Family head
27. Boston hoopster, for short
30. "Die Meistersinger" soprano
32. "Now ___ theater near you!"
34. Clark's "Mogambo" co-star
35. Alpine feature
37. 1981 Literature Nobelist Canetti
41. "Dagnabbit!"
43. College basketball tourney, for short
44. Totaled
45. Ashes, e.g.
46. Asian weight units
48. D.C. denizen
49. "For shame!"
51. Chicken general?
52. Skye of "Gas Food Lodging"
53. Norse underworld goddess
56. Level, in London
58. Atlas elevs.
60. Vigilant
62. Cow catcher
65. Badgered
66. 1998 NL M.V.P.
68. Harold Gray heroine
70. Architect William van ___
71. ___ patriae
72. Fence feature
73. Beam intensely
74. Acts
75. Armies

DOWN
1. Blockhead
2. Cooking fat
3. Curved arch
4. Swimming
5. Irregular
6. Blocks
7. "___ Little Teapot"
8. Friend of Porky
9. And others, in other words
10. "Like ___ of bricks!"
11. Man, for one
12. Calendario page
13. Inveigled
21. Secy. Abraham's dept.
23. Edits
25. Fill
27. Insincere talk
28. "Did you ___?!"
29. Household god
31. Get a load off one's chest
33. ___ maison (indoors): Fr.
35. Nail down
36. Are, in Arles
38. Chinese leader?
39. Egyptian sun god
40. "___ Enchanted Evening" ("South Pacific" song)
42. Asian celebration
47. ___ Linda, CA
50. Ankle bone
52. Really digs
53. Every 60 minutes
54. "Waterworld" girl
55. Weighs down
57. Leaf pore
59. Refuse
61. Linguistic symbol
62. 1968 Chemistry Nobelist Onsager
63. Cuckoos
64. Attack with a lance
67. Farm female
69. Some Caltech grads, for short

Solution on page 365

Perplexing 62

ACROSS

1. ___death (overwork)
5. Redcap's burden
9. Depress, with "out"
12. Sacred image: Var.
13. Paella pots
15. Pressure unit
16. Art supplies
17. African antelope
18. "Dedicated to the ___ Love"
19. Empathize
21. Shakes, for short
22. Comes out with
23. Chip-making supply
25. Manages, with "out"
27. "American Buffalo" playwright
30. "___ be an honor"
32. Heavy ___
36. Nasdaq debut
37. "Friends" baby
39. 1957 Jimmy Dorsey hit
40. Egg holders: Abbr.
42. Angler with pots
44. Like a stuffed shirt
45. *Sports Illustrated*'s 1984 Sportswoman of the Year
47. Fan club focus
49. Mid 11th-century date
50. Indo-___
51. Didn't hold
52. Heretofore
54. Loaded
56. Judicial proceedings
58. "Country Gentleman" Atkins
61. "I see!"
63. Sponge again
67. "The Shelters of Stone" author
68. "Savvy?"
70. "Leaving Las Vegas" actress
71. Lap dog, for short
72. Intimate
73. People: Prefix
74. ___Mae (Whoopi's "Ghost" role)
75. Box
76. Bombshell Diana

DOWN

1. Christian name
2. Tom Joad, e.g.
3. Exaction
4. Reduced
5. Big boo-boo
6. ___ Khan
7. Elated
8. Put (away)
9. ___gratia (in all kindness): Lat.
10. Chemistry Nobelist: 1934
11. 3-D tests
14. Mont. neighbor
15. Horseshoes players
20. British poet laureate Nahum
24. Element of change
26. First name in comedy
27. Millionths of a meter
28. More fitting
29. Hall of fame
31. Connie's portrayer, in "The Godfather"
33. Early Reynolds role
34. As ___ (usually)
35. For real
38. Blokes
39. Breaking capacity, briefly
41. Shake up
43. John's "Hairspray" role
46. CIA's sea-going arm
48. When repeated, like some shows
51. Fix, as a pump
53. Mouthed off to
55. Verne voyager
57. Minotaur's land
58. Crime boss
59. Shaded
60. Reggae's ___-Mouse
62. "How to Make an American Quilt" author Whitney ___
64. "___ be in England . . ."
65. Essen basin
66. Uncle ___
69. Kind of wheel

Solution on page 365

Perplexing 63

ACROSS

1. Man from UNC.L.E.
5. Personal interest
9. "Careless Hands" singer, 1949
14. Islamic VIP
15. Detective, at times
16. "Barry Lyndon" star
17. Long car, for short
18. "Biscuit" introduced in 1912
19. "Wellaway!"
20. It may be AM or FM: Abbr.
21. "Finnegans Wake" wife
22. "Got it!"
23. Puts forward
26. Cousin of a gull
29. Sue Grafton's "___ for Lawless"
30. Early capital of Macedonia
34. "Sunflowers" setting
37. Some horses
40. Androgynous "SNL" character
41. Hammermill unit
42. They form bonds
43. El ___, Texas
44. Crash site?
45. Looks out for, maybe
46. What "-vore" means
47. Coins
49. '60s grp.
50. Bones, anatomically
52. Ancient region of France
56. Word form of "man"
59. "Render therefore ___ _Caesar . . ."
61. Doll
62. Nancy's opposite number, once

64. "Star Trek" crewmember
65. Cluckers
66. ___ space (the sea)
67. Azerbaijan's neighbor
68. Grammy winner India.___
69. Like smokestacks
70. "No problem!"
71. Closefisted

DOWN

1. Hot stuff
2. Does away with
3. Describes
4. Coronado's quest
5. Brown ermines
6. Clears
7. Creditor's claim
8. Drink with a straw
9. ___ fault

10. Connected, in a way
11. Actor Stephen et al.
12. Nutmeg skin
13. Sommer in the cinema
24. I, O, or U, but not A or E: Abbr.
25. "___ for Rocket": Bradbury
27. Dark times, to poets
28. Places for forks: Abbr.
31. Cross words
32. Ed.'s request
33. Noun-form ending
34. Some Dada works
35. Get as a result
36. Fill the hold
37. A.A.A. recommendation
38. Salesman's dest.
39. Early times
42. Copper heads?

43. "Que ___?"
45. Sue Grafton's "___ for Alibi"
46. People people, for short
48. Waist band
49. "Citizen Kane" actor Everett ___
51. European autos
52. Floral fragrance
53. "All done!"
54. Ancient land on the Aegean
55. Goose genus
56. Onassis and namesakes
57. Prefix with technology
58. Bedrock pet
60. Island in Goto Archipelago
63. End for honor or bound
65. Liu Pang's dynasty

Solution on page 365

Perplexing 64

ACROSS

1. Buggy terrain
5. Radical Hoffman
10. Crack
14. Vidov in "Wild Orchid"
15. Some love songs
16. Draped garment
17. Henry VIII's last wife
18. Cant
19. ___for one's money
20. Take to one's heart
22. Primes
24. Egyptian peak
27. Mr., abroad
28. "Against ___ when he was drunk": Shak.
31. ___canto
33. Maine's ___ Bay
37. Beat it
38. Beer, in a boilermaker
41. Alpine pass
42. 4 x 4, for short
43. Christmas sounds
44. South of Spain
46. Hit the + key
47. Memory unit, for short
48. Sales incentive
50. "Fantasy Island" prop
51. Jabber
54. Follow
55. Bel ___
57. Capek drama
59. Assailed
61. Current measures
65. Warm welcomes
69. German industrial district
70. Appropriate
73. Bite
74. Volvo competitor
75. Blackmore heroine
76. "___ben Adhem"
77. "M*A*S*H" milieu
78. Endured
79. Room at the top

DOWN

1. Ninny
2. It means "red" in Mongolian
3. Techie, traditionally
4. Go out
5. "I don't give ___!"
6. Sticker
7. Petition
8. ". . . like ___ not!"
9. "Women Who Run With the Wolves" author
10. Bowls
11. Famous Amos
12. Chill
13. Embargoes
21. Common aspiration
23. Parenthesis, e.g.
25. Brought down
26. Plural suffix
28. "A poem begins as ___ in the throat": Frost
29. Lord's Prayer
30. Popular watch
32. "Gil Blas" author
34. Locker room item
35. Systems of rules
36. "Return To Sender" is one
39. Vert.'s counterpart
40. Beaten path
45. Run off
49. Short haircut
52. Compact
53. Asian leader?
56. Lacking a key
58. Analyzes
60. Filled to excess
61. Kodak competitor
62. Bergman's last role
63. Nanny's aid
64. Opening
66. Derelict
67. Date-setting phrase
68. Board up
71. John, to Ringo
72. "Starpeace" musician

Solution on page 365

Perplexing 65

ACROSS
1. Gallivants
5. Michael's father-in-law
10. Hood
14. Award for "Curse of the Starving Class"
15. Silk pattern
16. Harbor, perhaps
17. Single
18. Let out
19. Forward
20. Backslide
22. Factotums
24. Smeltery waste
25. Fingers
28. Rest of the afternoon
30. Sly character
34. Derelict
37. Jabba the ___ of "Star Wars"
39. ___ notch
40. Comic strip dog
41. Off-color
43. "I ___ the opinion . . ."
44. Play favorites?
45. Method
46. Characters in "Macbeth" and "Richard II"
48. Moolah
50. Swear
52. Beta carotene, for one
54. They're often girded
58. Gobs
61. Affixes, in a way
63. Beliefs
64. Hedren of "The Birds"
67. Union at LAX
68. Elite Eight org.
69. Province west of Madrid
70. Elite police unit
71. Preserved
72. Apples, e.g.
73. It comes in cans

DOWN
1. Noggin
2. Daisy Mae's guy
3. How to get the operator
4. Rasta's messiah
5. Grounded birds
6. Introverts
7. BMOC, e.g.
8. Burning sensation?
9. Fires off
10. Beach shelter
11. Ancient Greek coin
12. Jack Benny catchphrase
13. Classic Fords
21. Penultimate letters
23. ___ cloud (comet zone)
26. Letter getter
27. Lacking play
29. "The sign of extra service" sloganeer
31. ___ the word (hush!)
32. Lodge sign
33. Big galoots
34. Virginia statesman
35. Broadway star Linda
36. Tiny arachnid
38. Phoenician trading center
42. TV's "___ 12"
43. Floor
45. Gds.
47. 1952 Olympics host
49. Targets
51. Big hit
53. Draft status?
55. "___ Man and He Danced with His Wife": Cher hit
56. Less
57. Scythe handle
58. Make, as a putt
59. Suffix with fluor-
60. "Do I have to draw you ___?"
62. Spanish river
65. Literature Nobelist Andric
66. "Mr. ___ Passes By": Milne

Solution on page 365

Perplexing 66

ACROSS
1. Beginning
5. Actress Arlene
9. Coat part
12. Mix
13. Newbery-winning author Scott ___
15. Ruse
16. Course
17. Dike, Eunomia and Irene
18. Frosty coating
19. Improvised
21. Former White House inits.
22. Gillette product
23. Short depository
26. Bleu hue
28. Bilko's rank: abbr.
31. High mark
33. Spruce
37. Volga, formerly
38. Entanglements
39. Smelting residue
40. Last call
42. "Cut it out!"
44. Lanford Wilson's "The ___ Baltimore"
45. Israeli leaders?
47. Sideshow performer
49. Beer barrel
50. Lesser cut, usually
51. Manhattan Project physicist
52. Faline's mother
53. Hang loose
55. Manage
57. Poultry
60. Cry of pain
62. Encircles
66. Requiem Mass word
67. Mount Narodnaya's range
70. Attack
71. Blue
72. Embroidered loop
73. Tutsi foe
74. Mauna ___, HI
75. Controvert
76. Oolong and souchong

DOWN
1. Amino acid
2. "When I was ___ . . ."
3. In the company of
4. With zero chance
5. Cartoon cry
6. Busyness
7. Munster man
8. Some pack carriers
9. Oceans
10. Crowd response
11. "___ Breckinridge"
14. "Breezy" star, 1973
15. Exodus figure
20. Plug, of a sort
24. Contractor's info
25. North Sea feeder
27. Tar Heels' sch.
28. Muchachas: Abbr.
29. Diplomat Boutros Boutros- ___
30. Used a VCR
32. Convention
34. Valuable find
35. Hyperion, for one
36. 1945 conference site
39. Teacher's request
41. Relieved
43. Bondman
46. "Deadwood" airer
48. Double checker
51. Showy
54. ___-garou (werewolf)
56. Put on clothes, once
57. All you can eat
58. Black-and-white sandwich
59. Gilda's Baba
61. Before card or cream
63. Profligate
64. Bank contents
65. Actor Erwin et al.
68. Chaney Sr. or Jr.
69. Dump

Solution on page 365

Perplexing 67

ACROSS

1. Brewer Frederick
6. Part of R.I.T.
10. Kirgiz city
13. One concerned with figures
14. "___ Said" (Neil Diamond hit)
15. Clog, e.g.
16. Corporate flunky
17. Bro
18. Home to a Colombian drug cartel
19. ___ on (log)
20. Deplorable
21. More precious
23. Enfants attend them
26. Decent
27. Miller Lite alternative
30. "Leaving Las Vegas" star
32. Be still, at sea
33. Emulate Buffy
35. Claiming word
39. Diminutive suffix
40. Dirty campaigner
43. Big mouth
44. In-box item
46. Jupiter, e.g.
47. Ham's place, perhaps
49. Unlocked?
51. Word with big or blue
52. Entree
54. Bogeyman
57. Straight
59. Geisha girder
60. Improvise
64. Energy units
65. Suffix with flex
67. More upscale
68. Young, in Greece
69. "Shake a leg!"
70. Lint collector
71. Richard Gere title role of 2000
72. Request from the stumped
73. New Hampshire college town

DOWN

1. Okra units
2. Cultural beginning?
3. Modern journal
4. "Keystone Kops" producer
5. Afternoon hour in Italy
6. Kind of basin
7. ___ Cologne
8. REN or DIR, in a way
9. Made haste
10. "Gibbsville" creator
11. Having a bottom
12. One who succeeds
15. Went up
20. G note
22. Graph of beats
24. Boardroom bigwigs
25. Lasting marks
27. Aluminum potassium sulfate
28. Denver elevation
29. Have the earmarks of
31. Affirmative vote
33. Beginnings
34. Charlie of the '60s Orioles
36. 2002 Literature Nobelist Kertesz
37. Howls
38. Popeye's ___ Pea
41. Year Helsinki was founded
42. Architect Mies van der ___
45. Have a one-track mind
48. Soothing medicine
50. "I suspected as much!"
51. ___ de coeur
52. More terrible
53. Bar
55. List preceder
56. Has ___ for (is skilled at)
57. Act the shylock
58. Highly amusing
61. Bad marks
62. "Count ___"
63. ___ the mouth of (kiss)
66. ASCAP alternative
67. Suffix with neat

Solution on page 366

Perplexing 68

ACROSS
1. Atl. relative
4. Canadian dollar bird
8. Burdened Titan
13. Feels punk
15. A movie star may carry one
16. Davis in "Cutthroat Island"
17. Insignificant
18. Homecoming comer
19. "Un Ballo in Maschera" aria
20. Convictions
22. French pronoun
24. Bust, so to speak
25. "Die Fledermaus" maid
26. Red shade
28. Break
30. Series of movements
34. Screenwriter Diamond
37. He played Ben
40. Transfer
41. Border
42. Painter of many Washington portraits
44. With a needle: Prefix
45. Year's record
48. "Goosebumps" author R. L. ___
50. Vous, familiarly
51. High
53. Up ___good
55. Existing
58. Belts
62. Result of a sack
65. Court figure: Abbr.
66. Apartment, often
67. All worked up
69. "Hurlyburly" playwright
71. "At Wit's End" author Bombeck
72. Asmodeus
73. Euripidean conflict
74. Nothing, in Nantes
75. Clubs: Abbr.
76. Everglades deposit
77. Big World Cup power: Abbr.

DOWN
1. Rigatoni or ziti
2. Hurt
3. "I Fall to Pieces" singer
4. Brings up the rear
5. "___ Mutual Friend"
6. Emulate Webster
7. "Civic Arousal" author
8. Gray, in a way
9. Earthly
10. Movie princess
11. Detractor
12. Mideast royal name
14. Certain silversides
21. Blue hue
23. "___ boom bah!"
26. Daughter of Saturn
27. Groundskeeper's supply
29. Clean (up)
31. Room to swing ___
32. Chalupa alternative
33. His: Fr.
34. 401(k) cousins
35. "Is so!" rebuttal
36. K-P connection
38. Actor Pendleton
39. Bluebloods
43. "Another Day on Earth" rocker Brian
46. "Friends" co-star
47. Cariou of Broadway
49. Massachusetts motto opener
52. "Traffic" org.
54. Person with a title
56. Harness part
57. Rocket section
59. Central courts
60. Breaker of a sort
61. Like "dis"
62. "___ Rose" (song from "The Music Man")
63. Bauxite and borax
64. ___ Club
66. Cost of living?
68. Capt.'s aide
70. Flapper wrapper

Solution on page 366

Perplexing 69

ACROSS

1. "The Naked Maja" artist
5. Caesar cohort
9. Menotti opera character
14. "O Sanctissima," e.g.
15. Flag down
16. Bear in "The Jungle Book"
17. ___ ed.
18. Cherry placement
19. Foucault's "This Is Not ___"
20. Celebrex manufacturer
22. Month: Abbr.
24. Minor invention
25. Queeg's command
27. Fighter at Chancellorsville
29. Dimin.'s opposite
31. Bond, e.g.
33. Cairo's river
37. "MS. Found in a Bottle" writer
38. "La ___": Camus
40. Put ___ to
41. ___ France
43. Link letters?
44. Slow
45. Allied (with)
46. Coffeehouse order
48. It may follow a dot
49. Writer Seton
50. Something to chew on
51. Prison guard, in slang
53. Copier tray abbr.
55. Having wings
57. Fraud finder: Abbr.
60. "Certainement!"
62. Blue
65. Luft in "Trapper John, M.D."
67. Patrick's "Ghost" co-star
69. Ouida's "___ of Flanders"
71. It's a long story
72. "___ a roll!"
73. "The Vampire Lestat" author
74. Commoners
75. "Face/Off" actress Gershon
76. "Let's Make a Deal" choice

DOWN

1. Econ. figure
2. Circus reactions
3. Groovy
4. Lorraine's partner
5. Goblet
6. Like some breakfast cereal
7. Half of a 1955 merger
8. Boxer's fare
9. Diminish
10. Atlas item
11. Arabic initial
12. Kachina doll carver
13. "Stay" singer Lisa
21. Grated
23. Squall
26. "ChiPs" star
28. It's often in contention
29. Condoleezza's predecessor
30. Slender
32. Hide
34. For this reason
35. Following along
36. Blue Moon of baseball
37. Galileo's birthplace
39. Helmsman of 1960s TV
40. One of the Furies
42. Bargain
47. Alexandra, e.g.
50. French vineyard
52. Slow down
54. Hoppers
56. Car lot clunker
57. Sonar spot
58. Cotton capsule
59. Cheese region
61. "Got it"
63. Peculiar: prefix
64. First name in fashion
66. Bag
68. Capitol Records owner
70. Czech. neighbor

Solution on page 366

Perplexing 70

ACROSS

1. ___ side of the coin
6. Follower of Fannie or Ginnie
9. British coppers
14. Sea World attraction
15. "___ job's worth doing . . ."
16. "Half ___ is better . . ."
17. "Air Music" composer
18. Price abbr.
19. Stock options?
20. Saw stuff?
21. Bud holder
22. CBS part: abbr.
23. Queen's county
25. Bigger than med.
27. Colette novel
30. Sotto voce remarks
35. Loan figure: Abbr.
38. Arboreal apes
40. Seating sect.
41. Tilden topper
43. Bygone big bird
44. Actress Kelly
45. ___ of Court
46. Security holder
48. Lou's partner
49. Fin de ___
51. Makes a touchdown
53. "Jurassic Park" mathematician ___ _Malcolm
55. Baked, in Bologna
58. Zwei cubed
61. Stove or washer: Abbr.
64. Lucre
66. Astound
67. Encyclopedia abbr.
68. Burt Reynolds film
69. Catlike
70. French shield
71. Atmospheres
72. Floats
73. "Pink Panther" films actor
74. Clearing

DOWN

1. Gov't. laboratory
2. Big bills
3. Like Siberian winters
4. Antidote, often
5. Coke's partner
6. Easily split mineral
7. Times to call, in ads
8. Chart holder
9. Annie Oakleys
10. City NW Tucson
11. Understanding
12. Kirk's rank
13. Bad grades
21. Deviate
24. Fraternity letters
26. Blast
28. Avatar of Vishnu
29. How anchovies are packed
31. Centennial number
32. Drab partner
33. Almond
34. Cousin of a herring
35. Greek letters
36. "Pretty please?"
37. Sharon's "Cagney & Lacey" co-star
39. The Oscars, e.g.
42. Corner key
44. "Love ___"
46. Actress Benaderet
47. SASE, e.g.
50. Petrol measures
52. Minnesota twin?
54. Central point
56. Colorful swimmer
57. Tons
58. Kelp, e.g.
59. Do
60. Publisher Henry
62. Somewhat, in scores
63. Choice assignment
65. Martin Luther King refrain
66. Earth, to moon
68. [That's awful!]

Solution on page 366

Perplexing 71

ACROSS
1. Shia, e.g.
5. Crazily
9. Intensely excited
14. Get ___ deal
15. Dance party
16. "Lemon Tree" singer Lopez
17. Ex-Spice Girl Halliwell
18. Cuddle in Coventry
19. ___ hand (assist)
20. Outside: Comb. form
21. Ferdinand, e.g.
22. Backdoor
24. ___ Island, NY
26. Emeril exclamation
27. Cooker
29. IBM compatibles
30. Giddyup!
33. Sheds
36. Deflation victim?
38. Fed. bill
40. Bee's charge
41. Had a life
42. Slate, for one
43. Actress Oakes of "CHiPs"
45. QB's goals
46. Highlanders
47. Jurassic, in a way
48. IV amounts
50. 1994 Costner role
52. The Divine, to da Vinci
53. Butters up?
57. Spectacles
60. One of Alcott's "Little Men"
61. Buddhist temple
62. Knockoff
63. Meth., e.g.
65. Darned
66. Big name in fruit juices
67. Auxiliary
68. Monk's abode
69. Deep gulf
70. "___ Indigo"
71. E. Coast highway

DOWN
1. Gurus
2. Establish
3. Runnymede document
4. ___-night double-header
5. Sleuth Lupin
6. Lots
7. Ab ___ (from day one)
8. Frat party purchases
9. In any case
10. Porgy
11. Farm cry
12. May event, for short
13. Debussy's "Air de ___"
21. Guns, in a way
23. "Bonanza" network
25. Schlepped
28. Red-spotted creatures
29. Chasers
30. Browser button
31. Kin to bf. or rom.
32. Head lines, for short?
33. '60s–'70s Italian P.M.
34. Fire ___
35. Soprano from Stockholm
37. Flit
39. Some tides
44. Hostility
46. Mom's mom
49. George in "Blind Date"
51. Let up
52. Auto damage
54. Aviary sound
55. Country rocker Steve
56. Needles
57. Grubby sort
58. President of France: 1954–1959
59. Cyber-junk
60. Dumb cluck
62. Nashville-based awards org.
64. Capital before Brasilia
65. TiVo forerunner

Solution on page 366

Perplexing 72

ACROSS

1. "Where America's Day Begins"
5. Mid's sch.
9. Clock std.
12. Garfield's middle name
14. Custodian's collection
15. Anchor
16. "___ Else But You"
17. Finely ribbed fabric
18. Marine menace
19. Seuss character
21. Forest's role in "The Last King of Scotland"
22. Big wheel at sea
23. Acting legend Hagen
24. "Coming Home" actor
26. Quick breads
28. He serves with Beetle
29. Post-explanation chorus
30. Disney's "Big Bad Wolf"
33. Innocent
35. Just above average
40. Clumsy fellows
41. "South Pacific" hero
43. Tennyson's "The ___ of Shalott"
44. "___gol"
46. Mother of Chas.
47. Gen. follower
48. ER skill
50. Prepare for action
52. Like Chippendale furniture
56. Choice location?
57. Void, in Vichy
60. Impulse carrier
61. Letters in a ring?
63. Captivate
65. Brownie, e.g.
66. Crossing light

68. Linen fabric
69. Irritable
70. Sierra Madre valley
71. Kind of barrier
72. Augustine's "De civitate ___"
73. Put on notice
74. "Bronx"/"thonx" rhymer

DOWN

1. Province in N. China
2. Tin can's target
3. Appetite arouser
4. Gershwin's "The ___ Love"
5. Pol. neighbor
6. Do an usher's job
7. Det. Sipowicz's org.
8. Venomous, as a snake
9. Bridge authority
10. Base of a pedestal
11. Colliery carriers
13. Army of the Potomac commander, 1863–65
15. Mantle top
20. First name in cosmetics
25. Vagabond
27. Trig. function
28. Kick
29. Require
30. Last king of Albania
31. Outside: Prefix
32. Acetone: Comb. form
34. "Cool" amount
36. Argued
37. Calif. hub
38. Kier in "Barb Wire"
39. Old cartoonist Hoff
42. Web mag

45. Duke's grp.
49. Huddle
51. Peewees
52. Blew a gasket
53. Rust or lime
54. Literally, "dwarf dog"
55. ___ child
56. Of the cheekbone
57. Mrs. Yeltsin
58. Wrinkly fruit
59. Hanger-on
62. Tijuana locale
64. Peter Sellers was one
67. Folks

Solution on page 366

Perplexing 73

ACROSS

1. "Aunt" with a "Cope Book"
5. "Of course!"
8. Like some loads
12. Caterer's creation
13. Had markers out
14. "Apollo 13" star
15. Cry like a baby
16. Adriatic port
17. Circle
18. Claim
20. ___ law
21. Lummoxes
22. Brandy designation letters
23. Assails
26. Grind
30. Adaptable truck, for short
31. Ceremonial burner
34. Interpretation
35. Bosox rivals
37. Journalist Kupcinet
38. Got the message
39. Conflicted
40. Like some felonies
42. Elvis's label
43. Distillate
45. Bloviates
47. Like the Who, in the '60s
48. They cover all the bases
50. Foul fare
52. Like some dinosaurs, today
56. ___ Kea
57. Clip
58. Go slowly
59. "Tattered Tom" author
60. ___ acetate (banana oil)
61. Bend at the barre
62. Low pitch
63. Work for eds.
64. 3:00

DOWN

1. Rachel's baby on "Friends"
2. Roger of "Nicholas Nickleby"
3. Gullets
4. Cause of hereditary variation
5. Be ready for
6. Long lunches
7. Situation favoring the server
8. Charger
9. Long-range weapon, for short
10. Two, in Lisbon
11. Fangorn Forest dweller
13. Slow on the uptake
14. Give a leg up
19. Univ. military programs
22. Alternate sp.
23. Seat of Silver Bow County
24. Community character
25. Mediums
26. Gives some juice to
27. In reserve
28. "Odyssey" enchantress
29. "___ a Man" (Calder Willingham novel and play)
32. Longest river in the world
33. Madrilenian Mrs.
36. Some zoophytes
38. His real name was Arthur
40. Part of a TV camera
41. Light reddish-brown
44. Kind of stock
46. Not even
48. League members
49. Case workers: Abbr.
50. Ball
51. Blockheads
52. Nanny's aid
53. Louisiana town
54. Commando weapons
55. Heated competition?
56. Shelley's "Queen ___"

Solution on page 367

Perplexing 74

ACROSS

1. Port container
5. Bauble head
9. "It's all __"
14. Mine, in Amiens
15. Tra trailer
16. "Texaco Star Theater" star
17. Bed deposit
18. Continental abbr.
19. Jazz trumpeter Ziggy
20. Bee chaser
21. Something to build on
22. Like logs
23. Hockey stat
26. Arty Big Apple area
29. Coll. aides
30. Faculties
34. Improvises, in a way
37. Borders
40. "__ I Won the War": 1967 film
41. Radiance, of sorts
42. Chili partner
43. Disney lioness
44. 1944 initials
45. Cover anew, as a plot
46. Odysseus, to the Cyclops Polyphemus
47. Get
49. Gradually slower, in mus.
50. Night fliers
52. Keyboard instrument
56. "What __!"
59. Coll. entrance exam
61. Gridiron stats
62. River to the North Sea
64. Vision: Prefix
65. Some are corny
66. ". . . could __ fat"
67. Does in
68. Cross letters
69. Word form of "sexy"
70. "O, gie me the __ that has acres o' charms": Burns
71. Norse goddess of fate

DOWN

1. "Julius Caesar" role
2. Fille's friends
3. Shoe parts
4. Caboodle's partner
5. Wingdings
6. "Caddyshack" director
7. "__ Her Go" (Frankie Laine song)
8. Troubles
9. Copper head?
10. Wrestling hold
11. First word of the "Aeneid"
12. Hammer part
13. Next to N. Car.
24. The Eagles' "Take __ the Limit"
25. Flier to Copenhagen
27. Bone head?
28. "__ So Fine"
31. Ersatz
32. Louisiana town
33. Pen, e.g.
34. Strawberry's field, once
35. Women's rights pioneer
36. Like crazy
37. Remote batteries, often
38. Buddy
39. Cologne conjunction
42. Loafer insert
43. Do, say
45. Cove
46. Lacking value
48. Out
49. Mix anew, as greens
51. Disfigure
52. "Princess Caraboo" star, 1994
53. Gregg grad
54. "__ is human . . ."
55. "The Addams Family" actor
56. __ bit (slightly)
57. Driver's choice
58. Anent
60. Shelter grp.
63. Friend of Tigger
65. Bygone auto ornament

Solution on page 367

Perplexing 75

ACROSS

1. More than trim
6. Water-to-wine site
10. Catch, as flies
14. 1988 Olympics locale
15. Nasdaq debuts
16. Hard up
17. Feverish fits
18. Native Nigerians
19. Abruzzi bell town
20. Hit hard
22. Cache
24. Those opposed
26. Charlotte-to-Raleigh dir.
27. Bring up the rear
28. Like some parties
31. Macerate
33. Middle X or O, perhaps
35. ___ Gardens
36. Crystal ball gazers
38. Diagonal spar
42. Overhead
44. Five-pin plug
45. Gage bestseller
46. Old German coin
47. "Easter 1916" poet
49. Persona ___ grata
50. Brisk knock
52. Marienbad, for one
53. Four gills
54. Band aid?
57. Mi followers
59. Director Vittorio De ___
61. Most accessible
63. "The Crucible" setting
66. Falstaff's recruit
67. NW California tribe
70. Talking bird of poetry
72. Handle: Fr.
73. NE Asian river
74. "___ 'clock scholar . . ."
75. Bakery selections
76. Germany's Graf ___
77. Cares for

DOWN

1. Cousin of calypso
2. Records
3. Jack-in-the-pulpit, e.g.
4. Inasmuch (as)
5. "___ luego!"
6. Second-century date
7. Alert, for short
8. Halter
9. Nod
10. Boom
11. The Plaza, e.g.
12. Place for a valve
13. "Holberg Suite" composer
21. "Jane ___": 1971 film
23. Ends
25. Far from posh
28. Three-hand card game
29. Seaport in N Honduras
30. Gone wrong?
32. Essays
34. Radar, e.g.: Abbr.
36. Attack from above
37. Pics
39. Italian artist Guido
40. Apprised of
41. Turn blue, in a way
43. Not "agin"
48. Japanese food fishes
51. Olive Garden selection
53. It can be hard or soft
54. Menachem's co-Nobelist
55. Labor leader George
56. Analyze, in a way
58. Site of a recent Popeye comic
60. 200 milligrams
62. 1 and 66
64. All square
65. Fix up
68. Mardi Gras, e.g.: Abbr.
69. North Yorkshire river
71. Directory data: Abbr.

Solution on page 367

Perplexing 76

ACROSS

1. Part of a comparison
5. Regarding: Abbr.
9. Common sense?
14. Baylor's home
15. Words to an "old chap"
16. Atmospheres
17. "The heat __"
18. Quart quartet
19. Crete's highest pt.
20. Flash light?
22. Allowances
24. Sawbucks
26. "MADtv" alternative
27. Condescending one
29. Vaporize
34. Foreshadowed
37. Off-season
39. Certain plaintiff, at law
40. __ reflection
41. Humdrum
42. Some diner orders
43. Beach apparel
44. Take __ (swing hard)
45. Crosswise, on deck
46. Unpaid debt
48. 1982 Michener epic
50. Manute of the NBA
52. Notched
56. Be sleepy
61. Let
62. Bit of gossip
63. Elusive creature
65. Summers abroad
66. "Do __?"
67. Keds feature
68. Film
69. Some apples
70. Flaws and all
71. Amt. of heat

DOWN

1. Emulate Chubby Checker
2. Waste maker, proverbially
3. __ squash
4. Serious
5. Chicago suburb
6. Big Ten powerhouse, for short
7. Is off guard
8. Sacs
9. Try
10. Remote option
11. Land of literature
12. "Charlie's Angels" actress
13. Pastoral expanses
21. River feature
23. Completely
25. Before wind or flare
28. One of the Barbary States
30. Gawk at
31. Beach site
32. Crumbly cheese
33. Opie's answer to Aunt Bee
34. "Life is __ dream"
35. Abbr. on some dials
36. Man of action
38. Arctic dwellers
41. Captain of industry
45. One of the "back forty"
47. Goes down
49. Mountaintop homes
51. 1972 Derek and the Dominos hit
53. Chest site
54. "Lovergirl" singer __ _Marie
55. Ranger, Pacer, or Corsair
56. Film genre
57. Prefix for carp
58. Cheese town
59. Voir __
60. Stew ingredients
64. Cable co. that merged with AT&T

Solution on page 367

Perplexing 77

ACROSS

1. "Bewitched" aunt
6. Saturnine
10. Opposite of ecto-
14. Leporine leapers
15. "___ Lonesome I Could Cry": Williams hit
16. Curb, with "in"
17. Dye-yielding shrubs
18. Hands
19. Reply to a storybook hen
20. Road hugger
22. Digging, so to speak
23. Big name in plastic
24. "Rob Roy" star, 1995
26. "Dallas" role
29. Cut closely
31. Hosp. ward
32. Minute groove
34. ___ Island National Monument
38. A little lower?
40. A bit, colloquially
42. ICBM container
43. Better trained
45. Bombay-born conductor
47. Coll. course
48. Backed
50. Gear for gauchos
52. Punish with an arbitrary penalty
55. Salon offering
56. Refuse, long ago
57. Capitol
63. Shakespeare's shrew
64. Snowman prop
65. Hatch from Utah
66. Insurance gps.
67. CB sign-off
68. Kind of beer
69. Faults
70. Flap
71. Sorrowful song

DOWN

1. Dover domestic
2. Actress Wood of "Diamonds Are Forever"
3. Dehydrated
4. Go through again
5. Lights into
6. Declarations
7. Father of Ahab
8. Cybercafe patron
9. Cedric the Saxon's ward
10. Two-time U.S. Open winner
11. Dodge compacts
12. "Likewise"
13. It may bring a tear to the eye
21. Exams for some srs.
25. Cain raiser
26. Elite alternative
27. Hail ___
28. "My Bodyguard" actor
29. Brought forth
30. Owns, biblically
33. "Coriolanus" setting
35. Light air
36. Hip parts
37. Inebriates
39. Intrepid
41. "___ Grows in Brooklyn"
44. Ocasek of the Cars
46. Breathing aid
49. Saddam Hussein, e.g.
51. Ethically neutral
52. Crosses with loops
53. Biscayne Bay city
54. Tim's "Aida" collaborator
55. Feather: Comb. form
58. Popular video recorder
59. Made fun of, in a way
60. Drive
61. Victory: Ger.
62. Professor Higgins, to Eliza

Solution on page 367

Perplexing 78

Solution on page 367

ACROSS

1. "___ Dancer" (Nureyev documentary)
5. Brit. award
8. Second-story man's crime
13. Expanded
14. "What happened next?"
15. First name in country music
16. Won over
18. Middle root
19. Raul's relative
20. ___ lab
21. Comes up
22. Included elements of
24. Bold type
25. 1967 NHL rookie of the year
26. Bribes
27. Notebook maker
30. Grafter's need
33. Actor Barry of "War of the Worlds"
34. Sons of, in Hebrew
35. Crescents
36. Bee: Prefix
37. Eucharist plate
38. "Well, well!"
39. ___ point (certain stitch)
40. Bedeck
41. It ends in Oct.
42. Implore
43. Game piece
44. Site of Joan of Arc's demise
46. Court battle?
49. Poster heading
50. Last: abbr.
51. Horse color
53. Infatuated with
54. Aeschylus trilogy
56. Hidden
57. It touches four Great Lakes: Abbr.
58. Curse
59. Pours
60. "Some ___ meat and canna eat": Burns
61. "Give me another chance," e.g.

DOWN

1. "___ Around": Beach Boys hit
2. "Boner's" aardvark
3. Red Bordeaux
4. Cow, maybe
5. Dragonfly
6. Three-time Masters champ
7. Anomalous
8. "___ not to reason why": Tennyson
9. Medieval guild
10. Sign, as an agreement
11. Fragrant trees
12. Clavell's "___-Pan"
15. Fix
17. Decks out
21. His blood was turned into a flower
23. Rot
26. ___ Rebellion of 1857–59
28. Jethro of TV's "The Beverly Hillbillies"
29. Voyageurs Natl. Park locale
30. Tried to get home, maybe
31. Codger
32. Dazed
33. M-1 rifle inventor
34. Former German state
37. Puts on a coat
39. "The Power and the Glory" novelist
42. Hoaxes
43. PC key
45. A wee hour
46. ___ deaf ear to (ignore)
47. Consummate
48. Hotel offering
49. Abraded
52. Okinawa port
53. Hood's heater
54. "Impressive!"
55. Tee, e.g.

Perplexing 79

ACROSS

1. It's just above G
6. Osman, for one
10. Drag
14. Craft
15. Silver's rider, for example
16. Angered
17. Real things
18. Rolled items
19. "M" director Fritz
20. Early anesthetics
22. "___ chic"
24. "Brokeback Mountain" director
25. Salt, to a chemist
27. Jones and Smith, maybe
29. Citrus source
33. The Mormons, initially
34. Stub ___
35. Landers and others
37. Slog
41. Boulogne-sur-___
42. Ski trail
44. Former Serbian capital
45. "___ Joe's" (sandwich board message)
48. Denials
49. Chinese leader?
50. Chinese brew
52. Breaks
54. Prizes
58. Historic Virginia family
59. HBO rival, in listings
60. ___ League
62. Court figure
66. ___-Flush
68. ___-Tass
70. Chip feature
71. Abbr. on a mountain sign
72. Lake ___ (Blue Nile source)
73. Archie, to Mike
74. "Buona ___" (Italian greeting)
75. "Show Boat" cap'n
76. Diamond and others

DOWN

1. "The African Queen" screenwriter
2. Pipsqueak
3. Neighbor of Pol.
4. Property receiver, in law
5. Remove forcefully
6. "Don't Bring Me Down" grp.
7. Attack deterrent
8. IV part
9. Turn over
10. Cartoonist Keane
11. Ph.D. hurdles
12. Zellweger of "Cold Mountain"
13. Beats (out)
21. Get rid of
23. Caesar and others
26. Colleague of Trotsky
28. Soundless communication: Abbr.
29. Unconvincing
30. Willow genus
31. "Beetle Bailey" creator Walker
32. TV journalist David
36. Frick's business
38. Have ___ to pick
39. Hollywood crosser
40. Those, in Tegucigalpa
43. City in North Rhine-Westphalia
46. Buddy, in slang
47. Father of Eos
49. Raphael's "___ Madonna"
51. Hindu beverage of immortality
53. Look through a keyhole
54. Curves
55. Oil source
56. Cartridge contents
57. "Paradise Lost" character
61. Boston or Chicago, e.g.
63. Year the National University of Mexico was founded
64. ". . . ___ in Kalamazoo"
65. Intelligence
67. ___ Toguri (Tokyo Rose)
69. Bit of sun

Solution on page 368

Perplexing 80

ACROSS
1. Really silly
6. Have no truck with
10. Possesses, old-style
14. Kind of ticket
15. Bad thing to do
16. Dept. of Labor part
17. Undersides
18. Football Hall-of-Famer Ronnie
19. "___ I say!"
20. Celebrate spring
22. Peeved
24. Diva ___ Te Kanawa
26. Hack off
27. Brownies' org.
28. Some VCRs
31. FAQ response
33. Big success
35. Yellowfin tuna
36. Lady friend in Italy
38. Anwar's predecessor
42. Manners
44. Brit's oath
45. Develop
46. Donne and Bradstreet
47. Certain navel
49. AT&T competitor
50. Ben-___
52. Bank worry
53. "Life is ___ dream"
54. Close-lipped
57. Java setting
59. Coin for Khamenei
61. 1962 Paul Anka hit
63. Delon in "Borsalino"
66. Put on
67. Start of many addresses
70. Calculator key
72. Leaning

73. He had a hammer
74. Between: Fr.
75. 1968 folk album
76. Anthem starter
77. Range rovers

DOWN
1. Gore and Green
2. Lowdown
3. "___ do you good"
4. Prime purchases
5. Anwar's successor
6. Debut of Oct. 1975
7. Yoo-___ (beverage brand)
8. Sammy Kaye's "___ _Tomorrow"
9. "Later!"
10. Bricklayers' equipment
11. For ___ (cheaply)

12. Massenet opera
13. ___ la vista
21. Ore carrier
23. Farthest point
25. English architect Jones
28. Way off
29. Ah follower
30. Right hand
32. Use elbow grease on
34. Gum glob
36. Take on
37. Pianist Schnabel
39. Type of housedress
40. I.R.A. part: Abbr.
41. Princess from Alderaan
43. Afr. nation
48. Cetacean genus
51. Hurry in the direction of
53. Street magician David

54. Soprano Nellie
55. Carrier name until 1997
56. Relating to form
58. Barbarians
60. Cairo crooner
62. "Eso ___" (Paul Anka hit)
64. Like some verbs: Abbr.
65. Odd fellow
68. ___ man
69. Butt in
71. Parisian possessive

Solution on page 368

Perplexing 81

ACROSS
1. French cordial flavoring
5. "I'm outta here!"
9. Airline to Amsterdam
12. Spruce scented
13. They're taken in court
15. Dullea of "2001: A Space Odyssey"
16. 911 responders
17. Bit of high jinks
18. "The Periodic Table" author Primo ___
19. Frog's place
21. "___ Are My Sunshine"
22. Galoots
23. Governessy
25. Like many radios
27. Tehran tongue
30. BBC rival
32. "A Natural Man" singer
36. Major label
37. Stoic school founder
39. Fatherland, to Flavius
40. Paint
42. Correspond
44. Does some tailoring
45. Like O'Neill's "Bound East for Cardiff"
47. Brush off
49. Never abroad
50. Private reply
51. Baseball's Piniella
52. Commits a deadly sin
54. Feeling
56. Brouhaha
58. Bay on Somersetshire coast
61. Pin ___
63. King of the fairies
67. High notes
68. Role for Hayes or Natwick
70. Opposite of A-OK
71. Like some checks: Abbr.
72. Perfume, in a way
73. No layabout
74. Naval inits.
75. Morse bits
76. Go astray

DOWN
1. In ___ (miffed)
2. "The Secret of ___" (1982 film)
3. Like some verbs: Abbr.
4. Online VIP's
5. Raccoon kin
6. "Saturday" author McEwan
7. Firm member: Abbr.
8. Buckeye
9. Maintain
10. As it happens
11. Dr.'s orders
14. Pond dross
15. Oregon tribesman
20. East of Calif.
24. Like some vases
26. Lobster ___ diavolo
27. Joint tenant?
28. ___ acid (protein component)
29. Winter coats
31. Bit of statuary
33. Small songsters
34. Cap
35. Ms. accompaniers
38. Fill up on
39. Little: Fr.
41. Least worldly
43. Ample, in dialect
46. ___ de coeur
48. Say too much
51. Inclined
53. Flips
55. Anjou alternative
57. Bounds along
58. Satyr, slangily
59. Big Bang brew
60. Viking's destination
62. Hawaiian coastal region
64. Fleece
65. Gothic arch
66. Neighbor of Swed.
69. Kyrgyz city

Solution on page 368

Perplexing 82

ACROSS

1. Hunted
5. Some Traci Lords movies
9. Fort Knox unit
14. "Let's ___"
15. A little of this, a little of that
16. Bridge bid, informally
17. Probability
18. 1984–88 skating gold medalist
19. Old "Hits the Spot" marketer
20. Contest
21. Drift off
22. Drudge
23. Covers up
26. Sixth-century year
29. ___ Memorial
30. 1979 Vanessa Redgrave title role
34. Harvesting machine
37. Dangerous toy
40. Refuse to share
41. Word in a Carly Simon title
42. Put in the cup
43. Jeanne ___
44. Media attention
45. Brought on
46. Yellowish brown
47. One of rock's Ramones
49. Bristle
50. Hole-making tools
52. Mammals like camels
56. Long-range weapon, for short
59. Hebrew bushel
61. D.D.E. predecessor
62. Detroit's county
64. Study, say
65. Clotho, e.g.
66. Picked, with "for"
67. Hacking tool
68. Part of Caesar's boast
69. Dependent
70. Cutlass, e.g.
71. CSA fighters

DOWN

1. Show
2. "The Age of Bronze" sculptor
3. Council member, perhaps
4. Chemical endings
5. Fresh snow
6. Hodgepodges
7. Ostentatious display
8. Big-name
9. Keystone figure
10. Lack of vitality
11. Take back, for short
12. Windows character set abbr.
13. Act the serf
24. "Anthem for Doomed Youth" poet
25. Draft board?
27. Eulogize
28. Starter: Abbr.
31. Become friendlier
32. Game ender, perhaps
33. Part of the CIA
34. All fired up
35. Decline
36. "Swoosh" company
37. Hunk's pride
38. Short order, for short
39. Form of earth
42. Stiletto, e.g.
43. "Two Years Before the Mast" author
45. Ayres in "Advise and Consent"
46. Suburban abbr.
48. Ill-fated
49. Cottonwood trees
51. Croatian leader?
52. "Grab ___!"
53. Climax of many action flicks
54. Take ___ at
55. Worries
56. Exultant cry
57. May in New Jersey, e.g.
58. Computer storage unit
60. Combine
63. Ice cream maker Joseph
65. Douglas, for one

Solution on page 368

Perplexing 83

ACROSS
1. British carbine
5. Ballot listing
10. But: Ger.
14. "Oops!"
15. Blood: Comb. form
16. Loudness measure
17. Ancient Syria
18. Principal pipes
19. French silk
20. Turns in
22. Fashions
24. "__ evil . . ."
25. Promo
28. Bikini tryouts
30. Animal with a black-tipped tail
34. Fast follower
37. Rat follower
39. Last word of "America, the Beautiful"
40. Communion, e.g.
41. Minneapolis-St. Paul suburb
43. First name in design
44. Nicole's "Cold Mountain" role
45. "Good one!"
46. Add zip to
48. "Gymnopedies" composer
50. Wide of the mark
52. Hi-fi successor
54. Durango dwellings
58. Cruelty
61. Narrow, in a way
63. "Put a sock __!"
64. Tomato blight
67. Pip
68. Jeanne d'Arc et al.: Abbr.
69. Filer's worry
70. Depilatory brand
71. 1974 Peace Nobelist
72. Gifts for donors
73. Mother of the Valkyries

DOWN
1. Takes off
2. Florida ZIP code starter
3. Growing out
4. Put forward
5. "__ here"
6. Minima
7. "What Kind of Fool __"
8. Bronze metal
9. Bridge seats
10. Hold
11. Godsend
12. "Idylls of the King" character
13. Roger of "Nicholas Nickleby"
21. Memorization
23. Medical advice, often
26. Knickknack holder
27. Fictional wirehair
29. ". . .__ saw Elba"
31. Suffix for abnormalities
32. __ Flite (bicycle brand)
33. French breeze
34. Eon divisions
35. It's set in Egypt
36. "P.D.Q., doc!"
38. Horace's handle
42. Box-elder genus
43. Have a table for one
45. Earns after expenses
47. Ending for confer
49. "No kidding?"
51. Dormmate
53. "Let __ Cake"
55. More reasonable
56. Have __ for
57. Perfect Sleeper maker
58. Puncture sound
59. Porch pier
60. Lighten up?
62. Turner and others
65. Brace
66. N.J. summer setting

Solution on page 368

Perplexing 84

ACROSS

1. Big busyness
4. Fozzie or Baloo
8. Cockeyed
13. Added
15. "Her ___" ("Miss Saigon" song)
16. Big name in watches
17. "Young Frankenstein" woman
18. Spanish card suit
19. Indemnify
20. Service group
22. Court call
24. British actress Sylvia
25. Buttinsky
26. Double-check
28. Bar examination?
30. Peruse again
34. Ernest's unseen friend
37. Hieroglyphics bird
40. Michael Crichton book
41. Tempe inst.
42. Some services
44. Central truth
45. "La Plume de Ma ___"
47. Kinfolk: Abbr.
48. Student housing
49. Code word for "S"
51. Allocate, with "out"
53. Fighting force
56. Lay away
60. Bone: Comb. form
63. "I'll take that as ___"
64. Fast
65. Limited support?
67. King Atahualpa, for one
69. Blemish
70. Shows
71. Just right

72. Spinners
73. "I Hated, Hated, Hated This Movie" author
74. Shaw's "___ and the Man"
75. French beverage

DOWN

1. Concord
2. Charity, often
3. Club publication
4. Kick out
5. Be human, perhaps
6. Mexican agave
7. Ready to be used again
8. From l. to r.
9. Orchestra leader
10. Cosby series
11. Country until 1939?
12. Some beans
14. "For Your Eyes Only" singer
21. Head lines, for short?
23. Artist Gerard ___ Borch
26. Strengthening rod
27. Jiffies
29. Fabrication
31. Inner, in combinations
32. Biology lab supply
33. Bad end
34. Distillery items
35. Morales in "Rapa Nui"
36. Ancient symbol
38. Expert ending
39. 1965 King arrest site
42. Dakota, once: abbr.
43. "Cats" monogram
46. Kind of park
48. Can't stand
50. Health org.
52. Game co. that originated Dungeons & Dragons
54. "West Side Story" role
55. Organ ___
57. Knotted neckwear
58. Kind of infection
59. ___ fly (pest of equines)
60. Kill ___ killed
61. 9000 automaker
62. Dam's mate
64. Back-hand compliments?
66. Grounded flier
68. ___-corder

Solution on page 368

Perplexing 85

ACROSS

1. "___ Rhythm," by Gershwin
5. Eaten
8. Peter and others
13. "Brave New World" drug
14. Half of a Heyerdahl title
15. Really bugs
16. Drooled
18. Elect
19. Cry of derision
20. CAT's cousin
21. Some dresses
22. Port on the Loire
24. Faun's cousin
25. Suffix with drunk or tank
26. Tiberius' 202
27. Biblical pronoun
30. Delmonico alternative
33. Carnera KOer
34. "See ya"
35. Cup part
36. ___ Saud
37. Fair-haired
38. Speak up?
39. ___ row
40. Utah's ___ Mountains
41. Cries of dismay
42. Dentist's order
43. Journalist Kupcinet
44. Steppes settler
46. Take to the cleaners
49. Fires
50. After
51. Comprises
53. Special Forces units
54. Protect from the cold
56. Sub
57. Fr. martyress, maybe
58. In ___ (stagnant)
59. Ups
60. Own, to a Scot
61. "Bah!"

DOWN

1. Paris suburb on the Seine
2. Disputed heights
3. D-Day beach
4. Hebrew T
5. Impaired
6. Women's soccer star Michelle
7. Fizzle
8. Bounty's destination
9. Obdurate
10. Claim
11. Explorer John and others
12. R.R. stop
15. Filled finger
17. Admission
21. Climb
23. 1980s White House name
26. Uncle Tom had one
28. Spook in Dogpatch
29. Luke was his disciple
30. "___ the morning!"
31. Conceal
32. Hot
33. Some gang members
34. Novelist Barker
37. News office
39. Meager
42. Mexican Indians
43. "Maybe"
45. "Love is blind," say
46. Orange soda brand
47. Lucky piece
48. Devour
49. Yours, to Yvette
52. Dickens's Mr. Pecksniff
53. A patient may say it
54. Language suffix
55. Charlie of the '60s Orioles

Solution on page 369

Perplexing 86

ACROSS

1. They're hard to get out of
5. Like chiffon
10. "Dark Angel" star Jessica
14. Not this or that, in Spain
15. Jazz pianist with eight Grammys
16. Henhouse sound
17. Bad mood
18. It's the law
19. It makes sense for some crabs
20. Sight from Mount Olympus
22. Savvy
24. Civil rights leader Medgar
27. Kayaker's need
28. Silas of the Continental Congress
31. Showy moths
33. Gentle ones
37. Kayoed
38. Death personified
41. Gouge, e.g.
42. Jazz group, for short
43. ___el Amarna, Egypt
44. Yes, to Yeltsin
46. ". . . or ___thought"
47. Bit of roofing
49. Pontiac, e.g.
51. Coll. major
52. Hawks
54. Horse bit
55. Neckline?
57. Hung. neighbor
59. 1994 Peace Nobelist
61. Consecrate
64. Honor
68. Fabrication
69. City SE of Milan
73. Pizza Quick sauce maker
74. Ending with cigar or disk
75. Knock for ___(daze)
76. "Terrible" one
77. Aussie bounders
78. Salon supply
79. Mao successor

DOWN

1. Santa ___, California
2. ___ Reader (eclectic magazine)
3. Kind of function
4. Glossy fabric
5. Brouhaha
6. Bricklayer's burden
7. "___ tu" (aria for Renato)
8. Common Market inits.
9. 1969 Dustin Hoffman role
10. Power structure
11. "Laughable Lyrics" writer
12. Boxing prize
13. PC programs
21. Forestall
23. Bad beginning?
25. Bridge over Venetian water
26. Conciliatory gift
28. Proscriptions
29. Ragtime's Blake
30. Even a little
32. Composed
34. Husband of Zipporah
35. Benefits
36. Where Queen Mab lies
39. Classified ad abbr.
40. Damp and chilly
45. Nathan and others
48. Famed New York eatery
50. Bug
53. Juliet, to Romeo
56. ___ Lindgren, creator of Pippi Longstocking
58. Annual parade honoree, for short
60. Brings in
61. Massachusetts town
62. Peace pact, 2/24/49
63. "___take arms against a sea of troubles": Hamlet
65. Gutter holder
66. "A Summer Place" star
67. Kind of bean
70. "Prince ___" ("Aladdin" song)
71. Ex-Yankee Guidry
72. Verbal jewel

Solution on page 369

Perplexing 87

ACROSS

1. "Yes, ___"
5. Large number
9. Car bar
14. Donald Duck, to his nephews
15. Explorer Heyerdahl
16. Where "Aida" debuted
17. "Laugh-In" segment
18. Rock rabbit
19. Held title to
20. Less ruddy
22. Good, to Gerard
24. Homer, to Bart
25. Opener
27. These: Fr.
29. Dated
31. Good buddies use them
33. B'way showing
37. Hard throw, in baseball
38. "Coffee ___?"
40. "Consumer Reports" employee
41. Ehud's successor
43. Mugger?
44. Habituate: var.
45. Don't mess with
46. Map detail
48. It breaks every morning
49. He crosses the line
50. Telekinesis, e.g.
51. Tabitha of MTV
53. Elbow-bender
55. All lit up
57. Spike TV, formerly
60. Ewe said it!
62. "Consumer Reports" employees
65. Put up
67. Gunks

69. Anthracite or lignite
71. Boots
72. Church calendar
73. Jazz (up)
74. Of service
75. "My Heart Will Go On" singer
76. Concert sites

DOWN

1. Greek letters
2. "My Way" writer
3. Galatea's love
4. "Misty" singer
5. First pope
6. Cicada sound
7. Thumbs up, in space
8. Grayish
9. Tea go-with
10. Choice marble
11. Drink garnish
12. Plastic ingredient
13. "Sweeney ___"
21. It's often underfoot
23. Lt. trainer
26. "1984" state
28. Attention ___
29. Georges who wrote "Life: A User's Manual"
30. Tummy trouble
32. Loud hits
34. Liszt's "La Campanella," e.g.
35. Played again
36. Rocker Glenn
37. Buds
39. "What's ___?"
40. Smelting chamber

42. Weakens, as support
47. "The NFL Today" analyst
50. Class action grp.?
52. Come back again
54. Bigger than big
56. Ring bearer
57. Drop ___ (moon)
58. Oceangoing, briefly
59. Like some decrees
61. "Yes, there is ___!"
63. Chancel cross
64. Ginza libation
66. Cards, on scorecards
68. "It must be him, ___ shall die"
70. Green stretch

Solution on page 369

Perplexing 88

ACROSS

1. Prefers, with "for"
5. Profit
10. Bridge support
14. Keep time, in a way
15. Key
16. Deli spread
17. ___-my-thumb
18. Sound from a bay
19. Bedfellow
20. Foster's river
22. Nostrum
24. "Bee Season" star
26. Drawing
27. Downed
30. Artichoke bud
32. Anchored fastener
36. Certain corp. takeover
37. Its motto is "Lux et veritas"
39. ___ duty (service)
41. ___ the Hoople (rock group)
43. Light ___ (feathery)
45. "Road" film destination
46. Polished
48. Comedienne Martha
50. "Jurassic Park" girl
51. Sammy Davis Jr.'s "I've Gotta ___"
52. Abbr. at O'Hare
53. Villa ___
55. Org. for a store
57. Actor Blore
59. High degree
63. Soccer shot
67. Dance partner
68. "The Canterbury Tales" pilgrim
70. Coleridge work
71. Lit ___
72. Build an embankment
73. Chicago paper, for short
74. "The Merry Drinker" painter
75. About
76. James nicknamed "Miss Peaches"

DOWN

1. "I Ain't Marching Anymore" singer
2. Team's burden
3. Seville snack
4. Drink up
5. "The ___ She's a Lady": Kipling
6. Call on
7. Cut short
8. Fete
9. People: Prefix
10. Apple that may be green or red
11. Bundle up
12. "The Clan of the Cave Bear" heroine
13. Country musician Clark
21. Choosing-up word
23. One-quintillionth: Prefix
25. Reef dwellers
27. "The moan of doves in immemorial ___": Tennyson
28. Little Boy or Fat Man
29. Head-___
31. A dog's age
33. Point of a story
34. Mount Narodnaya's range
35. Apartment window sign
38. "That's nice"
39. Assay
40. Set, in Somme
42. Actor Arnold
44. "Musta been something ___"
47. Check
49. An Adams
52. Heel over
54. Game similar to euchre
56. He caught Larsen's perfect game
58. Ashley's rival
59. NFL coach Jim
60. Blue dye
61. Bilko and York: Abbr.
62. Ballesteros of the PGA
64. Lowdown
65. Vent, in a way
66. Country name
67. Acad., e.g.
69. Ital. seaport

Solution on page 369

Perplexing 89

ACROSS
1. Sets
4. Mercury and Mars
8. Stressed type, for short
13. Popular fruit drink
14. Barbershop band
15. Like very few games
16. "___ voce poco fa" (Rossini aria)
17. King ___
18. Watts of "King Kong"
19. Island entertainer
21. Allotment: Abbr.
23. Laundry laborer
24. Sot's state
27. Before sweet or skilled
29. Arctic
31. Furniture wood
35. Lift
38. Part of A.M.P.A.S.
40. Comic actress Tessie
41. Actress Madigan
42. Having no master
44. He cleans the plate
45. "The Nanny" butler
48. Conn of "Grease"
49. Come clean, with "up"
50. Pool parties?
52. "Long time ___"
54. Union jack?
56. Back talk, slangily
59. When doubled, a Pacific capital
62. Oz. and kg.
64. Bacchante
66. Golden ___ (seniors)
68. Wonderland message
71. When "77 Sunset Strip" aired: Abbr.
72. Madison helped draft it: Abbr.
73. Maintains
74. South Africa's ___ Paul Kruger
75. Like some bodies on a beach
76. Asset for Tea Leoni
77. "Kidnapped" author's monogram

DOWN
1. Fall heavily
2. Chiantis, e.g.
3. Limited
4. "Little" car of song
5. Moon, e.g.
6. Village
7. Mr. Peanut attire
8. Setting for TV's "Newhart"
9. Apple polishers
10. Deck call
11. Margarita garnish
12. Affect emotionally
14. Aim improver
20. Monster, so to speak
22. IBM competitor
25. Norwegian king
26. Made grain-sized
28. Measure of conductance
30. "Beyond the Sea" singer, 1960
32. Actress Madlyn
33. Radiation dosages
34. Doesn't shut up
35. Brinker of fiction
36. Faux: abbr.
37. Actor MacLachlan
39. Pedestal parts
43. It's just one thing after another
46. Approve
47. Former French coin
49. Bash
51. Do darts
53. Chair man?
55. Appropriate inappropriately
57. About to receive
58. Seasonal air
59. Orderly in "Nurses"
60. Enthralled
61. Colin Powell, briefly
63. Copy to a floppy
65. Turns down
67. Most-used edition: Abbr.
69. Two-year-old sheep
70. "___ Miniver," 1952 film

Solution on page 369

Perplexing 90

ACROSS

1. Thrash
6. Has power over
10. Letters on a bomber
14. Have something at home
15. Campus group
16. Words before tab or temperature
17. Escalator feature
18. Lake ___ (Blue Nile source)
19. Hayes of "The Mod Squad"
20. Civic competitor
22. Masculine side
24. Rapa ___ (Easter Island, to locals)
25. Cartoonist Goldberg
27. Sink
29. Pasta topper
33. Post delivery: Abbr.
34. Donald and Ivana, e.g.
35. About: Abbr.
37. Less dicey
41. "The One I Love" group
42. "You cannot teach ___ to walk straight": Aristophanes
44. Regulus's constellation
45. Bonnie's beau
48. German title
49. Japanese fish delicacy
50. Rx prescribers
52. Most overcome
54. Keep from overheating, in a way
58. Break off
59. "Without a Trace" org.
60. Biblical kingdom
62. Refines
66. Clinton cabinet member
68. Ravel's "Gaspard de la ___"
70. "___ Isn't So" (Hall & Oates hit)
71. Brewery fixture
72. Hairy Himalayan
73. "The Fog of War" director Morris
74. Bob Hoskins role of 1991
75. Burns up
76. Letter taker

DOWN

1. Needs diapers
2. Fabled racer
3. Rate ___ (be perfect)
4. Button snakeroot
5. Football play
6. Frequent, in rhyme
7. "King Kong" co-star
8. Some babysitters
9. Batting position
10. Web address
11. Virtuous sort
12. Make void
13. Prima ___
21. Philippine plant
23. Magazine contents
26. Author Segal
28. Dam org.
29. Grand Marquis, for short
30. Jump on the ice
31. ___ Martin (cognac)
32. Court decree
36. Seven-time AL batting champ
38. Passage for Santa
39. Hosp. readouts
40. Lopsided win
43. Highland hillsides
46. Hip-hop's Run-___
47. Biblical land
49. Drawing, e.g.
51. Woody's wife
53. Subject of Abu Simbel statues
54. Naturals
55. Flanged girder
56. Dentist's direction
57. "Today" co-host
61. Snack
63. Instrument for Orpheus
64. Noun suffix
65. Manche's capital
67. Fossey subject
69. 1999 Frank McCourt memoir

Solution on page 369

Perplexing 91

ACROSS
1. "Here Is Your War" author
5. Act crabby?
10. ". . . and here it is!"
14. Ages
15. Geep
16. Ancient greetings
17. Boundless
18. Anklebones
19. LeBlanc of "Friends"
20. Repairman's offering
22. First act
24. Container weight
25. Chipmaker's substitute
26. Key rings?
29. Editorial feature
30. Fair-sized musical group
31. Battery units
32. Hebrew letter
35. Took too much, briefly
36. Peep show
37. "Ich bin ___ Berliner": Kennedy
38. Prefix meaning "bad"
39. Fasten again
40. He hit 61 in '61
41. Out of port
42. Chafe at
43. Faucet attachment
46. Corn ___
47. Leader born in Georgia
48. Fixed beam?
52. Base stealer's verdict
53. Nautical direction
55. Carrier whose name means "skyward"
56. Drs. Zira and Zaius, e.g.
57. "A Confederacy of Dunces" author
58. "Heart of Gold" singer Young
59. Only
60. Banana oil, e.g.
61. Color quality

DOWN
1. Asphalt
2. House votes
3. At sea
4. Qualified
5. Cool red giants
6. Cole Porter's "___Men"
7. French illustrator Gustave
8. ___Tunas, Cuba
9. Bleach
10. Least exciting
11. Stylistically bold
12. Block
13. "Per ardua ad ___" (Royal Air Force motto)
21. Ale ingredient
23. Jots down
25. Football Hall-of-Famer Merlin
26. "___ is as good as a wink"
27. West Indian kingfisher
28. Aces, sometimes
29. Opera ___
31. Spy, at times
32. Bad thing to blow
33. Has ___ with
34. Suit piece
36. Ring
37. Right of passage
39. Indian bread
40. Department store department
41. "The Kingdom and the Power" author
42. Heel
43. Home of the eri
44. Day's march
45. Decathlete Johnson
46. Socialite Mesta
48. Dirty coat
49. Akin to jejuno-
50. Been in bed
51. George Sand's "___ et lui"
54. +: Abbr.

Solution on page 370

Perplexing 92

ACROSS

1. Bollix (up)
5. Remini of "The King of Queens"
9. Water collector
13. Mine passage
14. Exile site of 1814
15. Kitchen gizmo
16. Move, in real estate
17. League: Abbr.
18. Kind of group, in chemistry
19. Queued up
21. Songlike
23. Three dots, in Morse
24. Head for business?
26. Busy hosp. areas
27. Department of eastern France
28. Boatload
30. Bothers
34. TV's "Green ___"
37. Checks out
39. Nigerian people
40. Nantes's river
41. Crumb
42. Montana, e.g., once
44. Vs.
45. Goes undercover
47. George's "Red ___"
48. Iggy has two
50. "Bambi" aunt
51. Hosp. staffers
52. East, in Essen
54. Bring to bay
56. Monopoly foursome: Abbr.
59. Floods
62. Strengthen
64. Van Dyke co-star
65. Auspices: var.
67. "___ in Berlin" (1960 jazz album)
68. Farm machine
69. "___ But the Lonely Heart," 1944 drama
70. Milk, to Monet
71. Timetable, for short
72. Activist
73. Office phone nos.

DOWN

1. Mme. Tussaud
2. British noble family
3. Miserly Marner
4. Adaptable aircraft
5. Pressure, in a way
6. "Someone ___ America" (1996 film)
7. "Washboard" muscles
8. Tennis's Mandlikova
9. Small turnover
10. "A God in Ruins" novelist
11. Literally, "numbered"
12. Adept
15. Match
20. Birds sacred to Thoth
22. Russo in "Outbreak"
25. Eye
27. ___ Arann (Irish carrier)
29. Kilns: Var.
31. Banquet
32. Above, in Augsburg
33. Breed
34. Like a bump on ___
35. Deal with successfully
36. Fully developed
37. Mint
38. Bags
43. They, in Marseille
46. "Our Gang" dog
49. Zoomed
51. More compact
53. End of the road?
55. Marie Antoinette, e.g.
56. Chill
57. On again
58. Blinds, essentially
59. Good, long bath
60. After North or South
61. Thrill, so to speak
63. Marketing leader?
64. Disk space, in a way
66. Gunk

Solution on page 370

Perplexing 93

ACROSS

1. Coaster rider's cry
5. Isn't gentle with
9. Broken
14. Count, now
15. Others, in Latin
16. Admission of defeat
17. Cuxhaven river
18. Brooklet
19. Land of a black falcon
20. Token
22. The senses, e.g.
23. Screen
24. "Fiesque" composer
25. Roughen up
28. Windfalls
32. Grimalkin
33. Hoist again, as a sail
34. Cries on seeing a cute baby
35. Calculate astrologically
36. Word form of "silk"
37. Smeltery waste
38. Some linemen: Abbr.
39. Anglers' hopes
40. Comic strip canine
41. J. Paul Getty autobiography
43. Candy brand
44. Gofer
45. Crinkly green
46. Texas/Louisiana border river
49. Noah Wyle's "ER" role
53. One doing heavy lifting
54. Sainted pope called "the Great"
55. Arias
56. Indy family name
57. Browns
58. TV's "___ Ant"
59. Cross
60. 60 grains
61. Sondheim award

DOWN

1. "TV Guide" span
2. In good health
3. Kathryn of "Law & Order: Criminal Intent"
4. Babar or Horton
5. Flaunt
6. Analogous
7. Trick
8. Part of R.S.V.P.
9. Delay
10. Noted support group
11. Drop down?
12. This, in Taxco
13. Obsolete
21. Fries, maybe
22. Pre-exam feeling, maybe
24. Large-eyed lemur
25. Capital on the Bight of Benin
26. Crows
27. Big name in wine
28. Gascon cap
29. Big name in jewelry
30. Apprised
31. Some NCO's
33. Fix, as a bow
36. The taking of Troy, e.g.
37. Derides
39. No place for an epicure
40. Ward of "The Fugitive"
42. Small piano
43. King's bane
45. Reykjavik coin
46. Cottontail's tail
47. "Artaxerxes" composer
48. Four-string instrument
49. Honey
50. Baum canine
51. Carolina university
52. Frosted
54. Inc., overseas

Solution on page 370

Perplexing 94

ACROSS
1. First computer programmer
6. Big Board letters
10. Fabric rib
14. Oat genus
15. "None of ___ business!"
16. The same
17. Accomplishments
18. Fortran or Cobol
19. Hayes of "The Mod Squad"
20. Toasting term
22. Hardin-Simmons University site
24. Advertise
26. Ursuline, e.g.
27. Ship rope
28. Short depository
31. Banquet
33. Big race sponsor
35. Cabinet acronym, once
36. Emmy-winning Lewis
38. Accept
42. Chromosome
44. "Frasier" role
45. Building block
46. Thomas ___ (ancient ballad)
47. Legislate
49. Item in a photog's file
50. Hairpiece
52. Friday preceder
53. Four-time Indy winner
54. Watch attachment
57. Biological duct
59. Brown & Williamson brand
61. High point
63. System of shorthand
66. 1984 Peace Nobelist
67. Base of a crocus stem
70. Corrupt
72. Mr. Miniver in "Mrs. Miniver"
73. Astonished
74. Stud declaration
75. Counseling, e.g.
76. Seats with kneelers
77. Put in stitches

DOWN
1. "___ Boys" (1983)
2. First name in fashion
3. Be offensive, in a way
4. High, in a way
5. Kind of spray
6. Big Apple inits.
7. ___-hoo
8. Red Sea nation
9. Darkness personified
10. Heir lines?
11. Cutting down, after "on"
12. 1974 title role for Dustin Hoffman
13. Quizmaster
21. Plentiful
23. Because
25. "The House of Blue Leaves" playwright
28. Fan sound
29. Lamarr of "Samson and Delilah"
30. Didn't sink
32. Trident feature
34. Boll
36. Fight
37. "The Compleat Angler" author Walton
39. "___, Nanette," 1925 musical comedy
40. Comply with
41. Col. command
43. "What's ___?"
48. Flow stopper
51. Tank top
53. Take to the cleaners
54. Sell for
55. Fertilization site
56. Kind of nut
58. Simon Legree's creator
60. Big name in fishing gear
62. Cut of beef
64. Eat like a mouse
65. Beaufort scale category
68. VCR button
69. "ER" roles
71. Law degree

Solution on page 370

Perplexing 95

ACROSS
1. Flatten
5. Bone head?
9. Short haircut
12. Brilliant feats
14. Custard concoction
15. Made tracks
16. Beyond the fringe
17. Repeat offender
19. Jarrett of Nascar
20. "Wellaway!"
22. Corrode
23. Broadway opening
25. Ovum, e.g.
26. Print. process
28. Draw
29. It's all wound up
30. Make over
32. ___ Peres, Mo.
33. Put the kibosh on
34. Kind of ice
37. Spreads
39. Novelist Barker
41. Rub
43. Druid, e.g.
44. Corrigenda
45. Barely sustain
47. Eleanor, to Theodore
48. Boxers Max and Buddy
49. '60s radical grp.
52. It has a prominent bridge
54. Said "!@#$%"
56. Sugar suffixes
57. Stimulate
58. "Embraced by the Light" author
59. "Henry & June" role
60. Former Fords
61. Lacunae

DOWN
1. Monitor image
2. Playboy
3. Makes obsolete
4. "Car Talk" network
5. "The Rights ___"
6. Cut the cheese
7. Charge
8. Abbr. at the bottom of a letter
9. Straw hat
10. Busy
11. "The Divine Miss M"
13. "Miracle on 34th Street" director
15. Join forces
18. Province
21. Camp seat
24. McBride of "Boston Public"
25. Hefty competitor
26. Drug derived from ergot
27. Clanton gang leader
28. City rtes.
30. Angry reaction
31. Business card abbr.
33. Big zero
34. Tab, e.g.
35. Some have 4WD
36. Even so
37. Row
38. Eroded
39. Game stick
40. "Ally McBeal" actress
41. Melodic pieces
42. Home of the Beck's Beer brewery
43. Part of a price
44. Collapsed company of 2001
45. Slackened
46. Dirigible parts
48. Ring activity
50. Boring one
51. Regards
53. Draft org.
55. Card

Solution on page 370

Perplexing 96

ACROSS

1. Club of song
5. Leigh Hunt's "Abou Ben ___"
10. Like some batters
14. Pollute, say
15. Billy Joel's instrument
16. NBA's Kukoc
17. Breakfast chain, for short
18. Painter Andrea del ___
19. 10 jiao
20. Dos, e.g.
22. Bump
24. Kennedy's secretary of state
26. Carpenter's tool
27. British ___
30. Area of responsibility
32. Bewitched
36. Coll. in Troy, NY
37. Daredevil name
39. Make fit
41. Disorderly crowds
43. Cymru, e.g.
45. Lawless role
46. Some computer keys
48. Carve
50. Part of NCAA: Abbr.
51. A head
52. Brahman title
53. Four Holy Roman emperors
55. Harry Potter's Hedwig, for one
57. Scene of heavy WWI fighting
59. 1959 Neil Sedaka hit
63. Oktoberfest toast
67. Knot maker
68. "___ far, far better thing . . ."
70. Purple shade
71. Word form of "middle"
72. Anchor ring
73. Big screen name
74. Stick in one's ___ (rankle)
75. Conductor Kurtz
76. Abbr. at the bottom of a page

DOWN

1. Dogs haven't got one
2. "Hawaii Five-O" locale
3. Juniors' dance
4. Current amount
5. Lhasa ___ (dogs)
6. Cinco de Mayo, e.g.
7. Dwell upon
8. Bag
9. Made farm sounds
10. Dict. info
11. Rise
12. Insect
13. Feminine force
21. Bait-and-switch, e.g.
23. Benson or Pound
25. "Fish Magic" painter
27. "___ la Douce" (1963)
28. Future fern
29. Seventh sign
31. Part of a tennis court
33. ___-en-Provence
34. Fold
35. Old TV sidekick
38. Bugs
39. Active ingredient in marijuana
40. Cheers
42. Coll. major
44. Deferral
47. Horse's halter
49. Garden worker
52. Many
54. Start of two Henry Miller titles
56. Dash off
58. Contraction
59. ___ and terminer (criminal court)
60. The Crystals' "___ Rebel"
61. Boast
62. Transportation to NYC
64. Battle of the bulgy?
65. Confident words
66. Libretto
67. HBO competitor
69. Go after, in a way

Solution on page 370

Perplexing 97

ACROSS

1. "Can ___?"
5. "___ soit qui mal y pense"
9. "To fear love ___ fear life": Russell
13. Duma votes
15. Carl Sagan's "The Dragons of ___"
16. Kebab holder
17. Milk-Bone biscuit, e.g.
18. Boorish sort
19. Thompson of "Family"
20. Put a coat on
22. Not so likely
24. City of Belgium
26. ". . . ___ mouse?"
27. E-address ending
28. Brave opponent
29. "If He Walked Into My Life" musical
32. "Coming Home" subject
34. Air-monitoring org.
35. Jim Croce's "I Got ___"
37. Antibiotic target
41. Soft ball brand
43. Factions
45. Opening time, maybe
46. "___ Lover," Bobby Darin hit
48. Skin: Prefix
50. NYC airport
51. ___ 180
53. Da's opposite
54. Celtic Neptune
55. Inner ear?
58. Flight coordinators: Abbr.
60. Dizzy
62. Where Peachtree Street is
64. Chmn.'s cousin
65. Complain
66. Movie pioneer
68. Rhythmic dance
72. At one time, at one time
73. Plain of Jars land
74. Patty Hearst's alias
75. Comedian Rudner
76. Actor Ray of "The Marrying Kind"
77. Shindig

DOWN

1. Acct. addition
2. Norse war god
3. Drone, e.g.
4. Story of France
5. Didn't break
6. "Deep Space Nine" officer
7. Prefix with surgeon
8. Professional trainee
9. "That ___ you!"
10. Avalanche
11. Flowed to and fro
12. Hokkaido city
14. Blot
21. Lists
23. "Serpico" author
24. Persona non grata
25. "Do ___?"
28. Divide
30. Domestic
31. North Sea port
33. Atlas abbr.
36. Haunted: Var.
38. Mark on the moon
39. Actress Georgia
40. Body shape
42. Rage
44. Campaign tactic
47. Bewail
49. Motionless
52. Fifth-century scourge
55. What Highlanders fling
56. Cheri of "S.NL"
57. Sanctified
59. Lock site
61. Cornerstone abbr.
63. Colgate lotion
64. Baja bread
67. Flaky fish
69. "___ Bicycle Built for Two"
70. Musical notes
71. "Nonsense!"

Solution on page 371

Perplexing 98

ACROSS

1. ___ of thumb
5. Matador's victim
9. Bird sound
12. Jejuna neighbors
13. "Try ___ see"
15. Kansas town
16. Top
17. Bright circle?
18. Digits
19. "Dragonwyck" writer Anya
21. Plop or plunk preceder
22. Gazelle gait
23. Newshawk's asset?
26. Blow the whistle
28. Little, in Leith
31. Raid targets
33. Rock poet Smith
37. Massenet's "Le ___"
38. Greenland base
39. Back at sea
40. Lick ___ promise
42. Capri, e.g.
44. Make clearer, perhaps
45. Land
47. Bear's cry
49. ___-eyed
50. Dropped the ball
51. "Sweet!"
52. Fashion letters
53. Aida, for one
55. Charity
57. "South Pacific" girl
60. "Do the Right Thing" pizzeria owner
62. As ___ resort
66. Mont Blanc, e.g., locally
67. Company
70. Word form of "hipbone"
71. "All You ___ Is Love"

72. Bespectacled comedian Arnold
73. "Brave New World" drug
74. Like some discounted mdse.
75. Conscriptable
76. Given the O.K.

DOWN

1. Cookout fare
2. 1997 Fonda role
3. "___ we forget . . ."
4. Popular brand of stationery
5. "Meet the Press" host Russert
6. Capri suffix
7. Social standing
8. Geneses
9. Geezer

10. Blue Bonnet, e.g.
11. Brewer's equipment
14. Brave
15. 1959 Ricky Nelson hit
20. "Forget it!"
24. Arrive, as darkness
25. Spanish pronoun
27. Groovy platters
28. Daunt
29. One who gets the lead out
30. Summer
32. "___ Calloways" (Disney film)
34. Singer Pendergrass
35. Small combos
36. Chip giant
39. Finnish architect Alvar ___
41. Put on guard

43. Detective's need
46. Inaugural oath starter
48. "Come Back, Little Sheba" wife
51. Approaching
54. D-day craft
56. "I Still See ___" ("Paint Your Wagon" tune)
57. Word form of "wool"
58. "The Sopranos" actor Robert
59. Little, e.g.
61. Advance
63. Drooping
64. Nerd
65. "Wind in the Willows" hero
68. "Take ___"
69. Org. for drivers

Solution on page 371

Perplexing 99

ACROSS

1. County west of Tipperary
6. Crafty
10. Mo preceder
13. Wisconsin college town
14. Court plea, briefly
15. ___-Pei (dog)
16. "___ of robins . . ."
17. Two, in Lisbon
18. ___ Bear
19. Dotty
20. Foot, to Fabius
21. ___ and feathered
23. Wingdings
26. Cambodian cash
27. Branch of Islam
30. Angler's concern
32. Flaps
33. "Whoso diggeth ___ shall fall therein": Proverbs 26:27
35. Baryshnikov's birthplace
39. Maupassant's "___ Vie"
40. Supremely spooky
43. "And how!"
44. Arthur and others
46. Small songbirds
47. Find new tenants for
49. Cal. column heading
51. Mums
52. Word form of "feather"
54. Go
57. Venus's sister
59. Bouncers' requests
60. Hogwash
64. "It's ___ Dad" (1961)
65. Campus figure
67. ___-Prayer
68. "My bad"
69. "___ ain't broke . . ."
70. Alan and Cheryl
71. Scores: Abbr.
72. Soap star Linda
73. Assault

DOWN

1. Mountain goat's perch
2. Filmmaker Wertmuller
3. Take one down ___ ___ (humiliate)
4. "Will & Grace" maid
5. "The Lord of the Rings" creature
6. "Alive" setting
7. Catbird seat?
8. Second-century year
9. Central computer
10. Percentage
11. Place for a pin
12. Toward the mouth
15. Comparatively quick
20. Jack of clubs, in loo
22. Suffix with drunk or tank
24. Bone: Prefix
25. Dumps
27. Bang the big toe
28. Grind, maybe
29. Aftermath of a brainstorm
31. "___ time"
33. Commence
34. Set (against)
36. "Nuns on the Run" star
37. Attendee, in combinations
38. Isles
41. "Les nuits d'___"
42. Musical syllables
45. Mounts
48. Annual, as Mediterranean winds
50. Caterer's coffeepot
51. AWOL pursuers
52. Reform Party founder
53. Course hazards
55. Protest action from the '60s
56. Beef up
57. What to do "in the name of love"
58. Hydrochloric, e.g.
61. Chaps
62. Dated, formerly
63. After the hour
66. "Son ___ gun!"
67. U.S.P.S. limbo

Solution on page 371

Perplexing 100

ACROSS

1. Is wildly unstable
6. "B.C." cartoonist
10. Five-time U.S. Open champ
14. Development sites
15. Mary's "South Pacific" co-star
16. "Othello" fellow
17. Airs
18. Game played with four-foot-long mallets
19. Lab vessel
20. Unencumbered
22. Stephen, in France
24. Hidden valley
26. Vet, e.g.
27. "I'm so glad!"
28. Bryant's team, for short
31. "Be prepared" org.
33. Big palooka
35. Helen Thomas' org.
36. Utah's ___ Canyon
38. Born yesterday, so to speak
42. Purport
44. Calif. neighbor
45. Dependable
46. Newsboy's cry
47. Philosophy
49. Bring together
50. 1901 novel set in India
52. "It's cold!"
53. In use
54. Trig. function
57. Track pick, informally
59. "___-ho, and a bottle of rum"
61. Checks
63. Nez ___
66. Edit menu choice
67. Jacquard product
70. Below, in poesy
72. Go bad
73. "As I see it," in chat rooms
74. Pact signed by Bush and Clinton
75. Hobart loc.
76. Captain of literature
77. Alaskan tongue

DOWN

1. Deborah's "The King and I" co-star
2. Hearing-related
3. Cry out loud
4. Sandinista leader
5. Kind of rug
6. With it, once
7. ___ dye
8. Hot under the collar
9. Terribly affected
10. "Had enough?"
11. Not fair?
12. Capital of Guam, old-style
13. House speaker before Gingrich
21. South of S. Dak.
23. Rejoinder to a doubter
25. "Bye Bye Bye" band
28. Three islands in the Firth of Clyde
29. Culmination
30. Business that makes little money
32. Bitter tasting
34. Toy magnate ___ Schwarz
36. Mensa requisite
37. "___ Heartbeat" (Amy Grant hit)
39. Stevedore's org.
40. Struggles
41. Christian Science founder
43. Tolkien creature
48. Discontinue
51. Like some rebates
53. Northern
54. Coin word
55. Andrea Doria's domain
56. Spider nest
58. Treasure guardian
60. Auburn tint
62. Absolute value
64. ___ noir
65. Brute leader?
68. Electrical unit
69. Bossy remark?
71. Pillbox, e.g.

Solution on page 371

Perplexing 101

ACROSS

1. Blanchett of "The Aviator"
5. Digs in twigs
9. Bomber plane org. from 1946 to 1992
12. Author Robert ___ Butler
13. Departments
15. Algeria neighbor
16. Inclination
17. Import
18. "The Plague" setting
19. "A Garden of Earthly Delights" author
21. Bernadette, e.g.: Abbr.
22. Inventeur's need
23. Charlie Brown's expletive
26. "So ___ to you, Fuzzy-Wuzzy": Kipling
28. Article written by Marx
31. Milker's targets
33. Bikini blast
37. NYC subway line
38. Bandar ___ Begawan (Brunei's capital)
39. Actress Stevens
40. Four-footed TV star
42. "A Lonely Rage" author
44. Hardly pastel
45. Some fishermen
47. Clears
49. "Ishtar" director
50. Changes back
51. Eastern wrap
52. ___ flash
53. Bibliographic abbr.
55. Smell ___ (be suspicious)
57. Highland toppers
60. Feline, to Tweety
62. Assailed
66. Came to earth
67. ___-Unis
70. Casa chamber
71. Cataract site
72. Four-time Australian Open champ
73. Blacken
74. 100 qintars
75. Bucks, e.g.
76. "Aladdin" prince and namesakes

DOWN

1. Detroit's ___ Arena
2. Epithet of Athena
3. Boy Scout's need
4. Key word
5. "One Mic" rapper
6. "___ he drove out of sight . . ."
7. Chamber workers: Abbr.
8. Preferences
9. Red chalcedony
10. Avis pair
11. Cannes showing
14. Expert in futures?
15. Wet
20. Exams for srs.
24. Lock, of sorts
25. Miffed
27. Fast no more
28. Coins
29. Court decree
30. Ancient monument
32. Coronet
34. Lacquer ingredient
35. "McSorley's Bar" painter
36. Roberts of "That '70s Show"
39. When haroseth is eaten
41. Abominates
43. 100 kurus
46. Alphabet sequence
48. Limitless quantities
51. On the docket
54. Stuttering actor Roscoe
56. Giuseppe's wife in "The Gondoliers"
57. Farfetched
58. Sheltered, in a way
59. Stole material
61. Chaucer chapter
63. Old Chinese money
64. Asia's Trans ___ mountains
65. Crew members
68. Concert souvenir
69. Belarus, once: abbr.

Solution on page 371

Perplexing 102

ACROSS
1. "Philadelphia" director
6. End piece?
10. Ball girl?
13. Edgar or Hugo
14. Walt Kelly comic
15. Counter offer
16. All's partner
17. Russia's Sea of ___
18. Jersey, e.g.
19. Bearded beast
20. Clinker
22. Confederacy
23. Rorschach pattern
24. Put away, in a way
26. Place side by side
29. ___ Rose
30. Jupiter's counterpart
31. Managed
35. Planted oats
39. A cabinet dept.
40. Low island
41. Little, in Lyon
42. Tiny time period: Abbr.
44. Aligned
46. Bit of banter
47. Oberhausen "Oh!"
49. Demands
51. Highlight
55. Sidewalk Santa, e.g.
56. Negative campaign feature
57. Colorful lizard
59. Some ALers
62. Oenologist's interest
63. Engine sound
64. Derisive gesture
66. Jed Clampett's daughter
67. Dog
68. Representative
69. Fraternal fellow
70. Field calls
71. Ann-Margret, by birth

DOWN
1. TV's "Deputy ___"
2. McGregor of "Star Wars" films
3. Word on a Japanese tanker
4. "Rocky III" actor
5. Corsair and Citation, for two
6. Eyeball benders
7. Nincompoop
8. Stravinsky and others
9. Yom ___ (Jewish holiday)
10. Sinker
11. "Dombey and Son" woman
12. Clean up
15. Drinks a toast
21. Film director Nicolas
22. It sells, they say
23. Bison genus
25. It may be cut and dried
26. Muezzin's call to prayer
27. Identifies
28. Unalloyed
32. PC reader
33. ___ lepton (physics particle)
34. "Later"
36. Crude group
37. ___ Bank
38. "Darn it!"
43. Informer
44. Cal. column
45. Believe
46. Philip. neighbor
48. Bull's-eye: Abbr.
50. Short holidays?
51. Name on a check
52. Nancy of "Access Hollywood"
53. Johnny Cash's "___ the Line"
54. Singer Abdul
55. They cover all the bases
58. Cultivate
59. Followed Louganis
60. Mob member
61. Largest of the Inner Hebrides
63. Army E-3
65. Compass dir.

Solution on page 371

Perplexing 103

ACROSS

1. Planted oats
5. Less ruddy
10. "Krazy" one
13. 1965 NCAA tennis champ
14. Poem title start
15. Small salmon
16. "Why should ___ you?"
17. Frame job
18. Hubbard of Scientology fame
19. Period of immaturity
21. Rafter connectors
23. Insults
25. Hearty entree
26. Karnataka, once
28. Children's author/ illustrator Asquith
29. Getty Center architect Richard
30. Barrymore in "Bad Girls"
32. Followed Louganis
36. Drain
37. Part of a winning combination
38. Eggheads
39. Buffet
40. "Minimum" amount
41. Finger
42. Whit
43. Unsaturated alcohol
45. Summer fare
48. Origin of a phoenix
49. Creepy feeling
51. Henry Clay, for one
55. Basted
56. To this point
58. De ___ (from the beginning)
59. It may be fatty
60. Dress up
61. Lacking play
62. Cambodian coin
63. Do
64. Bill producers

DOWN

1. Teammate of Spahn
2. Northern capital
3. "Say ___"
4. Accounting figure
5. Phony
6. Cooler
7. Some Balts
8. Place for pins
9. Lift
10. Holy text
11. "Oh, give me ___ . . ."
12. Oceans
15. Jazz singer Laine
20. Brilliance
22. Small ammo
24. Kind of sale
26. Steno task
27. Sounds from pounds
28. Day break?
29. Confronted
31. Cleaning cloth
32. Wish list opener
33. Aware of: Slang
34. Cello's ancestor
35. A abroad
38. Feminist Germaine
40. Apple variety
42. Good times
44. Full of complexities
45. Model Gabrielle
46. Field marshal Rommel
47. Marmalade ingredient
48. With respect to
49. Spanish pronoun
50. Ice cream parlor treat
52. Just so
53. Female gamete
54. Falls apart
57. Finesse

Solution on page 372

Perplexing 104

ACROSS

1. Clip
5. Macaw
10. Zoology dept.
14. Rogers and others
15. Man at the top of Microsoft
16. Ending with buck or stink
17. Constitution: Abbr.
18. King and others
19. Novel's essence
20. Lodger
22. Computer program input
24. Got ready to drive, with "up"
26. Ed.'s in-box filler
27. Blockheads
30. Absorbed, as a cost
32. "Take ___ a sign"
36. Coal holder
37. Ad headline
39. Ornamental shrub
41. Grille protectors
43. "These Dreams" band
45. Actor's goal
46. Mountaintop homes
48. Disrespect
50. Fell for a joke
51. "La Scala di ___" (Rossini opera)
52. TV remote abbr.
53. "Backdraft" crime
55. Gabriel, for one
57. Battle of Lake ___, 1813
59. Put out
63. They're history
67. Binds
68. Was out
70. Month after Shevat
71. Disney sci-fi film, 1982
72. Borden bovine
73. Prefix with hertz
74. Elated
75. Set, as a price
76. Anthologies

DOWN

1. Duff
2. Capital
3. Blue hue
4. All that's left
5. Colored marble
6. End of an Irish lullaby
7. Just barely
8. Call a spade a hoe?
9. Helpers: Abbr.
10. Chance occurrences
11. "House of Dracula" director ___ C. Kenton
12. Carrot, e.g.
13. Big belly
21. Cape
23. "It can't be tasted in ___": Dickens
25. Chip's pal
27. "Dancing Queen" band
28. Horse fathers
29. Catcher
31. Bait
33. End
34. Fast horses
35. Comic introduction?
38. Physical sounds
39. Bourbon and others: Abbr.
40. Business letter abbr.
42. Brood
44. Asthmatic sound
47. Whence the Magi, with "the"
49. 1940s–'50s All-Star Johnny
52. Fishhook attachments
54. Soprano Scotto
56. Flummoxed
58. Like bonds
59. De Valera's land
60. "You're putting ___!"
61. "___ It A Pity?" 1933 song
62. Secretary, e.g.
64. Former British colony in Arabia
65. 1814 Byron poem
66. Ladies of Sp.
67. Word proc. predecessor
69. "Trivial Pursuit" piece

Solution on page 372

Perplexing 105

ACROSS
1. Glorify
5. "Battlestar Galactica" commander
10. Animation unit
13. Hebrew bushel
14. Cornerback Sanders
15. The Crystals' "___ Rebel"
16. Harbor alert
17. Longest constellation
18. Peeling potatoes, perhaps
19. Cue ball, e.g.
21. Volunteered
23. Turkish bread
25. First name in Mideast politics
26. Cheat
28. An end to sex?
29. Macduff, e.g.
30. Fontanne's partner
32. Units of power ratio
36. Hunt in Hollywood
37. Partner, with "the"
38. Nutritious beans
39. Wastes
40. When repeated, an old TV sign-off
41. Early times
42. Dog holder
43. Drifted
45. "___ Better Be Tonight": Mancini song
48. Get more out of
49. "Oklahoma!" gal
51. Pounds
55. Show fully
56. Mosque heads
58. Fiber-yielding shrub
59. All the rage
60. Bright-eyed Couric
61. Ruhr refusal
62. John ___ Passos
63. German town
64. Misses

DOWN
1. "I'm game"
2. Per
3. "Oops!"
4. Article starters
5. Cleave
6. Hamlin's "L.A. Law" co-star
7. Right hands
8. Poetic time of day
9. Shrink
10. Prefix with grade
11. Gravelly ridge
12. Friday's org.
15. Little Joe's brother
20. Up
22. Cole Porter's "___ Loved"
24. Rocker Gregg
26. Child, for example
27. Better ___
28. Have covered
29. But, briefly
31. Coffeepot
32. Backfire
33. Lake ___, lowest point in Australia
34. Set down
35. Draft inits.
38. Bang up
40. Bores
42. Blackout
44. Get-go
45. Its license plates say "Famous potatoes"
46. Spelling and others
47. Hic, ___, hoc
48. Ranch in "Giant"
49. Opening run
50. "While ___ it . . ."
52. Olive in a Caesar salad?
53. Be hopping mad
54. D.C. group
57. Prefix with summer or winter

Solution on page 372

Perplexing 106

ACROSS
1. Part of MHz
5. Religious title: Abbr.
9. "Groovy!"
12. Western lizards
13. Like some points
15. Bygone player
16. Exec, slangily
17. Lower
18. Lilac, for one
19. Cheryl of "Curb Your Enthusiasm"
21. Call
22. L',toile du ___, Minnesota's motto
23. Western friend
26. Fungal spore sacs
28. M.p.h.
31. Eunuch's charge
33. Skating category
37. Cap material?
38. Actor Mark ___-Baker
39. 3.26 light-years
40. 1920s chief justice
42. "Vissi d'arte" opera
44. Sony acquisition of 2002
45. Drawer
47. High-rise locales
49. Rocky point
50. Car with "horse collar" grille
51. Mattress brand
52. Foot soldiers: Abbr.
53. Kiri Te Kanawa, e.g.
55. Like early LPs
57. Like some games
60. DWI-related test
62. Provide
66. "Be My Love" crooner
67. "The Brady Bunch" housekeeper
70. Foot
71. Has chits out
72. Debaucher
73. Columbus discovery
74. Strengthen
75. Winner of five consecutive Wimbledons
76. Black, to Browning

DOWN
1. Command to a team of sled dogs
2. Pin holder
3. Grid stat
4. "It's ___ in the right direction"
5. Juilliard deg.
6. Bro, e.g.
7. Growl
8. Do some tailoring
9. Pet name
10. ___ effort
11. Clint Eastwood film: 1988
14. Field guides?
15. Capital of the Solomon Islands
20. "Heartland" autobiographer Mort
24. "Nick of Time" singer
25. 1962 Joseph Wiseman role
27. Book reviewer, for short
28. Aqua ___
29. Modern greeting
30. They're thrown during a fight
32. Come afterward
34. Disciple's query
35. Took back
36. Wolf
39. Casals or Picasso
41. Decorates '60s-style
43. Burn the midnight oil
46. Hearst's captors: Abbr.
48. Ago, in Aberdeen
51. Aquanauts' haunt
54. Corp. recruits
56. In abeyance
57. Acknowledge
58. Gilda's Baba
59. "Fred Basset" cartoonist Graham
61. Gaston of baseball
63. Apply paint with a sponge
64. Boss on a shield
65. "My Country" author
68. "Tetramusic" composer
69. .0000001 joule

Solution on page 372

Perplexing 107

ACROSS

1. Fundamental
6. "Heartbreak House" writer
10. Aesir leader
14. "To fetch her poor dog ___"
15. Fabled loser
16. Angry talk
17. "___ Smile Without You": Manilow hit
18. Prefix meaning "both"
19. Down in the dumps
20. Cough syrup amt.
21. French door part
23. Stair parts
25. Fifth, e.g.: Abbr.
26. Dewey, e.g.: abbr.
27. Even
28. Umbrian town
32. Make a splash
33. Markers
34. Cricket need
35. Gregarious: Comb. form
40. Cat sound
41. Indian
42. Hospital count
43. Granddaddy of all computers
45. Speech fillers
46. Eyelashes
47. Bowlers
49. Raymond of "Dr. Kildare"
50. Ore. summer setting
53. School media depts.
54. D-day craft
55. French rocket
57. Be fond of
58. British rule over India
61. Skedaddles
62. Prefix for stat
64. Geneva's river
66. Hard to grasp
67. A little night music?
68. Ridicule
69. Endure, in Edinburgh
70. Ooze, in Orkney
71. "Stand and Deliver" star, 1987

DOWN

1. Entice
2. Basic skills
3. ___ on a rope
4. That girl in "That Girl"
5. Disregard
6. Classic western
7. Harness part
8. Short trader?
9. Nut
10. Moons, e.g.
11. Longtime Chicago mayor
12. Accustom (to)
13. Military trial, briefly
22. Prefix with culture
24. Little pains
26. Choir section
28. Arthritis symptom
29. Kicker's target
30. No-no's opposite?
31. "___ Boy" ("Tommy" song)
32. Ways to go
34. Fights
36. Eastern ties
37. Art collectibles
38. Romeo's last words
39. Start of "The Star-Spangled Banner"
44. "Rush Hour" star, 1998
46. Humor
48. Parries
49. Colo. hours
50. Summoned
51. Varnish additive
52. Boxer's dream
54. No longer caged
56. "___ sow . . ."
57. "Blow" star
58. Bulg. neighbor: Var.
59. Before mundi or regni
60. "West Side Story" gang
63. Japanese yes
65. "2001" robot

Solution on page 372

Perplexing 108

ACROSS

1. Fancy name appendage
4. Hippie gathering of a sort
8. Additional
13. Actress Madlyn
15. ___ Beach, FL
16. Prepare, as mushrooms
17. Coward of note
18. "Fudge!"
19. Conservative starter
20. Goes off
22. Four times a day, in prescriptions
24. Record label in TV ads
25. Hearty entree
26. Jams
28. Certain undergrad
30. "Species" creature's objective
34. Aries or Taurus
37. Earsplitting
40. Winter warmer
41. Key opener?
42. Tidbits
44. Keystone figure
45. Anatomical sac
47. Censorship-fighting org.
48. Newton fraction
49. Polishes
51. Can
53. Candy bar contents
56. Gift ___
60. Nunn and Neill
63. Hoover, e.g., informally
64. Albeniz piano work
65. Shake like ___
67. Classic Fords
69. Nibble
70. Opposite of sur
71. Rested
72. "Burning Giraffe" painter
73. Brad Pitt thriller
74. Certain NCO
75. Grant-giving grp.

DOWN

1. Sea birds
2. Lacking
3. File
4. Certain briefs
5. Ending for market or profit
6. Dinar earner
7. Instruction for casual dress
8. Big Ten sch.
9. Addresses
10. Jabba the ___ of "Star Wars"
11. Bien-___ (well-being): Fr.
12. Dairy product label
14. Fort Bliss city
21. Fight finisher
23. Start of S. Carolina's motto
26. Birch of "American Beauty"
27. D.C. donors
29. Al Fatah's org.
31. Gross
32. It precedes one
33. Goggle
34. Police dept. alerts
35. "Nope"
36. Bore
38. Trojans' sch.
39. Type of glazed pottery
42. Jorge's hand
43. Him, to Henri
46. Able to feel
48. Protect
50. Blazer, e.g.
52. Knock over, so to speak
54. Irritates
55. Assume the role of
57. Slave's response
58. Seater's beat
59. Coastal Brazilian state
60. ___ serif
61. Baby wipes additive
62. Mr. Griffin
64. "___ that special?"
66. Boggy lowland
68. Archaeological site

Solution on page 372

Perplexing 109

ACROSS

1. Ancient Italian
6. Army address
9. Flightless birds
14. Aptly named author
15. ___ Alamos, NM
16. Old, yet new
17. Spain's Gulf of ___
18. Assembled
19. Capital of Pas-de-Calais
20. Flying saucer alternative
21. "Mon Oncle" star
22. Ballerina, in a way
23. East German secret police
25. "We ___ Family"
27. Inscribed stone
30. Stone cutter
35. Barker and Bell
38. Punta ___, Chile
40. It was left on the Titanic
41. Energetic risk-taking type, so it's said
43. Laugh syllable
44. Asian palm
45. "___ go!"
46. Writer Fallaci
48. Ralph Rackstraw, e.g.
49. Gauge
51. Boxes
53. New Guinea port
55. Lance
58. ___ breve (2/2 time)
61. Preserve, in a way
64. ___ unto himself
66. Really vexed
67. La lead-in
68. Dior creation
69. Car dealer's offering
70. Lab abbr.
71. Big name in skin care
72. Fast times
73. Hatchery supply
74. Curl the lip

DOWN

1. Grampuses
2. Christmas ___
3. Academy student
4. Puma rival
5. Pince-___
6. "Summer and Smoke" heroine
7. Pound, e.g.
8. Old Roman port
9. Violent, perhaps
10. "My ___!"
11. To be, in French class
12. Sandarac tree
13. 1975 Abba hit
21. Ticket info, maybe
24. Depots: Abbr.
26. Dorm leaders, for short
28. Annealing oven
29. Author Nin
31. ___ financing
32. Bubbly name
33. Ancient strongbox
34. Kansas City newspaper
35. Powers in "Benghazi"
36. Aphrodite's consort
37. Goes unused
39. Not give ___
42. Abilene-to-Waco dir.
44. Modern Maturity grp.
46. She-bear: Sp.
47. Democratic donkey designer
50. Schedules
52. Immure
54. Spanish 101 verb
56. Frankenstein cry
57. Indian dignitary
58. Exactly, after "to"
59. "Ryan's Daughter" director
60. "Jelly's ___ Jam"
62. Comic strip "___ & Janis"
63. Chantilly product
65. It goes with wash
66. Word before and after "in"
68. Years, to Yves

Solution on page 373

Perplexing 110

ACROSS

1. Back
4. Clique
8. Argonaut who slew Castor
12. Auto graphs?
14. "Are not!" comeback
15. Hokkaido people
16. Capone's nemeses
17. Con game
18. Mother of Hermes
19. Prime
21. Castile neighbor
23. Election time: Abbr.
24. Gives a seat to
26. "Mr. Belvedere" actress Graff
28. Medium, maybe
31. Classic opener
32. Make ___ of
33. Hatcher role
36. Tony winner Neuwirth
40. "Arabian Nights" menace
41. Show scorn
44. Blast
45. So, in Sorrento
47. Bug tail?
48. Word form of "gland"
50. Expose, poetically
52. Dispositions
54. Some medical procedures
57. Salon employee
59. "If only ___ listened . . ."
60. Mlle., in Mallorca
62. Poker player's declaration
66. Broncos kicker Jason
68. Shipping hazards
70. East of Ariz.
71. Favor one side?
72. Folding words
73. Cassette contents
74. Poison conduit
75. Barrier breakers
76. Paycheck abbr.

DOWN

1. Qtys.
2. Monkey business
3. Kadett maker
4. Clock standard: Abbr.
5. Half-cocked
6. Vespers preceder
7. Disco dancer
8. "How dry ___"
9. "Cheers" role
10. Charged atom
11. Smooth-spoken
13. Bad looks
14. Flower with a showy head
20. Coach, e.g.
22. Never, in Neuss
25. People person
27. Court ploy
28. "Traffic" cop
29. 1847 story of the South Seas
30. P.I.s
31. Code-breaking govt. group
34. Antipoverty agcy.
35. Badinage
37. Former Israeli president Weizman
38. Cause of misery
39. Heroic poetry
42. Dumfries denial
43. Home run, slangily
46. + or - item
49. "The Story of Civilization" author
51. Endings to some e-mails
53. Elite
54. Book keeper
55. "Queen of Salsa" Cruz
56. Give ___ (care)
57. Arises
58. The Lightning-Struck Tower, for one
61. Aaron's 2,297
63. Noncommittal words
64. Half of quatorze
65. Struck out
67. New car stat
69. Gloomy one

Solution on page 373

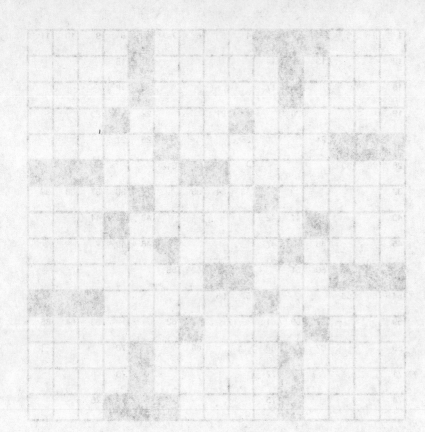

Perplexing 10

Solution on page 373

ANSWERS

Section 1: Mildly Tricky Puzzles

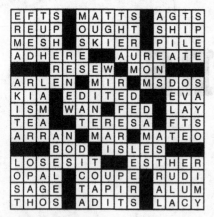

Mildly Tricky 1

Mildly Tricky 2

Mildly Tricky 3

Mildly Tricky 4

Mildly Tricky 5

Mildly Tricky 6

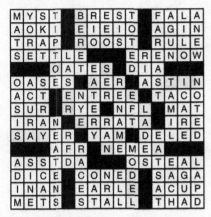

Mildly Tricky 7

Mildly Tricky 8

Mildly Tricky 9

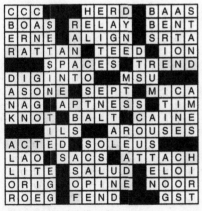

Mildly Tricky 10

Mildly Tricky 11

Mildly Tricky 12

Mildly Tricky 13

Mildly Tricky 14

Mildly Tricky 15

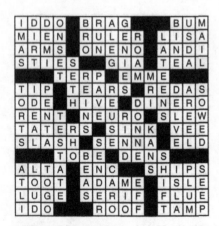

Mildly Tricky 16

Mildly Tricky 17

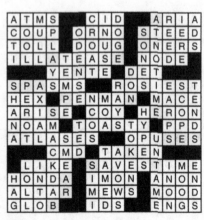

Mildly Tricky 18

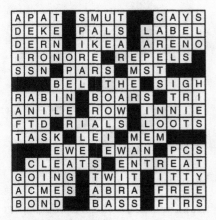

Mildly Tricky 19

Mildly Tricky 20

Mildly Tricky 21

Mildly Tricky 22

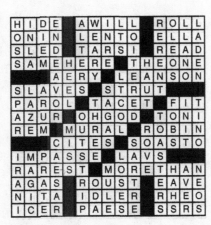

Mildly Tricky 23

Mildly Tricky 24

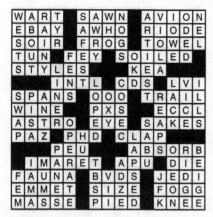

Mildly Tricky 25

Mildly Tricky 26

Mildly Tricky 27

Mildly Tricky 28

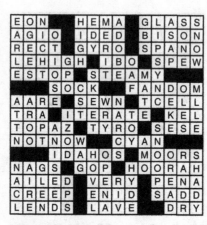

Mildly Tricky 29

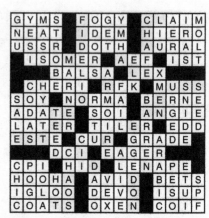

Mildly Tricky 30

Mildly Tricky 31

```
N I P . . B U R G . P O N E
I L I A . S A B E R . E G E R
P I C S . L A I N E . S E A N
S E T T E R . . D E B E E R S
. . . R U S E S . K A T . . .
S A P O R . L I S . S A C R A
I S I S . L O C A T E . H O D
E S Q . M A P . I O S . L S U
N Y U . A G E N D A . F O I L
A R E A S . D I N . F L E E T
. . . D U C . H O S E A . . .
C A M E R A S . . T B I R D S
A T O P . S A U T E . L I E U
I M E T . A S N E W . S M E E
N E T S . S H A Y . . E D Y
```

Mildly Tricky 32

```
C Y S . . S H O P . H A R P O
L E M A . C A R A . O N E I L
A S I T . A T I T . I N B E D
R E T T O N . O H M . E S T E
A S H E S . A N O I N T . . .
. . . S O O N . . L E T H A L
S L A T . B O T H . N E A T O
Y O W . M E D I A T E . N O B
S P A R E . E L L S . P S I S
T S G A R P . . L P G A . . .
. . . P L E A S E . S T P A T
N A B S . T L C . T A T A M I
E A R T H . O R C A . I T O N
W H E A T . N E O N . E C U A
T S A R S . G E O G . H R S
```

Mildly Tricky 33

```
N O T I F . P U P S . J A M S
U P O N E . O K A Y . O B O E
B E G A T . L E T S . V E R E
. L A R E D O . S T E E L E D
. . O S U . D Y E D . E L Y .
F L A W . K A I . M I G . . .
L O X . R E W E D . C O R P S
A B I D E . E C O . T O U R S
M E L O N . D A R T S . B O G
. . . M O W . S K A . D E F T
L I D . W E P T . F I E . . .
E T E R N A L . S T O P U P .
V A S E . S A K I . N O T E R
E L E M . E Y E R . I S I T I
R O X Y . L A G S . C E L E B
```

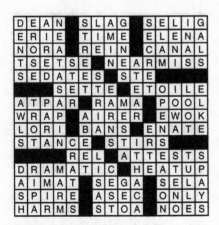

Mildly Tricky 34

```
D E A N . S L A G . S E L I G
E R I E . T I M E . E L E N A
N O R A . R E I N . C A N A L
T S E T S E . N E A R M I S S
S E D A T E S . S T E . . .
. . . S E T T E . E T O I L E
A T P A R . R A M A . P O O L
W R A P . A I R E R . E W O K
L O R I . B A N S . E N A T E
S T A N C E . S T I R S . . .
. . . R E L . A T T E S T S
D R A M A T I C . H E A T U P
A I M A T . S E G A . S E L A
S P I R E . A S E C . O N L Y
H A R M S . S T O A . N O E S
```

Mildly Tricky 35

```
S U D S . C O R D . A S T O P
C L A W . O K I E . L E O X I
U N U M . L A F F . G E N E T
B A N . L Y T E . D K N Y .
A R T E M I S . R A Z E . . .
. . . W O E . . T O R P O R
O W L E T . S H O V E . A M B
H E A R . L E A F S . F I N I
T A U . M A Z D A . M I D I S
O R D A I N . . D U B . . .
. . . S A K S . R E D S T A R
H U G S . T K O S . Y M A .
A B O I L . R E A P . F R E T
L E T G O . I P S O . L O B O
F R O N T . P I T T . U L A N
```

Mildly Tricky 36

```
S E N T A . I S A S . A C O W
I C I E R . D A L E . S O R A
R O N E E . E P I C . T R I S
. N E T T L E . S A L I E N T
. . E E E . A T N O . A G E .
A P A R . N I T . T A M . . .
T E L . S A L E S . T A B B Y
T A B L E . L A P . H O R A E
A S S E T . E L I S E . I R A
. . . T O N . O N O . E E N S
T A P . S E C T . M C S . . .
A G R E E T O . L E A P E D .
T A I L . T R Y A . R I L E D
E N N E . E G A N . L A M A S
R A T A . D I N G . A L O F T
```

Mildly Tricky 37

Mildly Tricky 38

Mildly Tricky 39

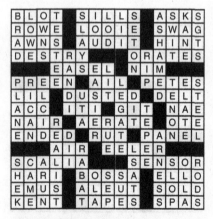

Mildly Tricky 40

Mildly Tricky 41

Mildly Tricky 42

Mildly Tricky 43

Mildly Tricky 44

Mildly Tricky 45

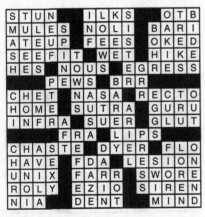

Mildly Tricky 46

Mildly Tricky 47

Mildly Tricky 48

Mildly Tricky 49

Mildly Tricky 50

Mildly Tricky 51

Mildly Tricky 52

Mildly Tricky 53

Mildly Tricky 54

Mildly Tricky 55

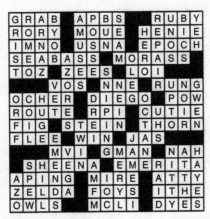

Mildly Tricky 56

Mildly Tricky 57

Mildly Tricky 58

Mildly Tricky 59

Mildly Tricky 60

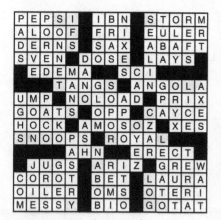

Mildly Tricky 61

Mildly Tricky 62

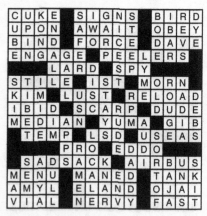

Mildly Tricky 63

Mildly Tricky 64

Mildly Tricky 65

Mildly Tricky 66

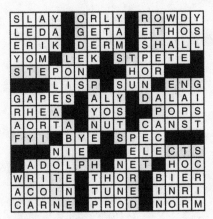

Mildly Tricky 67

Mildly Tricky 68

Mildly Tricky 69

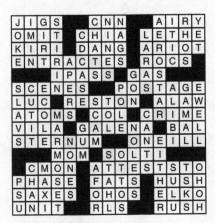

Mildly Tricky 70

Mildly Tricky 71

Mildly Tricky 72

Mildly Tricky 73

Mildly Tricky 74

Mildly Tricky 75

Mildly Tricky 76

Mildly Tricky 77

Mildly Tricky 78

Mildly Tricky 79

Mildly Tricky 80

Mildly Tricky 81

Mildly Tricky 82

Mildly Tricky 83

Mildly Tricky 84

Mildly Tricky 85

Mildly Tricky 86

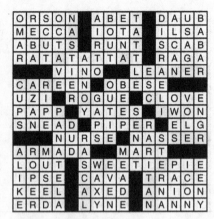

Mildly Tricky 87

Mildly Tricky 88

Mildly Tricky 89

Mildly Tricky 90

Mildly Tricky 91

Mildly Tricky 92

Mildly Tricky 93

Mildly Tricky 94

Mildly Tricky 95

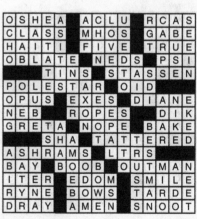

Mildly Tricky 96

Mildly Tricky 97

Mildly Tricky 98

Mildly Tricky 99

Mildly Tricky 100

Section 2: Challenging Puzzles

Challenging 1

Challenging 2

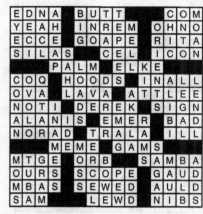

Challenging 3

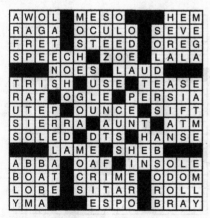

Challenging 4

Challenging 5

Challenging 6

Challenging 7

Challenging 8

Challenging 9

Challenging 10

Challenging 11

Challenging 12

Challenging 13

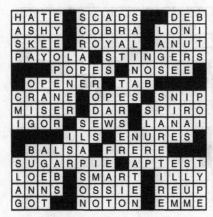

Challenging 14

Challenging 15

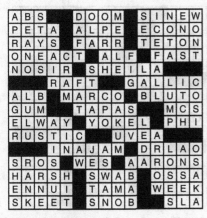

Challenging 16

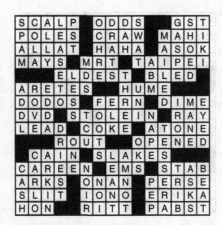

Challenging 17

Challenging 18

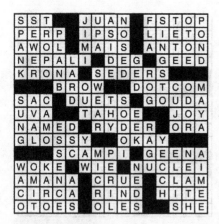

Challenging 19

Challenging 20

Challenging 21

Challenging 22

Challenging 23

Challenging 24

Challenging 25

Challenging 26

Challenging 27

Challenging 28

Challenging 29

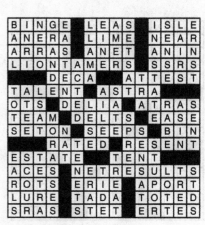

Challenging 30

Challenging 31

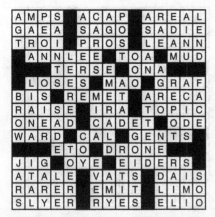

```
AMPS   ACAP   AREAL
GAEA   SAGO   SADIE
TROI   PROS   LEANN
 ANNLEE  TOA   MUD
  TERSE   ONA
 LOSES   MAO   GRAF
BIS  REMET  ARECA
RAISE  IRA  TOPIC
ONEAD  CADET  ODE
WARD  CAL  GENTS
   ETO  DRONE
JIG  OYE  EIDERS
ATALE  VATS  DAIS
RARER  EMIT  LIMO
SLYER  RYES  ELIO
```

Challenging 32

```
BNEG   RCMP   YAWPS
BODY   EROO   AGREE
GRIM   SAIL   KOALA
USC   EMLY   RYES
NETTLES   PABA
   EIK   SEEFIT
BABEL  ORBIT  ICH
PRIM  FEELS  VEER
OON  DIDNT  MISDO
ENDRUN  AME
   CHEF  BREWSKI
SNCC  CLEO   TOV
KIROV  LULU  ZERO
ENOLA  ERIN  OPER
DECAL  FEED  OSAY
```

Challenging 33

```
STIR   SAGS   TRILL
HOME   ACRE   ROLEO
AMAH   SHAQ   ATEAT
DECEASED   SITARS
   ABED   PILE
STERES   SERENADE
CRASS  SHEER  SEN
OISE  STARE  SSNS
OPE  SAENS  SEATO
TELLALIE   SENDER
   AMEN   REST
LOTTOS   PARSIFAL
ANITA  BANE  NALA
DONEN  ARON  ELEC
DRESS  PANE  LAST
```

Challenging 34

```
CLAN   WAWA   ALD
OASIS   CPAS   CREW
SYLPH   SRIS   ATEE
TEASEL   IFI   GIRL
ARN  BALL  SLYEST
   KARL   MIB
FORA  COPA  OHMIC
LOIN  HYENA  EBRO
UNDER  DRAB  HAVE
   EDS   GOBS
ARABLE  MERL  PTA
GOGO  AJA  TECHIE
ATAD  RAND  SLOMO
ZAPS  MISO  SATIN
ESE   ELEM   PODS
```

Challenging 35

```
TIMER   ABLE   ATOP
ENERO   SEEN   BONE
AGANA   PEST   ATEN
SALESREP   RISERS
   STER   TYNE
SLAT  DATA  ADELA
HEROES  ELIS  NAN
AVI  LEONINE  OTT
REE  MARS  SCATHE
PESTO  BEST  TEED
   EROS   CARE
TEASER   RELEASES
ENCL  ALAN  ALITO
COCA  MIME  MOLTO
SSTS  APPS  STOUT
```

Challenging 36

```
AQUA   LARKS   TWI
CURT   EXALT   HERA
HASP   SLIER   AHEM
TIARAS   NEEDLESS
   ENEMY   TOLET
URSINE   ACH
OKIES  TECH  DIVE
PENNE  EFT  LIVEN
SSGT  TOGS  ORANG
   WAR  ARGENT
 NABOB  ISAAC
FOREWARN   INTOWN
ARCA  SUDAN  HIRE
TMEN  CHIDE  INIT
SAD  OREAD  TKTS
```

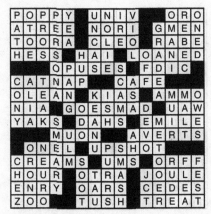

Challenging 37

Challenging 38

Challenging 39

Challenging 40

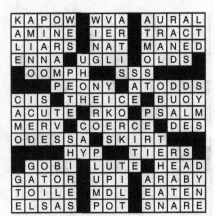

Challenging 41

Challenging 42

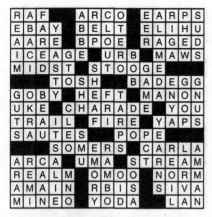

Challenging 43

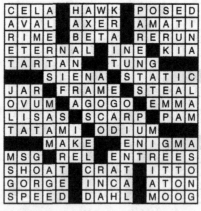

Challenging 44

Challenging 45

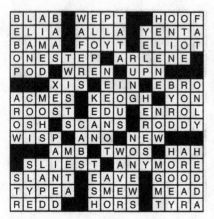

Challenging 46

Challenging 47

Challenging 48

Challenging 49

```
R I D   D A S H   D A I R Y
E V E S   A P I A   U L N A E
C A L M   D U E L   B A S I N
O N E I D A   T L C   D O N S
N A S T Y   S E E R E D
  H E L P   T A I C H I
S E C   S O A K S   U N M A N
I B O   G N A T S   O R T
P R M A N   S L O O P   N P R
S O O N E R   O W L S
  N E A R E D   O C A L A
F L E E   H E N   S T A L E R
A U N T S   A L G A   P O E M
D I C T A   D A U B   E N Z O
E S S E X   S I T U   G A R
```

Challenging 50

```
H A T S   A B A B A   M A R G
A W H O   R A V E L   D A B A
N A I L   S H I R E   S H I M
D Y N A M O   D E P R E S S
  C I N C   F H A
M O D E S   H A T   Y A L U
T H O   T H A N   D E L A N O
S Y N S   O T E R I   G U S T
T E N A N T   N U N S   R E T
S E G O   S T E   Y E A R S
  M O E   D E N S
A D H E R E S   L E T H A L
O H I O   C O R N Y   H E M I
P O O P   A U T O S   E X A M
T Y R E   S T A G E   R A J A
```

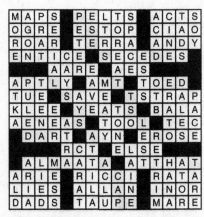

Challenging 51

```
M A P S   P E L T S   A C T S
O G R E   E S T O P   C I A O
R O A R   T E R R A   A N D Y
E N T I C E   S E C E D E S
  A A R E   A E S
A P T L Y   A M T   T O E D
T U E   S A V E   T S T R A P
K L E E   Y E A T S   B A L A
A E N E A S   T O O L   T E C
D A R T   A Y N   E R O S E
  R C T   E L S E
A L M A A T A   A T T H A T
A R I E   R I C C I   R A T A
L I E S   A L L A N   I N O R
D A D S   T A U P E   M A R E
```

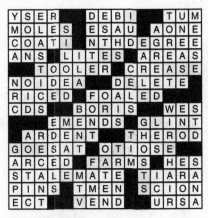

Challenging 52

```
Y S E R   D E B I   T U M
M O L E S   E S A U   A O N E
C O A T I   N T H D E G R E E
A N S   L I T E S   A R E A S
  T O O L E R   C R E A S E
N O I D E A   D E L E T E
R I C E D   F O A L E D
C D S   B O R I S   W E S
  E M E N D S   G L I N T
  A R D E N T   T H E R O D
G O E S A T   O T I O S E
A R C E D   F A R M S   H E S
S T A L E M A T E   T I A R A
P I N S   T M E N   S C I O N
E C T   V E N D   U R S A
```

Challenging 53

```
R O B L E   S C O T   C O D A
I V I E S   A L P O   O A R S
B E T A S   S U I T   S K I T
  R E S E E K   N A S T I E R
  E N L   D E L A   E D O
S I T S   H A R   S U P
K O H   R I L E D   N O R A H
E L A T E   F A Y   A L U L A
D A T E S   A D A M S   S T U
  A I T   E D A   C H I T
B E D   S A I D   C H A
A N I S T O N   R E A R E D
L O G O   I D I O   D E C A F
E L I A   S I N O   S E R V E
R A N K   M A I M   T R U E R
```

Challenging 54

```
O R A L   A R A T   R A S T A
M I N E   T A C O   A S E A T
B A I N   A C E R   T A N T O
  S L O A N E   A M E   D I M
  R E E D S   O R S
S T E R N   T I S   A L E F
I T O   A D M E N   S M E A R
S E E I T   A R R   C E A S E
A L I N E   R E E S E   S T D
K E N T   S L O   I N S T S
  O N S   S A N T A
L A D   O A T   L A S S I E
A L E R O   A S I T   S O S O
M I L A N   B R E R   E N T O
S E I N E   S A N A   D E A F
```

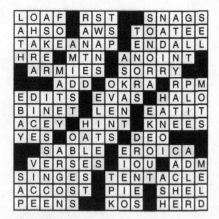

Challenging 55

Challenging 56

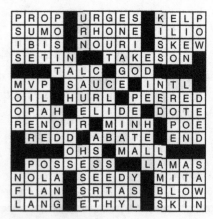

Challenging 57

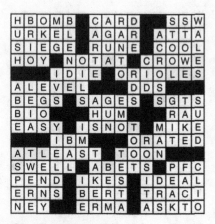

Challenging 58

Challenging 59

Challenging 60

Challenging 61

Challenging 62

Challenging 63

Challenging 64

Challenging 65

Challenging 66

Challenging 67

Challenging 68

Challenging 69

Challenging 70

Challenging 71

Challenging 72

Challenging 73

Challenging 74

Challenging 75

Challenging 76

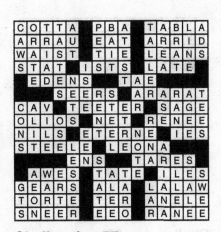

Challenging 77

Challenging 78

Challenging 79

```
R P G S   C A A N ■ ■ ■ T M C
U E L E   E B B E D ■ T A U R
S K A T   S C O R E ■ A C T I
S E D A N ■ ■ Y E W ■ R T E S
■ ■ T A M E ■ I S N T ■ ■ ■
S P F ■ R O A L D ■ S A M A R
C H O ■ Y O R E ■ H A R A R E
R O S H ■ S L A V E ■ E R I C
I N S A N E ■ P E N H ■ L S U
P E E L E ■ I S E R E ■ O E R
■ ■ T O A D ■ P I N S ■ ■ ■
C A N E ■ R E C ■ ■ S T A L L
A U E R ■ M A R N E ■ A B I E
G E L S ■ S L O A N ■ S E R F
E L L ■ ■ S P E C ■ H E A T
```

Challenging 80

```
E G G A R ■ C U P S ■ O S S O
S O A V E ■ A G R I ■ C H A P
P A G E S ■ R O O F ■ H A R T
■ D E N I S ■ S T O O L I E
■ ■ U N I T ■ E E C ■ L S D
H Y P E ■ S O L ■ R E W ■ ■
I A L ■ T I T A N ■ A B O I L
T R E V I ■ E C O ■ N A N C E
E D D I E ■ M E A L S ■ N A V
■ S U B ■ S H O ■ T O N I
I R V ■ P E T ■ S A K E ■ ■
D E E P S E A ■ D E E P S ■
T U T U ■ T M E N ■ A H A L F
A S T R ■ L I K E ■ T E N O R
G E E R ■ E L E V ■ S E T G O
```

Challenging 81

```
M I R A ■ L E K ■ ■ N A T O
I M A X ■ C U R E ■ D E T O X
S A K I ■ R C M P ■ O U T D O
S M E L L A R A T ■ S T U D
■ ■ L A V E S ■ I E R ■ ■
O F L A T E ■ ■ G O R I L L A
V I E ■ E N B L O C ■ N A U T
A T T A R ■ O B E ■ C O R G I
L I M B ■ L E S S O R ■ G E L
S N E A K E R ■ ■ R E T O R T
■ ■ T E M ■ A P T E R ■ ■
■ F E T E ■ S T E E P E D I N
L O G O N ■ H A N G ■ N O S E
A G G I E ■ U L N A ■ C N B C
Y G O R ■ E L Y ■ ■ H A N K
```

Challenging 82

```
O S H E A ■ M O B S ■ L A N E
T H O S E ■ A N A P ■ A H E M
T E A K S ■ Y E T I ■ M E R C
■ A R I O S O ■ O N L E A V E
■ ■ M P H ■ F R E E ■ D E E
I T S O ■ U R L ■ T I M ■ ■
S H E ■ O N E A M ■ C O N C H
L U N A R ■ D R U ■ A N E R A
A D D L E ■ D E S K S ■ E A N
■ ■ Y I P ■ U S N ■ E R G S
C I D ■ D A M P ■ O C T ■ ■
I N A C A S T ■ S T U A R T
G U R U ■ T I D Y ■ G L O A T
A R I L ■ O D I N ■ A I O L I
R E N T ■ R A Z E ■ T I M E S
```

Challenging 83

```
C R A B ■ R I I S ■ B E A R
H A V O C ■ U S M C ■ A T M O
I N G E R ■ D U P E ■ W H I M
■ ■ R I V E ■ E N C L O S E
■ P A S E O ■ L I B ■ S H O
P E N ■ R I G S ■ C E L ■ ■
O A K ■ S L A T E ■ R E A C H
O R L E ■ A S I D O ■ B A L M
F L E E R ■ P L E B E ■ R I O
■ ■ C I A ■ T R E X ■ O N S
O W S ■ B R R ■ S A I N T ■
P R A Y S T O ■ J E L L ■ ■
A O N E ■ E G G O ■ T I N C T
R T E S ■ R U N S ■ S A U T E
T E R M ■ Y E P S ■ C T R S
```

Challenging 84

```
B O C A ■ A F R O ■ ■ G N U
I P O D ■ T A U R O ■ P O O R
B A L D ■ A S N E R ■ O T R A
B L E E P ■ ■ T A D ■ P H I L
■ ■ D I S C ■ D O I T ■ ■
P O R ■ T O O T S ■ M A R L A
I L A ■ H O P I ■ C E R E A L
E S M E ■ T A T E R ■ T I N O
T E E N S Y ■ L Y E S ■ N G O
A N N A N ■ T E E T H ■ A E F
■ ■ B L A H ■ R E A D ■ ■
B R E L ■ H E H ■ ■ G E T A T
A I D E ■ A R A B S ■ B O D E
I M U S ■ S A R A H ■ A F A R
L A C ■ ■ M E N U ■ R U M P
```

Challenging 85

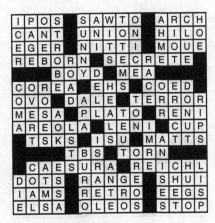

Challenging 86

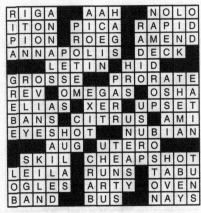

Challenging 87

Challenging 88

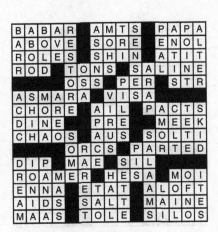

Challenging 89

Challenging 90

Challenging 91

Challenging 92

Challenging 93

Challenging 94

Challenging 95

Challenging 96

```
G R I M   G A D S     G P A
R O S I E   I T O O   B E E F
I D L E D   S O I R   A N T I
S E I N E S   O N T   B E E R
T O P   M O S T   I N E S S E
    T A U T   D E E
T O P E   S O T O   A M P A S
U R I S   E L M E R   P A P P
T O A S T   E S S O   A C T H
    A C S   S A G A
S T A B L E   T O R R   T O M
H O L E   A D O   S E L E N A
I D E E   S U N S   T O N E R
P A C S   E R G O   A C T I I
S Y S   S A A B   H O N E
```

Challenging 97

```
A M M O   P E D I   S T U M P
M O O N   A X I S   T A B O O
B O L O   G E N L   E P E E S
I C A N S O   T E A P A R T Y
T H R E A D S   T I P
    S K A T E   R E P L A N
W I L T S   O N M E   I A G O
I D E O   E L G A R   E W E R
D O V E   B I E R   W A N D A
E L Y S E E   L I B E L
    G R R   A E R A T E D
O D O M E T E R   D E M U R E
T A C O S   H I V E   O L O F
I N H O T   A F E W   D I D O
C O S T S   B E T S   E P E E
```

Challenging 98

```
F A S   F L A B   H O M E R
E L E M   R A B E   E N U R E
L I D O   A B B A   Y A L I E
L E A R N T   I L K   G E E K
A N N A S   D E S I R E
    S C O W   M A R S H A
H E S S   H E A P   U S H E R
A T A   T O E N A I L   A M P
S U G A R   B Y R D   T W O S
P I A N O S   L O K I
    O P P O S E   I M A G O
C H E T   F D A   A D I D A S
A M A H L   D Y E R   N I T A
N O S E E   L S A T   G O O K
I S E R E   Y O R E   S R A
```

Challenging 99

```
C L O N E   S C A M   H U T
A I L E Y   P Y R O   B O N Y
D E I C E   I S N O   E R I K
S F O   L A T T E   C A S T E
    H E B E   L I O N E S S
C R E A T E   D D E
O O Z E   L I E N S   D S C S
V M I   W A Y   P A H
E E O C   M O N T H   H O V E
    O D O   A B A T E D
A S H H E A P   S L A Y
H O O E Y   A L O E S   C O L
M A W R   P R O D   S P U M E
A P I E   O K L A   E A T E N
D Y E   P A L S   T R E N T
```

Challenging 100

```
F O G U P   C H I A   C A M S
G O N N A   P I N T   I M A N
S H A L T   L E T O   G I D E
    S T A H L   O N E S T A R
    C E O S   W O N   Y T D
P U C E   C P I   F A D
I C H   P O O N A   B O I N G
E L I S E   O B S   L A B O R
T A P A S   L A T K E   E M I
    C E N   D I T   T T O P
R E P   T O L   R E B A
A C E T A T E   L I M P S
Z O R A   N O A H   R A L P H
E L K S   O R B E   C R O C E
D E S K   W A R Y   H A D A T
```

Challenging 101

```
A M A S S   A M I S   S I R S
R E N T A   D A R E   A S A N
C A N A L   A D E N   A T R I
    D O S E S   S T A R L E T
    E M T S   T O T   E E S
A R B S   A L B   N E S
D E L   A R E A S   S T E P S
A N T E S   D A T   T O N I O
R E S T S   S E A T S   D S L
    E I S   D I R   B O A S
S A D   S A S   R I T E
T R E S T L E   S A A B S
A T M O   S E L L   S T A I D
B O O B   A T O E   S E A R S
S O N S   S O S A   O N S E T
```

Challenging 102

Challenging 103

C	L	A	R	O		I	D	E	A		E	S	S	O
S	I	R	E	N		N	E	X	T		T	A	C	K
A	D	A	G	E		K	I	T	H		A	T	O	I
	S	T	I	N	G	Y		R	O	U	T	I	N	E
		M	D	I		L	A	M	P		N	E	S	
M	O	P	E		R	H	E		E	C	O			
I	N	I		E	D	I	T	H		A	R	B	O	R
M	A	C	H	U		F	S	U		S	C	A	R	Y
I	N	T	E	R		I	L	L	A	T		L	G	E
		W	O	P		I	A	M		R	A	Y	S	
F	O	B		P	O	M	P		I	N	E			
L	A	S	C	A	L	A		K	N	O	T	T	S	
O	K	I	E		Y	O	K	E		R	I	A	L	S
A	I	D	E		P	R	I	G		T	R	I	A	D
T	E	E	S		S	I	N	S		H	E	L	P	S

Challenging 104

A	L	A	E		S	L	A	M		A	L	A	M	O
A	S	E	N	S		A	S	O	U		R	A	R	E	D
C	O	I	L		T	A	U	S		S	N	A	R	E
A	N	O		E	T	T	E			C	B	E	R	
P	E	N	A	T	E	S		S	U	P	E			
	L	A	N			S	T	R	E	S	S			
S	L	A	T	S		T	I	L	E	S		S	A	O
A	E	R	O		I	O	T	A	S		T	A	I	L
S	A	N		A	L	O	S	S		P	H	I	L	E
S	H	E	R	E	E			A	D	E				
		E	R	R	S		A	T	T	E	S	T	S	
O	R	G	S		T	O	R	O		T	A	T		
D	O	L	E	S		O	P	E	D		D	O	N	E
A	L	E	N	E		R	E	E	D		O	L	I	N
S	E	E	D	S		E	L	L	S		N	E	A	T

Challenging 105

O	K	I	E		S	C	R	E	W		S	N	O	W
W	A	N	T		T	B	O	N	E		A	I	D	A
E	T	C	H		A	S	P	C	A		S	K	I	S
R	E	H	E	A	R		E	A	R	T	H	E	N	
		N	U	T	S		S	E	I					
P	A	T	E	R		U	A	E		R	U	L	E	
R	B	I		A	I	M	S		S	E	N	O	R	A
O	N	E	G		S	P	O	R	E		D	E	R	N
T	E	T	O	N	S		N	O	G	O		W	E	D
	R	O	B	E		P	E	A		D	E	E	D	S
		V	S	O		M	O	E	N					
	A	P	P	E	A	S	E		A	D	E	P	T	S
G	D	A	Y		R	A	B	A	T		S	O	A	P
Y	E	A	R		A	D	A	M	E		C	O	R	A
P	E	R	E		N	A	N	A	S		O	L	A	Y

Challenging 106

K	I	W	I		M	O	O	E	D		R	A	S	P
M	C	A	T		M	A	H	R	E		E	L	O	I
A	I	L	S		E	T	O	N	S		S	O	W	N
R	E	L	A	P	S	E		A	R	O	U	S	E	
T	R	A	D	E		R	A	S	C	A	L			
		E	N	D	S	I	T		R	E	A	R	M	
O	C	T	A	N	E		M	A	D	E		J	O	E
N	O	E	L		E	L	E	N	I		R	A	I	D
C	O	E		A	R	I	D		E	D	E	R	L	E
E	T	N	A	S		S	A	N	D	A	L			
		R	E	L	A	T	E		R	O	G	E	T	
S	I	L	I	C	A		T	I	N	C	A	N	S	
O	M	O	O		T	H	O	T	H		A	L	D	A
L	O	O	S		K	O	A	L	A		T	O	U	R
I	N	M	E		A	S	K	E	D		E	P	P	S

Section 3: Perplexing Puzzles

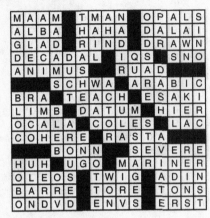

Perplexing 1

```
S N C C   P O L A B   H U R L
N O A H   E B O N Y   E L E A
A G R I   S E R T A   W E I R
P O O R A T   D E I G N E D
      A S O F   U R E
B O S C H   A P P   M C L I
U A W   Y U L E   P S A L M S
R T E S   S L A K E   N A P A
P E A L E D   B O N D   N E U
  S T Y X   K O O   A S O L D
    A R R   P A W N
  S C H M E A R   S N A P U P
C H O Y   A M E S S   R O L O
B I N D   T E S S A   L M N O
S M E E   A R T S Y   Y E A H
```

Perplexing 2

```
M A A M   T M A N   O P A L S
A L B A   H A H A   D A L A I
G L A D   R I N D   D R A W N
D E C A D A L   I Q S   S N O
A N I M U S   R U A D
    S C H W A   A R A B I C
B R A   T E A C H   E S A K I
L I M B   D A T U M   H I E R
O C A L A   C O L E S   L A C
C O H E R E   R A S T A
    B O N N   S E V E R E
H U H   U G O   M A R I N E R
O L E O S   T W I G   A D I N
B A R R E   T O R E   T O N S
O N D V D   E N V S   E R S T
```

Perplexing 3

```
E R O S   S A G A S   D A D S
L E G O   I R I D O   Y O Y O
D U E L   N A G A T   N U N N
  P E A H E N   T O A T E E
  C A W   G R O O M
K E E N   R O E   M I C A H
J O T   N E E D E D   C A L M
A A A   A T V   B O D   N E O
B L T S   D E P O S E   T R S
S A S H A   R O K   F A S T
  I F E E L   W E S
C O M E B Y   S E R A P H
H A U L   I G E T A   P O U R
A R I D   N I G E R   I S E E
S S R S   G L A S S   N Y S E
```

Perplexing 4

```
C L A S P   G N U   S P A W N
H O S E A   O O N   A L G A E
E A S E L   B O L   L E E R Y
R D A S   T Y K E   L A R D
  S M I T H   T G I
  N E R D S   R E A L M S
S S E   N U A N C E   W I N O
A H E A D   V I A   A S N O T
L A R F   R E T H A W   C P O
A H O R S E   S N A R L
  E M P   H Y A T T
B O L T   O A K S   M A R Y
T O R U S   P B A   C I L I A
O C A L A   P U T   O N E N D
S A L U T   A T A   M A R I A
```

Perplexing 5

```
D I P   R E M O   N E A R S
E R O   A Y E A R   E R I E S
E O S   D E E R E   S I R E N
S N I D E   L O A   T E D S
  S T E E L E   S A A R
  A M E N S   A R E O L A
A M A N   A L A N   R A N I N
D E L   P A L E D   T E D
E T A I L   I E R E   S O D S
E S D R A S   S O L E A
  E D H S   S E T S T O
A S A P   E T A   T H O R A
M O R E S   A S I D E   N O P
A L E A N   R E N D S   I N E
S E A T O   T A O S   C O T
```

Perplexing 6

```
I M P   A F R O   A P O C
M I E N   S L E E K   F A R R
O C R A   H U L L O   L I S I
K E T T L E   L A K E   N E B
  T E E N S Y   T A T A S
H A V E O N E   T C U
A H O R N   M U N I   G L U M
I S L   A M E R I C A   E L I
R O T H   C A I N   D E A N S
  U N S   T R O I K A S
O A S E S   S C H O O L
A D U   F L E A   G R E A T S
T I S H   I N U S E   E F I K
H E A R   F O D O R   N I D I
S U N S   T R A Y   G Y P
```

Perplexing 7

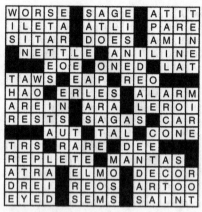

Perplexing 8

Perplexing 9

Perplexing 10

Perplexing 11

Perplexing 12

Perplexing 13

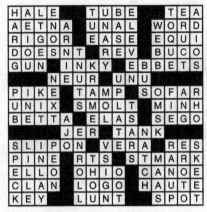

Perplexing 14

Perplexing 15

Perplexing 16

Perplexing 17

Perplexing 18

Perplexing 19

Perplexing 20

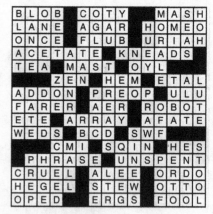

Perplexing 21

Perplexing 22

Perplexing 23

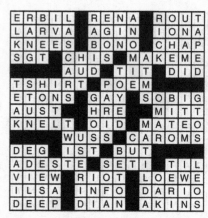

Perplexing 24

Perplexing 25

Perplexing 26

Perplexing 27

Perplexing 28

Perplexing 29

Perplexing 30

Perplexing 31

Perplexing 32

Perplexing 33

Perplexing 34

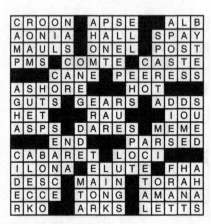

Perplexing 35

Perplexing 36

Perplexing 37

Perplexing 38

Perplexing 39

Perplexing 40

Perplexing 41

Perplexing 42

Perplexing 43

Perplexing 44

Perplexing 45

Perplexing 46

Perplexing 47

Perplexing 48

Perplexing 49

Perplexing 50

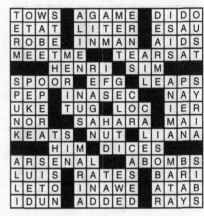

Perplexing 51

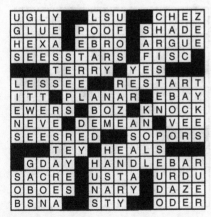

Perplexing 52

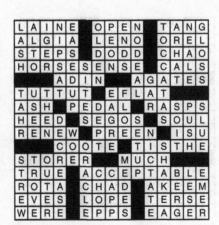

Perplexing 53

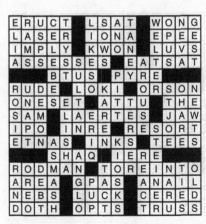

Perplexing 54

Perplexing 55

Perplexing 56

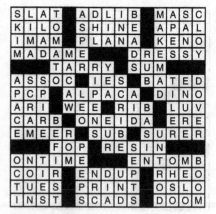

Perplexing 57

Perplexing 58

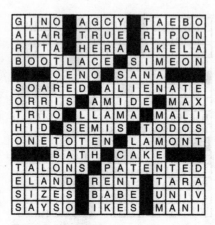

Perplexing 59

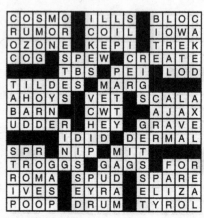

Perplexing 60

Perplexing 61

Perplexing 62

Perplexing 63

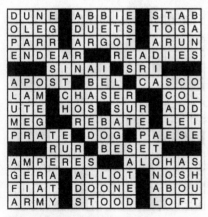

Perplexing 64

Perplexing 65

Perplexing 66

Perplexing 67

```
PABST  TECH   OSH
OGLER  IAMI   SHOE
DRONE  DUDE   CALI
SIGN  SAD  DEARER
     ECOLES  CLAD
AMSTEL   CAGE
LIETO  SLAY  DIBS
ULE  SMEARER  MAW
MEMO  DEUS  ONRYE
     BALD  CHEESE
  DISH  SCARER
LINEAR  OBI  VAMP
ERGS  IBLE  NICER
NEOS  CMON  INNIE
DRT  HINT  KEENE
```

Perplexing 68

```
PAC  LOON  ATLAS
AILS  AURA  GEENA
SLIM  GRAD  ERITU
TENETS  TES  RAID
ADELE  CERISE
   TAME  SONATA
IAL  LORNE  DECAL
RIM  PEALE  ACU
ANNAL  STINE  TOI
STONED  TONO
   INESSE  SWATS
LOSS  ATT  RENTAL
IRATE  RABE  ERMA
DEMON  AGON  RIEN
ASSNS  PEAT  ARG
```

Perplexing 69

```
GOYA  COCA  AMAHL
NOEL  HAIL  BALOO
PHYS  ATOP  APIPE
SEARLE  OCT  FIB
   CAINE  REB
CRESC  SPY  OHIO
POE  PESTE  ANEND
ILEDE  URL  LENTO
SIDED  LATTE  COM
ANYA  CUD  SCREW
   LTR  ALATE
BBB  OUI  EROTIC
LORNA  DEMI  ADOG
ILIAD  IMON  RICE
PLEBS  GINA  DOOR
```

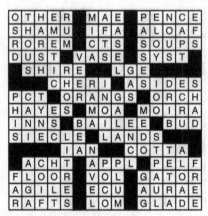

Perplexing 70

```
OTHER  MAE  PENCE
SHAMU  IFA  ALOAF
ROREM  CTS  SOUPS
DUST  VASE  SYST
  SHIRE  LGE
   CHERI  ASIDES
PCT  ORANGS  ORCH
HAYES  MOA  MOIRA
INNS  BAILEE  BUD
SIECLE  LANDS
   IAN  COTTA
ACHT  APPL  PELF
FLOOR  VOL  GATOR
AGILE  ECU  AURAE
RAFTS  LOM  GLADE
```

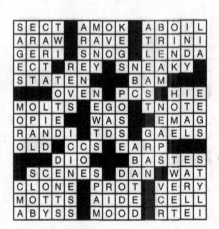

Perplexing 71

```
SECT  AMOK  ABOIL
ARAW  RAVE  TRINI
GERI  SNOG  LENDA
ECT  REY  SNEAKY
STATEN  BAM
   OVEN  PCS  HIE
MOLTS  EGO  TNOTE
OPIE  WAS  EMAG
RANDI  TDS  GAELS
OLD  CCS  EARP
   DIO  BASTES
SCENES  DAN  WAT
CLONE  PROT  VERY
MOTTS  AIDE  CELL
ABYSS  MOOD  RTEI
```

Perplexing 72

```
GUAM  USNA  GST
ABRAM  KEYS  MOOR
NOONE  REPP  ORCA
SAMIAM  IDI  HELM
UTA  DERN  SCONES
   ZERO  OHS
ZEKE  LAMB  CPLUS
OXES  EMILE  LADY
GOTTA  ELIZ  EXOD
   CPR  GIRD
ROCOCO  MENU  NUL
AXON  WBA  ENGAGE
GIRL  WALK  TOILE
EDGY  OJAI  SONIC
DEI  WARN  NASH
```

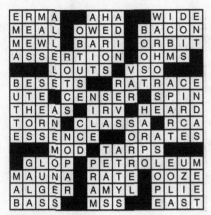

Perplexing 73

Perplexing 74

Perplexing 75

Perplexing 76

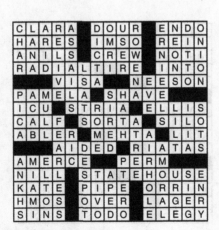

Perplexing 77

Perplexing 78

Perplexing 79

Perplexing 80

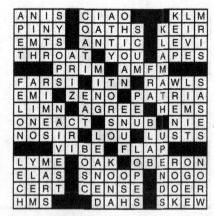

Perplexing 81

Perplexing 82

Perplexing 83

Perplexing 84

Perplexing 85

```
I G O T   H A D     T S A R S
S O M A   A K U   E A T S A T
S L A V E R E D   C H O S E N
Y A H   N M R   A L I N E S
  N A N T E S   S A T Y R
    A R D   C C I I   T H Y
T B O N E   B A E R   C I A O
O U N C E   I B N   B L O N D
P R A Y   S K I D   U I N T A
O Y S   O P E N   I R V
  T A T A R   F L E E C E
A R D O R S   A L A   H A S
A T E A M S   I N S U L A T E
H O A G I E   S T E   A R U T
H I K E S   H A E   U M P H
```

Perplexing 86

```
R U T S   S H E E R   A L B A
O T R A   C O R E A   P E E P
S N I T   E D I C T   P A L P
A E G E A N     S M A R T S
      E V E R S   O A R
D E A N E   I O S   L A M B S
O U T   R E A P E R   T O O L
N B A   T E L   D A H   S O I
T I L E   O T T A W A   E N G
S E L L S   O A T   L A S S O
    A U S   P E R E S
A N O I N T     E S T E E M
Y A R N   P A R M A   R A G U
E T T E   A L O O P   I V A N
R O O S   T I N T S   D E N G
```

Perplexing 87

```
M A A M   S C A D   S T R U T
U N C A   T H O R   C A I R O
S K I T   P I K A   O W N E D
A S H I E R   B O N   D A D
    I N T R O   C E S
P A S S E   C B S   P E R F
P E G   O R T E A   R A T E R
A R I E L   H A M   E N U R E
L E T B E   I N S E T   D A Y
S C A B   P S I   S O R E N
    S O T   A F I R E
T N N   B A A   R A T E R S
R A I S E   G O O S   C O A L
O U S T S   O R D O   H O K E
U T I L E   D I O N   O D E A
```

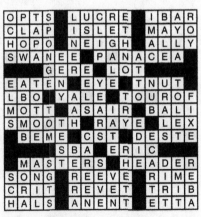

Perplexing 88

```
O P T S   L U C R E   I B A R
C L A P   I S L E T   M A Y O
H O P O   N E I G H   A L L Y
S W A N E E   P A N A C E A
    G E R E   L O T
E A T E N   E Y E   T N U T
L B O   Y A L E   T O U R O F
M O T T   A S A I R   B A L I
S M O O T H   R A Y E   L E X
  B E M E   C S T   D E S T E
    S B A   E R I C
M A S T E R S   H E A D E R
S O N G   R E E V E   R I M E
C R I T   R E V E T   T R I B
H A L S   A N E N T   E T T A
```

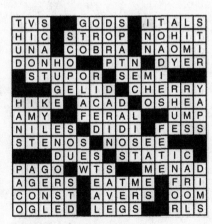

Perplexing 89

```
T V S   G O D S   I T A L S
H I C   S T R O P   N O H I T
U N A   C O B R A   N A O M I
D O N H O   P T N   D Y E R
  S T U P O R   S E M I
    G E L I D   C H E R R Y
H I K E   A C A D   O S H E A
A M Y   F E R A L   U M P
N I L E S   D I D I   F E S S
S T E N O S   N O S E E
    D U E S   S T A T I C
P A G O   W T S   M E N A D
A G E R S   E A T M E   F R I
C O N S T   A V E R S   O O M
O G L E D   L E G S   R L S
```

Perplexing 90

```
W H A L E   O W N S   U S A F
E A T I N   F R A T   R A N A
T R E A D   T A N A   L I N C
S E N T R A   Y A N G   N U I
    R U B E   S C U T T L E
M A R I N A R A   E N V
E X E S   C I R C   S A F E R
R E M   A C R A B   L E O
C L Y D E   H E R R   F U G U
    M D S   T E A R I E S T
A I R C O O L   W E A N
F B I   M O A B   S M E L T S
R E N O   N U I T   S A Y I T
O A S T   Y E T I   E R R O L
S M E E   I R E S   S T E N O
```

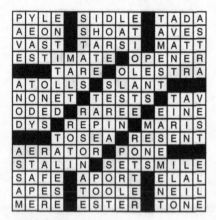

Perplexing 91

Perplexing 92

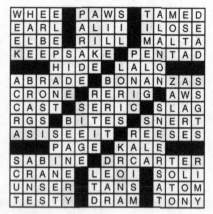

Perplexing 93

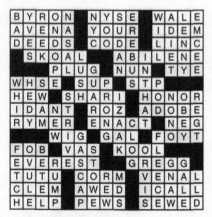

Perplexing 94

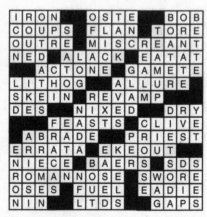

Perplexing 95

Perplexing 96

Perplexing 97

Perplexing 98

Perplexing 99

Perplexing 100

Perplexing 101

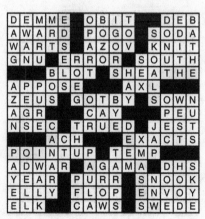

Perplexing 102

Perplexing 103

Perplexing 104

Perplexing 105

Perplexing 106

Perplexing 107

Perplexing 108

Perplexing 109

Perplexing 110

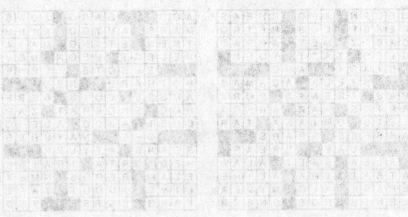